Sofia Gubaidulina

RUSSIAN MUSIC STUDIES
Malcolm Hamrick Brown, founding editor

SOFIA GUBAIDULINA

A Biography

Michael Kurtz

Foreword by Mstislav Rostropovich
Translated by Christoph K. Lohmann
Edited by Malcolm Hamrick Brown

Indiana University Press
Bloomington and Indianapolis

Published with the generous support of the Paul Sacher Foundation.

This book is a publication of

Indiana University Press
601 North Morton Street
Bloomington, IN 47404-3797 USA

http://iupress.indiana.edu

Telephone orders	800-842-6796
Fax orders	812-855-7931
Orders by e-mail	iuporder@indiana.edu

Original title: Sofia Gubaidulina--Eine Biografie
© 2001 Verlag Freies Geistesleben & Urachhaus GmbH, Stuttgart

Revised and expanded
First English edition © 2007 by Indiana University Press
All rights reserved

The paper used in this publication meets the minimum requirements of
American National Standard for Information Sciences—Permanence of
Paper for Printed Library Materials, ANSI Z39.48-1984.

Manufactured in the United States of America

Library of Congress Cataloging-in-Publication Data

Kurtz, Michael, date
  [Sofia Gubaidulina. English]
  Sofia Gubaidulina : a biography / Michael Kurtz ; foreword by Mstislav
Rostropovich ; translated by Christoph K. Lohmann ; edited by Malcolm
Hamrick Brown. — 1st English ed., rev. and expanded
      p. cm. — (Russian music studies)
  Includes bibliographical references and index.
  ISBN 978-0-253-34907-1 (cloth : alk. paper) 1. Gubaidulina, Sof'ia
Asgatovna. 2. Composers—Biography. I. Title.
  ML410.G9463K8713 2007
  780.92—dc22
  [B]
                                                          2006102062

1 2 3 4 5 12 11 10 09 08 07

For Vitia, Petia, and Ritva with Gratitude

It is not my desire to express an idea, but to give
expression to the spiritual form of an emotion
steeped in life itself.

It does not matter to me whether or not I am modern.
What is important is the inner truth of my music.

I have no doubt that women think and feel differently
than men, but it is not very important whether I am a
woman or a man. What matters is that I am myself and develop
my own ideas strictly toward the truth.

Sofia Gubaidulina

Contents

Foreword

Mstislav Rostropovich

We both studied at the Moscow Conservatory, but she was there after my time. I heard her name early on—she stood out, and I knew she was extremely talented. She is a woman who walks a straight path—without compromises, but she is very modest. In my opinion, that is the only way to cut your own swath and have a successful career. At that time she composed children's music and things of that sort to make ends meet. But she stands by those works.

In my career to this very day I have received piles of compositions for the cello and I don't throw any of them away. Among them are many amateur compositions that have been dedicated to me. In Moscow Sofia never asked me to perform one of her pieces, but she did write a work for my student, Natalia Shakhovskaya. I attended the concert and afterward invited the composer and performers to my apartment, where we sat in the kitchen. This slender and beautiful Tatar woman is phenomenally gifted, and even then in our kitchen it was clear to me that she would have a splendid career.

Only after I went into exile did I become more familiar with some people I had known earlier only in passing. Among them was Alfred Schnittke. Shostakovich and Solzhenitsyn took up much of my time during my final years in Moscow, and when I arrived at the conservatory my colleagues averted their eyes or avoided meeting me. Even friends pulled back and did not want to appear on stage with me. It was not until I started living in the West that I became better acquainted with Sofia, Alfred, and Giya Kancheli.

As I look at her life two things become apparent. On one occasion we played together at her house in Appen. I had never experienced anything like it and have never forgotten it. At first I held back, but then I played whatever came to mind. I discovered that Sofia is intrigued by particular sounds and colors, regardless of the instrument or its cultural origin. Second, I saw a manuscript in her study that resembled an engineer's drawing—something for a plane like the Concorde or for a computer. There was an abundance of carefully drawn lines. I asked her about it, but all she said was "Never mind, that's my business." Both these situations are characteristic of her work and her taste.

At that time I gave Sofia a small present. People usually simply say "Thank you" and go on to the next topic. But Sofia gave me a present in return, one that was even more precious than mine, and her response more gracious. To me, her purity reflects her human qualities. I once sent her a telegram, or perhaps I phoned her, to say: "I am gradually coming to the end of my career, and all the great composers have written something for me—except you." And I repeatedly asked her to promise that she would do so. In 1995, after her successful festival in Paris, I suggested to *Radio-Télévision Française* that the station commission one of her works. It eventually turned out to be *Sonnengesang*.

Sofia had a brilliant idea for this work: to render the life of a human being as the life of a saint. Although the church has many saints, only St. Francis of Assisi shines like the apostles. St. Francis, in *Sonnengesang*, at first praises and glorifies the entire creation—the sun, the moon, and the elements—and in the end he celebrates death. Sofia presents all this in her music, giving sound to the radiance and the glory. Of course, inherent in this work was the difficulty of developing an appropriate musical structure that would reflect the various elements—first the sounds praising the sun, then the moon, and so on. It had to be a logical form, like that of the human body, well proportioned and orderly. Sofia succeeded in creating this form with an exceedingly good sense of time. In my view, only two other composers have that sense of time: Beethoven and Shostakovich. Though they may have written some inferior pieces, their sense of the proportionality of time is brilliant. Since 1941 I have performed onstage as if electrified. If I play at a full 220 volts, I leave the audience behind and they start leafing through their programs. I then have to haul them back with an iron rake, but then I let them go again so they can once more find themselves. I was delighted to see this same sense of time and proportion in Sofia—her work breathes and beautifully unfolds in time.

Sonnengesang permits me to take another step as a cellist, as I play percussion as well. I did so once on an earlier occasion—an anniversary—but that was more in fun. It is quite new and different when I work on the cello with small wooden mallets; it changes my playing. At the first climax of the work I hit the tam-tam several times. It almost drove me crazy not to be able to play the cello but to be a percussionist. At the end of the piece, when I play the glorification of death in the highest registers, tears come to my eyes. I am deeply moved by the ending.

I remember one particular rehearsal of *Sonnengesang*. The choir is singing, I am playing onstage and see Sofia's face in the concert hall, her mouth silently speaking the words, her entire soul moving along with the work. She tells me everything she wants to say, because she knows precisely what she wants. She is also someone who has no problems with fame and prestige, and that is very rare. Shostakovich once asked me: "When you are onstage and someone throws a stone at you, what do you do?" "I stay" was my answer. "That's exactly right.

Music has no generals, no higher and lower ranks. True musicians are all soldiers fighting together at the forefront of music." Among these "soldiers of music" Sofia Gubaidulina is one of the most honest, loyal, and brilliant, and her entire life is dedicated to the art of music.

Preface to the American Edition

This book was written in an attempt to build a cultural bridge between Central Europe and Russia. That mutual understanding among cultures is the basis of a humane and civilized world was impressed upon me in the years after World War II, when the Iron Curtain ran straight through Central Europe, dividing the world's major powers into two camps: my home country, the Federal Republic of Germany, and the United States among those in the West, and the former Soviet Union among those in the East. Thus contacts between East and West became difficult, at times impossible, preventing the West from a clear understanding of the Soviet Union. Indeed, the Soviet Union and communism were often simplistically seen as identical.

I am delighted that this book will now appear in the United States, and I am deeply grateful to Laurel Fay for her support of this project in translation. A specialist in Russian and Soviet music, she has been connected with Sofia Gubaidulina for many years both professionally and personally. I also appreciate the decision by Indiana University Press to publish this translation at a time of funding shortages and cutbacks in support of many cultural projects. Professor Malcolm Brown, whose distinction as a scholar of Russian and Soviet music is too well known for me to repeat here, deserves special thanks for including this biography in his Russian Music Studies series.

I have expanded the original text for the American translation by making a few minor additions. One is a section on a "conspiratorial meeting" in Moscow in the fall of 1982, which the composer Peter Michael Hamel recollects in his contribution to this biography. A second added section concerns Gubaidulina's collaboration in a performance by Gidon Kremer of Luigi Nono's "La lontananza nostalgica ..." in Salzburg in 1995. A third is a recollection by Cynthia Phelps in which she gives her impressions of performing as one of two excellent solo violists in Gubaidulina's *Two Paths*. Lastly, the American edition includes two new sections detailing important events between the fall of 2000 and Easter 2004 regarding the Boston premiere of *Light at the End* under the direction of Kurt Masur; the narrative of these events also looks ahead to the year 2005. In this context I have emphasized the premiere, in Hamburg, of Gubaidulina's major composition, the complete cycle of the *Passion and Resurrection According to*

John, for which a brief retrospective was written by Richard Armbruster, the artistic director of "das neue werk" at North German Radio. I gratefully acknowledge Peter Michael Hamel, Cynthia Phelps, and Richard Armbruster for their contributions to this book.

I also thank all those who provided assistance with this expanded American edition. Besides Sofia Gubaidulina, Pyotr Meshchaninov, Hans-Ulrich Duffek, and Laurel Fay, many others answered my questions in conversations, by phone, and by e-mail: Richard Armbruster; Cecilia Cartellieri (Alte Kapelle, Forum für Kunst und Kultur, Hamburg); the composer Reinhard Flender (Hamburg); the music scholar and reviewer for the *Boston Herald,* Keith Powers; the journalist Irina Perfenova (Berlin); the director of the Freiburg experimental studio of the Heinrich-Strobel Foundation, André Richard; and the artistic administration coordinator of the Boston Symphony Orchestra, Alexander Steinbeis.

As for the overall translation from German to English, I was well served by my translator, Christoph Lohmann, and am very grateful for his exceedingly precise and accurate work regarding both content and language. I particularly appreciate his patience in working with me on many additions and revisions necessitated by new facts and data in the final phase of the translation.

Introduction

Sofia Gubaidulina belongs to the generation of composers who were born during the 1920s and 1930s. The Western representatives of that generation in Cologne and Paris, in Milan and New York, as well as in Tokyo, influenced the development of music in the 1950s with their radical experiments. Germany began to take notice of developments in Eastern Europe at the beginning of the 1960s, and names like Ligeti and Penderecki soon became well known. Somewhat later, Denisov and Schnittke began to be mentioned here and there; together with Gubaidulina they are now generally regarded as the Russian "musical avant-garde." As a composer, Sofia Gubaidulina is a "late bloomer" in her generation; she was virtually unknown in the West until the 1980s and did not achieve international renown until the 1990s.

I first met Sofia Gubaidulina during the 1986 Berlin Festival Weeks, a few days before the premiere of *Stimmen . . . verstummen . . .* We had agreed to meet in her hotel for an interview, and she came downstairs at the precise time of our appointment to excuse herself: her earlier meeting with three women was running a bit late, and would I mind waiting about fifteen minutes? The ensuing one-hour conversation I had with her was quite amazing. Not many of her colleagues from the West would have been willing to talk about improvisation in such thoughtful detail, about the creative process with such specificity, or about religion with such candor. In April 1989 I visited Denisov, Schnittke, and Gubaidulina in Moscow; I had known Denisov through correspondence since the 1970s and had met him in Germany in the early 1980s. This first trip to Russia opened up a new world for me, and I decided to write about Sofia Gubaidulina. It was a challenge not only to understand the life and work of this particular woman as a composer but to render the Russian cultural milieu of the twentieth century in its complexity and confliction. One must understand that Russia and the Soviet system have little in common, even though Western commentators during the Cold War era often regarded them as one and the same. Russian music and literature have always fascinated me, particularly because of the intensity of experience, the suffering, and the creative impulse that characterize Russian culture. The search for man's spiritual and moral roots has pushed artists up to and beyond the boundaries of human inquiry. Religion—or, as Simon Rattle referred to it in our interview on Gubaidulina, "all this looking up"—is an essential part of Russian existence. What we in the West would disparage as speculation or mysticism is entirely acceptable in Russia. When I told Gubaidulina at that time about my plan to write her biography, she promised her support and assistance, but it was not until the summer of 1997 that I was able to commit myself fully to this project.

Gubaidulina's work, as well as the background and origin of her music, have so far not been extensively studied. Besides several interviews and a few analyses of individual works, two books have made her the subject of study. The first is an Italian monograph by Enzo Restagno and Valentina Kholopova, originally published in 1991 and issued in Russian translation five years later, to which I am deeply indebted even though some minor corrections were necessary. The second is a thorough study, made in the 1990s by the Moscow musicologist Valeryia Tsenova, of the "rhythm of form" in Gubaidulina's works (German translation, 2001).

Since 1990 I have had many conversations with Sofia Gubaidulina. Her husband Nikolai Bokov, Pyotr Meshchaninov, and Victor Suslin have provided me with much detailed information about her years in Moscow. I am deeply grateful to all of them. I also conducted almost eighty interviews with relatives, friends, musicians, and composers in ten different countries. The following is a list of my interviewees, with the location of the interview in parentheses; many interviews were conducted in multiple sessions and were followed up with correspondence, telephone calls, and other communications. I thank them all for their contributions: Asgad Gubaidullin, the composer's late father (Kazan); her sisters Ida and Vera Gubaidullina (Kazan and Moscow); her daughter, the late Nadezhda Alexandrova (Moscow); Mark Liando, the composer's first husband (Moscow); and Nikolai Bokov, her second husband (Paris). Among her teachers, the following must be mentioned: Natalia Segel (Kazan) and her late composition teachers Albert Leman (Moscow) and Nikolai Peiko (Moscow). Friends from Gubaidulina's early years include the composer Elizaveta Tumanian (Moscow); the two pianists, Olga Stupakova (Moscow) and Henrietta Mirvis (Moscow); and the musicologist Valentina Kholopova. I spoke with the following composers: Andrei Volkonsky (Aix-en-Provence); Elena Firsova and Dmitri Smirnov (London); Viacheslav Artyomov (Moscow); Alexander Vustin (Moscow); Marek Kopelent (Prague); Václav Kučera (Prague); Yuji Takahashi (Kamakura); Toshio Hosokawa (Tokyo); and Irina Shostakovich, the composer's widow (Cottbus). The conductors I interviewed included Simon Rattle (Berlin); Charles Dutoit (Düsseldorf); Kurt Masur (New York); the late Yury Nikolaevsky (Bochum); and Reinbert de Leeuw (Amsterdam). Gennady Rozhdestvensky chose to answer my questions in writing, but unfortunately his response provided little information.

The following musicians answered my questions: Alexander Bakhchiev (Moscow); Alexei Liubimov (Bochum, Paris, Kuhmo); Ivan Sokolov (Moscow, Cologne); Pierre-Yves Artaud (Paris); Valery Popov (Moscow); Friedrich Lips (Moscow); Elsbeth Moser (London); Gidon Kremer (Cologne); Yury Bashmet (Cologne); Mstislav Rostropovich (Cologne); Vladimir Tonkha (Moscow); Natalia Gutman (Moscow); Natalia Shakhovskaya (Moscow); David Geringas (Dortmund); Boris Artemiev (Moscow); Mark Pekarsky (Moscow); Irina Kotkina (Hamburg); Rubin Abdulin (Kazan); Friedemann Herz (Düsseldorf, Bochum); Leonid Chumov (Moscow); Mayumi Miyata (Tokyo); Kazue Sawai (Tokyo); Lydia Davydova (Moscow); Valentina Ponomaryova (Moscow); and Bruce Weinberger (Weimar). Other artists and poets included the film script writer and storyteller Rosa Khusnutdinova (Moscow); Gennady Aigi (Moscow); the late Francisco Tanzer (Düsseldorf); and Vladimir Yankilevsky (Paris). I also met with the following musicologists, festival managers, organizers, and publishers: Laurel Fay (New York); Hannelore Gerlach (Berlin); Olga Bugrova (Moscow); Felix Meyer (Basel); Detlef Gojowy (Unkel); Ulrich Eckardt (Berlin); Gerard McBurney (London); Veijo Varpio (Helsinki); Grigory Frid (Moscow); Seppo Kimanen (Helsinki); Jean-Pierre Armengaud (Paris); Jürgen Köchel (Bochum); Hans-Ulrich Duffek (Hamburg); André Lischke (Paris); and Emma Kerr (London). And, finally, Dmitri Lissitsyn (Moscow); *Starosta* Nikolai Alexandrovich (Moscow); and Erich van der Vossen (Amsterdam). I also gratefully acknowledge information I received by letter, telephone, telefax, or e-mail from Rosita Wouda of the Schönberg Ensemble (Amsterdam); Michel Karsky (Paris); Mie Miki and Georg Friedrich Schenck (Landgraaf); Christoph Caskel (Cologne); Tatiana Sergeeva (Moscow); Patricia Adkins Chiti (Rome); Roswitha Sperber (Heidelberg); Richard Steinitz (Huddersfield); Igor Ganikowski (Eitdorf); Elizabeth Wilson (Giaveno); Boris Berman (New Haven); Frangis Ali-Sade (Berlin); Alexander Ivashkin (London); Elmer Schönberger (Amsterdam); Rainier Rocchi, secretary of the *Fondation Prince Pierre de Monaco* (Monaco); and Christian Eisert (Stuttgart). In the last stage of writing I received much appreciated assistance from Ludmilla Tikhomirova (Moscow), who did some local research and obtained information from Alfred Ratsbaum, Ivan Ogonov, Gennady Savliev, and Ida Garanina. Many thanks also to Yoichi Usami, who was my interpreter in conversations with Mayumi Miyata and Kazue Sawai, making it possible for me to take notes in German at the time we spoke. Jurriaan Cooiman and Ivan Sokolov conducted interviews on my behalf with questions I had prepared for them (with Kurt Masur, on May 3, 1999, and with Boris Artemiev). For original English translations of texts in languages other than German for this American edition, I am most grateful to Professor Malcolm Hamrick Brown (Russian), Frances Karttunen (Swedish and Finnish), Brigitte Lent (Italian), and Christoph

Lohmann (French). In the spirit of collegiality, I express my warmest gratitude to three experts on Sofia Gubaidulina and her music: Valentina Kholopova (Moscow), Dorothea Redepenning (Heidelberg), and Laurel Fay (New York). They all provided me with important information, but I am especially indebted to Laurel Fay for her unstinting support.

I am also grateful to the following individuals for writing down their thoughts and recollections for use in this biography: Kalevi Aho, Werner Barfod, Valentina Kholopova, Laurel Fay, Galina Grigorieva, Vera Gubaidulina, Sergei Yakovenko, and Enzo Restagno. Archival research in Moscow was not completely successful; for example, the minutes of the Wednesday meetings of the Commission for Chamber and Symphonic Music [*Komissiia kamernoi i simfonichesko muzyki*] "cannot be found," according to information I received from the Composers Union. But I am indebted to the Moscow Tchaikovsky Conservatory for providing me with copies of examinations and graduate school documents and to Russian State Radio for giving me the recording dates of several compositions that I had requested. I also received valuable information from the East European Research Center (Forschungsstelle Osteuropa) at the University of Bremen; the Centre de Documentation de la Musique Contempraine: France (Paris); and the music publisher Ricordi (Milan). For receiving me as a guest researcher, I am grateful to two publishing houses: Chant du Monde (Paris) and Boosey & Hawkes (London). The Paul Sacher Stiftung (Basel) gave me permission to study original scores and manuscripts, and I am most thankful for the excellent conversations I had with Felix Meyer. Similarly I thank my friend Hans-Ulrich Duffek of Sikorski Music Publishers, who opened his company's archives to me and promptly answered all my questions. Permission was generously granted by Enzo Restagno and Elizabeth Wilson for quotations from their respective books, *Sofia Gubaidulina* (1991) and *Shostakovich: A Life Remembered* (1994). Last but not least, special thanks go to my sponsor and to the foundations that supported my work as well as the American edition of this biography: Gemeinnützige Treuhandstelle e.V. (Bochum); Hausser Stiftung e.V. (Stuttgart); iona stichting (Amsterdam); Rudolf Steiner Fond für wissenschaftliche Forschung (Nuremberg); Stiftung Kunst und Kultur des Landes Nordrhein-Westfalen (Düsseldorf); Belaieff Stiftung (Frankfurt); Paul Sacher Stiftung (Basel); Schirmer Music Publishers (New York); the Office of Research and Graduate Development, Indiana University (Bloomington).

Sofia Gubaidulina authorized this biography and read the entire manuscript.

Michael Kurtz

Sofia Gubaidulina

1 | Ancestors

Tatarstan: Russians and Tatars of the Middle Volga

Russia, the mysterious giant empire between Europe and Asia, has sometimes been called the "multiethnic state of the eastern hemisphere."

Even now, after the collapse of the Soviet Empire, more than a hundred different nationalities, each with its own language and culture, live within its boundaries. Today the Tatars are the second largest ethnic group, outnumbered only by the Russians. This diversity has often led to conflicts with the rulers, not only under the tsars but also during the Soviet regime. Yet all contacts with Russian culture, all situations where it was possible to bridge the differences, were fruitful and enriching. Many famous "Russians" of the twentieth century can trace their origins back to other cultures at least through one parent; for example, the mother of the Orthodox priest and scholar Pavel Florensky was Armenian; Chingiz Aitmatov is Kyrgyz but writes in Russian; and many influential Russian artists from Chagall to Pasternak have Jewish ancestry.

"As fate would have it, I am half-Tatar and half-Russian. . . . It was the hand fate dealt me and that's the way it is," says Sofia Gubaidulina, who was born in Tatarstan, the daughter of a Tatar father and a Russian mother.[1] She spent her childhood, youth, and first few years as a student in the capital, Kazan, about a night's train ride east of Moscow, and did not move to the Soviet capital until she was twenty-three.

The Republic of Tataria, formerly Tatarstan, lies on both sides of the middle Volga and north of its eastern tributary, the Kama, a substantial river more than eleven hundred miles long. The republic is part of the enormous Russian plains extending from the Pripet Marshes of Belarus all the way to the Ural Mountains. The dimensions of that country are vastly different from those of small and tidy Western Europe: Russian distances are measured not in hours but in days of railroad travel, and the climate is equally overwhelming in its extremes. Short,

1

hot summers are followed by long, cold winters with bone-chilling temperatures that often keep the Volga and Kama frozen between November and April. Russians are fond of this melancholy landscape, whose beautiful seasonal colors have inspired many songs and poems. Tatarstan itself appears as a mere speck on the map of the Russian Federation, no larger than any of the Baltic states; its population is half-Tatar and a little less than half-Russian. These two ethnic groups share a dramatic history: three hundred years of "Tatar yoke" on one side and, on the other, a long and painful period of "Russification" following the conquest of Kazan by Ivan the Terrible. Both sides were guilty of violence, oppression, and brutality.

Those who imposed the Tatar yoke, however, were not the direct forebears of today's Tatar population. The Old Russian chronicles use the term "Tatar" in reference to the Mongolian riders who crossed the Volga in the thirteenth century and leveled Kiev and Moscow, although the majority of the invaders were Turkic Kipchaks from southern Siberia. Turkic languages soon spread among the "Golden Horde," as the enormous Mongolian Empire came to be known, and not much later their khan converted to Islam. In the fifteenth century, as the Golden Horde began to disintegrate into several smaller empires, the khanate of Kazan blossomed into a flourishing center of Islamic culture. It had its own distinct literature, historiography, and architecture, and the Kazan Tatars—merchants, artisans, scholars, and spiritual leaders—formed its cultural elite. Originating from a mixture of Turkic Kipchaks, Bulgarians, and Finns who had settled on the banks of the Volga, these Kazan Tatars—with a healthy admixture of Mongolian blood in their veins—were the forebears of today's Tatars in that region.

After the collapse of the Soviet Union, nationalist sentiments rose like wildfire in many of the republics, resulting in some instances in an extreme and destructive form of chauvinism. When Sofia Gubaidulina, then living in Switzerland, was asked in the early 1990s whether Russians or Tatars were her chief admirers, she replied: "Not Tatars, and only fifty percent of Russians."[2] Also, in a conversation with the Swedish musicologist Jöran Fant, she commented on the excesses of nationalism: "For instance, people deny me . . . and others our right to life because we have both Russian and Tatar blood—are 'halfbreeds.' . . . They think halfbreeds must be destroyed and killed. . . . That's what they say in newspapers and declare in speeches. This nationalism is really nasty."[3] But, meanwhile, the Tatar rulers have paid tribute to their world-famous composer. In December 1993, when Gubaidulina visited Kazan for several performances, she stayed in the government's official guest residence, received an honorary degree from the Kazan Conservatory, and was given a sable fur jacket by Prime Minister Mintimir Shaimiyev. In the days of the tsars such a fur was a symbol of imperial favor.

Gubaidulina has never identified with either Tatar or Russian nationalism: "For me, the important thing is not nationality but humanity as a whole."[4] Looking back on her childhood and youth, she can actually point to four important cultural influences. Her earliest teachers were mostly Jews belonging to the cultural elite of that time. German culture inspired her musical and literary interests. She grew up speaking Russian and absorbing Russian culture both under her mother's influence and as a result of prevailing political conditions. But the Tatar element—her paternal heritage—has always been a part of her background that she has greatly respected.

Her Grandfather, a Muslim Imam; Her Father, a Soviet Engineer

The village of Bayryaka and its namesake river are located at the southeastern edge of Tatarstan. The village lies among gently rolling fields of rye and potatoes, meadows, and small patches of woodland. The land is a transition between the Russian plains and the foothills of the Ural Mountains. In the days before the revolution, Bayryaka had about a thousand farmsteads belonging to Tatars and Tatar-speaking Bashkirs living peacefully together, and it had a substantial Muslim school, the Medrassa "Gubaidiya," which was founded by and received its name from Hasrat Gubaidulla. Gubaidulla was his surname, and Hasrat the honorific title used in addressing spiritual leaders. He was the imam of the principal mosque in the village, its officiating priest, an authority in matters of religion and law, and (if necessary) a physician. His father, Ibrahim, had come to Bayryaka from a Bashkir village at the end of the eighteenth century; he became an imam and saw to it that a two-story stone mosque would be built. The forebears of five generations have been identified by the names listed on a cover sheet of an Arabic manuscript belonging to the family, but there are no further details about them. The first among them was one Maytibi, who appears to have lived at the turn of the fifteenth to the sixteenth century.

The son of the founder of the medrassa in Bayryaka was another imam— Gabdulgali Gubaidullin—who established the family's name. With the purchase of 262 *desiatin* (about 28,000 acres) of land, his generation became wealthy landowners with a large retinue of servants. At Gabdulgali's death in 1901 (he had grown blind in old age), his son, Masgud, became the new imam. Sofia Gubaidulina's grandfather, Masgud Gabdulgalevich Gubaidullin, must have been a remarkable person—intelligent, cosmopolitan, practical, yet deeply religious. He had been trained at a Muslim academy in Bukhara (Uzbekistan) and visited Mecca on a pilgrimage. A gifted orator in both Tatar and Russian, he also spoke

Arabic, Turkish, and Uzbek. Until the Russian Revolution, Tatar education was the responsibility of the spiritual leaders. After having been installed as an imam, Masgud Gubaidullin traveled to St. Petersburg, where he received permission at an audience with Minister Sergei Witte to establish a "Society for Progressive Muslims." He took an active part in its work, particularly in the education of Muslim girls. But he also extended his influence beyond his own country by heading the regional office of the American International Harvester Company in Samara, which supplied the area with agricultural machinery, and a man from his medrassa worked as a mechanic for the company. The imam's secret wish to translate the Koran into his native language was never to be fulfilled beyond a few scattered passages.

At the outbreak of the revolution, Masgud Gubaidullin took a cautious position. He rejected the communist ideology on intellectual grounds, as it did not agree with his philosophical and political views. Like so many others, he thought about emigration, but a large number of villagers gathered at his farm and, after a lengthy discussion, begged him not to leave. Before he died of typhus at age forty-seven in January 1921, he was still able to be of help to the village during the civil war. While on his sickbed he received a letter from a religious friend in Ufa, but he was unable to understand its content. The Mufti of Ufa, the highest Muslim spiritual leader in the European part of Russia, had died and Gubaidullin was in line to succeed him.

The revolution and the beginning of the Soviet state, with its propaganda of a utopian future, deeply affected the next generation, even though young people witnessed the atrocities of the civil war and the early dictatorial measures of the Communist Party cadres. The imam's eldest son, Asgad Masgudovich Gubaidullin, the composer's father, born in 1903, belonged to that generation. As a child attending the Muslim elementary school, he had learned Arabic before enrolling in the public Russian-Tatar village school that his father had originally built and later became instrumental in reopening. Asgad Masgudovich studied at night in the local medrassa. In 1916, recognizing his son's technical gift, his father enrolled him in the Russian technical school in Bugulma, the county seat. It was considered an excellent school, with a German principal, a large supply of learning materials and equipment for physical exercise, as well as instruments for a brass band. After the imam's death, his widow struggled along but told her son: "Our economic situation does not scare me—you must get a university degree." Because his father had not become a supporter of the new regime and Tatarstan was little more than a provincial backwater in the huge Russian Empire that had been shaken to its foundations by the revolution, it was not easy for the twenty-year-old boy to gain admission. He had heard about a group of Tatar students in Berlin, but, despite his efforts to join them, he never realized his wish to study in the German capital. After a long wait, a place finally opened up for him in Moscow, the new capital, and in 1922 the imam's son began his studies in geodetic engineering at the Geological Institute [Gorno-geologicheskii institut] in Moscow. The following years were a time of hard work, hunger, and deprivation.

In 1927, when the future geodetic engineer was working as a surveyor in a small Tatar village, he made the acquaintance of a young Russian woman his own age. Fedosia (Fenya) Fyodorovna Elkhova had grown up in a country village and became a teacher. Her mother lived in Novye Chelny, not far from Naberezhnye Chelny on the Kama. The village no longer exists today, and all we know about Fedosia's ancestors is that her mother was a farmer and her father a laborer. During the chaotic years of the revolution the fourteen-year-old girl, holding her younger sister by the hand, ran away from home to join the Komsomol, the Communist Youth Organization. She cared for orphans during the first few Soviet years and then enrolled in a teacher-training school. She told Asgad that she had just been divorced and was expecting a child. They liked each other and began a friendship that survived several months of separation, while Asgad completed his studies in Moscow and Fenya took courses in Kazan. After a period of steady partnership, during which Vera and Ida were born, the couple registered their marriage in Chistopol on February 12, 1932. In the Tatar Autonomous Soviet Socialist Republic it was an act of courage for a Tatar to take a Russian for a wife. Until well into the war years, Asgad's family refused to accept her, and they even told him, "Leave your wife and turn the children over to us; we'll bring them up." For the imam's son, however, that was inconceivable.

At about the time when Asgad started his family he noticed how his relatives in Bayryaka suffered as a result of forced collectivization and their persecution as kulaks—the disparaging term the new regime applied to wealthy landowners. At first his family was forced to give up their land; then they had to sell their cattle to meet the Party's demands for large payments; and finally their house was confiscated, making them move into the bath house. In 1929 Asgad's mother and two of his brothers who had lived with her in Bayryaka left the village to find quarters with friends in Central Asia. But they never reached their goal: the train was raided, the luggage of all its occupants confiscated, and all the occupants locked up in a church without food. A week later they were packed into another train, taken to a fishing village on the Aral Sea, and put to work. The sons were drafted into the military in June 1941, and the mother was not allowed to leave the village until 1945. Only in the late 1990s did the family learn that this "labor camp," in which every inmate was deprived of his passport, was one of the islands in Stalin's Gulag Archipelago.

In March 1930 Asgad Gubaidullin found a small apartment in a wooden house near the river in Chistopol on the Kama, where he and his family settled down, even though as a geodetic engineer he had to do much traveling. In the summer of 1931, while on a trip upriver to the area between Yelabuga and Sarapul, his third daughter was born in Chistopol. This event is factually recorded in the memoirs he wrote in the 1990s: "We had a good tent and until late autumn roamed around our parcel of land like nomads. Thus occupied, I received the news that Sonia had been born on October 24—in spite of a few problems we successfully concluded our work."[5] Sofia Gubaidulina later called it "a quirk of fate" that, of all places, she was born in Chistopol,[6] where ten years later the poet Marina Tsvetaeva came to her tragic end.

After Hitler's invasion of the Soviet Union in 1941, Tsvetaeva had sought refuge in Tatarstan. However, unlike other members of the Writers Union who had settled in Chistopol, she could find neither lodging nor assistance and had to take a room in Yelabuga on the other side of the river, where she committed suicide a few days later. Sofia Gubaidulina, who always felt close to Tsvetaeva's poetry and tragic fate—both women share a forthrightness of character and a passion for artistic creativity—later presented a portrait of the poet in *Hour of the Soul,* her concerto for percussion and mezzo-soprano. She also dedicated five choral pieces to the poet, setting Tsvetaeva's poems to music.

Having advanced to the position of chief triangulator at the State Geodetic Survey of Tatarstan, Asgad Gubaidullin decided to spend the winter of 1931–32 with his family in Chistopol, intending to work through the materials of his latest survey; however, another urgent assignment required him to spend time away from home. In her later years Sofia Gubaidulina was deeply touched by the following episode, as it was so intimately related to her own life.

The aviation combine of Kazan was one of the largest projects of the First Five-Year Plan. An airport covering more than eleven square miles as well as a water pipeline and a high-tension wire connecting a power plant to the Volga were to be constructed, and Asgad Gubaidullin, as the responsible survey engineer, had scheduled one year for the completion of his project. The young man of twenty-eight and his team of forty staff members were, however, presented with an enormous challenge: although his estimate was officially accepted, the team was suddenly faced with the demand that the survey had to be completed in just over three months, regardless of the weather. They faced great difficulties caused by deep snow and a lack of roads, typical conditions of a Russian winter. To move horses, humans, and machinery required immense effort. Struggling to push through the deep snow, three horses died in one night. Levels and balances ceased to function accurately in the freezing cold. The brilliant sunshine endangered the workers' eyesight, and one of the young women suffered temporary blindness. Unable to meet deadlines, the team had to accept assistance from a professor and his students from the Geodetic Institute of the University of Kazan. On his return to Kazan to evaluate the collected data, Asgad Gubaidullin and his crew worked in three shifts around the clock. During the final phase, he had to stay up night and day to settle questions and resolve problems among the three groups. In the end, however, he succeeded in transmitting the completed survey by courier to Moscow on time.

The accomplishment of this task reflected the unselfish idealism and total, almost fervent, dedication that Asgad Gubaidullin brought to his work. With a slight shift in nuance, it served as an early inspiration and source of energy for his daughter, Sofia, who would later comment: "I think he passed some of this quality on to me, and it is almost as if fate has called on me to accomplish the impossible. I always have the feeling that I too have set myself a goal that is far beyond my strength."[7]

The Year 1931—An Interjection

The year of Sofia Gubaidulina's birth has no particular significance in the history of the Soviet Union—it is no more than the midpoint of the "Great Leap" of the First Five-Year Plan, which forced enormous changes in Russian life and culture. If the composer, like Anna Akhmatova,[8] were to write a few personal reflections about the year of her birth, they might read as follows:

> I was born on October 24, 1931, in Chistopol, the town where Marina Tsve-taeva might have lived. At that time Shostakovich, living in peace and quiet on the Black Sea, was at work on his opera *Lady Macbeth of Mtsensk*, five months after Alois Hàbas's quarter-tone opera *Matka* had had its successful premiere in Munich. It was the year in which two buildings became symbolic of the spirit of the century in the West and the East: in May 1931 the grand opening of the Empire State Building celebrated the world's tallest building; in November the Communists razed the Cathedral of Christ the Redeemer [Khram Khrista Spasitelia] in Moscow, a church that could be seen from almost all parts of the city. It was to have been replaced by a monumental Palace of the Revolution, but that was never built. The name Gubaidulina comes from my Tatar forebears on my father's side, industrious and religious people, who, for generations, held the office of imam in their local mosques. My parents gave me a Greek first name—Sofia. Although I am a mixture of different cultures, as a composer I have always looked to what is universally human.

Following the relatively liberal period of the New Economic Policy (NEP), the Soviet regime began to enforce its brutal control over all aspects of life with the First Five-Year Plan in October 1929.[9] It was a time of forced collectivization in agriculture as well as persecution of the kulaks. In May 1932, half a year after Sofia's birth, the Party launched an antireligious "five-year plan" with the goal of tearing down all religious structures throughout the Soviet Union and eliminating the word "God" from the Russian language as a medieval relic used for the oppression of workers and peasants.[10] It was Stalin's major thrust against both peasants and Christians, who, for centuries, had been the pillars of Russian culture. The Russian peasant's deep love for his "mother earth" is legendary, and the name he has given to himself, *krestianin* (bearer of the cross) speaks for itself. The Christian faith was deeply ingrained in the everyday life of all classes and expressed itself in the pervasive use of religious icons and church liturgies as well as the veneration of the patriarchs of the church. After the revolution, however, the Christian philosophies of such thinkers as Berdyaev, Bulgakov, and Florensky (the latter two were priests) had no chance of surviving. Berdyaev and Bulgakov had to emigrate together with many other members of the intelligentsia; Florensky became a victim of the Gulag. The suppression of the Church and the oppression of the peasantry resulted in the death of millions.

Beginning in April 1932 the Communist Party extended its ideological control over artists and writers, requiring that they form unions and insisting that they write encomiums to the new Soviet state. Writers were among the first who were forced to adhere to "Socialist Realism," and the Party's unrelenting enforcement of the concept led to both moral degradation and intellectual hypocrisy. Only those of unusual fortitude of character and vision were able to stick to their own course. When the Writers Union invited Boris Pasternak in the summer of 1932 to the Ural Mountains to write in praise of Collectivization, he refused to write a single line but then suffered many months of depression.

2 | Childhood and Youth, 1932–1949

Kazan: The Gate between East and West

While working as a surveyor at the airport, Asgad Gubaidullin learned that he would have a new assignment in the republic's capital, Kazan, starting in the spring of 1932. In his new position as an engineer with the People's Commissariat for Agriculture, he found a small apartment in the Russian part of the city—two rooms with a kitchen—and Fenya and their three daughters soon joined him there. For a while they boarded his younger sister and then one of Fenya's sisters. The family's home was now at 29 Ulitsa Telmana (Thälmann Street), Apartment #6, on the top floor of a three-story wooden structure, where Sofia would live until 1954.

Because of its location on the Volga, the "river of Russian rivers," Kazan developed into one of the foremost cities of commerce and culture between Russia and the Orient. About half its inhabitants are Tatars, the other half Russians, with several minority groups mixed in: Bashkirs, Chuvashs, Mari, Armenians, Jews, and Kalmyks. For Moscow, Kazan had served as "Russia's Gate to Asia" ever since its conquest by Ivan the Terrible. For the Tatar population it had always been a gate to the West. It contained every ethnic group of the huge empire, and in this mixture of languages and cultures in and around the city the pulse of life beat so fast that uprisings and rebellions always simmered just beneath the surface. Pushkin loved the Oriental flavor of this city with its Kremlin and Orthodox churches, its mosques and bazaar. He came here to collect materials for his *History of the Pugachov Rebellion*. During the last third of the nineteenth century, Kazan and its university became the seedbed of revolutionary ideas. The tsar's ubiquitous spies infiltrated the university and the general population, ruthlessly suppressing any sign of subversive activity. It was here that the young Maxim Gorky lived at that time, finding "his universities" in remote, filthy basements or in a room behind a bakery, where students, impoverished day laborers, and

9

tradesmen engaged in heated arguments and exchanged forbidden books. Today Kazan has twelve institutions of higher education in addition to its respected and renowned university—one of the first to be founded in Russia. The city can claim a roster of famous names: Nikolai Lobachevsky, the pioneer of non-Euclidian geometry; Lev Tolstoy, who briefly studied Oriental culture and law at the university; and Lenin, the founder of the Soviet state, who participated in a protest demonstration as a law student, was arrested, and had to leave the university and the city after serving a short prison term. Among the city's native sons is Feodor Chaliapin, Russia's famous bass, who performed on all the great opera stages of the world. He grew up in poverty and participated in the battles fought every winter between young Tatars and Russians skating on Lake Kaban, which separates the Russian from the Tatar part of the city. He sang first as a choirboy and later as a cantor in Kazan's Church of St. Varlaam.

Up to the time of the revolution, only four Tatars had studied at the university, because, under the tsars, the cultural life of the city was predominantly Russian. Such important representatives of Tatar culture as the historian Shakhabeddin Merdzhani, who dedicated himself to bridging the two cultures, or the poet Ğabdulla Tuqay, an early modernist, remained largely unknown outside Tatarstan.

During the Soviet era Kazan's appearance changed dramatically. Like everywhere in the Soviet Union, ornate Party buildings as well as drab department stores and apartment complexes sprang up all over. After the end of World War II, Kazan's uniform urban sprawl spread over the adjacent countryside, and the city's population reached more than a million. The construction of several dams changed the appearance of the Volga, widening the riverbed to five miles. In earlier years the river, with its boat docks, had been visible in the distance, but since the 1950s it has touched the edge of the city.

Music School: The Holy Temple of Childhood

When the Gubaidullins arrived in Kazan in 1932, the city had a population of about 250,000. Of the sixty Orthodox churches all but two had been closed, destroyed, or put to other use by the Communist Party. From the very start, the family suffered deprivations; the severe famine of that year was the result of forced collectivization, and in many South Russian villages all children under the age of two were doomed to starvation. Sofia's father's income was below average and barely sufficient to feed the family, and for years life was hard and reduced to the bare necessities.

Ulitsa Telmana—its prerevolutionary name had been Popova gora (Priest's Hill)—was a quiet side street with wooden houses, backyards, and sheds that have survived to this day. These were the living quarters of craftsmen and workers of all stripes and expertise. In one direction and around a few corners one could reach the Kremlin; in the opposite direction the little street led directly to Ploshchad' svobody (Freedom Square), which would soon be part of young Sofia's daily walk to the Children's Music School [Detskaia muzykal'naia shkola] and later to the Kazan Conservatory.

Sofia grew up in a strict but loving family. The youngest of three, she often felt alone. On days when the family visited the local bath, Mother accompanied the two older sisters (three were too much to handle), and Father took care of the youngest. Although her sisters were not much older than she, they were the "big ones," and the littlest was to keep a certain distance from them. Although Sofia was a bit shy, at times she demonstrated a fiery and explosive temperament. Not much given to children's games or playmates, she lived in her own world. Whenever the rest of the family went out, she liked to stay at home to indulge in her own dreams and imagination.

Ulitsa Telmana was a world of grim poverty. The sheds and garbage piles in the backyards left no room for greenery, and the little girl could escape the wretched surroundings only by looking up at the sky and the drifting clouds. "I clearly remember," Sofia later recalled, "how I used to sit in that bare courtyard staring at the sky—and I began to live there. The earth disappeared someplace else, and I seemed able to walk across the sky."[1]

Yet in this gray, dreary world of her backyard, someone made the five-year-old forget everything. Just a few doors down the street lived a young man—maybe seventeen or eighteen years old at the time—who the children teasingly called "Shurka Durak" (Shurka the Knucklehead). He was mildly retarded and did not have a job, but he played the accordion with talent and verve. His audience in the neighboring backyards or by the carousels at the fair consisted mostly of old women (the babushkas) and children, among them the youngest daughter of the Gubaidullins. Sonechka—just one of the affectionate names by which Sofia was known at home—at first listened spellbound to the sounds of Shurka's instrument but soon began to dance to them: "It was an unconscious improvisation that came to me from who knows where."[2] And before long she followed him everywhere. One of the babushkas, whose daughter-in-law taught piano at the local Children's Music School, noticed the young girl's talent as a dancer and talked to her mother. Sonechka and her sisters were taken across the street to see Ekaterina Pavlovna Leontieva, who, after testing their musical talent, agreed to provide daily piano lessons at her own apartment for both Sonechka and Ida. At the same time it made sense to submit applications for admission on behalf of the two girls to the Children's Music School, where especially gifted schoolchildren took intensive instrumental and musical instruction in the afternoons.

Sofia later remembered the day when she was introduced to the headmaster Ruvim Lvovich Poliakov:

> Everything was fine except for my age—I was only five. I suddenly felt a terrible danger. To wait a whole year at that time seemed a catastrophe to me. I grasped the leg of his [Poliakov's] trousers and started pleading with him, tears in my eyes, to accept me. I remember it vividly. My life hung by a thread. Maybe that instant was so dramatic because I already knew even then that music was my salvation. But . . . Poliakov was very understanding and said, "All right, let's give it a try."[3]

At first their mother took the young girls to their lessons, but later they were on their own. Sonechka often sported a fashionable middy blouse, but under it she wore a quilted vest, as she tended to be sensitive to the cold and was susceptible to the sniffles. On the way to the music school—first in the center of Ploshchad' svobody, then at the entrance to the school—Sonechka always experienced two special moments: "In those years the big square was completely empty, and the cars drove around on the outside. As I crossed it, I looked up at the sky, and, reaching the center, I always began to feel as if I had left the pavement and was walking in the sky. After the square, after a few more blocks, a right turn, and there would be my school—my temple."

Pushing open the door in a mood of eager anticipation, the little girl would be welcomed by a colorful patchwork of musical sounds. Songs, etudes, scales, or arpeggios on the piano emanated from every room. The school became the holy temple of her childhood, and Ruvim Poliakov and Ekaterina Leontieva, who taught with dedication, skill, and high professionalism, became the "gods" she loved and honored. Poliakov, a cellist who had studied at the St. Petersburg Conservatory, had been forced to leave the city on the Neva after taking his examinations because he was a Jew. He moved to Kazan, one of the first cities east of Leningrad and Moscow that was open to Jews. There he founded the Children's Music School in 1933 and did much important work for the city's musical culture. Speaking in retrospect of her musical training, Gubaidulina mentioned both his name and Ekaterina Leontieva's with evident gratitude for having taught her "to love Bach, Mozart, and Beethoven";[4] they planted "the seed of purity and dedication to art . . . in the hearts of future musicians."[5]

"Music Naturally Blended with Religion"

Although Sofia's parents were not particularly musical, they heartily supported their daughters' talent. Her father felt that "every educated person must have some musical training," and for that reason her parents bought a baby grand made by Slessar, a local manufacturer. This purchase must have been a considerable sacrifice, but in those days baby grands were cheaper than uprights because most apartments were too small for them. The day it was delivered was like a High Holy Day for the six-year-old girl, and the composer later remembered it as "the most powerful experience of my life."⁶ Taking up a good half of the room, the instrument brought an air of cosmopolitan culture to the little apartment in Kazan and gave a decisive new impetus to the life of the youngest daughter.

At Ekaterina Leontieva's, Sonechka played only simple children's pieces within the range of two octaves, but soon she encountered an unexpected variety of tone and color. She could play in the highest and lowest registers both on the keys and inside the instrument, as she and her sisters tried everything—placing paper, pieces of cloth, and pencils across the strings. When Ida sat down to play, "I could even crawl under the piano and feel as if I were in a vast, empty sanctuary where music would surely resound at any moment."⁷ There was always something new and amazing, and the little girl plunged into this world with abandon. At that time a question came to her mind: Why am I always playing such poor little pieces, when there is such a wonderfully rich world of sounds?

"Several folders of music for beginners," she later recalled, "lay around Ekaterina Pavlovna's studio. In my naïveté I assumed that this repertoire for beginners was all there was to the world of music."⁸ She decided, therefore, that, "since mankind suffers such deprivation, I'll do some composing myself. Why not?! I knew it would be endless hard work. . . . I already understood a lot even then. And I prayed to God to give me this path in life—I promised to do whatever work was required."⁹

By a curious historical coincidence, just at the time when the two sisters Gubaidullina were doing their childlike experiments on their baby grand, the twenty-six-year-old American composer John Cage was writing his first piece for prepared piano, *Bacchanale*—perhaps more for pragmatic than artistic reasons. Cage and Gubaidulina briefly met on two occasions sixty years later in Leningrad and New York, and expressed their mutual respect and admiration, despite the Russian (Eastern) and American (Western) differences separating them. As we will see, this would later have important musical consequences for Gubaidulina.

It was probably the summer before Sofia entered the music school that the family spent time in Nizhny Usslon, a village in the hills on the other side of the Volga. Because of their limited means, they normally remained in Kazan during the summer. This time, however, they were able to find lodgings on a farm, where Sofia happened to notice a simple icon of Christ in a corner. Despite the state's vigorous campaign to repress religion, some people remained true to their faith and its symbols. The West has nothing comparable to the Russian icon, but it is of central importance in the lives of Orthodox Christians: it offers protection, strength, and inspiration and serves as a window to God's realm. Sofia, however, did not know who was represented on the farmer's icon: "For a long time I had been praying in our Kazan courtyard—a completely irrational prayer; but suddenly I understood the connection between my prayer and that icon. It wasn't some sort of mystical experience; it was simply the same thing. All excited, I asked my mother: "Who is that? Who is that?"[10]

> Being naïve, I blurted out everything to my parents, and when they realized I was religious, they were horrified. This was forbidden! So I started hiding my emotional, religious life from the grownups, but it continued to thrive within me. Music naturally blended with religion, and sound, straightaway, became sacred for me.[11]

Sofia's parents were so worried, however, that they packed up and left the farmhouse the very next day.

Years of Terror, Illness, and War

Stalin's secret police, which later became the KGB [Komitet gosudarstvennoi bezopasnosti (Committee for State Security)], had by now set up a nationwide network of terror and surveillance. His political purges were already under way and reached their traumatic climax in 1937. Hardly a family escaped without having one of its members or a neighbor taken away, among them Evgeniya Ginsburg, who first worked as a local Komsomol Party organizer and then as a history instructor at the University of Kazan. She was to spend eighteen years in various prisons and labor camps. Gubaidulina was later among those in Ginsburg's Moscow apartment listening to the author reading from her manuscript, "Journey into the Whirlwind" ["Krutoi marshrut"], and it was this experience that confirmed her suspicions about the camps. "Even in our home," Gubaidulina remembered,

> we were constantly in fear that the 'Black Raven' [Black Maria] would come and get our father. In those years our lives changed, and it didn't become clear to me until much later what was gradually taking place. It happened in three stages: at first a number of topics became taboo at home; then people stopped saying things but they were still thinking them; and finally they submitted to whatever the state decreed. Today it seems to me that our fear was even worse than imprisonment—because it paralyzed and eventually killed the spirit and any kind of creativity.

Surprisingly Sofia's father, the son of a religious leader and wealthy landowner, escaped both prison and labor camp. There was, of course, the inevitable visit of an acquaintance wanting to recruit him for the Party; the visitor had brought a doll and some chocolate for Sonechka but failed in his recruitment effort. Also, Asgad Gubaidullin and his wife had to appear for a hearing at his place of work to listen to a litany of absurd accusations. At home Fenya asked her husband, "Why didn't you say anything? Those were nothing but lies!" "They knew they were lies," he replied, and nothing came of it.

He often said that "silence is golden," and his silences, a sign of his Tatar character, protected him against Stalin's apparatus of terror. At any rate, that is how his seven-year-old daughter saw it when she was allowed to accompany him on surveying trips to the surrounding countryside.

> We trudged through woods and along streams mostly in complete silence. Being from the Orient, he loved silence, and these excursions forged a deep and mysterious bond between my father and me. Perhaps he didn't even feel it or wasn't particularly conscious of it, but I never experienced anything so profound again in my later life. I inherited that love of silence from him—I, who love both peace and silence.

Silence, it should be pointed out, is an expression of hospitality and a part of normal etiquette in Tatarstan: a guest is greeted and then asked to share food at the table; silence reigns and conversation is only allowed to develop slowly. It is a polite way of not asserting oneself.

At home Mother was in charge of what was allowed, what wasn't, and what one was supposed to do, and she was always ready to explain these rules. She organized and supervised the day's activities and seemed never to rest. Father was usually on field assignments; his almost religious dedication to his work made him a model. He worked for a better future, if only for his children. He was aware, of course, of the deception, manipulation, and corruption of the outside world, but he was true to his own ethical standards, and all three daughters remember him as the family's moral authority. When Vera, the oldest, asked one day why the family lived in such poverty, perhaps even greater poverty than many of their neighbors—even though all other aspects of family life were thoroughly satisfactory—Mother told her, "Young lady, we do not steal and neither will you."

The sisters progressed rapidly in their piano lessons. As early as 1938, on the occasion of the fifth anniversary of the Children's Music School, the local paper, *Komsomolets Tatarii,* printed a picture of the "young pianists." Two years later they gave a public recital as part of a Bach festival at the auditorium of the Music Gymnasium. Following the choir, several soloists performed, and Sonechka played a suite. That same year the sisters took part in the "Olympic Games of the Republic for Children's Productivity," and two notices appeared in the paper. The issue of June 2 shows their picture, and a review appeared five days later: "The two little sisters, Sania [Sofia] and Saida [Ida] Gubaidullin [*sic*], demonstrated an excellent ear for music as well as good technical skill. Sania's tiny fingers brought Kuhlau's *Variations* to life in clean, crisp tones that were pleasing to the ear."[12]

At this time the family acquired a new Eberg grand piano. It was only a slight improvement over its predecessor, but no efforts were spared to promote the children's development. The youngest was then composing a number of piano pieces, writing them down, playing them in improvisations, and giving them names like *The Lark* or *The Windmill*, following the example of Tchaikovsky's *Children's Album* [*Detskii al'bom*]. As Mother supervised the day's activities—elementary school, music school, piano practice—her reaction tended to be brief and to the point: "Stop tinkling, girl!" But Father typically displayed a more reasoned paternal kindness: he was under the impression that his little daughter still did not really know the original themes and, when they would take a walk together, he would lecture her.

At age ten Sofia kept her wish to be a composer to herself. "I often prayed in those years—at home, or when I was alone in the yard or in the woods.... Once when I saw a shooting star I made a wish to be a composer, even though I was unable to express it in so many words. I had played music by Mozart, Gnesin,[13] and others—but it wasn't really clear to me that these were real people. I was already being presented on stage as a child prodigy, but my consciousness was still dim. The wish to compose was deep inside me, but I was small and shy. So I prayed that God would show me a way out of this confusion, but I did not know how."

In June 1941 the German army invaded Russia, taking the country by surprise and unleashing chaos and suffering. Government ministries, university departments, and even entire factories were relocated to the center of the country. With streams of refugees moving eastward, the population of Kazan increased by a third during the first months of the war. Asgad Gubaidullin continued his field trips and his wife turned her kitchen over to the refugees, adding six women and children from Voronezh to the household; the men lived at the factory. Expecting nightly bombing raids by German planes, the neighbors took turns standing guard with buckets of water. But Kazan was spared. Schools stayed in session despite the severe winter weather; the children, bundled up to their ears, found the ink at their desks frozen solid. The music school had to move; its facilities were needed for a military hospital, where the girls later played on several occasions to entertain the wounded. Food was available only with rationing cards, and Mother had to resort to bartering the family's possessions for potatoes as she scoured the surrounding country for victuals. But there was no end to the shortages, and things got so bad that some of the refugees in the kitchen died of starvation. "People were dying before my eyes," Sofia later recalled, "and the worst of it was that we were unable to help them because we had nothing to eat ourselves."[14]

By the spring of 1945, with the end of the war in sight, everyone breathed a sigh of relief. Months of malnutrition, however, had taken its toll on the children, especially the youngest, who was stricken with a case of malaria that was treated with *akrikhin* [a patent medicine produced by a Soviet pharmaceutical company that survives to this day with the name Akrikhin]. Her condition worsened—she insisted on staying in the dark, responded to questions with strange answers, and experienced temporary memory loss, to the point where her mother had her hospitalized. The diagnoses ranged from poisoning to incipient schizophrenia, with the suggestion that she be committed to the Kazan Psychiatric Hospital—a plan that fortunately, in the end, came to nothing. Mother, in her distress, turned to prayer and promised to have her child baptized if Sofia recovered. She herself had been Christened in the Orthodox Church but had lost her faith when, as a small girl, she had had to confess her own sinfulness over and over again, even though she did not feel sinful at all. Now the wife of a member of the intelligentsia, she dared not go to church herself and therefore asked a neighbor to light a candle, say a prayer, and return with a consecrated wafer. The neighbor brought it to the hospital and told the young girl, "Here, eat this." After two months Sofia's condition improved enough for her to practice a Mozart minuet on the hospital piano. By the time she was allowed to return home, her mother had forgotten all about the baptism, but Sofia insisted on going to church. Her schoolmates, however, were all Young Pioneers, a Soviet-era political organization for children, and a local baptism would have had serious consequences. So, one Sunday, mother and daughter secretly set out on a trip down the Volga toward Selenodolsk to find a certain village where Fenya Gubaidullina knew of an appropriate church. But the priest was drunk and somehow failed to understand them. Ida, Sofia's older sister, later recalled a second attempt somewhere near Tsaritsyn (formerly Stalingrad, then Volgograd), but here the church was closed "for renovations." Sofia's mother felt that enough was enough: "We have given it a try—let's leave it at that." But that did not end the matter for her youngest daughter.

In those years Sofia took long walks in the countryside to experience nature and feel the earth under her feet. On one of her walks she saw a slow-moving freight train nearby and noticed that the cars were loaded with glass with people sitting on top. They turned out to be German prisoners of war who threw pieces of glass at her. She managed to dodge the glass, but could feel the intensity of the men's hatred. "None of us was to blame for what happened," she later remarked; "it was one of those historically defined moments."

In May 1946 Sofia graduated from elementary school and finished her years at the Children's Music School. Fifty years later Natalia Adolfovna Segel, a department head (*zavuch*) at the school, remembered the girl—by then world-famous—for two character traits in particular, elaborated below: "Sofia

Asgatovna was probably not our best pupil, but she was creative—perhaps the most creative who had ever attended our school. When she played onstage, the music infused her entire being. At that time we felt it was simply because she was a child, but unlike others she never lost it—it stayed with her."[15]

First Lessons in Composition from Nazib Zhiganov

Sofia entered the Kazan Music Gymnasium in the summer of 1946. The four-year program, which she and her classmates actually completed in three years, prepared students for admission to the conservatory. Besides general subjects, the curriculum consisted of instrumental lessons and courses in advanced music. That very summer the conservatory of the republic's capital had officially become the Tatarstan Graduate School of Music, with Nazib Gayazovich Zhiganov as the new director. The thirty-four-year-old Tatar composer, a graduate of the Moscow Conservatory, was a Party member. Some years earlier he had called attention to himself by writing an opera on the Pugachov Rebellion using motifs from Tatar folk music. *Kachkyn* (Rus., *Beglets;* The fugitive), which had its premiere in 1939 on the occasion of the opening of the Kazan Opera, was considered to be the first Tatar opera. As part of Stalin's policy of nationalities, Tatar State Philharmonic Hall had opened its doors in 1937; two years later the Tatar Composers' Union came into being; and now Zhiganov established himself in the city as the central figure of Tatar music.

Like elsewhere in the Soviet Union, music education in Kazan was focused on the early and superior training of new generations of musicians, and Zhiganov assembled a small group of students from the Music Gymnasium in preparation for his composition class at the Tatarstan Graduate School of Music. Sonechka, on hearing about it, was thrilled but too shy to come forward or tell about her early attempts at composing. Maria Alexandrovna Pyatnitskaya, the new and sympathetic piano teacher of the Gubaidulina sisters, heard of it from the more audacious older sister, Ida, who told her about Sofia's compositions. "Oh, so you're also doing some composing?" she asked Sonechka at the next opportunity. "Well, yes—" "Do you have anything you could show Nazib Gayazovich?" "Well, yes—" Finally, a short sonata in the style of Mozart convinced the director of her talent, and Sonechka, while still attending the Music Gymnasium, was admitted to his special course. The class started out with five students—two girls and three boys—but soon Sofia was the only one. Zhiganov turned out to be her favorite teacher during her years at the Music Gymnasium, and Gubaidulina later referred to him, almost sentimentally, as "my first musical love affair." Naturally Zhiganov wanted this new generation of young composers to develop an interest in their Tatar musical heritage. Gubaidulina later explained that Tatar music "could be heard everywhere at that time—as folk music and as compositions—on the radio, in the streets, on holidays. Willing or not, I soaked it up."[16]

But even in those early years she thought of herself as "a universal human being," and any limitation to Tatar or any other particular music would have been too confining. "I was not deeply introspective and thought that [Tatar] pentatonics would constrain me."[17] In those years she wrote a variety of works: songs to texts by Pushkin, Fet, and Tiutchev; variations for string quartet; a sonatina for piano; and—her first large composition—Piano Variations on the Tatar Folksong *Epipe*. The young composer performed this 1946 bravura piece on several occasions with great success. Nikolai Ivanovich Peiko, who later was to become Sofia's composition teacher in Moscow, heard her at a performance of young musicians in 1948, when he was attending a conference in Kazan.

In her third year at the Music Gymnasium, Sofia suddenly felt exhausted as a result of her creative efforts and had to interrupt her composition classes. She had pushed herself too far. "Perhaps at that age one shouldn't work so hard at composing," she observed in the mid-1980s, during an interview for a Finnish journal with the composer Vladimir Agopov, who spoke with her just before her departure on her first trip to Helsinki. "Nowadays, when twelve-year-old children come to see me, I tell them to stop composing, to leave it until later. A child first needs to accumulate a fund of experience on which she can then draw without exhausting herself."[18]

But there was another reason why the sixteen-year-old girl was ready to set aside composition for a while: the All-Union Congress of the Union of Soviet Composers[19] met in Moscow for the first time in April 1948.

Zhdanovshchina—Cultural Life under Party Dictatorship

During the "Great Patriotic Par," when the Party had to deploy all available human resources in the battle against Hitler's army, artists existed in a relatively liberal climate. "Patriotic forces" were being mobilized in every sphere of life, and Party control was somewhat relaxed. But only one year after the war ended, Stalin ordered his ideological henchman and cultural spokesman, Andrei Zhdanov, to step up the fight against "cosmopolitanism and formalism." The resulting policy, and process, of cultural purging later came to be known as the *zhdanovshchina*. The Party demanded only simple and folk-oriented works of art, fundamentally different from the "abstract formalism" of the decadent, bourgeois West. Soviet life, supposedly well on its way to a classless society, was to be depicted in optimistic and idealized representations. Every departure from this doctrine, every individual pursuit of creative freedom, was suppressed and eliminated. Anyone who did not submit was subject to persecution and denied the right to perform or publish, resulting in economic deprivation and social isolation. Operating with cold deliberation and brutality, Zhdanov and his Party apparatus spread fear throughout the land.

The reprisals began in 1946 and were first aimed at writers like Mikhail Zoshchenko, the acclaimed satirist of the 1920s and 1930s, and Anna Akhmatova, the grande dame of Russian poetry who was particularly celebrated by the intelligentsia. Using these big names as a deterrent, the campaign of defamation and vilification in the press lasted for a year.

Then it was the turn of filmmakers, actors, and directors, and toward the end of 1947 dark clouds gathered over the composers. Stalin not only had discovered political errors in *The Great Friendship*, an opera by one of his countrymen, Vano Muradeli, but he disliked the music. His reaction became the basis of a sweeping campaign that began in January 1948 with a meeting in Moscow lasting several days. It resulted in the blacklisting of such "formalist composers" as Shostakovich, Prokofiev, Khachaturian, Miaskovsky, Popov, and Shebalin, beginning a period of ideological deep-freeze. Following a Party resolution and a meeting of the Moscow Composers Union in February, Soviet musical life became strictly regulated and controlled by the All-Union Union of Soviet Composers. It held its first congress in April 1948 and subsequently proclaimed the guidelines for all matters of cultural policy: pleasantly melodious music reflecting the realities of Soviet life. The thirty-seven-year-old Tikhon Khrennikov, a Party member, was appointed Secretary General of the new union. His credentials included the 1939 opera *Into the Storm [V buriu]*, which for the first time presented Lenin as a character on stage. As early as January, he had attacked Shostakovich, Prokofiev, and other composers of renown; and only a few months later he took on the formalists of the West—Hindemith, Berg, Messiaen, even Britten—and vilified Stravinsky. It all culminated in his final and chief assault on Shostakovich, who eventually lost every position he held, including his professorships at the Leningrad and Moscow Conservatories, causing him serious financial troubles. The performance of new compositions became all but impossible, and a large number of older works were blacklisted. Tikhon Khrennikov, who would remain as Secretary General of the union into the 1990s, almost single-handedly determined the nature and history of Soviet musical life.

Soon congresses were also held in Tatarstan and the other republics. The Composers Union in Kazan did not have its own meeting place but met in the same building that housed the Children's Music School, which the Gubaidulina sisters entered every day. At these meetings the union members criticized composers and their works, passed resolutions, and pilloried disagreeable rivals. Zhiganov himself came under fire, and the younger generation lost its sense of direction and creative energy. The seventeen-year-old Sofia was already familiar with the score of Shostakovich's opera *Lady Macbeth of Mtsensk* and was very fond of it. She had also discovered Shostakovich's Second Piano Trio and practiced it with her friends. Gubaidulina later talked about the shocking experiences of that time with the English author and cellist Elizabeth Wilson:

> We grew up at a time when everything around us became one unending question. We were obsessed with asking questions, because at the time there was a complete absence of information about everything from politics to art. The crude attacks on literature and music that appeared in our press were utterly bewildering. One day you're in love with a story by Zoshchenko or a poem by Akhmatova; then suddenly they're proclaimed 'bad' and 'terrible,' and their works are aggressively attacked in all the major newspapers.

It's now difficult for people to imagine what a young person felt in such a situation. Suppose that you are fourteen or fifteen years old, you discover with delight a particular work by Shostakovich, and suddenly it turns out that this work is suspect, even dangerous. You are left with an urgent question, and there is no answer to be had anywhere.[20]

After her successful final examinations in the spring of 1949, it became clear that Sofia was on her way to the conservatory. Her older sister was already enrolled as a piano student, and although Sofia did not register in the composition department, she too was about to study the piano.

3 | At the Kazan Conservatory, 1949–1954

Piano Classes and First Encounters with the Communist System

Sofia Gubaidulina began to take piano classes at the Kazan Conservatory in the fall of 1949. Her teacher was the Muscovite Leopold Genrikhovich Lukomsky, who spent ten days every month in Kazan to teach his students. Now nineteen years old, Sofia decided to concentrate on playing the piano and give up her dream of studying composition. But she was determined to broaden her general understanding of music by studying theory of harmony, playing from orchestral scores, and instrumentation (taught by Zhiganov). Two foreign-language courses were required as part of the five-year program, and Sofia chose German, which she had already begun in school. There were, of course, also the required annual courses in Marxism-Leninism that began with Marx's *Communist Manifesto* and Lenin's major works. In his *Left-Wing Radicalism: A Childhood Disease* [*Detskaia bolezn' "levizny" v kommunisme*] the founder of the Soviet state argued that lies were an acceptable means of defense in emergencies, a position deeply offensive to the young woman's moral sensibility. "That was a real eye-opener on the whole system for me—we were supposed to lie—and lies were the basis on which the system was built." At the end of the first semester the instructor announced a course in "Philosophical Topics" for the following semester, and Sofia eagerly anticipated reading Socrates and Plato. However, not yet familiar with the system's terminology, she ended up taking a course in dialectical materialism. A short while later Sofia had her first personal encounter with the Soviet system, in which economic and cultural institutions and activities were, without exception, controlled by Party functionaries. During her second year the presiding officer of a new student organization was to be elected, and the instructor for Marxism-Leninism asked the students for nominations:

I put in the name of a very active Jewish fellow student; it greatly displeased the representative of the Party, and he made his point perfectly clear. Because of Stalin's nationality policy in those days, the Tatars ranked highest in Kazan, then came the Russians, then the other nationalities, and the Jews were at the bottom. Later, in Moscow, it didn't matter much whether you were a Jew or a Russian. When we got to the election, I voted for the Jew because I wanted to retain my personal freedom. But the person elected was a Tatar woman who was neither very intelligent nor particularly active. All this had reverberations for me, even touching my family. The Party man complained to my father that his "impudent daughter" had had the cheek to nominate a Jew, and my father confronted and reprimanded me. It cast something of a shadow on the relationship between me and my father, whom I otherwise respected and loved without reservations.

The musical fare in Kazan in those first postwar years was rather provincial, even though some Moscow artists visited from time to time, and Sofia Gubaidulina still fondly remembers piano evenings with Rosa Tamarkina or Bella Davidovich. Whatever contemporary music the programs featured was limited to unproblematic works by such composers as Shostakovich, Prokofiev, or composers of the Soviet era not well known abroad. The opera theater performed mostly works by Verdi, Rimsky-Korsakov, and Tchaikovsky, but they did not leave lasting impressions on the mind of the young music student. In those early years at the Conservatory Wagner's operas were her favorites, especially *Lohengrin*, *Parsifal*, and the *Ring*, but she got to know them only from their scores. She had little comprehension of the German text, but the music made a deep impression. In the Kazan of those years one had to make do with scores and books.

Lukomsky's piano class covered the classical-romantic repertoire that was then the usual fare in the Soviet Union, with special emphasis on Russian composers. Sofia studied the concert literature and presented herself onstage with Mozart's Piano Concerto in C Minor, K. 491, in a hall on Ploshchad' svobody. She soon followed up with Haydn's Concerto in C Major, Rimsky-Korsakov's Piano Concerto in C♯ Minor/D♭ Major, as well as the Second Concerto in G Minor, Op. 22, by Saint-Saëns. At times, Lukomsky gave her some fatherly advice, saying on one occasion: "Listen to everybody, but never follow anyone," as if he had already sensed the uncompromising nature of his dark-haired, tireless student. He must have had a high regard for her, as he invited her to Moscow between terms, giving her access to the big world of the nation's capital. She was allowed to read in his library, study scores, and listen to music at the conservatory. Hermann Abendroth conducted a concert in the Great Hall of the Conservatory [Bol'shoi zal Moskovskoi konservatorii], and students were allowed to sit in on the rehearsal at no cost. Sofia also heard the composition student Edison Denisov and one of his fellow students, Elizaveta Tumanian, play one his works for two pianos, and she listened to the young Andrei Volkonsky, who was in Shaporin's composition class. Lukomsky fell ill in the summer of 1951 and could no longer travel and teach his classes in Kazan, but Sofia used this occasion to study and play scores with redoubled energy.

Maria Yudina and a Special Piano Evening in Kazan

Trying to find a replacement for Lukomsky, Zhiganov considered another Muscovite, Maria Veniaminovna Yudina. She was an outstanding pianist and important authority in her field—her repertoire extended from the classical to the modern period—as well as a woman of strong personality and opinions. Eighteen years old in 1917, the year of the revolution, she had committed to her diary a personal confession that could just as well have been Sofia's credo at age twenty: "I know of only one path to God: through art. I don't mean to say that my path is universal. I know there are other roads. But I sense that for me this is the only one. Everything divine and spiritual first reveals itself to me through art, through one of its branches—music. It is my confession!"[1] Five years later she was offered a professorship to teach piano in Leningrad, and even so great a pianist and teacher as Heinrich Neuhaus, whose students included Sviatoslav Richter and Emil Gilels, told Pasternak at that time that he felt like nobody compared to Yudina. Yudina maintained her religious commitment against all political pressures—actually once going up against Stalin himself[2]—but, like her friend Pasternak with whom she corresponded, she was almost miraculously spared imprisonment and the Gulag. During World War II, Yudina worked as a volunteer in military hospitals and performed almost daily on the radio, playing works by Russian composers but also Bach and Beethoven. The Party, however, considered her a dangerous and decidedly undesirable person. Because she was not allowed to travel in the West, she remains to this day largely unknown outside Russia.

On November 12, 1951, Maria Yudina gave a concert in Kazan,[3] featuring Beethoven's Piano Sonatas Op. 26 in A♭ Major, Op. 27, No. 2, in C♯ Minor (*Moonlight Sonata*), and Op. 31, No. 2, in D Minor (*Tempest*). The concert hall must surely have been filled to the last seat, for a concert by Maria Yudina always meant a performance well beyond mere technical brilliance. Onstage the artist usually wore a dark dress resembling a nun's habit, and her religious approach to music was evident in her manner of playing. It is said that people came to her performances as to church services, and Sofia Gubaidulina was among those who went to the conservatory that evening. With the audience already in their seats, Sofia happened to be walking down the hallway leading from the Artist's Room to the stage just as Maria Yudina, evidently feeling unobserved, briefly stopped at the stage door to bow her head and make the sign of the cross. This small but significant gesture gave Sofia courage and confidence, as it demonstrated that even in a hostile religious environment one need not feel abandoned.

Despite the concert's great success, Maria Yudina was not offered a position at the Kazan Conservatory. She had just been released from teaching at the Moscow Conservatory, as the Party objected to the religious influence she exerted over her students. It was feared that this outspoken and uncompromising artist would face similar problems in Kazan. "As a teacher," Gubaidulina later said, "Maria Veniaminovna was very authoritarian, and one could feel almost oppressed by her; today I am glad that she did not come to Kazan at that time." In the 1960s, however, the composer and the pianist got to know each other rather well in Moscow.

Piano and Composition Lessons:
Grigory Kogan and Albert Leman

The search for a new piano teacher at the Kazan Conservatory lasted until the spring of 1952 and concluded with the appointment of Grigory Mikhailovich Kogan. He was on the piano faculty of the Moscow Conservatory and, like his predecessor, fulfilled his teaching duties in Kazan during monthly visits. An outstanding performer and scholar of the piano, he appeared as concert pianist and lecturer on a wide range of topics related to the keyboard. His favorite repertoire comprised the French clavicinists Rameau and Couperin, whom he rendered with great subtlety on the piano. Sofia progressed rapidly under his guidance, studying Bach's *Wohltemperiertes Klavier* and Beethoven's Piano Sonata in Bb Major, Op. 106 (*Hammerklavier*) and his Sonata in F Minor, Op. 57 (*Appassionata*). She also gave performances of Bach's *Brandenburg Concerto* No. 5 in D Major, Beethoven's Piano Concerto No. 3 in C Minor, Op. 37, as well as Rakhmaninov's Piano Concerto No. 2 in C Minor, Op. 18. Kogan gave her excellent advice about practicing, advice that was founded on his scholarship:

> Never practice when you are tired. In a state of fatigue any effort to wind up a ball of yarn will result in tangled threads. But when you are awake and alert, you'll produce a clean, tight thread of thought that will be firmly tied down in your subconscious mind. And that thread will permit you to play well when you appear onstage. Fatigue causes the thread to loosen and expand, and a wide thread leaves the subconscious less firmly engaged—there will be slippage resulting in mistakes. Our memory is rather weak, but the subconscious is tremendously strong.

This advice applied not only to performing but also to composing. Although Kogan did not teach composition, "his extensive knowledge of art and his original approach to a musical text strongly influenced my decision to become a composer."[4]

Although Kogan never spoke of it, his relationship to his student seems to have had a particularly strange twist. Sofia apparently reminded him of his wife, who had died under tragic circumstances. She had been a gifted pianist who suffered from such severe stage fright that she never performed publicly. When her husband was on his concert tours she stayed at home suffering unbearable nervous tension, and on one of these occasions threw herself down a flight of stairs. The program Sofia studied under Kogan's direction was the same one that his wife was to have performed onstage, including Liszt's *Totentanz,* for piano and orchestra, and Prokofiev's *Sarcasms,* for solo piano, Op. 17. "Perhaps he tried to find out what could be achieved with such works," Gubaidulina later speculated; "the lessons, at any rate, were very intense. I learned about the circumstances only much later and by complete coincidence." Like Lukomsky, Kogan invited his student to Moscow, and on one of these visits he happened to be on tour and had given his apartment key to the pianist Nina Svetlanova, who, as a child, had been his wife's piano student. During a long night's conversation in Kogan's apartment Svetlanova, also noting the strong resemblance between Sofia and Kogan's wife, revealed the background of Gubaidulina's piano program. In that same conversation Sofia learned about the composition department at the conservatory and, in particular, about Yury Shaporin's class and his three students, Andrei Volkonsky, Rodion Shchedrin, and Evgeny Svetlanov—Nina Svetlanova's husband, who later, for many years, conducted the State Symphony Orchestra of the USSR. Shaporin's students were divided into three distinct groups: a small circle of avant-gardists around Andrei Volkonsky; a group of Party loyalists and adherents to Socialist Realism that strongly opposed the avant-garde; and a group positioned between the other two whose members, including Shchedrin and Svetlanov, assumed the appearance of the avant-garde and engaged in the study of modernism but in fact aspired to the conveniences of life within the establishment. This account gave Sofia Gubaidulina, even while still only a student in Kazan, a clear picture of the situation in Moscow.

Gubaidulina never experienced stage fright as a performing pianist; to the contrary, she loved being onstage and felt deeply fulfilled by performing a great musical work to which she could give herself with her entire being. She was so captivated by composing, however, that in her third year at the conservatory she took composition as an elective from Albert Semyonovich Leman, a pianist and composer at the conservatory. Born in 1915, Leman had studied under Mikhail Fabianovich Gnesin in Leningrad but had to be evacuated to Kazan in 1942 when Leningrad was under siege. Much later, only a few years before he died, Leman commented on his former student who had meanwhile become world famous:

I remember Sofia Gubaidulina as an extremely intelligent and gifted and also very beautiful student. When she was still quite young she played Chopin's Fantasy in F Minor [Op. 49] with me. She was a gifted composer and a gifted pianist—she had the makings of a virtuoso performer. But her heart was set on composition, and she was then writing, among other things, variations for piano somewhat in the manner of a beginner. She understood all my explanations and every demand I made and she was remarkably studious and dedicated: she was an artist to her fingertips. When she completed her studies, I did everything in my power to get her admitted to the Moscow Conservatory.[5]

The years in Kazan from that point on were marked by a conflict between performance and composition. Repeatedly people encouraged or comforted Sofia by telling her that Rakhmaninov and Stravinsky both composed and performed onstage. "But that was not possible for me. When I concentrated on composing, I neglected the piano, and when I gave everything I had to the piano, it sapped the energy I needed for composition. Also, because my training in both was not yet complete, I had to choose between two paths." Kogan was convinced that his student should become a pianist, probably because she played with great expressiveness ranging from deep tenderness all the way to demonic fervor. Certain that she had the makings of a virtuoso performer, he was ready to open every door for her, even one leading to graduate studies with Heinrich Neuhaus in Moscow.

Life as a Student, a Scholarship, and a Delegation from Moscow

Music, however, was not all there was to life. Sofia Gubaidulina participated in sports and in the social life of her fellow students whenever her busy schedule permitted. Vera, her oldest sister, who was then a medical student at the local university, later remembered,

> Often a gang of her schoolmates, always noisy and cheerful, appeared in our home. Less often, at the Institute of Medicine, as soon as Sonia appeared you would notice it immediately and hear "Sonia is here!" And there she was already at the piano improvising, surrounded by young people caught up in the spirit and mood of the music, cheerful, happy, and full of enthusiasm. She had become famous among the intellectuals during her years of study in Kazan, starting with [the Children's] Music School, and even I had become aware of it. During my first years at the Kazan Institute of Medicine, many of my instructors would ask, with interest, "Aren't the Gubaidulina girls yours sisters?" ... The girls were welcome in any of the good homes. They were always shining examples, but constantly busy "up to their ears." They never had a free moment.[6]

The early morning hours were reserved for practice, and Sofia, with Zhiganov's special permission, usually worked in one of the free classrooms at the conservatory, even during the summer break. On one occasion the janitor discovered the supposedly offending student and wanted to throw her out. Bothered by the interruption, she told him of Zhiganov's permission, but the custodian was not about to change his mind. She flew into a rage and, eyes flashing, picked up a nearby chair and threw it at the intruder. The janitor got the point and withdrew. When she told her parents about the incident, her father let it be known that it was this very man who had reported him to the Party in the 1930s and thereby precipitated an official hearing.

During the Soviet era scholarships were used as a reward for exceptional achievements not only in science and technology but also, and particularly, in the arts. Among the fourth-year piano students at that time were two viable candidates: Boris Yevlampov, a Russian, and Sofia Gubaidulina. A picture of Grigory Kogan and the young woman with the Tatar name appeared in the local paper of December 19, 1952, on the occasion of the award of a Stalin Scholarship being granted to the "Komsomol girl" Sofia Gubaidulina. Referring to her competitor, she later commented: "We were about equal at the piano, but in all the other subjects I had received a 5 [the best grade], whereas he had a few 4s and 3s, and he also had a drinking problem. Perhaps I won on the basis of the overall evaluation, but I rather suspect that because of Stalin's policy of nationalities they wanted to feature a Tatar name."

Leman's composition class—in which Sofia was working primarily on a violin concerto—provided a new impetus for resolving her inner conflict. In 1953 a delegation from Moscow arrived in Kazan. Headed by an official from the Ministry of Culture by the name of Shaveiko, the delegation was to scour the provinces for talented composers in an effort to implement the Party Resolutions of 1948 and to advance overall cultural policies. Sofia and two fellow students were selected for travel to Moscow to be examined in three areas—performance of a work written by the student, solfège, and a general oral examination. The standards were very high, and Sofia, after three days of intense preparation, stress, and almost no food, was close to total exhaustion. After the examination was over, she nearly fainted and barely made it to the dining area for a bowl of soup. But a few spoonfuls revived her, and she finally learned that she was the only one to pass the examination. This result made it possible for her to begin her studies in composition at the Moscow Conservatory in the summer of 1954.

A Geology Student from Kazan Who Writes Poetry

Groups of students carrying briefcases, rushing from one class to another at any one of the numerous universities and institutes, were very much a part of life in Kazan. The students of that postwar generation were ill-fed and ill-clothed, and lived extremely modest lives. In the war years and immediately after life was hard, and students gratefully accepted anything that might lift them above the gray deprivations of everyday Soviet existence. Soldiers who had returned from the war spoke about a distant and unfamiliar Europe, and German "booty films" could now be seen in local theaters. Hollywood films had arrived as part of the American lend-lease program, and Oleg Lundstrom and his big band played jazz on Ploshchad' svobody. He was the son of immigrants to Shanghai whom Stalin had permitted to return, but rather than allowing them to settle in Moscow, they were assigned to live in Kazan. The decisive event, of course, was Stalin's death on March 5, 1953, which brought the glimmer of life to a country that had been paralyzed for three decades.

Mark Liando, then a geology student at Kazan's famous university, wrote in his autobiography about the changing atmosphere at that time:

> Dances were often held at New Year's and in early spring. In winter we'd go cross-country skiing to the hilly banks across the Volga, all the way to the Sviiaga River and the ancient city of Sviiazhsk, founded by Ivan the Terrible. In summer we'd go out to the Volga, its islands and sandy beaches in the backwaters. . . . Together with the "foreign" students from North Korea—a marvel in themselves!—"Shanghai" jazz made its first appearance in the city. . . . We were wild about dancing to "Chattanooga Choo-Choo," "Saint Louis Blues," and "Caravan" on the squeaky old parquet floor of the former Nobles Club, later the Officers Club, on Ploshchad' svobody.[7]

Mark Liando was attending the 1953 New Year's Eve ball of the Furriers' Club when he spotted a student in the crowd, "a rather skinny girl in a bright red frock. Long black corkscrew curls framed her delicate, sensitive Tatar face. A small, determined chin. A birthmark on her cheek. Her steady gaze—fathomless. . . . Frezi Grant, gliding across the dreadful nighttime waters in her dainty slippers, suddenly appeared before me; in those years I was a great Alexander Grin fan."[8]

Too shy to ask the "Tatar girl" for a dance, Liando followed her when she left the ball and struck up a conversation in the snow on Ploshchad' svobody. He was surprised to learn that she studied composition and told her that he was a budding geologist but sometimes wrote poetry. "Then I accompanied her to a narrow street lined by log houses in the old city of Kazan, exactly where I was headed, where my family lived; we were almost neighbors."[9] Mark was introduced to Sofia's family, and the two began a romantic relationship, with Mark perhaps more committed than she. They spent much of their free time together, watching German films, visiting the theater, and listening to concerts:

> During our walks S. G. would tell me about musical form, sonata-allegro form, polyphony, the functions of Wagner's *Leitmotive*. . . . We talked about literature. About the difference between what appeared on the pages of journals and life as it surrounded us. "You know what," she said, "they've tried yet again to enlist me in some sort of Komsomol work!"—"Well, so what did you do?"—"I told them that for me it was study, study, study, morning, noon, and night!" Then she let out a resounding laugh.—Occasionally I would try to sing something Neapolitan or an aria; she would accompany me at the piano, insisting that I steer clear of wrong notes. She had perfect pitch. At times she would play some classical piece or something of her own for me. Her expressivity and accuracy were fantastic. Many people even today regret that she did not make a career as a performer. . . . Now and again, my heart pounding, I would pull from my pocket a sheet of doggerel dedicated to her and read it. She would listen, her dark eyes gazing into the distance. And all of a sudden I came to the acute realization that she was striving with all her being to reach some goal that only she could see, just like Grin's Frezi, "going her own way." . . . I was still confused and searching, and I understood that we probably would not be together for long.[10]

Final examinations at the conservatory were held in June 1954. Sofia performed the program she had studied with Kogan: Liszt's *Totentanz* for piano and orchestra, Beethoven's *Appassionata*, Bach's Prelude and Fugue in A♭ Minor from the *Wohltemperiertes Klavier* (book 1), and several preludes by Kabalevsky. Her examination behind her, Sofia and Mark spent the summer together in Zhelanga on the Volga. Her years as a student in Kazan were over.

Sofia Gubaidulina's father,
Asgad Masgudovich Gubaidullin.

Sofia Gubaidulina's mother,
Fedosia Fyodorovna Elkhova.

Ekaterina Pavlovna Leontieva's class. Sofia, above left of Leontieva, leaning on her teacher's knee.

Gubaidulina at the piano (1936–37).

Gubaidulina with her piano teacher, Grigory Mikhailovich Kogan.

The three sisters with their mother. From left, Vera, Ida, and Sofia (1950).

Sofia as a student at the Moscow Conservatory (1955).

Sofia with her daughter, Nadia (1965).

4 | At the Moscow Conservatory, 1954–1959

"The Thaw" and Orientation in Moscow

With Khrushchev's rise to power in the fall of 1953, a new political era began in the Soviet Union. Stalin's death meant the end of the worst period of *zhdanovshchina,* when students' rooms in the dormitories of the Moscow Conservatory were searched for forbidden musical scores. Now artists and scholars were allowed certain minimal freedoms, ushering in a decade that soon became known in both East and West as "The Thaw," after the title of Ilya Ehrenburg's 1954 novel, *Ottepel'.* Two years later, in February 1956, Khrushchev gave his famous "secret speech" at the Twentieth Party Congress revealing Stalin's crimes for the first time. A large number of prisoners and camp inmates were released and rehabilitated. That same year saw the opening of a Picasso show at Moscow's State Pushkin Museum of Fine Arts [Gosudarstvennyi muzei izobraziteľ'skikh iskusstv imeni A. S. Pushkina]—an exhibition of "decadent" Western paintings in one of the top art museums of the Soviet Union that would have been unthinkable just a few years earlier.

Moscow has always been a magnet for people from the provinces, not only for Chekhov's famous "three sisters." In 1918, after the Soviet revolutionary government had moved from the tsar's residence in St. Petersburg to the Kremlin in Moscow, the city became the central command post of the Communist Party. But, above all, Moscow, with its proverbial "forty times forty churches," was the cultural heart of the nation, where the very best artists and scientists lived and interacted. Anyone intent on learning from them, anyone wanting to feel the pulse of contemporary Russian culture, could have only one goal: to live in Moscow. At the time of the Thaw the capital had an official population of about five million, but that did not account for all those who lived there illegally without registering. Obtaining the much-desired *propiska* (residency permit) was difficult, as the Party checked each and every application because of the enormous housing shortage. Countless families still lived in the so-called *kommunalkas* (communal apartments) in terribly crowded conditions. Large apartments dating back to tsarist time had been subdivided, with occupants sharing both kitchen and bath facilities. People married established Moscow residents just to become eligible for housing.

Sofia Gubaidulina began her studies at the Moscow Conservatory in the fall of 1954. She had received a small scholarship and, like most beginning students, was sharing a room with four others in a dormitory on Dmitrovskii pereulok, not far from the Bolshoi Theater in central Moscow. The city boasted two major music schools at the time. One was the venerable Tchaikovsky State Conservatory, so named because Tchaikovsky had taught music theory and composition there, when the conservatory enjoyed the patronage of the tsars. The other, the Gnesin Institute, founded by members of the Gnesin family of musicians, started out as the most important private music school in Moscow but, after World War II, was officially recognized as a postgraduate institution. Several professors who had lost their positions at the conservatory during the 1948 purge were able to resume their careers at the Gnesin Institute, among them the remarkable Maria Yudina. The faculty of the conservatory included such world-class musicians as the violinist David Oistrakh and the pianist Heinrich Neuhaus, whose instruction of technique and interpretation was of the highest caliber.

All students at the conservatory, without exception, were required to take piano lessons. But Sofia Gubaidulina, having already passed her piano examination in Kazan, was admitted to the more advanced piano class of Yakov Izrailevich Zak, a Neuhaus student and highly respected teacher. At the time Sofia's sister, Ida, was in her final year of graduate studies with Zak, which is equivalent to third-year postgraduate studies, the course work required of doctoral students. Besides Shostakovich, who had been forced out of the conservatory in 1948, three composers formed the top national tier: Dmitri Kabalevsky, Yury Shaporin, and Aram Khachaturian. But these famous composers were complemented by several excellent teachers: Nikolai Peiko and Vissarion Shebalin, Edison Denisov's teacher. Sofia Gubaidulina decided to enroll in the composition class of Yury Alexandrovich Shaporin, a dignified, elderly, bald gentleman who had enjoyed the successful premiere of his major opera, *The Decembrists* [*Dekabristy*], at the Bolshoi Theater only a year earlier. Just at the time when Gubaidulina began working with Shaporin, Andrei Volkonsky quit "for medical reasons." In truth, he had refused to subject his compositions to Party control and, during his examination, did not provide the answers his professors wanted to hear. Clearly he was not going to pass. Shaporin, however, remained kind and gracious to Volkonsky, even supporting him financially.[1]

"When I arrived in Moscow in 1954," Gubaidulina commented later, "they had lifted the prohibitions and stopped searching the dorms at the conservatory. It had also become possible again to listen to Stravinsky and Hindemith in the archives."[2] A few years older than most of her fellow students, Gubaidulina had a clear sense of her goals and made demands on her teachers. Although her living conditions were extremely modest, she knew she could now plunge into a rich musical life as never before. Old and new works by Shostakovich were again being performed in Moscow, among them his song cycle, *From Jewish Folk Poetry* [*Iz evreiskoi narodnoi poezii*]; Günther Ramin, the Thomas Kantor from Leipzig, conducted Bach's *Passion according to St. John;* and occasionally Maria Yudina appeared in concerts.

Shaporin's composition class, however, was a vast disappointment to Sofia. He could read notes in extremely high and low registers only with great difficulty, and his criticism of her work was skewed and biased. When she submitted her efforts to him, he would only say, "That's no good, but perhaps it could go like this," and then he would improvise on the piano in the style of Rakhmaninov. With suppressed anger and resentment, she decided to change instructors and found an ally in Gennady Saveliev, another Shaporin student. One winter day the two set out for Ruza, a small town about sixty miles west of Moscow, to look up Dmitri Kabalevsky in the town's creative retreat (Dom tvorchestva) owned by the Composers Union.

The fifty-year-old composer received them graciously but leafed through their compositions without comment. To their request to be admitted to his class, he replied, "There is nothing I can do," as he was allowed to teach only one student at the conservatory and that spot was already filled. "Probably it was fortuitous that Kabalevsky turned me down. A wise and intelligent man, he likely suspected that I would not be happy with him." Having missed the last bus to the station, the two students walked several hours on that cold winter night to catch the train back to Moscow and arrived early the next morning.

But Gubaidulina did not give up at that point. According to Elizaveta Tumanian, then in her final year of studying with Nikolai Ivanovich Peiko and later to become Sofia's close friend,

> A young woman came to my door one day, wanting to know what sort of teacher Nikolai Ivanovich was. I said that his teaching was thoroughly professional and he himself greatly respected—but that he dominated his students. It was not easy to get along with him because he could be ironic, even sarcastic, and had driven some of his students to tears. Sofia listened and then replied: "I work hard and I'll take my chances with him." She believed that life was a continual learning process.[3]

Shaporin had already sensed that something was amiss with his student and commented to the dean of the composition department, Semyon Bogatyryov: "This girl scares me. She looks at me with such angry eyes." So, without further questions, the dean authorized the change. In 1991, when Enzo Restagno, the artistic director of the festival Settembre Musica, asked Gubaidulina about Shaporin, she provided an insightful perspective that revealed him as a victim of the Soviet system:

> This whole thing, in my opinion, was typical of life in the Soviet Union at that time. The most intellectually gifted and talented members of the intelligentsia in Russia were ruthlessly destroyed. And it was essential to fill that vacuum as quickly as possible to create hospitable conditions for the emergence of a new class of intellectuals. The "lucky ones" were offered a straight path to immediate success. They got the biggest state prizes, and the ministry paid top prices for their work. But, alas, those "lucky ones" couldn't handle their good fortune. They were unprepared and therefore had no other choice but to put up appearances and to "puff themselves up." They had plenty of talent but their abilities fell far short.... [Shaporin's *The Decembrists* is the work of] a professional, without a doubt, and it is said that it is the result of many years of labor, but exactly how things happened, nobody knows. The opera has kept its secret.[4]

When the new academic year began Sofia Gubaidulina became Nikolai Peiko's composition student.

Composition Classes with Nikolai Peiko

In the summer of 1955, at the start of her second year, Gubaidulina moved to the student residence at Srednii Kisslovskii pereulok, directly behind the conservatory. Sharing a double room, she remained at this address until her graduation in 1959. At long last, after a year's delay, her composition classes could begin.

Nikolai Ivanovich Peiko, born in 1916, became an assistant to Shostakovich in 1944 and had been teaching composition at the conservatory ever since. His work was influenced by his teacher, Nikolai Miaskovsky, as well as by Prokofiev and Shostakovich, and he took an interest in Bashkir folk traditions. Later, in the 1990s, Peiko commented on his composition classes:

> Twice weekly I taught at the conservatory, although students in their first and last year took three lessons a week. They brought their own compositions and performed them; some of them were very good pianists. There was criticism and analysis, and finally I would suggest some improvements, making an effort to be specific. For instance, if a student had not completely worked through his material or composed a weak coda, I would show him examples ranging from Haydn to Miaskovsky, my teacher. In those days records and tapes were still scarce, so

my students—and sometimes I—played their works four hands. Even today I think this is better than just listening—playing is much more active. Each class had two or three students. Miaskovsky's classes were larger, and that was better because you had an audience right from the start.[5]

While Albert Leman had been a rather gentle teacher who used encouragement and praise, Peiko's lessons were a challenge. As Gubaidulina recalled:

Nikolai Ivanovich Peiko and Albert Semyonovich Leman were completely different teachers—in fact, opposites. Albert Semyonovich motivated his students to do their best, and even someone of mediocre ability would show excellent results with him. Nikolai Ivanovich always came down hard on his students; his criticism was intense and frequent. Even some excellent students were unable to take it and left him, as, for instance the very talented Albanian Tschesk Sadeja. I don't know which method is better—both were good. Nikolai Ivanovich was harsh with the men, maybe a little less so with women. It wasn't always easy for me, but I was happy.

Peiko was tolerant of twentieth-century music, even though he was not at home in that world. "Somewhat later I analyzed Schönberg's *A Survivor from Warsaw*, as well as Mahler and Stravinsky—and, of course, Taneev and Rimsky-Korsakov. 'Constructivism' is even there, not only in Berg and Schönberg. It is found in Taneev's polyphony and in Rimsky-Korsakov's harmony."[6]

Mark Liando came to Moscow at the same time as Sofia. He had found a position as a geologist in the Ministry of Metallurgy that required him to travel from the Baltic to the Pacific. So they saw each other only on weekends, and not at all for many weeks during the summer. They were married on January 22, 1956, but there was no hope for an apartment to share. At first he lived with an aunt in Moscow, but later he moved to a small room in Peredelkino, which required a daily commute to the city.

Peredelkino and "Phacelia," a Poem by Mikhail Prishvin

Peredelkino, the "town of authors and writers" west of Moscow, was made famous by Pasternak; it is where the tragedy of his Nobel Prize played itself out in 1958, when, after first responding with great joy and pride, he later, presumably on his own, "rejected" the prize because of the meaning the award represented in his society. Lying between patches of birch and pine in the countryside, Peredelkino can be reached in twenty minutes by train from the Kiev Station in Moscow. Farther along the tracks, after crossing a small river, one reaches the village of the Writers Union with its houses, student residences, and dachas for writers and other prominent figures.

"Sometime about 1956," Mark Liando notes in his autobiography,

> I rented a small attached room in the little wooden house of a drunkard inventor, in Peredelkino not far from Moscow near the well-known writers' colony. . . . A bottle of wine, oranges, some cookies, a bunch of snowdrops on the bedside table in a vase belonging to the landlord. Embraces on a lumpy coil-spring bedstead with nickle-plated "eyes" that resembled a Triassic lizard's. Afterward we would stroll through the meadows and over the hillsides of Peredelkino above the river and have dinner at the local *stolovaia* [public dining hall], then return again to our kennel. . . . We could hear the inventor and his wife fighting on the other side of the wall.[7]

On these walks Mark and Sofia would occasionally spot Pasternak, dressed in a long overcoat, strolling through the woods or along the river. His dacha was near the village close to the river. Liando, still writing poetry at home and while traveling, tried to establish contact with young writers:

> S. G. and I sometimes attended their literary evenings. I remember a student of medium height with Asiatic features, a face "from the forest," who spoke with a rasping voice, pondering what he had to say. He was Chuvash and went by the name of Gena Lisin. He and, to some extent, I had "Volga roots" in common. Later he translated his name into Chuvash and he became the now famous avant-garde poet Gennady Aigi.[8]

They read classics like Shakespeare and Goethe but also Hermann Hesse and Thomas Mann's *Doktor Faustus,* as well as poems by Pasternak, Mandelstam, Tsvetaeva, and Rilke. In the spring of 1957 they read Mikhail Prishvin's prose poem, *Phacelia* [*Fatseliia*]. Prishvin died in 1954, but he—together with a small number of other writers—had become popular in the Soviet Union, escaping the pressures of the Soviet system by writing about nature. In a mood of romantic love, Mark and Sofia called the river Phacelia and started working together as lyricist and composer, with Mark drawing on Prishvin's long prose poem to create a six-part fragment. At Sofia's request, he added some lines of his own for dramatic contrast. She set the texts to music and wrote the orchestral score, creating a cycle of six concert songs that combine sensitivity to the experience of nature with the melancholy of lost love. A little more than a year later this composition was performed at the conservatory under the direction of Emin Khachaturian, with Tamara Petrova as soloist. A recording for radio and several broadcasts followed soon thereafter, apparently enjoying some popularity. At the time of her final examination in 1959, Gubaidulina included *Phacelia* in her dossier of required submissions.

Playing the Piano and Working on Compositions

Weekends at Peredelkino provided Gubaidulina with the elixir of life: nature and quiet peace; Moscow, a city of five million, could offer neither. The dormitory was a lively place full of the sounds of students practicing their instruments. Between classes she would either retreat to her room (having worked out an alternating schedule with her roommate) or sit on a bench in the park trying to concentrate on her work. The best time for collecting and preparing herself was her daily practice session at the piano during the morning hours, a routine she had been strictly following ever since her days as a student in Kazan.

"I practiced each morning for two or three hours at the conservatory," Gubaidulina later commented:

> The practice rooms and classrooms were unoccupied between seven and nine or ten o'clock. Although I was often hungry, those were the "sacred hours" that put me in a state of pure meditation, somewhat like the condition described in *The Story of a Russian Pilgrim*. It was the most important time, the high point of my day. From there I would go to the cafeteria for a small breakfast to begin my daily schedule of lectures and seminars—the less agreeable parts of my life.

Gubaidulina has kept these "sacred hours" throughout her life, except that, eventually, composing took the place of playing the piano. So when, in the 1990s, she spoke of composing as "a kind of worship service," she also had in mind those earlier morning hours of focused introspection.

At he end of her third year at the conservatory Sofia finally had to make a decision that was long overdue. Perhaps the excellence of Peiko's composition classes and the success of *Phacelia* helped her to reach the choice she made. At any rate, in the summer of 1957, she quit her piano class with Yakov Zak and concentrated completely on composition. What the future of the pianist Sofia Gubaidulina might have been remains a matter of speculation. She probably would have excelled as an interpreter of great expressiveness. Henrietta Mirvis, who was a fellow student in Zak's class at the conservatory and won a prize at the Salzburg Mozarteum in 1956, and who is now on the piano faculty at the Moscow Conservatory and has performed in Japan and the United States—commented on Sofia's abilities as a pianist in words that recall Natalia Segel's opinion of her pupil in the Children's Music School in Kazan:

> Sonia was not so fond of romantic piano music—not Chopin, but Schubert. She loved grand and exalted, as well as modern music—Shostakovich. As a pianist she probably did not have truly outstanding technique but total dedication and excellent taste. Most of all, she was a profound musician and at the same time disciplined. When Sonia was playing—for example, Schubert's late G Major

Sonata [D. 894]—it was as if she were praying—her performances were always like prayers.[9]

It may seem that Gubaidulina's life as a student was that of a recluse, but that is only partly true. To concentrate without distraction on her work as a composer she needed absolute solitude; but another side of her life may come as a surprise. In the June 25, 1956, edition of *Sovetskii muzykant,* the conservatory's publication, which has nothing to do with music, there is a photo of Sofia Gubaidulina: the first-prize winner in gymnastics at the "Spartakiad" of Moscow's institutions of higher learning. Valentina Kholopova, a friend and student of musicology at the time who later wrote extensively about Gubaidulina's work, was familiar with Sofia's interest in sports and her habit of taking long walks. One might add that for this composer there have always been latent connections between sports and music, a motif reminiscent of earlier days in Kazan:

> Sonia always looked smartly athletic, and for her it was important to be in good physical shape. "The physical can in itself give rise to the creative," she believed. In her youth she loved tennis, and a tennis racket often peeped out of her satchel. While giving birth to her musical ideas, she would take long walks. She called it "working at her profession" and referred to her walks as "strolls through the sky." While still living in Kazan . . . she loved to look up, her head flung back, and see nothing but the sky, no building anywhere around. Later she made every effort to take similar walks in the broad clear-cut areas in the woods near Moscow. During winter, cross-country skiing always appealed to her. How many times we skimmed like the wind together over the snow-covered fairyland of the woods in the Moscow countryside, wallowing in the snow and in the poetic beauty of the landscape.[10]

Friday Evenings at Shebalin's

Even if Peiko was critical and ironic as a teacher, he respected his student and her dedication. Every now and then he would invite her to his home for dinner. A casual comment he made on one such occasion reconciled Sofia to the severity of his teaching. "As we got out of the taxi, Nikolai Ivanovich said, in passing: 'I'm constantly criticizing you, but you are developing nicely.' That gave me strength to carry on for the next several years." In their home Mrs. Peiko provided a good balance, softening his severe manner. During these visits, teacher and student would often play Mahler symphonies or Peiko's own compositions set for four hands, and occasionally he would challenge her to a game of chess.

Peiko encouraged and supported his student in many ways well into the time of her graduate studies, establishing important contacts for her and introducing her to his circle, which included the Friday evening gatherings at Vissarion

Shebalin's. Shostakovich greatly respected Shebalin as an outstanding teacher; as a composer, he was a representative of moderate modernism. In 1948 he had refused to toe the line and consequently lost his position as the director of the conservatory.

As Gubaidulina later recalled,

> In my third year Nikolai Ivanovich introduced me to Shebalin, who was then a grand figure on the musical scene. Each Friday, composers, performers, and musicians gathered at his home, a custom dating back to the time of Prokofiev and the music critic Pavel Lamm. Shebalin's wife, an accomplished hostess, took care of food and drinks but not before we had played music for two hours. Lev Naumov and his wife as well as Nikolai Ivanovich and I would play the piano together—for example, symphonies by Prokofiev and Shostakovich. Then we would all sit down at the table and start drinking vodka. It was fascinating to be among these famous people: Shostakovich's two sisters would join us, and Sviridov and his wife came once. A man of enormous talent, Sviridov struck me as arrogant and self-inflated, and he did not treat his wife well. On one of these Friday evenings I joined the Komitas Quartet in a performance of my Piano Quintet.

Gubaidulina had composed this work in her third year, and a committee of the conservatory had selected it for a public performance. The Komitas Quartet, the top string quartet from Armenia, with the composer at the piano, gave the first performance in November 1958, and it was probably this event that led to a repeat performance at Shebalin's home.

Encouragement from Shostakovich and Final Examination

Dmitri Dmitrievich Shostakovich was a revered father figure for a whole generation of composers and musicians. Addressing him in the Russian manner as Dmitri Dmitrievich, many hundreds of students showed him their works and asked for his counsel and help during the last twenty years of his life. In the West people may be respectful and admiring of the arts, but in Russia, especially Moscow, illustrious artists command admiration and fervor bordering on religious devotion. This Russian trait could not be extinguished during seventy years of Communist dictatorship; if anything, it became more pronounced. Already during her years in Kazan, Shostakovich and his Piano Trio No. 2 in E Minor, Op. 67, had become favorites for Sofia, but in Moscow she came to revere him as a model. "I met Shostakovich on several occasions and hung onto his every word."[11] Shostakovich, however, was a model not because of his music but because of his way of thinking and acting. "It was his psychological makeup that attracted me. When I now look back to that time, it is clear to me that I could not have lived or breathed without Shostakovich—he was that important for me."[12]

It was Peiko who had arranged a brief meeting with Shostakovich. Peiko had asked his friend, Shostakovich, to listen to the symphony his student had written the previous year as her final examination project. In the spring of 1959, a few weeks before the examination, Sofia and her teacher came to Shostakovich's apartment on Kutuzovskii prospekt, and she played her symphony on the piano.

"He listened to it," Gubaidulina later recalled,

> and made some remarks, generally praising the music. But what struck me most was his parting phrase: "Be yourself. Don't be afraid to be yourself. My wish for you is that you should continue on your own, *incorrect* way." One phrase said to a young person at the right moment can affect the rest of his or her life. I am infinitely grateful to Shostakovich for those words. I needed them at that moment, and felt fortified by them to such an extent that I feared nothing, and failure or criticism just ran off my back, and I was indeed able to pursue my own path.[13]

Final examinations were held in June 1959. June 11 was the date for judging all submissions, and on June 17, following examinations in the usual required subjects, Sofia took an oral examination on Richard Strauss's *Don Juan.* In addition to her symphony, she had submitted four other works: *Phacelia,* the 1957 Piano Quintet; two movements for chorus based on Russian folk songs; and a 1959 Piano Concerto that she and her friend and fellow student Olga Stupakova, a graduate student in Zak's class, played together on two pianos. The examination committee, headed by Shostakovich, consisted of twelve members: Alexander Sveshnikov, the director of the conservatory; Semyon Bogatyryov, the dean of the Department of Musicology/Music Theory; as well as three musicologists and seven composers—among them Shaporin, Shebalin, Chulaki, and, of course, Peiko, who later commented on the committee's judgment:

> Her diploma work, the symphony, was a very gifted piece. Of course it was somewhat immature, as is true of most [young] composers. It is true of my own works written when I was a student. The one possible exception is Shostakovich's diploma work, his First Symphony. Someone suggested a 5—'outstanding,' the highest grade—for the examination; however, Shaporin and the two musicologists Keldysh and Skrebkov were not happy, and said: "There are still certain formalist tendencies." To which Shostakovich, the committee head, replied: "I do believe that Sofia Asgadovna is very talented and deserves a grade of 'outstanding.'" The two musicologists were willing to agree, but Shaporin persisted, saying, "I have my doubts." Shebalin suddenly became quite exercised and told him: "So why don't you stuff your doubts and sit on them." A grim-faced Shaporin finally conceded: "All right, I'll also vote for a 5."[14]

On June 19 the Great Hall of the Conservatory was filled for a festive occasion. Professor Nikolai Pavlovich Anosov conducted the eighty musicians of the

Moscow Philharmonic Orchestra in a performance of all the successful diploma works by the graduates, among them Sofia Gubaidulina's symphony. Then it was all over. However, Sofia's successful completion of her examination with the highest possible grade was still to have unpleasant ramifications for Peiko. Although Shostakovich and Shebalin had been able to support their colleague on the examination committee, controversies apparently continued behind the scenes. Peiko was relieved of his position at the conservatory. Because he also taught at the Gnesin Institute, the official, though disingenuous, explanation was that such dual appointments were against policy, even though such appointments were then commonplace in Moscow. The real reason—which also had been the basis of Shostakovich's comment about the "*incorrect* way"—was probably the award of "outstanding" to a composer whose works strayed too far from the 1948 Resolution. One can glean this much, at any rate, by reading between the lines of an article by Mikhail Chulaki in the August 1959 issue of *Sovetskaia muzyka,* in which he discusses the eight composition graduates of that summer. In his piece, entitled "Young, New Growth," the section on Gubaidulina is about twice the length of that covering the other composers. It initially praises *Phacelia,* though not without a few caveats. Then Chulaki continues, referring to the symphony and the piano concerto:

> Obviously the young composer is now engaged in seeking for herself new means of musical expression, and in the process betraying a certain neglect of melodic possibilities. That is a pity, especially since the composer shows absolutely no lack of melodic gift. In the symphony, for example, the melodious lyricism of the principal theme, in the character of a pastorale, is captivating. However, it soon disperses in "generalized formulas of melodic motion" and returns again only at the very end in its enchanting original form.[15]

Of course, it cannot be determined with absolute certainty whether Chulaki wrote under duress or whether he freely arrived at the same judgment.

Students with excellent grades generally received recommendations for a postgraduate degree candidacy, and for this purpose Sofia Gubaidulina applied to Vissarion Shebalin. This meant extensive admission examinations in the fall term, the same situation in which Sofia's friend in musicology, Valentina Kholopova, found herself. Kholopova later reported:

> In 1959, when we were both taking the exams for admission into the *aspirantura* at the Moscow Conservatory, she [Sofia] proposed: "After the last exam let's walk around the entire Garden Ring!" The seven admission examinations were very long and exhausting: an oral exam in one's specialization (or, for composers, an audition of an original work), a written fugue, a formal analysis of some complicated orchestral score, history of Russian music, history of foreign music, a

foreign language, and some Marxist subject. But the intended marathon did not happen for an unexpected reason. After the last exam, Sonia—[16]

had a baby.

5 | Searching for Her Own Way, 1959–1965

Tomilino

Already a year before his wife took her final examinations, Mark Liando had moved out of his temporary quarters in Peredelkino. Weary of so much loneliness, he had built a house for himself and Sofia with the help of his father and some friends in the summer of 1958. It was a wooden structure in the Finnish style located in Tomilino, a Moscow suburb on the road to Riazan; thin wooden walls divided the interior into several rooms. Number 20 Polevaia ulitsa had earlier been the address of his parents' dacha, which had been destroyed by German bombers during the war. Situated in a quiet neighborhood at the edge of town, it overlooked a field and a rising hillside topped by a twelfth-century church. The young couple enjoyed the quietness of their home and its natural surroundings, but during the first few months of Sofia's final year at the conservatory her dormitory room still served as a necessary foothold in the city.

Then, after the birth of their daughter on November 2, 1959, Gubaidulina and her yet unnamed child moved to Tomilino. In her characteristic way of combining thoroughness with intuition, the young mother settled the child's name by asking all visitors to write their suggestions in a notebook. After a substantial list had accumulated, Gubaidulina announced that nominations were closed and that "her name is Nadia"—the short version of Nadezhda, the Russian word for hope.

Babies, of course, introduce many changes in a couple's life: although the father's daily work routine may not change much, the mother's life is greatly altered. Over the next several months Sofia was on her own much of the time, especially while Mark was away on geological expeditions. Playing or composing music was out of the question, and during the cold, dark season of the year, life in the country was anything but romantic. The house had only a single stove, and it had to be nursed along with peat, wood, and coal. There was an outhouse, and water had to be fetched from across the street—shod in rubber boots during the spring and fall, as the "street" was little more than a large mud puddle. They had no telephone, but there were skis, a rented concert-grand piano, and a shelf with a solid stock of books, including the Bible and a number of officially prohibited volumes. "Sometimes after the fire died down," Gubaidulina later recalled, "I just sat down and cried. And when Nadia started crying on a quiet evening, I would sit down at the piano and play Beethoven's *Hammerklavier* sonata or recite poems by Pasternak until she went back to sleep."

The year following her final examination was a period of crises and radical change. Not only practical problems and frequent loneliness got her down, but she felt that her creative impulses were blocked and that music was receding to an irretrievable distance. According to her friend Olga Stupakova, "Sofia always felt ill when she could not compose; she suffered when other things got in the way."[1] Just as composing could lift her to exhilarating heights, during these months she plunged to depths of depression, even to the edge of suicide. Only by sheer force of will did she pull herself out of this depression.

Making everything worse, it turned out that the prospects for continuing her marriage to Mark Liando were not bright. The geologist and poet himself later explained, with candid self-criticism, the reasons that led to their separation:

> [We] were too different, both psychologically and intellectually, and, besides that, our lives were headed in entirely different directions. S. G. possessed an incredible, laser-like will and relentlessly pursued her composing, her concerts, her meetings with performers and devotees of new music. . . . [W]hen I was a child the families of the intelligentsia had servants. By her side—true, not always even that—she had only an odd, rather infantile . . . husband, intellectually immature and chaotic, who also hated the half-troglodytic existence, who was no whiz as a handyman like an engineer or a man from the village might be (although my fieldwork as a geologist had certainly taught me something!), and, to make matters worse, a man determined to escape his profession in a direction with no financial prospects whatsoever, into literary studies.

Liando continued: "I already felt superfluous, forgotten. At concerts, and in the company of musicians and her admirers, I suddenly felt like some tedious appendage, like the shadow of this already famous wife."[2]

By the end of her maternity leave late in the spring of 1960 Gubaidulina had come to a firm decision about her family's future. Nadia would be brought up by her grandparents in Kazan, and she herself would move back to Srednii Kisslovskii pereulok, into her double room in the residence hall. After a period of ups and downs, her marriage to Mark Liando gradually evolved into mutual friendship but ended in divorce in 1964.

The Wave Runner and *The Magic Flute:*
Two Promising Ballets

During the final phase of her life with Liando, the composer and the writer collaborated on one more project. Sofia wanted to try her hand at the classical Russian genre of ballet music. However, disinclined to begin such a work without some hope of having it produced, she asked Yury Alexandrovich Fortunatov, her instructor for instrumentation, for advice. He told her: "I know a lady who teaches at GITIS [Gosudarstvennyi institut teatral'nogo iskusstva (State Institute for Theatrical Arts)], Nina Chefranova; she would suit you very well." Located on a street that ran parallel to the one where the student residence was located, GITIS was the oldest Russian school for acting, directing, and criticism. Nina Chefranova taught a master class in the Department of Ballet Choreography, and Fortunatov soon arranged a meeting between Sofia and this forceful, somewhat authoritarian, and at times rather sentimental woman, who was at least ten years older than the composer. They got along well from the start, and their friendship lasted until Chefranova's untimely death in 1971. Mark Liando had suggested the basic theme for the ballet, and, with Chefranova's expert assistance, he wrote a libretto for a full-length production based on Alexander Grin's *The Wave Runner* [*Begushchaia po volnam*]. An author who enjoyed widespread popularity during much of the twentieth century in Russia, and, in those days, Liando's favorite, Grin created in this story a suspenseful fantasy tale combining seafaring, adventure, and romance. Its central figures are the protagonist Thomas Harvey, the dark, mysterious Frezi Grant, and the sailing ship *The Wave Runner*. Gubaidulina worked on this ballet in five scenes during the entire period of her candidacy.

Gubaidulina's relationship with Chefranova brought about a second request for ballet music. It came from an Albanian student working with Chefranova and preparing for his final degree project—a libretto based on the Albanian folktale "Tana's Flute" ["Fyell I Tanës"], also known as "The Magic Flute," a story of love and death. The Albanian expected to be appointed as ballet master at the Tirana State Theater in Albania, and he was looking for a composer so that his work could be staged upon his return. After reading the libretto, Gubaidulina agreed to compose the music, and after her return to the residence hall in the summer of 1960, created the new work in a matter of weeks. With no other students present during the summer and Sofia eager to get back to work, conditions were perfect. The music pleased the Albanian, and he returned to Tirana carrying in his bags the score of *Tana's Flute* [*Fleita Tany*] (or *The Magic Flute* [*Volshebnaia svirel'*]).

First Experiments, First Contacts with Instrumentalists

The beginning of her candidacy period in the summer of 1960 was Gubaidulina's first step toward a life as an independent composer. The stipend and free lodging she received gave her three years free of practical worries such as making a living. Candidates enjoyed a more relaxed relationship with their professors than did the strictly regimented younger students, and they were expected primarily to work independently. The hours with Vissarion Shebalin, during which they discussed issues and problems of contemporary music, lasted only a year; because of his failing health, Shebalin preferred to stay in his dacha in Nikolina Gora. He died in May 1963, before the end of Sofia's period of candidacy.

Peiko's instruction, although generally liberal, had focused on thematic compositions, and his student had willingly gone along. As was then customary, he expected an initial theme, subsequently to be developed and varied. But now Sofia had opportunities to follow her own impulses, to probe the range of her own talent, and—until her Piano Sonata of 1965—she tried different genres and small experiments. Among the eight pieces on the list of works she submitted at the end of her candidacy period are the two ballets already mentioned; a one-act opera, *Joker King* (a subtle parody of Khrushchev's corn cultivation program); theater music for Jean-François Régnard's *Le Joueur* [Rus., *Igrok*], a film score (more on this later); an Adagio and Fugue for Violin and Large Orchestra; and two small chamber music pieces. These last two, each about five minutes long and dating from 1960, are more like compositional finger exercises, but they are rather significant "signposts along the way"—experiments in two areas that are repeatedly found in Gubaidulina's later work: her persistent search for particular sound effects and new, striking instrumental timbres as well as the fiery and explosive rhythm of her Tatar temperament. The first work was simply named Four Pieces for Electronic Instruments [*Chetyre p'esy dlia elektronnyikh instrumentov*]. To earn some pocket change, Sofia played in a sound studio that produced recordings of "electronic instruments" for films and radio. There was even an Ensemble for Electronic Musical Instruments [Ansambl' elektromuzykal'nykh instrumentov] at the All-Union Radio Network [Vsesoiuznoe radio, Gosteleradio SSSR], under the direction of Viacheslav Meshcherin. His instrumentation consisted of a variety of so-called electronic instruments then widely used by popular musicians and film composers in Moscow. Some of these instruments had been developed at the end of the 1950s in the Moscow Experimental Factory for the Production of Musical Instruments [Moskovskaia eksperimental'naia fabrika muzykal'nykh instrumentov]: the "Ekvadin," a type of electronic organ, developed by Andrey Volodin, and the "Kristadin," a semiconductor device with a range of five octaves. In the summer of 1960 the inventor Igor Simonov had presented the Shumofon (*shum* = noise) at an exhibition in Moscow's Sokolniki Park; it could produce sounds ranging from bird song to the roar of turbines. Gubaidulina wrote compositions not only for these three instruments but also for electronic "chambertone clavier," electronic-mechanical glockenspiel, and electric guitar. Her composition for six electronic instruments, however, remained an incomplete experiment. She was not the only one at that time to try her hand at these new methods. That same year Alfred Schnittke began, but never completed, a concerto for electronic instruments, and he used electronic instrumentation again in his *Poem about the Cosmos* [*Poema o kosmose*] (1961). These instruments did not last long, however, as the sounds they produced were too similar and could not be modulated in dynamics.

Gubaidulina's second experimental piece, Intermezzo for Eight Trumpets, Sixteen Harps, and Percussion (originally titled *The Invisible Drummer* [*Nevidimyi barabanshchik*]) deserves special attention. It is preceded by a quotation from Mayakovsky, a poet one would normally not associate with this composer: "Our God is the march, our heart the drum." A highly placed official at the Moscow Conservatory by the name of Lapshin, who had previously been at the Ministry of Culture, requested that Gubaidulina write a piece with instrumentation of her own choosing. At the time she still occupied an officially respected position as a young composer who had been awarded a degree with distinction. The piece was to be performed at a student concert in the Small Hall of the conservatory [Malyi zal Moskovskoi konservatorii]. "It was important for me at that time," the composer later commented, "to try something with unconventional instrumentation, but I was also motivated by a certain degree of spite and sarcasm. So I chose this absurd instrumentation and preceded it all by a fitting quotation from Mayakovsky. The piece was a bit of an experiment in rhythm and dynamics. The beat of a *barabán*, the Russian word for drum, runs in a quarter-and-half-note ostinato through the whole piece—which, by the way, was actually performed, as Lapshin had promised."[3]

In the early 1960s Sofia Gubaidulina underwent a simmering process of change, gradually moving away from the influence of the teachers and role models of her student years to a greater effort to learn about music written by her Western contemporaries. At that time anyone interested in the new music of the West stood outside the officially legitimate music world and had to work underground. A central figure in this context was Andrei Volkonsky, around whom a small circle of the Moscow intelligentsia had begun to gather in the second half of the 1950s—not only musicians but writers and painters. Friends in the West supplied him with recordings, scores, and books, making him the secret and unofficial agent of classic modernism and postwar Western music. In 1956–57 he had written *Musica stricta,* generally considered to be the first twelve-tone composition of the postwar Soviet era; it officially premiered in May 1961, in Gnesin Hall, with Maria Yudina at the piano.[4] In the late 1950s Volkonsky had experimented with Evgeny Murzin's legendary ANS tone synthesizer [ANS are the initials of Alexander Nikolaevich Scriabin], at the Scriabin Institute, where Volkonsky worked on film scores. His apartment in Studentcheskaia ulitsa was a lively and casual meeting spot for listening to music and for discussion. There were literary evenings when Volkonsky read Kafka, Ionesco, or Beckett to his friends. Although Sofia was not much inclined to join these gatherings, she sometimes overcame her shyness, went to Volkonsky's apartment, and borrowed records from him. She was always welcome, but apparently the music did not leave much of an impression, because later Gubaidulina recalled: "I don't remember what recordings I borrowed, but those names probably didn't mean anything to me then."

Four Pieces for Electronic Instruments was not Sofia Gubaidulina's only contact with the world of electronic and synthesized sound. A few months after she wrote this work she made her first visit to Murzin's music laboratory at the Scriabin Museum, which five years later was officially established as the Experimental Studio of Electronic Music [Eksperimental'naia studiia elektronnoi muzyki] According to Gubaidulina, Murzin was a fanatically dedicated scientist, completely consumed by his ideas. An engineer and colonel in the Red Army who always dressed in uniform, he worked at a secret military installation. He loved Duke Ellington's music and Scriabin's late works, which he—together with the composer Leonid Sabaneev—saw as a precursor of a pitch continuum or slide, and microtonality. In the late 1950s, after much hard work, he had completed a light-electronic synthesizer [*fotoelektronnyi sintezator*] for a seventy-two-fold subdivision of an octave. Analogous to the "moving pictures" of the cinema at a rate of twenty-four or thirty-six frames per second, the human ear would register the impression of a sound continuum. In the residence that served Scriabin during the last years of his life—11 Vakhtangova ulitsa, located near the Arbat—he had been given two small rooms in which to perform his experiments. "This was the place that attracted young musicians like me," Gubaidulina later remembered, "even before there was a laboratory for electronic music. We went there to hear pianists like Yudina, Neuhaus, and Sofronitsky. It was also where Pasternak and Balmont read from their poetry. The Scriabin Museum was an intellectual center we all loved."[5]

Nikolai Peiko had suggested that visit, when he told his former student about his friend Murzin and his ANS-synthesizer, and then added: "Murzin is looking for new composers and musicians who will dedicate themselves with every fiber of their body to the potential of his synthesizer." On hearing that, Gubaidulina hoped to be able to draw graphic representations of her ideas for compositions on glass (more on this later). But once she actually faced the synthesizer, she realized that everything was more complicated than she had expected. Murzin talked about the need to be grounded in theoretical concepts and, pointing to a young man, said: "He's the one who knows everything." Only seventeen years old, Pyotr Meshchaninov had come to the studio for the first time in 1960 after reading a newspaper piece by Murzin, and since then had worked in his spare time on problems of sound continuity and microintervals. The first meeting between the music theoretician and the composer did not last long. After listening to his introductory lecture, she said, candidly, "This young man does not explain things very well!" And with that the session ended. Her brusque manner, however, was mostly an act of self-protection. The problem was not that she refused to be instructed by such a young person; rather, she was a composer, not a musicologist, strongly intuitive rather than intellectual. Although Meshchaninov was seriously dedicated to his subject, he was still only beginning to formulate his theory. And Gubaidulina, fearing that she might lose her intuitive ability if she were to be drawn into theoretical issues, stepped back from both Meshchaninov and Murzin.

Meshchaninov began to develop his theory at the same time that Ligeti wrote *Apparitions* and *Atmosphères* and Stockhausen worked on *Carré*, but he did not know either at the time. Sound texture or "sonoristics," as Meshchaninov later called it, was in the air, and could also be heard in the works of Cerha, Penderecki, Scelsi, and others. The first satellites were orbiting the earth, and Yury Gagarin would soon shatter physical barriers with his first space flight, reaching orbital height. Ligeti's works and similar "sonoristic" music have a cosmic quality—the sound seems to emanate from an orbit—and thus they are closely related to the idea of a sound continuum. But this needs further investigation.

Sofia Gubaidulina also began collaborating with instrumental interpreters during this time of her candidacy—primarily with pianists for her Piano Concerto and the Chaconne for Piano of 1962. Although today she counts the Concerto among her juvenilia, it must have been a significant departure from the hackneyed compositions adhering to Party guidelines. Victor Suslin, later a close friend and colleague and one of the three musicians of the ensemble Astraea of the 1970s, related the following story. In 1959, while still a pupil himself at the Kharkov Music Gymnasium in Ukraine, Suslin heard Gubaidulina's name mentioned for the first time:

> Vladimir Libin, then a student at the Moscow Conservatory, had come on vacation to Kharkov; he was sounding off in front of his friends about an interesting and "ultramodern" piano concerto he was then learning. It was music in the style

of "Shostakovich-Hindemith," more modern than anyone else was writing, he declared with an air of superior knowledge; and all of us provincial boors pricked up our ears. . . . He played excerpts from it, and I liked it immensely.[6]

Henrietta Mirvis, who could play the Piano Concerto from memory, made the work part of her repertoire at the time. This friend of Gubaidulina's and former fellow student in Yakov Zak's piano class was just at the beginning of her career, which made it difficult to include the work of a young, uncompromising composer in her performances. She therefore suggested to Gubaidulina to play the Concerto for Shostakovich: "Dmitri Dmitrievich could have recommended us for a performance at the Philharmonic but Sofia replied: 'No, I will not return to old works.' She had no interest in public success. All she wanted to do was compose, compose, compose. If her works were performed, that was fine; if not, it was just as well. Then she would simply compose another one."[7] Over the next few years, Henrietta Mirvis performed the Concerto two or three times, including a performance with the Novosibirsk Philharmonic Orchestra [Novosibirskii akademicheskii simfonicheskii orkestr, Novosibirskaia gosudarstvennaia filarmoniia], on January 24, 1964, in Novosibirsk, with Arnold Katz conducting. But when she proposed it for a concert tour of Romania, it was officially stricken from the list and replaced with a work by Rakhmaninov.

Given Gubaidulina's rigorous and austere attitude toward her earlier work, she may have been entertaining some other thought. In the summer of 1960 Shostakovich joined the Communist Party, a move that puzzled many of his friends and admirers. It must have been a profound shock for Sofia, for it took many years for her to accept Shostakovich's decision. Thirty years later she said to Elizabeth Wilson: "I now realize that the circumstances he lived under were unbearably cruel, more than anyone should have to endure. He had overcome the most important trials, but when he allowed himself to relax, he succumbed to weakness. But I accept him, for I see him as pain personified, the epitomy [sic] of the tragedy and terror of our times."[8]

Distancing oneself from Shostakovich, however, was part of the natural evolution of the younger generation. After completing their musical education, their horizons widened and they looked for new guides and role models (more on this later).

The 1962 Chaconne for Piano was Gubaidulina's first commissioned piece and the only work from the period of her candidacy that she includes today in her list of works. Marina Mdivani, a student of Emil Gilels from Soviet Georgia [Gruziia] who lived in the room next to Sofia's in the student residence, had asked her for an original piano work. Mdivani had received First Prize at the 1961 Concours international de piano Long-Thibault in Paris and became a "laureate" and recipient of the Fourth Prize in piano at the 1962 International Tchaikovsky Competition [Mezhdunarodnyi konkurs imeni P. I. Chaikovsogo] in Moscow, where the foremost young pianists of the world competed against one another. It was the first time Gubaidulina let herself be inspired by another musician's artistic personality. Mdivani, according to the composer, "played forceful chords and had a vivacious temperament,"[9] performance characteristics that Gubaidulina sought to make the most of in the resulting Chaconne—historically a stately sixteenth-century dance for lute or guitar. But only the introduction harkens back to the historical model: an eight-bar theme comprising a chord progression that undergoes variations ranging in style from solemn stateliness through impulsive drama to quiet lyricism. In 1969, following the Piano Quintet and *Allegro rustico* for flute and piano, the Chaconne became the third published score by Sofia Gubaidulina. The latter was frequently performed at that time, not only by Marina Mdivani but also by other Soviet pianists, in performances both in Russia and France. A recording soon became available. Today this work remains as fresh as ever. It is the composer's earliest work to be included in eurhythmic performances in the 1990s. Werner Barfod, a noted eurhythmist and long-time director of the Nederlands Eurythmie Ensemble in The Hague, explains why he included the Chaconne in the ensemble's repertoire:

> Ever new spheres of sound evolve in the Chaconne, leading to ever new spheres of the soul and unexpected layers that captivate the listener as well as the interpreter. The very first chord in its second register encompasses the entire sound range of the piece. Even with its extreme chord registers, its rhythms, tempi, and dynamics, the music nevertheless remains humanly comprehensible and soul-fulfilling. We experience a grappling with human existence, if we completely surrender to its development, a grappling with man himself and his innermost balance, his human center and verticality. It always calls for finding a new position, making new decisions, remaining centered, even if the challenges become superhuman. It is these qualities that make this piece so relevant and authentic, especially in its eurhythmic representation.[10]

First Successes, First Disappointments

In the second year of her candidacy Sofia Gubaidulina submitted *Phacelia* [*Fatseliia*] with her application to the Composers Union, and she was admitted. This organization functioned, at the Soviet state level, as the all-union union under the leadership of Tikhon Khrennikov, but there were chapters in each republic—and in the larger cities, for example, the Moscow Composers Union—that were in charge of local musical culture. Closely connected to the Central Committee of the Communist Party and to the Ministry of Culture, the Union's General

Secretary, Khrennikov, represented official Soviet cultural policy, but—regardless of the lip service it paid and the compositions it brought in line with Party ideology—the organization could make life easier for its members. It ran several composers' creative retreats in Karelia, on the Black Sea, and even close to Moscow, where members were allowed to do their work or simply relax at very little cost for room and board. In cases of illness or other emergency situations, "Muzfond" (Muzykal'nyi fond, affiliated with the Union) could provide assistance and even loans. The Union also had its own music and book publisher, "Sovetskii Kompozitor," that published a scholarly journal, *Sovetskaia muzyka,* and a popular periodical, *Muzykal'naia zhizn'*. Beyond that, the Union organized concert series for members and music festivals for the general public. Finally, through its various committees, it served as an ideological watchdog, controlling the performance of its members' compositions abroad, as well as the production of scores and sheet music. At that time the chapter in Moscow, the Moscow Composers Union [*Soiuz moskovskikh kompozitorov*] had about four hundred members (including music scholars) and was steadily growing; membership throughout the Soviet Union stood at about thirteen hundred.[11] Any artist who was not a member of an appropriate national union might have to face court proceedings in critical situations. Every citizen, according to Soviet law, had to prove that he was engaged in socially productive employment, or else he would be branded as a "parasite." For instance, Joseph Brodsky, a poet from Leningrad who was not a member of the Writers Union, was sentenced to five years in exile.

In 1962 Gubaidulina began to be recognized as a composer of national stature. *Sovetskaia muzyka* printed an extensive article about her work in its February issue, and ten months later she shared her first Meet-the-Composer evening with Alexei Nikolaev. The February article was written by Victor Bobrovsky, a lecturer in musicology and music theory at the Moscow Conservatory, and titled, encouragingly, "Open All the Windows!" ["Otkroite vse okna"]. Bobrovsky was particularly interested in the music of the younger generation, attending their concerts and participating in meetings of the Society of Students and Scholars [Nauchnoe obshchestvo studentov i aspirantov]. The inclusion of numerous examples and detailed descriptions of individual works in his article show that he had studied Gubaidulina's compositions carefully. Covering everything from *Phacelia* to *The Magic Flute,* he concludes his discussion by stating that hers is an "exceptional talent." Although some of the praise and criticism sounds dated today, the following passage is still of interest as it points to Gubaidulina's fondness for contrasting structures—a dualism that, for her, is the very foundation of the world and of human existence:

> The more one analyzes Gubaidulina's works, the more one clearly senses the two polar extremes of thematic imagery, each comprising a characteristic complex of expressive techniques. The fire of inspiration burns incessantly in her music—but it is inspiration tinged with melancholy. No youthful rapture over the beauty and poetry of life, rather an elemental force of volcanic energy, rage, indignation, and at times embittered sarcasm. This music is fiery, direct. In the final analysis, one can interpret it as an indirect, mediated affirmation of noble, humanistic, metaphorical images, as a reaction against the negative aspects of reality. The opposite extreme is represented by a "pure," rather coolly aloof lyricism, an often impassive solitude. Such episodes evoke images of desolate, snow-capped mountains. But along with this goes a characteristic refinement and whimsicality.[12]

Gubaidulina considered this first critical analysis of her work as accurate and positive encouragement.

On December 15, 1962, with the Chaconne for piano already completed, the second in the series "Meet-the-Composer Evenings for Young Composers" [Molodye kompozitory: Avtorskie vechera-vstrechi] took place in Gnesin Hall. The first part of the concert was dedicated to Sofia Gubaidulina and featured three pieces of her chamber music: the Piano Quintet, with the composer at the keyboard; *Phacelia,* a piano version, again played by the composer and sung by Tamara Petrova; and the premiere of the Chaconne, with Marina Mdivani at the piano. The evening was probably a nice success for Gubaidulina, even though the reviewer for *Sovetskaia muzyka* commented on the "modest and inhibited interpretation" of the four young string players and felt that the range of feelings in *Phacelia* was both too subjective and too narrow. But he praised Marina Mdivani for her exuberant and brilliant playing of the Chaconne.[13]

Sofia's candidacy came to an end at the beginning of 1963, and she had to confront the question of earning a living. Some of her colleagues dealt with this problem by playing scores or teaching music analysis or instrumentation at the conservatory or other institutes. Others found positions in the editorial offices of the two state music publishers, "Muzyka" and "Sovetskii Kompozitor." None of these appealed to Sofia: teaching did not suit her reclusive nature, and she saw editorial work as too dull and time-consuming; she wanted to work on her own compositions. A third, well-paid possibility was to write music for films. Completing an assignment would guarantee several months of financial security—and Gubaidulina was later able to live on as little as a hundred rubles a month. Writing film scores, however, was extremely arduous work with strict deadlines and the demand to conform to detailed requirements of style, mood, and length of compositions. On the other hand, film scores were not subject to censorship; they even offered considerable freedom for experimentation. But everything depended on the approval or disapproval of the director, and directors tended to consider scores as having no more than secondary importance.

Nikolai Peiko helped to open doors to the world of film. A former fellow student, Andrei Sevasrianov, was a music editor in the State Documentary Film Studio [Gosudarstvennaia studiia dokumentl'nykh fil'mov], and Peiko recommended Sofia to him. As early as December 1960, she had written her first film score for the studio's production of *The Peasant Women of Riazan* (*Baby Riazanskie*),[14] a propaganda remake of a popular film by the same title from the late 1920s by Olga Preobrazhenskaya. The new version showed a model dairy *kolkhoz* in the Riazan region, where the women had not only fulfilled the state-mandated plan but, with great effort and total dedication to socialism, exceeded it. Sofia's time at the studio ended in a scandal, however, and the cruel reality of life under socialism claimed another innocent victim. It turned out that the production statistics of the actual *kolkhoz* in Riazan had been meddled with, causing its director to commit suicide, the studio to abandon its film project, and Gubaidulina, who had delivered her score well before the deadline, to walk away without a kopek for her effort. Between then and the years of perestroika, however, she successfully completed the scores for at least twenty-five films—documentaries, cartoons, and a number of feature films.

The Peasant Women of Riazan was not her only disappointment in this line of work. The promised ballet production in Tirana also dissolved into nothing after the Albanian's departure. The reason for this failure, however, was not the choreographer's unreliability but a fraternal squabble between Moscow and Tirana. In the aftermath of frictions between Khrushchev and Mao Zedong, the Soviet Union had broken diplomatic relations with Albania in June 1960, a move kept secret at first. When the rupture became public knowledge, neither side saw any possibility of producing the work of a Moscow composer in Tirana. To this day the ballet score—which, for Victor Bobrovsky, had "made the deepest impression of all Sofia Gubaidulina's work"[15]—has remained unperformed and remains in the archives of the Paul Sacher Foundation in Basel.

Gubaidulina completed her degree candidacy promptly and efficiently in the summer of 1963 by submitting *The Wave Runner,* arranged for piano, and by successfully passing all required examinations. She could now move on to another phase in her life.

Ever since her expectations for a performance of *The Magic Flute* in Tirana had been dashed, she harbored the hope that it would some day be performed. The mother of her neighbor at the student residence, a woman from Leningrad with many connections, told her at the time: "You write music and I'll sell it." In the spring of 1967 she told Gubaidulina about a ballet master at the Leningrad Maly Opera and Ballet Theater [Leningradskii akademicheskii Malyi teatr opery i baleta], and Sofia traveled to the city on the Neva with the piano score in her luggage. She played it for Konstantin Boyarsky, and for the second time a ballet master liked her music and promised to perform the ballet. Delighted, she returned to Moscow, only to experience disappointment for the third time: in the fall she received news from Leningrad that Boyarsky had quit his position at the Maly. Thirty years later she was able to provide a different perspective on these early disappointments:

> Today I am convinced that my triple misfortune was for the best. It probably protected me from premature success before I reached maturity and independence as an artist. I was good as a composer—my work, at any rate, was technically flawless and full of good ideas. Someone could have said: "O, that's nice, keep doing it!" But I had not yet achieved mental and spiritual maturity. I needed greater depth and self-knowledge. After all the pressures of studying with Peiko and completing my candidacy, I needed peace and time to find myself.

On her visit to Leningrad, wandering through the city to view its architecture, Gubaidulina discovered a mosque. Although women were not allowed to enter, the guard, noticing her Tatar features, admitted her, asked her to remove her shoes, and let her sit in a corner to listen quietly. About twenty men, simple folks with their everyday worries about life, had gathered, sitting cross-legged and staring at their hands. As Gubaidulina later recalled,

> The mullah recited a passage from the Koran, a short one to begin with, which was met by silent meditation. The second passage, with a richer melisma, was again followed by a period of contemplation. The melodic quality grew more complex with each succeeding passage, and the silences became longer and longer. The climactic phrase, highly ornamented, unfolded like a melody in full flower. The silences between the passages created an almost ecstatic mood, and after one more meditation the service was over.[16]

This first experience of a Muslim worship service touched her deeply: "It became clear to me how important it is for human beings to enter into such a relationship with God." At the same time she felt that some deep inner roots connected her to this ceremony—roots that her conscious mind was not yet able to grasp.

Two Important Relationships

In the summer of 1963 Gubaidulina rented a room at 62 Leninskii prospekt and began her life as a freelance composer. Vera Mikhailovna Svetukhina, her landlady, was an elderly, educated Orthodox Christian and a physician who had once taught at Lomonosov University. Her small apartment on two floors was something of a luxurious curiosity in the larger Soviet context. It was located on the narrow side of a large apartment building and had its own separate entrance. Sofia occupied the lower room that was furnished with a piano, but life with Vera Svetukhina was not without its problems. For three years Gubaidulina was unable to do her work without interruptions. Vera Svetukhina had very likely worked as a physician in Stalin's Siberian Gulag[17] and had developed a nervous disorder in those years—but this whole topic remained strictly taboo until perestroika:

> When I sat at my desk working, she would knock on my door. Vera Mikhailovna was lonely and suffered from some kind of nervous condition. She constantly asked for my attention and sympathy, and I always had to come up with new ways to comfort her. When I refused to do so, she would scold me: "You don't love me anymore!" In those days she used me as her psychiatrist.

During the first few months at Leninskii prospekt, Gubaidulina lived without financial difficulties. She had received a first prize of several hundred rubles at the 1963 All-Union Competition for Young Composers [Vsesoiuznyi konkurs molodykh kompozitorov] for her duet for flute and piano, *Allegro rustico*. In December of that same year it had also been performed as a compulsory piece at the All-Union Competition for Wind Players [Vsesoiuznyi konkurs dukhovykh instrumentov], an important event at which two hundred instrumentalists from twelve different republics competed. The first prize went to the flutist Albert Ratzbaum (then living in Riga) and the pianist Hermann Braun. The premiere of *Allegro rustico* took place in October 1963 in Moscow, with flutist Eduard Shcherbachov, an outstanding student of the flutist Nikolai Platonov, and Gubaidulina at the piano.

Around the beginning of 1964, having learned that Maria Yudina had been admitted to Pervaia Gradskaia Hospital on Leninskii prospekt, Gubaidulina decided to visit the revered pianist. It may have been her earlier experience in Kazan that prompted the otherwise reticent composer to take this step, or it was the pianist's fiery temperament and uncompromising personality that attracted Gubaidulina. Despite a thirty-year difference in age, the two musicians were much alike in this respect, and their Christian faith and dedication to music were the two pillars on which both their lives rested. At that time Yudina corresponded with Stockhausen and Adorno in Germany and with Boulez in Paris. And when Luigi Nono came to Moscow in the fall of 1963 (as a member of the Italian Communist Party he had no problems obtaining a visa), she not only accompanied him and Andrei Volkonsky to see Murzin and his ANS tone synthesizer at the Scriabin Museum but welcomed him into her home. Gubaidulina's decision to see Yudina at the hospital was the beginning of a warm friendship, which was marked not so much by the frequency with which they saw each other as by the intensity of each visit. Six years later, moreover, their friendship strongly affected Gubaidulina's religious life.

Mark Liando arrived one day at the new apartment accompanied by a fellow student in philosophy who also wrote poetry. The two had participated in the last unofficial poetry readings on Mayakovsky Square in 1963 and were taken into custody to have their papers checked by the militia. With his blue eyes and blond hair, Nikolai Bokov, who went by the nickname Kolya, looked more like a Scandinavian than a Russian. With wit and histrionic talent he would satirize the current regime, to which he had been opposed since his school days. This first encounter between this attractive young man and the dark-haired composer evidently ignited a passion that continued through many more visits from Kolya and eventually led to a serious romance in the spring of 1964. But for the time being they had to deal with two extended periods of separation. For two years following his graduation from high school, Kolya had worked during the day and taken evening courses in philosophy at Lomonosov University. Now, in the summer of 1964, he was sent to Kazakhstan for three months as a truck driver to qualify as a full-time student. This was to be followed in December by a tour of military duty.

The list of Gubaidulina's works for 1964 contains only film scores—two for documentaries and one for a feature film. Her score for *We Explore the Ocean* [*My otkryvaem okean*] turned into an unexpected endurance test. Facing his own deadlines, the director demanded twenty minutes of music within three days—something evocative of the sea. For once, good luck was on her side: Vera Svetukhina was away and a neighborhood store happened to have received a shipment of tangerines. Armed with five pounds of the rare fruit, Sofia retreated to her desk and managed to deliver the score before the deadline. The extraordinary effort, however, induced complete exhaustion requiring a lengthy period of recovery.

That fall the music for her first feature film, *Believe It or Not* (*Khotite, vert'e— khotite, net*), took Gubaidulina to Yalta to work on location. She used that occasion to visit Kolya Bokov for a few days before he returned to Moscow to begin his studies in philosophy. Kolya was not simply a student but was deeply engaged in the dissident movement and in *samizdat* [from *samo-izdatel'stvo*, meaning self-publishing outside official channels, a coinage ironically analogous to *gosizdat*, short for the "state publishing enterprise"]. Even before going to Kazakhstan, Kolya had prepared the publication of a twelve-page typed transcript of the trial and sentencing of the poet Joseph Brodsky. Now he placed on Sofia's desk at Leninskii prospekt two typewriters, each holding seven sheets of the thinnest typing and carbon papers. Between the typewriters lay Pasternak's *Doctor Zhivago*—a Russian edition printed in Italy which he had obtained from Liando by circuitous routes via Paris. One day, as Kolya and a fellow student, Valentin Shalenko, were working there, unexpected visitors arrived. The entrance to the apartment could easily be seen from all sides, and apparently some overly eager neighbors, annoyed by the frequent visits of young men at a young lady's apartment, had called the militia. Leninskii prospekt was a main route for official traffic from Vnukovo Airport to the Kremlin and therefore subject to careful surveillance.

Bokov later recalled,

> When the bell rang, Valentin immediately disappeared into the upstairs toilet. The officials checked my identity card, and asked: "What are you writing there?"—"I'm preparing for my exams." The militia in those days was still inexperienced and naïve and I was still carefree and cheerful. They expected to find arms, and when I told them, "Please, feel free to search the entire apartment, even the toilet," they thought I was making fun of them and left.[18]

The *samizdat* edition of *Doctor Zhivago* remained unfinished for several months after Kolya began his military service on the Soviet-Chinese border in December. But in April 1965 he returned to Moscow. He had used his histrionic talent for what today would be considered a Catch-22 caper: after a month's service in uniform he was admitted for tests at the psychiatric clinic of Khabarovsk—and three months later he received his discharge. Soon after his return from the Far East, Sofia Gubaidulina and Nikolai Bokov took out their marriage papers in Moscow.[19]

Tackling Twelve-Tone Music and a Piano Sonata

1965 was a watershed year for Gubaidulina and her music. Having laid up some savings from three compositions for film the year before, she was now able to work independently for a while. The first work of this period was her Sonata for Piano, completed in 1965, a piece that demanded long and careful preparation. It was the last of her compositions in which she drew on traditional forms, albeit freely and eclectically. The three classical sonata movements reveal a multiplicity of fresh and imaginative ideas for motifs, rhythms, and performance techniques. The first movement, for example, features prominent jazz rhythms, and parts of the second, slow movement are played directly on the strings inside the piano. Moreover, this sonata is the first result of Gubaidulina's efforts to wrestle with Schönberg's *Anleitung zur Komposition mit zwölf nur aufeinander bezogenen Halbtönen*. For a long time she had left this forbidden fruit in Soviet musical life untouched, much longer than her colleagues Denisov, Schnittke, Silvestrov, or Pärt, all of whom had worked in the spirit of the Second Viennese School for shorter or longer periods of their careers. The first fragmentary pieces of information about twelve-tone music reached her and her fellow students in the 1950s. Some of the names were known, and here and there a few scores had come to hand, and perhaps even a recording or two. In his biography of Schnittke Alexander Ivashkin notes that, as early as the mid-1950s, Schnittke studied scores from the Second Viennese School and did little exercises in twelve-tone technique on his daily railroad commute between Valentinovka and Moscow. But he soon laid these aside, realizing "that it did not help to solve the crucial problems of 'dynamic form,' satisfactory syntax and 'breathing' in a work of art."[20]

Edison Denisov had initially focused his attention on Stravinsky and Debussy. Near the end of the 1950s, when the French pianist Gérard Frémy—at the time one of his neighbors in a student residence—showed him the score of Webern's String Trio, Denisov's reaction was still quite critical; he felt that the music was artificial and downright bad. One of the major events in Moscow's music world had been the visit by the Canadian pianist Glen Gould in May 1957. Gould played two concerts of works by Schönberg and his students, among them Webern's Piano Variations. Afterward he accepted questions about his program choices. Gubaidulina, then a third-year student, heard the program:

> The Great Hall of the Conservatory was half empty for the first concert—nobody knew who this Glen Gould was. When the students wanted to go to the second concert, the hall was overflowing.... He had an interpreter, but it wasn't all that important to understand everything he said. His manner of playing, his touch, his phrasing were more expressive than anything he could have said.[21]

A short while later Maria Yudina made Webern's Variations for Piano part of her repertoire and performed the work at a semi-official concert at the Scriabin Museum. In the early 1960s still more information became available: scores, books, and records, hidden in the baggage of friends or even diplomats, found their way through cracks in the Iron Curtain. But twelve-tone music, just like any "decadent Western art," faced major problems in the world of official culture. Andrei Volkonsky, who, according to his own statements, favored "strict twelve-tonalism" in the years 1956–61, became the object of criticism by politically assimilated friends and by the press. At the Third All-Union Congress of Composers of the USSR [Tretii Vsesoiuznyi s'esd kompozitorov SSSR] in Moscow, in March 1962, the large number of attacks on dodecaphony ranged from Kabalevsky's mild and paternal rejection all the way to the sharply worded ideological tongue-lashing delivered by Khrennikov, the organization's First Secretary, who would also comment negatively on the Estonian Arvo Pärt's *Necrologue* [*Nekrolog*]. These attacks, however, remained a sideshow at the proceedings at the Congress, even as they proved that the 1948 Party Resolution was still in force. The main business of the Congress was the celebration of the achievements of Soviet music during the past five years.

"I was afraid," Gubaidulina later said, "that this twelve-tone technique did not suit me, and for that reason I used it only in practice. In Moscow we were then studying a Polish translation of a work by René Leibowitz; also Herbert Eimert's *Lehrbuch der Zwölftontechnik* and Hanns Jelinek's *Anleitung zur Zwölftonkomposition.*"

There are a number of reasons why Gubaidulina began to wrestle with twelve-tone music four or five years later than the colleagues mentioned above. On the surface it may have had something to do with her general work habits: she prepares herself intensely and carefully for each new work—if necessary on a wide range of related topics—because each new area of interest, each new idea she takes up, is not simply a matter of intellectual curiosity but an existential challenge to her whole being. Also, given her more delicate and sensitive feminine nature, she works more slowly than her male colleagues, although she is capable of working through the night to meet deadlines when necessary. Her reservoir of physical strength runs dry more quickly, and she always requires ample time for regeneration. The chief reason for her late grappling with Schönberg's technique, however, was most likely her good sense of keeping her distance from influences for which she was not yet ready—as had been shown by her visit to Murzin. She would speak about the consequences of all this twenty-five years later in her conversations with Enzo Restagno:

> My relationship with serialism did not develop in the same way as that of other composers, especially Schnittke and Denisov. They actively sought out this technique and went through an important phase with it. I, on the other hand, approached dodecaphony as a researcher, analyzing it as eagerly and thoroughly as one would any historical period. I plunged into this technique just as I plunged into the style of strict sixteenth-century counterpoint or later into tonality. For me, dodecaphony was already a fully matured and possibly even historically complete tradition, and for this reason I set myself the task of moving beyond it. Some composers of my generation lived in this tradition and others went beyond it; I am one of the latter.[22]

The Piano Sonata that Gubaidulina herself performed on several occasions was dedicated to Henrietta Mirvis in gratitude for her friendship. A small episode a few years later revealed Gubaidulina's thinking about Schönberg's technique at that time: Yakov Izrailevich Zak had assembled his present and former students in his classroom at the conservatory. The students performed, and Gubaidulina played her Piano Sonata, prompting Zak, who liked and respected his former student both as a person and as a musician, to ask: "Why do composers use twelve tones?" To which she replied: "There are always rules one needs to overcome. Twelve-tone music is like a heavy chain that composers lay upon themselves in the manner of Russian Orthodox ascetics, to surmount pain and suffering."—"And if the composer actually masters the technique?"—"Then he will take upon himself a new burden."[23]

Regarding twelve-tone music, a comment needs to be made about Gubaidulina's relationship with the Romanian-born Philip Herschkowitz, a student of Anton Webern who left Austria during the Third Reich and, after a long and circuitous route, came to Moscow. The story goes that he was the intermediary between a number of Moscow composers and the Second Viennese School, and in this context one can often hear Gubaidulina's name mentioned. But this is only part of the story. After he and Gubaidulina met they exchanged a few visits in the late 1960s and early 1970s—Kolya Bokov later remembered a long session at Herschkowitz's when they listened to recordings of Wagner's *Ring*—and Gubaidulina recalled,

> Philip Herschkowitz had a strong personality full of surprises. I would have liked to hear him say something about Webern and Schönberg, but when we saw each other he talked only about classical harmony and analyzed Mozart and Beethoven from Webern's perspective. I was a little concerned about getting drawn into his sphere of influence. When I invited him to a concert of recent works, he declined, saying, "I'm already married."

In February 1965 Gubaidulina received a letter from the Ministry of Culture [Ministerstvo kul'tury]. The head of the Department of Music invited her in for a conversation, but although she was only thirty-three, she made a courageous decision: "I knew what was going to happen. They wanted music for the Komsomol [Kommunisticheskii soiuz molodëzhi = Communist Youth League] and the Party, and I didn't go." That sort of work paid very well, and Sofia's refusal put her in some painful financial straits until the advent of perestroika. The delicate problem of writing music for the Party and the power establishment was occasionally a topic of conversation among composers. Karen Khachaturian, the nephew of the famous Aram, would sometimes invite Sofia out for a meal, realizing that she was in need. During one of these restaurant outings, he expressed a view fairly common at the time: "I write a piece to please them, and then I write what I like." Understandably no one wanted to live in penury, but Gubaidulina could not play that game: "You prostitute yourself once," she felt, "and you've lost everything."

6 | A Late Artistic Birth, 1965–1970

The "Sixties Generation"

Sofia Gubaidulina belongs to the generation that came of age in the 1960s. During "the Thaw" this "sixties generation" witnessed the public condemnation of Stalin's crimes, terror, and cult of personality. Those of this generation were eager to get at the truth—and not only about the past: they wanted assurance that the past horrors would not be repeated. Fascinated by all that was happening on the other side of the Iron Curtain, they were equally determined to break out of their enforced isolation. Vasily Axionov, a native of Kazan and son of Evgeniya Ginsburg, expressed these views in stories such as *A Ticket to the Stars* [*Zvezdnyi bilet*] in which his protagonists were no longer Komsomol heroes enthusiastically fulfilling five-year-plan objectives but new, attractive character types representing an appealing mixture of cosmopolitanism, youthful energy, and healthy skepticism. But in the spring of 1964, even before the end of the Khrushchev era, the trial of the poet and later Nobel Prize winner Joseph Brodsky proved that any hope for change, let alone greater freedom, was illusory. Khrushchev's fall in October marked the beginning of the reactionary Brezhnev era, with its return to strict Party control over all aspects of life. Although dissidents were no longer executed, those who did not submit to the new order were persecuted, sent to labor camps or psychiatric institutions, or—like Solzhenytsin and others—forced to emigrate. The Brezhnev era caused the third wave of emigration from the Soviet Union, where the KGB, serving as a second government, generally enforced its rule through blackmail, lies, theft, assault, even murder. For the third time, fear was running rampant: people chose their words carefully on the telephone and knew just which books to remove from their shelves at the least sign of danger. During the last phase of "The Thaw," groups of writers and artists had spontaneously sprung up, and in the early 1960s scholars and members of the technical intelligentsia joined them. Dissidents and civil rights advocates began to be active against a renewal of harsher political measures, providing assistance over the next few years with remarkable dedication and moral courage to those who needed it, always risking arrest and imprisonment. *Samizdat* ("self-publishing") was also just beginning at this time. Manuscripts that had gathered dust on the desks of the state-run publishing houses or had no chance of passing censorship were distributed in typed copies and later by microfilm. Countless underground texts were then circulating for secret midnight readings, more copying, and recirculation; and, as of the late 1960s, the *samizdat* journal, *Chronicle of Current Events* [*Khronika tekushchikh sobytii*] played an important role. The chief objective of the dissidents' activities was not to attack the system itself but to call for strict adherence to constitutionally granted rights and privileges. Thus the *Chronicle* reported calmly and factually on violations of Soviet law printing eyewitness accounts of important trials of the period; by so doing, many political prisoners were freed and others were saved from the inhuman conditions of the labor camps.

Through Kolya Bokov and his circle of friends, Sofia Gubaidulina became involved with the dissidents. She was grateful for the fresh intellectual breeze of this environment and supported the dissidents' activities to the best of her abilities, but as a composer she had little to contribute to political action programs. Kolya often returned home with some friends, sharing with them the sparse contents of his refrigerator and letting them use the bathroom as a darkroom for developing microfilms. Poised in stark contrast to today's world of instant global communication is Gubaidulina's explanation of what she and her friends at that time considered absolutely essential to their lives:

> Two very simple things were most important to us at that time ... to get information about the world—truthful, not falsified—and to stop lying. The "sixties generation," which took on the job of *samizdat,* was obliged to do great things. It isn't all that clear to the present generation or sufficiently appreciated nowadays, since all information is now accessible and open. But we sat up all night copying out the *Chronicle of Current Events* simply to know what was really going on.... And we knew they might knock on the door and catch us.[1]

The external pressures of the system and the growing resistance among the population changed Gubaidulina in ways that had a lasting impact on her compositions. A sustained inner process of self-discovery culminated in the composition Five Etudes for Harp, Double Bass, and Percussion, which she wrote in 1965 after completing her Piano Sonata. The work developed in a multi-tiered, multifaceted process that would result in her final independence from her earlier models and teachers, especially Nikolai Peiko, whose opinion had always held much sway with her. Committed to her own rich imagination and wrestling with an abundance of musical material that could no longer be formed and shaped following traditional principles, Gubaidulina arrived at a radical conclusion: "Until then, I had wanted to write for the theater, to compose ballets, symphonies. . . . But then I understood: no, absolutely not. I need to write miniatures, miniatures in a whisper. I picked instruments that have almost no sound. The harp, a quiet, gentle instrument; the string bass is purposely muted; the percussion instruments are also treated the same way, so that the score calls for very few sounds. It was from this moment I realized that I would pay no attention at all to anybody else. I would do what I liked. . . . That doesn't mean, of course, that afterward I only expressed myself in a whisper."[2]

Less can be more—and with that radical turnabout Gubaidulina had broken the spell. Her decision to tone down her compositions was, she later explained, also a commitment to a path toward greater inwardness and depth: "Perhaps the purpose of our actions today is not to invent more and more novelties; the filters need to be turned on, not the generators. (The twentieth century has already had enough innovations, be they timbral, textural, or whatever.) It's time to give something up, in order to work *inside* the material, not just *with* it, to get a feel for its inner resistance and make use of it."[3] Somewhat surprisingly Gubaidulina used this metaphor of the generator and the filter again, several times, when discussing her late "artistic birth" in the early 1990s.[4] And no less a person than Karlheinz Stockhausen also once said that among composers Gubaidulina is a filter rather than a generator; yet he could hardly have known of her own earlier comments, which were published in Russian. This choice of phrase, however, is not only a comment on two distinct concepts of composition; Gubaidulina's usage points toward the fundamental differences between male and female. For her, this "birth" was a twofold process of finding her own language: the remarkably long time of artistic gestation was, for her, closely related to her self-discovery as a woman.

About Female and Male

Gubaidulina spoke on this subject with some hesitation after noticing, during her first travels in the mid-1980s, that women composers in the West had formed associations and arranged festivals, and that certain publishers issued works only by women. She had never seen anything like it in the Soviet Union. Russian history and culture have known strong women figures, and during the years of the Soviet regime Gubaidulina never experienced oppression or exclusion as a woman. She devoted much thought to this matter and grappled with a wide array of perspectives, ranging from Otto Weininger's *Geschlecht und Charakter* all the way to Carl Gustav Jung's thoughts about female *animus* and male *anima*.

In the early 1990s she gave Göran Fant a rather detailed account of her process of self-discovery when she was thirty-four years old, offering at the same time her views of women and men:

> I am convinced that male and female consciousness are two quite different things. But that is complicated by the fact that no person is either purely a man or purely a woman. To determine what is typically masculine and typically feminine seems to me an immensely important area of research. Within myself, I sense a very distinct femininity. . . . I remember how it was for me when I was young. It was very difficult for me to articulate my thoughts in words. It was so painful to have to express something in words. . . . All my thoughts came to me at the same time, forming something like a vertical thought structure. Instead of a line, I experienced a vertical form. I would say something and felt at the same time that it wasn't right. It was a real tragedy for me, this pileup of disparate thoughts; I wanted to express all levels simultaneously, but of course that was impossible. So I chose the last thought and voiced only that—and it was very painful. I believed that a man does not experience such a disordered consciousness, that for him things are simple and clear, that his thoughts are horizontal and linear. This led me to conclude that the ability to think vertically is peculiarly feminine. My consciousness contains much darkness; it is not suffused with light. Men's thinking, on the other hand, is bright, logical, and very clear. My vertical thinking comes from my feminine nature. Only with great self-discipline have I learned to concentrate at the uppermost layer of my verticality and to articulate it. It took me a long time to understand that it is necessary to do so, that not all layers are equally important, that it is impossible to include everything, and that the vertical must be transformed into the horizontal. It was only then that I learned to speak coherently—even to live.[5]

Gubaidulina has sometimes, and quite accurately, been called a musical mystic. The ancient mystics also believed that the inner world of the soul was a feminine entity: the soul was the bride who strove for union with the groom, the divine seed within man that was to grow and thrive. A poem by the Spanish mystic St. John of the Cross (San Juan de la Cruz, 1542–1591), describing this process through a series of images, has the significant title *The Dark Night of the Soul*. Gubaidulina loved the solitary, still hours when she could submerge herself in that dark inner world, the realm of the soul, which she experienced as rich and creative but also as dangerous and treacherous, a world she took great pains to protect against all disturbing, rational influences. Not surprisingly she is an admirer of Meister Eckhart (Johannes Eckhart [c. 1260–1327]), has read and reread his sermons, and took Rilke's "Ich liebe die Nächte . . ." from his *Stundenbuch* as a text for her First Cello Concerto. In the 1990s she initially planned to set some of Novalis's writings on music to fulfill a commission for the Schönberg Ensemble of Amsterdam, because this Romantic poet made the dark world of the soul the center of his creative work. His lines—"The mysterious path leads inward. Eternity with all its worlds, the past and the future, either lie within us or are nothing. The external world is the world of shadows, casting its shadow over the realm of light"[6]—speak of the same sphere that Gubaidulina calls feminine verticality. Vertical and horizontal, the soul's realm of night and day, intuition and rationality—all these will be recalled later when Gubaidulina speaks about her own creative process, the "transformation of time."

Five Etudes for Harp, Double Bass, and Percussion

Gubaidulina's five "miniatures in a whisper" do not represent a radically new departure in their handling of musical material as do, for instance, Pierre Boulez's *Structures I* or Morton Feldman's earliest graphic aleatoric scores. Her work, by comparison, seems almost conservative. Toning down her music and parting ways with her teachers and her past were deeply liberating experiences, but the changes in compositional technique, rather than being at the heart of her transformation, instead were the means to an end. For this reason, these five miniature exercises—and this is how "etudes" should be understood here—result in remarkable and contrasting character pieces, which nevertheless form a distinct unity based on subtle interaction among instrumental timbres, lively rhythms, and performance techniques. In simple motifs and pitch successions, the three instruments speak sometimes with and sometimes against one another in a conversation of extraordinary colorations. The dynamic markings rarely exceed a "whisper," ranging from *mezzo piano* to *piano* to *pianissimo* (three of the etudes end with the marking *morendo,* one with *ritardando*). The rhythms are striking, characterized by frequent changes in beat, together with polyrhythmic and (in one instance) aleatoric elements. A number of deftly calibrated percussion solos feature marimba, tambourine, side drum, small cymbal, and the four bongos. Although the tonal structures are generally intuitive, the third etude, and more extensively the fifth, reveals elements of twelve-tone technique. In the context of what was otherwise pompous official Soviet music, these etudes must have had a most welcome cleansing effect. Valentina Kholopova, at any rate, felt that, in the basic conception of these five instrumental miniatures, "one can detect the influence on the composer—an influence that is not overt or obvious, but still to the highest degree beneficial—of Anton Webern's early works ... in particular his Opp. 6 and 10 for orchestra."[7] The passages for percussion vividly express Gubaidulina's Tatar temperament, but in the Moscow of her day they only seemed vaguely exotic. Just as she had produced unusual sounds on her baby grand as a child, she continued in these pieces to explore each instrument—harp, double bass, and percussion ensemble—for new possibilities. The instrumentation she chose for the Five Etudes exemplified in itself a thoroughly unconventional departure.

Gubaidulina created astonishing nuances of sound and color in this work, all emanating from the distinctive aura of these particular instruments. This quality characterizes her work as a whole. Later she would comment on this aspect by speaking of her almost mystical relationship with a musical instrument: "An instrument is a living being; all the echoes of our subconscious are invested in it. When a finger touches a string or a bow touches the bridge, a transformation occurs; a spiritual force is transformed into sound. My quasi-religious approach to an instrument is a gift, and I try to strengthen it within me."[8] To assume, however, that all this comes about easily from natural talent and female sensibility would be a mistake. Her treatment of each instrument—even in her student days—has always been based on "a process of hard professional work," as she explained in 1981. "Always and everywhere I've been studying the possibilities of instruments and their combinations—in classes at the conservatory, at concerts, in scores—but mainly by taking chances myself and by personal association with musicians."[9]

The first musicians Gubaidulina collaborated with were the well-known Moscow percussionist Mark Pekarsky, who at the time was still a student at the Gnesin Institute, and Boris Artemiev, bassist at the State Symphony Orchestra of the USSR [Gosudarstvennyi simfonicheskii orkestr Soiza SSR], the premier orchestra of the Soviet Union. It was not easy to find musicians who would perform compositions like the Five Etudes, as the unorthodox score required much preparation. Neither fame nor additional engagements were likely to follow, and the pay—if any—was more symbolic than substantial. Pekarsky, who by then had already begun his famous collection of exotic percussion instruments, met Gubaidulina for the first time at Edison Denisov's. Denisov had told him about "this interesting young composer," who was just working on a piece for harp, double bass, and percussion. In Pekarsky, Sofia found a skilled and versatile musician and, beyond that, a man of wit and humor. "I invented some new techniques for the Five Etudes," Pekarsky later recalled; "for instance, a marimba-tremolo played simultaneously with one mallet from above and one from below. I was very proud of myself and thought I'd discovered America. But later I found out that this way of playing had already been used."[10] It was the beginning of a long friendship and extensive collaboration, during which Gubaidulina wrote several pieces for Pekarsky and for the ensemble he founded in 1976. These were performed in the Soviet Union, and later in concert tours in the West. Not long after they had met, Pekarsky asked Sofia for a piece for his degree recital; she obliged with a Sonata for Two Percussionists, a work she revised many times until 1966 but never to her ultimate satisfaction. In his 1967 book, *New Trends in Soviet Music* [*Nové proudy v sovětské hudbě*], Václav Kučera argues that Gubaidulina conceived this Sonata as a counterpole to Stockhausen's *Zyklus*.[11] This Sonata, however, did not have its premiere until December 1991 in Moscow, on the occasion of a weekend of concerts, arranged by Mark Pekarsky, in honor of the composer's sixtieth birthday. The celebration, running under the title "In the Beginning Was Rhythm" [*V nachale byl ritm*], featured all of Gubaidulina's works for percussion alone as well as her chamber music with percussion.

As for Boris Artemiev, a former fellow student at the Moscow Conservatory, Gubaidulina explored with him such performance techniques for the double bass as *col legno* (playing with the wooden side of the bow) and *ricochet* (bouncing the bow off the strings), and she experimented under his supervision with a variety of glissando techniques.[12] The harpist for the first unofficial performance of the Five Etudes in March 1966 was Vera Savina, also of the USSR State Symphony Orchestra. Pekarsky, however, had to cancel, as he did not have all the necessary instruments and was on tour at the time.[13] He was replaced by Valentin Snegiryov, another member of the State Symphony Orchestra.

The Moscow Commission for Chamber and Symphonic Music [Komissia kamernoi i simfonicheskoi muzyki]

The beginning of 1966 was a time of political turbulence. In a February show trial that received considerable international attention, two writers, Andrei Siniavsky and Yuli Daniel, were, respectively, sentenced to seven and five years of imprisonment and labor camp for "anti-Soviet agitation and propaganda." They had published their writings under much publicized pseudonyms in the West, Siniavsky as Abram Terts, Daniel as Nikolai Arzhak. Protest demonstrations took place in front of the Justice Building in Moscow, and the dissident movement got ready for action, because the trial was symptomatic of a much larger situation. The possibility was bruited about that the upcoming Twenty-Third Party Congress might ratify resolutions to rehabilitate Stalin. This sufficed to rally twenty-five renowned scientists, scholars, and artists to send a letter to Leonid Brezhnev, protesting any possible restoration of Stalinism. The distinguished writer Konstantin Paustovsky, noted theoretical physicist and member of the Academy of Sciences Andrei Zakharov, popular film director Mikhail Romm, and prima ballerina assoluta Maya Plisetskaya numbered among the signers.[14]

During these turbulent weeks, Gubaidulina had her own little trial by fire. On March 30 the three musicians noted above—Artemiev, Savina, and Snegiryov—performed her Five Etudes for discussion and critique for the Commission for Chamber and Symphonic Music. Usually about twenty or thirty members of the Composers Union attended these regular sessions on Wednesday afternoons. Visitors were also welcome, and on good days as many as fifty might be in the audience. Usually two or three works by members from Moscow would be performed and discussed, with a stenographer taking notes. The room was equipped with two grand pianos and an audio recorder, and the score lay open on the table. When the discussion had progressed sufficiently, the judges would make a crucial decision: Would they have the score and its instrumental parts printed at the expense of the official *Muzfond* for distribution to potential conductors and instrumentalists (privately owned printing or copying devices was strictly prohibited), and would they recommend the work for a concert series of the Moscow Composers Union? Bitter battles were fought in these sessions until well into perestroika days, and in the discussion of the Five Etudes no holds were barred. Gubaidilina had the support of friends like Schnittke and Denisov and also some younger composers. A few older colleagues supported her as well; especially Sergei Razoryonov and Boris Kliuzner (the latter having left Leningrad because of difficulties with the music bureaucracy) were favorably disposed toward the younger generation and particularly fond of Gubaidulina. On that particular afternoon they argued "relentlessly about the exoticism of the whole thing, about its sound in general, its instrumentation"[15]—and, naturally, they got into the perennial issue of "melody." "What we call melody," Razoryonov argued, "doesn't exist here. But everything is so logical—whatever follows seems to build on what came before—it is absolutely convincing. Furthermore, there is another interesting aspect: although there is no melody, the whole piece is emotional and appeals to our sensibilities."[16] And Boris Kliuzner commented elsewhere: "It was the composer's special talent that turned even the drums into something poetic."[17] The happy result of that Wednesday session was that the Five Etudes was performed on several occasions, among them the evening concert of March 13, 1967, at the Concert Hall of the Composers Union [Kontsernyi zal Doma kompozitorov], which also featured works by Victor Suslin, Grigory Frid, Boris Kliuzner, and others. Surprisingly Gubaidulina's Piano Sonata was also performed at that event, with Maria Gambardian as soloist. With hundreds of composers working in Moscow, it was quite unusual that a composer would have two works on the same program—and Nikolai Peiko may once again have pulled some strings. He was one of the secretaries of the Moscow Composers Union, as well as a member of the regular Wednesday sessions.

Only three weeks after the critical session, on April 21, 1966, the Five Etudes had its premiere in the Concert Hall of the Composers Union. Grigory Frid, who had probably participated in the discussion of the work, arranged for an evening of Gubaidulina's music under the auspices of his Moscow Youth Musical Club [Moskovskii molodëzhnyi muzykal'nyi klub].

Grigory Frid and the Moscow Youth Musical Club

In 1965 Grigory Frid founded the Moscow Youth Musical Club as part of the Moscow Composers Union. Many young people, including future scientists and engineers, took out a year's subscription and attended regular Thursday club sessions between October and May. A large number of them renewed their subscriptions year after year, so that the audience gradually increased in age. The club still exists today and celebrated its thousandth performance in 1999. The Thursday evening gatherings played an important role in Moscow's musical life up to perestroika, as many works that were not officially sanctioned could be performed and discussed there. Gennady Aigi later paid tribute to these evenings by referring to them as the "*samizdat* of music." A man of cosmopolitan taste and superior education, Grigory Frid was also an excellent organizer with a gift for diplomacy. He selected a theme for each evening, introduced the program, and conducted the ensuing discussion with great skill. The club functioned as a first-rate music encyclopedia for those in attendance, with topics ranging from portraits of individual composers and definitions of musical movements both past and present all the way to interrelationships between art and science. Some evenings were dedicated to great interpreters, and others focused on topics the audience had suggested, for example, "Music and the Subconscious," "Music and Painting," or "Music and Cybernetics." Almost all well-known Soviet composers and musicians took part in Frid's evenings, or at least attended performances; even Shostakovich could now and then be counted among the guests. The latter's song cycle, *Five Romances on Texts from Krokodil Magazine* Op. 121 (ca. 1966), opened the thirteenth session of the club, on April 21, 1966, which was dedicated to Gubaidulina's music. Frid knew that on this evening he was exposing his young audience to something quite unusual. Following his introductory comments, Gubaidulina played her Piano Sonata, and then the three musicians from the State Orchestra performed the Five Etudes. When it was over, the audience reacted with tense uncertainty. The public discussion that followed focused on Gubaidulina's music but also involved Webern and Stockhausen, possibly because Frid had mentioned them in his introduction. When a young man in the audience commented, "I don't believe that what we just heard can still be called music," Frid tactfully replied: "If we can't call this music, then we also can't call other things music, for example, Stockhausen."[18] At times, when Frid had to justify himself before some Party functionary of the Composers Union, the discussions resembled a high-wire act. As Frid recalled in the late 1990s,

> Five Etudes was not the only work we premiered; we also gave the first performance of Denisov's *Laments* [*Plachi*], Schnittke's First String Quartet, and his

Second Sonata. Of the 400 members of the club, perhaps 380 had quite traditional musical tastes and were not interested in modern music. My position was particularly difficult, because I stood between the Party on one side and, on the other, the many Moscow composers who also didn't like modern music. The Party told me: "Nobody likes this music—so what are you doing?" Had I not been a Party member myself, the club would have been shut down promptly. Khrennikov didn't know a thing about modern music, but he was on my side and told me, "You've got to be very careful."[19]

In the summer of 1966 Gubaidulina traveled to the Caucasus Mountains, where Stanislav Govorukhin was working on his film *Vertikal*. She had been commissioned to write the film score. The leading role was played by Vladimir Vysotsky, who had had a career at the Taganka Theater and then achieved enormous popularity as a film actor and song writer. Many of his melancholy, aggressive, and critical songs, with his own guitar accompaniment, were played throughout the Soviet Union in unauthorized recordings. This film was a melodrama about the dangers and adventures of mountaineering. Gubaidulina enjoyed her time in the Caucasus, sharing the film crew's life in tents. She participated in the actual filming, with crew and guides on ropes reaching altitudes as high as the clouds. A short while after the filming, Vysotsky appeared for a work session in Moscow to talk about an orchestral accompaniment to one of his songs.

Because living conditions at Leninskii prospekt had become difficult, Kolya and Sofia looked for new quarters. They lived for a while with Kolya's mother on Lomonosovskii prospekt, but in the summer of 1966 they found a small apartment owned by the Composers Union at 28 Studentcheskaia ulitsa. Andrei Volkonsky and Edison Denisov lived nearby. The one-room apartment was part of a communal residence with three parties sharing a kitchen and a bath, but a grand piano stood in Gubaidulina's room.

A Visitor from Prague and a Trip to Zagreb

Soon after the couple moved to their new apartment, the Czech composer and musicologist Václav Kučera, a former fellow student, came for a visit. He and Denisov had studied composition in Shebalin's class at the Moscow Conservatory, and Kučera had now come from Prague to do research on a book about Soviet modernism since the Thaw. When he and Schnittke had sat together in Denisov's apartment talking about which of their Moscow colleagues should be written up in the book, Denisov said: "You must get to know Sonia's music. She's become a great composer." He immediately reached for the telephone and arranged a meeting between them. "I was surprised," Kučera later commented, "because I still remembered Sofia as just a young student. When we met, she played her Piano Sonata for me, a very original, expressive piece. She has always been a fine pianist."[20]

Kučera's eighty-page book, *New Trends in Soviet Music* [*Nové proudy v sovětské hudbě*], was published in April of the following year, 1967, in Prague. One must be grateful for this work, for in Moscow at the time and in Prague a year later one could never have written about these composers, who, in trying to find their own unique style, were continually in conflict with the authorities.[21] Kučera discussed Gubaidulina's work in one and a half pages and included her photograph.

On February 25, 1967, the same three musicians who had earlier played the Five Etudes—Artyomov (double bass), Savina (harp), and Snegiryov (percussion)—presented its official "premiere" (as indicated in the evening's printed program) in the Small Hall of the Moscow Conservatory. This performance had been arranged by Nikolai Platonov, who had liked Gubaidulina's work ever since *Allegro rustico*. It was an evening in the prestigious series Contemporary Chamber Music [Sovremennaia kamernaia muzyka] of the Moscow State Philharmonia [Moskovskaia gosudarstvennaia filarmoniia], a concert organization that enjoyed great popularity. In addition to Gubaidulina's work, the program featured the premiere of Viacheslav Artyomov's *Two Northern Songs* [*Dve severnye pesni*], and works by Hindemith, Prokofiev, Stravinsky, and Walter Piston. After the performance Andrei Volkonsky approached Sofia backstage, kissed her, complimented her, and thanked her for her new composition. Of the three musicians, Boris Artemiev was particularly fond of the Five Etudes. At his request Gubaidulina, somewhat earlier, had written *Pantomime* for double bass and piano, which she dedicated to him.

Two and a half months after that concert, Gubaidulina went abroad for the first time. The program of the Fourth Music Biennial Zagreb, 1967, International Festival of Contemporary Music [Muzički biennale Zagreb], listed a matinée performance of the Five Etudes on May 20, 1967, together with Hans Werner Henze's *Lucy Escott Variations,* Aribert Reimann's *Spektren* for piano, and several works by Yugoslav composers. Gubaidulina must have been delighted and excited about the trip to the old Croatian capital. Besides the already well-established International Warsaw Autumn Music Festival [Warszawska Jesień: Międzynarodowy Festiwal Muzyki Współczesnej], the Zagreb Biennial was the second festival of contemporary music within the Iron Curtain where composers, performers, and critics from East and West could meet for eleven days of lectures, press conferences, receptions, and as many as four concerts per day. Under Tito's regime of relative independence from Moscow, Yugoslavia was enjoying greater freedoms than the rest of the Communist camp. The composer Milko Kelemen had organized the entire event; as a student of Wolfgang Fortner, he had many contacts in the West. The program included not only old and new Yugoslav compositions but also works by such Western avant-gardists as Boulez, Nono, Stockhausen, Ligeti, Cage, and other big names. There were also performances of electronic music and two seminars on modern instrumental techniques, Aloys Kontarsky of Cologne offering the piano course and Heinz Holliger, the Swiss composer and virtuoso performer, the oboe course. (In the 1980s and 1990s Holliger had conducted several of Gubaidulina's works.) At the 1967 festival, Western critics were particularly excited about the participation of the "modernists from the USSR,"[22] for, in addition to Gubaidulina, several other Soviet colleagues had traveled to Zagreb. Commenting on works by Denisov, Schnittke, Silvestrov, Volkonsky, Shchedrin, and several others, Hans Heinz Stuckenschmidt, the most respected German music critic, wrote that these "Soviet modernists, who are trying to establish connections to the compositional techniques of the Western avant-garde, have two things in common: a deeply emotional expressivity and a fundamentally tragic disposition. In this regard they seem to be closer to Russia's soul than someone like Prokofiev or the brilliant Shchedrin."[23]

Two cantatas, Denisov's *Sun of the Incas* [*Solntse Inkov*] and Volkonsky's *Laments of Shchaza* [*Zhaloby Shchazy*], were especially well received, and Stuckenschmidt praised their brilliant and sensitive renditions. When Gubaidulina arrived at the concert hall for the rehearsal of her work, she was shocked to learn that the members of the ad hoc "chamber ensemble" were apparently rehearsing *a prima vista,* at first sight. Whatever the reason was—whether because of a poorly arranged rehearsal schedule or a lack of interest and commitment—she reluctantly decided to cancel the performance. This unfortunate experience, however, was not unique and probably was the result of an overly ambitious program. Stuckenschmidt, accustomed to Western standards of organization, commented: "The massive program in many ways fails to live up to its advance billing. Offended prima donnas have departed, and scheduled works have been abbreviated or rewritten because of insufficient rehearsal time and the specter of performances that run on forever." All these factors led him to conclude that, "despite the organizers' efforts to get it off the ground ... the festival as a whole is inadequate and incoherent."[24] But Sofia, who had come to Zagreb from a life of isolation in Moscow, surely experienced those days quite differently, in spite of the debacle of the Five Etudes. She had lived with canceled performances before and would experience them again in the future—for example, as noted, the derailed ballet performance in Leningrad later in 1967. Important festivals like in Zagreb or Warsaw often provoked envy and ill-will among the established Moscow composers, because festival organizers, both Eastern and Western, had no interest in their music. At times they used their connections to prevent their less well-known competitors from traveling to the festival or to torpedo performances of their works.

On her return to Moscow, Sofia carried a few small presents for Kolya: a volume of Nietzsche, two of Joyce (in English), and a book by Emanuel Mournier on French existentialism. Yugoslavia's greater freedom was also evident in its bookstores.

Night in Memphis [Noch' v Memfise] and Rubaiyat [Rubaiiat]

Gubaidulina was fortunate to be offered several commissions for film scores between 1967 and 1969. Roman Davydov, the director of a five-part animated film based on Kipling's *Jungle Book,* which became a success in theaters and on television under the title *Mowgli [Maugli]*, had originally approached Boris Tchaikovsky, but he declined the offer with the comment: "The best person for this work is Sofia Gubaidulina." In addition to *Mowgli*, she wrote the scores for two feature films directed by Stanislav Govorukhin and for another animation. The income from these assignments gave her the freedom to work independently at the end of the 1960s. Sufficient savings, however, were only one of the necessary preconditions for creative work; peace and quiet were even more important, and working on film scores was particularly demanding. Since the beginning of her relationship with Kolya, she had often sacrificed her privacy. She rose early in the morning; he was a night owl. She was very fond of him and he respected her work, but his activities and frequent visitors caused considerable havoc in their small efficiency apartment. The resulting tensions led to a one-year separation in 1968, and it was during this period that Gubaidulina began her next important work, *Night in Memphis.* She actually received some unexpected help at that time from three other people living in the communal apartments—a chauffeur and his wife (the latter ran the elevator), and a secretary. To these individuals, the composer must have appeared as a rather odd individual, not at all a normal figure in Soviet life. "It's strange," the chauffeur said one day, "you work all day long, but you have little to eat and hardly any money. That doesn't seem fair, and I certainly wouldn't live like that." Somehow this attitude must have affected all her neighbors, because a short while later the woman who ran the elevator started doing Sofia's cleaning, and the secretary included Sofia in the meals she cooked for herself. Sofia gratefully accepted these services.

The two cantatas *Night in Memphis* and *Rubaiyat,* composed in 1968 and 1969, respectively, belong together as a contrasting pair; they represent an important achievement of this period in the composer's development. Having completed the Five Etudes, *Pantomime [Pantomimma]*, and the Sonata for Two Percussionists, Gubaidulina wanted to experiment with a larger ensemble—solo voice and chamber orchestra. In *Night in Memphis* she wrestled with some of the ultimate questions of existence: death as "the center of human life" and man's acceptance of its inevitability. In *Rubaiyat* she dealt with the pain and suffering of human life and man's range of emotions, from despair to indignation, in confronting it.

Night in Memphis was composed in the year of the "Prague Spring," when the Moscow intelligentsia was anticipating a future of communism with a human face. But in August 1968 Soviet tanks rumbled through the streets of Prague, destroying all such hopes. Gubaidulina elevated to a higher level the anguish of these months and the questions it provoked about the pain of living in a world without escape. Pushing aside the limits of time and space in *Night in Memphis,* she looked to ancient Egypt, a civilization that had always intrigued her. She used inscriptions from ancient tombs, translated by Anna Akhmatova and Vera Potapova, as texts for her composition and arranged them to contrast in a seven-part cycle reflecting the ancient division between the world of the day and the world of the night, the world of humans and the world of the gods. For the ancient Egyptians, the eastern part of the land was the realm of day and of the living; people lived and tended the fields on the east bank of the Nile. The western side, with its pyramids and places of worship, represented the sphere of the spirit, the realm of the night. *Night in Memphis* opens with the soft but intense sounds of strings; above them, the repetitive tones of a muted trumpet and the flutter tonguing of a flute, used as a contrasting pair, are the only two wind instruments in the entire piece. The mezzo-soprano begins with an apostrophe to the night: "O, night, give me peace," and, from then on, mezzo-soprano and chamber orchestra are heard in alternation from the stage: the human soul speaks of its loneliness as it ponders death. A male chorus resounds mightily and massively from the back of the hall, its words—supported by tremendous cascades of percussion—appealing to the eternal world of the gods. Along with the male chorus runs a spoken text, which in the performances of the 1990s was played on tape. After the sixth part, in which death appears to the soul "as the healing of the sick, as a freeing from the imprisonment of suffering . . . as the fragrance of the lotus flower," the quiet, sustained dramatic tension of the work is resolved. The instruments play above a seemingly endless *pizzicato* arpeggio in the double bass as the soul reaches a state of harmony and peace:

> Calm your heart.
> May it forget the preparation
> For your enlightenment.
> . . .
> Lamentation will not save you from the grave.
> So celebrate the beauty of the day
> And do not exhaust yourself.

Look—no one has taken his possessions with him.
Look—none of the departed has returned.

Among Gubaidulina's early compositions, this cantata set in ancient Egypt is the most strictly structured work and also the most rationally organized according to twelve-tone principles. Its prime twelve-tone row, with its groupings of half steps in succession, betrays her study of Webern. She assigns the smaller intervals that can be sung—major seconds, minor thirds, and major thirds—to the human realm, fourths and tritones (supported by an active rhythm) to the realm beyond the human. The tone row appears both in dramatic linear *fugato* episodes and in harmonic blocks, the series in continual rotation. The absence of a tonic or a tonal center in the twelve-tone system often gives it a peculiar, suspensive quality, and Sofia Gubaidulina successfully integrates this approach with the subdued inner drama of the work. *Night in Memphis* was also her last work employing twelve-tone technique consistently.

Before composing the second of the two cantatas, Gubaidulina completed two other pieces: *Detto,* for solo organ, and a cycle of piano pieces, *Musical Toys* [*Muzykal'nye igrushki*], in which she looks back at her childhood, presenting pictorial miniatures that she would have liked to play as a child.

In *Rubaiyat* Gubaidulina turned to the Orient of the Middle Ages, feeling connected to its mystical philosophy through her Tatar ancestors. This cantata—with its title representing the plural form of the Persian *rubai* (the classic four-line form of Persian mystic poetry)—is the opposite of *Night in Memphis* in both theme and expression. In a translation by Vladimir Derzhavin, nine of these four-line verses by Omar Khayyam, Khaqani, and Hafiz, are gathered in seven parts of a single-movement work. It foregrounds the physical world, humanity's life on earth, and man's dialogue with God. Like Job's despair and quarrel with God about an unbearable human fate, it rises in three waves, moving from mourning and loneliness to passionate rebellion. But this cantata also resolves the struggle of the human soul in peace and reconciliation:

Be not frightened by the fleeting nature of this world.
Sit quietly in a corner and be content!
Focus your mind on the playfulness of fate.

Whereas *Night in Memphis* is controlled by strict dodecaphonic rationality, in *Rubaiyat* Gubaidulina relies completely on artistic spontaneity. The most remarkable aspect, however, is her treatment of the vocal part, which she uses for the deliberate deployment of a wide range of expressive elements. The female voice in *Night in Memphis* expresses itself only in song and spoken song; in *Rubaiyat,* the baritone voice has to master a number of techniques: (1) singing at a specified pitch; (2) breathing audibly in stronger and weaker breaths; (3) speaking; (4)

speaking with vocal glissando; (5) whispering; (6) whispering with glissando; (7) screaming; (8) singing falsetto; and (9) singing through a microphone.

Several important song cycles with ensemble accompaniment mark postwar Soviet music, and Jürgen Köchel correctly points to the premiere of Volkonsky's *Suite of Mirrors* [*Siuita zerkal*] (1961) as the beginning of postwar Soviet New Music. Volkonsky's other two cycles, *The Laments of Shchaza* and *A Traveling Concert* [*Stranstvuiushii kontsert*], and Denisov's *Sun of the Incas* and *Laments* must also be mentioned in this context. It may well be that Boulez's *Le Marteau sans Maître* served as a catalyst for the genre "voice and ensemble" and for some of the works written by Denisov, who had heard a recording of this Boulez composition at Shebalin's in the late 1950s. Also, in the late 1960s the recording of Luciano Berio's *Visage* was all the rage in Moscow. It combines an electronic sound track with various completely unorthodox sounds of a female voice, sung by the composer's wife, the American singer Cathy Berberian. Radio Italy, which had originally commissioned this recording, later banned it for alleged sexual innuendo and lewdness. Kolya Bokov remembered how Nina Chefranova was actually moved to tears when she listened to this record, exclaiming, "Boy, she's tops."[25] Its appearance revolutionized the high culture of Russian song, and it is entirely possible that it encouraged Gubaidulina to experiment with the tremendous potential of the human voice.

Finding venues for performing her two works in Moscow proved impossible. *Night in Memphis* did not have its Moscow premiere until twenty-one years later; *Rubaiyat* gathered dust on a shelf for "only" seven years until it was successfully performed for the Composers Union (more on this later).

The Experimental Studio at the Scriabin Museum

In January 1969 Gubaidulina was finally able to buy her own apartment, and she and Kolya moved to the northeastern part of Moscow. Large nine-story apartment buildings had recently been built only a five-minute walk from the Preobrazhenskaya ploshchad' metro station, and some of the apartments belonged to a co-op owned by the Composers Union. Apartment No. 130 on the seventh floor at 2nd Pugachovskaya ulitsa (Building 8, Block 10), with its two small rooms, kitchen, and utility rooms, would serve as Gubaidulina's refuge and workplace for the next twenty-two years. There was, of course, a small grand piano, which Olga Stupakova had discovered for her at a wholesale store. Other composers and artists lived in the same building, among them the collector Alexander Glezer, who would lend Gubaidulina some of the paintings from his collection of contemporary art. Also living at this address was the renowned musicologist Yury Kholopov, who had been working since the 1960s with his sister, Valentina, on a book about Anton Webern; the book, however, was only allowed to be published in 1984, nine years after its completion.

At this time Gubaidulina (as well as Denisov and Schnittke) began regular visits to the electronic studio at the Scriabin Museum to work on a piece making use of sonorities generated by the ANS tone synthesizer. After Murzin's laboratory had officially become the Moscow Electronic Studio, he had assembled an Artistic Council (Khudozhestvennyi sovet) as was commonly done with collective enterprises in the USSR. Its members were Pyotr Meshchaninov, the two composers Eduard Artemiev[26] and Alexander Nemtin,[27] as well as Denisov, Schnittke, and Gubaidulina. Stanislav Kreitchi, a technician in Murzin's studio, also served on the council. Whereas Meshchaninov, Artemiev, and Nemtin worked full-time at the studio, the others showed up only now and then. Since its official opening, the studio had been maintained by the recording company Melodya and the Soviet Ministry of Culture; it had been assigned its own rooms in the Scriabin Museum, enabling composers to put in a full day's work. There were two tape recorders, and Murzin had built an improved version of his ANS tone synthesizer. Because of his concept of sound continuity, the tones were not produced on a regular keyboard. Instead, Murzin worked with a glass plate that was painted black and lit from below; any area not covered by paint resulted in a tone. A vertical roller at the side could inscribe lines of varying thickness, making it possible to produce tones of any desired timbre. Gubaidulina began by doing research and preparing herself thoroughly, and Stanislav Kreitchi stood by to assist with all technical problems; but she soon realized that the apparatus was much too complicated for productive work. During the first few months Gubaidulina's thoroughness yielded important new acoustical insights regarding timbre and articulation, but after several months of hard work and unsatisfactory results, she decided on a new approach: she wanted to compose a work using the contrasts and transitions between synthesized tones and natural sounds and noises. For this project, Elizaveta Tumanian became her most important assistant. They taped laughter, sighs, and screams as well as the tinkling of small bells and fragments of a church choir, all of which underwent further processing in the studio. The result was a ten-minute, tape-recorded piece called *Vivente—non vivente,* in which a rich palette of "living sound" is slowly transformed into an array of synthesized tones, and vice versa.

On April 29, 1970, several electronic compositions from the studio were presented at a meeting of the Commission for Symphonic and Chamber Music [Komissiia simfonicheskoi i kamernoi muzyki]. Because experiments of this sort were frowned upon by the established composers and the music bureaucracy (who eventually closed the studio in 1975), Gubaidulina spoke up to present a brief on behalf of tolerance: "[This] music cuts a broad swath across many pathways, and none of these encroaches on one another."[28] The recording of this work available today lacks much of its original subtlety. In the 1970s a technician, intending to improve his income, copied high-quality archival tapes from the German Democratic Republic onto much poorer Russian tapes, as the former were in high demand on the black market.

During the first few weeks in her new apartment Gubaidulina became acquainted with someone who was to play an important role both in her art and her personal life. On December 23, 1968, Evgeny Murzin reported to his Artistic Council on a convention in Florence, where he had described the ANS tone synthesizer in a paper. This led to a *contretemps* between him and Pyotr Meshchaninov, who criticized the paper on several points. Gubaidulina felt that the critique raised important issues and suggested that Meshchaninov be given an opportunity to present his case more fully. Two weeks later, on May 29, after defining his criticism in greater detail, he presented his ideas to the council in a lecture. Then, six months later, Denisov invited him to give another lecture at the Composers Union. Gubaidulina was always in the audience.

She and Meshchaninov had met several months earlier at the home of Alexander Rabinovich, Meshchaninov's close friend from their student days together. Rabinovich, who liked Gubaidulina's Five Etudes, had invited her opinion of his opera after Dostoyevsky's *Crime and Punishment* [*Prestuplenie i nakazanie*], which he played on the piano for her and Meshchaninov on that occasion.

Meshchaninov and the Beginnings of an Elemental Evolutionary Theory of Music

Meshchaninov had actually wanted to become a composer and had come to Murzin's studio with that goal in mind. He earned his living as a pianist for the USSR State Symphony Orchestra—a distinguished position, especially considering that Moscow was full of first-rate pianists. He lived a private and withdrawn life, and his avocation was researching and developing his new theory of music, which was fostered by the potentialities of Murzin's ANS tone synthesizer.

Meshchaninov took as his point of departure the sound continuum created by dividing an octave into seventy-two equal units, which posed the question: What laws of acoustics apply to this phenomenon, and how are they related to the historical development of music as we have understood it? Because all commonly unifying laws of composition and traditional musical structures had been abandoned, Meshchaninov was "in search of lost musical material," as he later described his theory. Since that period a more far-reaching and multilayered theory of pitch, melody, rhythm, and harmony has been developed under the rubric "elemental evolutionary theory of music [*elementarnaia evoliutsionnaia teoriia muzyki*]," but at the time the theory existed only in rudimentary form with regard to pitch. (The ANS tone synthesizer was too inflexible in matters of rhythm and dynamics to handle the elemental substance, the *ur-noumenon*, in the domain of rhythm.) The *ur-noumenon* in the domain of pitch was the overtone series, the source from which each period derived its own historically defined intervals through a process of evolutionary development. Meshchaninov had read Ernö Lendvai's study of Bartók's *Miraculous Mandarin* [*A csodálatos mandarin*] in 1963, but he quickly realized how questionable it would be to derive a pitch set from the Fibonacci series. Hába's experiments with quarter tones also had no foundation, as they could not be developed from the evolutionary regularities of the musical material but were the result of purely arithmetical divisions of half tones. The attempts of the serial school to combine pitch and rhythm also seemed an inadequate and superficial approach to the problem. Meshchaninov therefore worked on the problem of pitch with materials from the classical period, then proceeded to the present and then backward to the more distant past. His research revealed that the development of pitch was defined by a consistent process of expansion, which always regenerated itself by the same principle, a principle he called "invariable transformation." As an aid to understanding, he devised a "geometrics of acoustics," in which tonal intervals were arranged vertically and horizontally in a grid of orthogonal cells. Each of the three major periods covered by his theory is characterized by a development revealing period-specific intervals that evolve successively from the overtone series: the "linear period" (up to the year 1600) with octave and fifth; the "harmonic period" (up to the beginning of the twentieth century) with fifth and third; and the "sonoristic period" (since the mid-twentieth century) with its qualitatively different and radically new development. Invariable transformation is always represented by a diagonal movement within the grid of intervals, freeing up a new cell. A change occurred, however, at the beginning of the twentieth century. Intervals that were clearly noticeable in the tonal realm can be detected in a chromatic structure only enharmonically through their surrounding field. The step from a chromatic to a micro-chromatic structure of the sound continuum, however, is a qualitative leap, as hierarchy of tone, interval, and chord has given way to a microtonal realm consisting of "tonal spots." Because of certain "compensatory" aspects, the function and meaning of the three elements of the "musical web"—melody, harmony, and rhythm—undergo a shift. Just as melody was fundament during the linear period and harmony during the harmonic period, so rhythm is the basic element of the sonoristic period (more on this later). Meshchaninov only presented his theoretical thinking for the first time eleven years later, in 1980, as part of a ten-part lecture series at the acoustics laboratory of the Moscow Conservatory. Among the small number of people who attended regularly were, besides

Gubaidulina, the scholars Yury Kholopov and Valentina Kholopova; Lev Termen (Léon Thérémin) came twice. In the 1990s Meshchaninov discussed his theory also in Germany (Bochum and Hamburg) and Switzerland (Dornach).

At his lecture in May 1969 Meshchaninov explained the development of pitch and his network of intervals during the classical, romantic, and modern periods. For the classical period, the perfect fifth and the major third were the "prime" or basic intervals from which everything else followed; for the romantic period it was the minor and major third; and for the modern period, up to Webern and Shostakovich, the minor third and major seventh. He demonstrated his principle of invariable transformation on the basis of these two developments.

In those years it was important for Gubaidulina to have the evolution of music explained as a coherent and unified process in which the same principle always creates new facets. She invited Meshchaninov to visit her and borrowed his notes for closer and more independent analysis. It was the beginning of an important relationship of fruitful collaboration between the theorist and the composer that has lasted to this day.

Baptism in the Orthodox Church and
Parting from Maria Yudina

Maria Yudina, though approaching seventy, remained active and full of plans for the future although her technique was no longer flawless. In the late 1960s she wanted to play new works by the young generation and proposed a concert cycle, titled "Variations," that would include an evening with Bach's *Goldberg-Variationen* (BWV 988), Liszt's *Variationen über Weinen, Klagen, Sorgen, Zagen* (S. 180), and a work with voice by Gubaidulina.[29] Yudina had asked the much younger composer to write a piece for this occasion, and Gubaidulina obliged with *Sayan [Saian]* (1967) for voice and piano, with texts by Velimir Khlebnikov.

Whenever the two women visited together, in addition to music they also spoke about matters of religion, and Yudina urged her friend to be baptized in the Orthodox Church. She thought it was important for Gubaidulina to be part of a religious structure and offered to be her godmother. These conversations eventually led to Gubaidulina's decision to be baptized, thereby redeeming the promise her mother had made during the first few months after the war. The baptism took place on March 25, in the Church of the Prophet Elijah on Obydennyi pereulok [Khram Ilii Proroka "Obydennogo"],[30] close to what once had been the Church of Christ the Redeemer [Khram Khrista Spasitelia]. Yudina knew the priest, Father Vladimir. Orthodox custom forbids any outstanding debts between the person to be baptized and her sponsor. Because Maria Veniaminovna had borrowed a small sum from the composer, Gubaidulina asked her former land-lady, Vera Svetukhina, who also attended Father Vladimir's services, to sponsor her. In the years to come Gubaidulina celebrated the major religious holidays and occasionally attended services at one of the churches near Preobrazhenskaya ploshchad'.

Eight months after her baptism, Gubaidulina received the news that Maria Yudina had died on November 19, 1970. It was customary in Moscow to pay tribute to important individuals in a civil ceremony at a public viewing of the body; the Gnesin Institute, however, where Yudina had held her last teaching appointment, refused to provide an appropriate hall. For a musician of her stature, the ceremony would normally have been conducted in the Great Hall of the Conservatory, but in the end nothing but the foyer of the Great Hall and the two cloakrooms on either side were made available, and only through Shostakovich's intervention. Many important—and especially young—musicians and academics came to the memorial celebration, and well-known artists and ensembles performed: Sviatoslav Richter, Maria Grinberg, Kirill Kondrashin and the Moscow Philharmonic Orchestra [Moskovskii filarmonicheskii orkestr], as well as Lydia Davydova and Alexei Liubimov.

Maria Yudina's death was a sad loss for Gubaidulina, as she felt a close spiritual affinity for this brave, deeply religious pianist. The admiration was evidently mutual and found expression in a short note Yudina wrote in 1968, two years before her death: "What is so captivating in Gubaidulina is her extraordinary purity in everything, her faith in her creative path, in people, in the beauty and truth of the world; she is absolutely full of honest and guileless intentions, evaluations, projects, deeds, words, and *works*. So, if I live I'll soon perform one of her remarkable works composed quite recently."[31] She never did. Gubaidulina later rejected her setting of Khlebnikov's texts; she did not believe that she was mature enough to write a work for a pianist of Yudina's stature.

Life with Kolya Bokov

While Gubaidulina was preoccupied with religious questions and her baptism, Moscow was humming with preparations for Lenin's hundredth anniversary. April 22, 1970, was to be a day of pomp and circumstance for which the entire city was to be decorated with red banners and posters. Moscow composers were preoccupied with works praising the founder of the Soviet state, his accomplishments and the places where he had been active. Poets were kept busy as well: after an extended visit to the Tatar capital, Evgeny Yevtushenko wrote his poem *Kazan University* [*Kazanskii universitet*], which he dedicated to Lenin's memory. As part of the regular visits between Sofia and her daughter, Nadia came to Moscow to see the Lenin Mausoleum on Red Square. Lenin's embalmed body, exhibited in a granite structure, was a chief attraction during that centennial year, drawing a line of visitors many blocks long. Although Sofia loved her daughter, she asked her husband to take Nadia, because Sofia not only disliked the crowds but also that kind of hero worship.

Kolya Bokov, who was a freelance writer in addition to his *samizdat* activity, used the occasion of his visit to the Lenin Mausoleum with Nadia to write a satire, *The Latest Time of Troubles; or, The Amazing Adventures of Vanya Chmotanov* [*Smuta noveishego vremeni ili udivitel'nye pokhozdeniia Vani Chmotanova*]. The protagonist is a Soviet citizen and the spitting image of Lenin, who, in a series of adventures, steals Lenin's mummified head from the mausoleum to turn it into hard-currency cash. The Party hierarchy is thrown into panic and chaos. Because of his astonishing resemblance to the former Soviet leader, he causes a minor public rebellion in the countryside and is eventually poisoned by the KGB as one of several candidates to take the place of the vandalized mummy. Widely distributed through the *samizdat* network, this absurdly fantastic narrative enjoyed great popularity and soon appeared in the West both in the Russian original and in German, French, and Italian translations. In addition to his many prose pieces, Kolya wrote poetry, philosophical papers, and short plays in those years. Every now and then Sofia's kitchen or Olga Stupakova's apartment would serve as a stage for impromptu theatricals in which Kolya, switching from one part to another, improvised hilarious dialogues between Lenin and his wife, Krupskaya.

His output for *samizdat* was remarkable, as he produced not only reams of typed and mimeographed scripts but also microfilm copies. Sofia's bathroom at No. 2 Pugachovskaya ulitsa was his workshop and dark room, where he copied Adorno's *Einleitung in die Musiksoziologie: zwölf theoretische Vorlesungen* and the collected works of Andrei Siniavsky. Other publications—some originating in other Moscow bathrooms—included Akhmatova's *Requiem*, Rilke's *Marienleben* (in a translation from the 1920s), Florensky's *The Pillar and Ground of the Truth: An Essay in Orthodox Theodicy in Twelve Letters* [*Stolp i utverzhdenie istiny: Opyt pravoslavnoi teoditsei v dvenadtsati pis'makh*], and all of Solzhenitsyn's writings. Even more risky and incendiary were books by such authors as Abdurakhman Avtorkhanov, who had emigrated during World War II: *The Origin of the Party Apparatus* [*Proiskhozhdenie partokratii*], a history of the Party, and *The Technology of Power* [*Tekhnologiia vlasti*], which was a study of Stalin's assumption and exercise of power. These books stood at or near the top of the Index of anti-Soviet literature, and they would cause Gubaidulina considerable trouble a few years later.

In early July 1970 Jürgen Köchel, an editor at Sikorski Music Publishers in Hamburg, took his first trip to Moscow. Besides visiting Shostakovich, he looked up a number of other composers who were on the publisher's list, and he had his first meeting with Gubaidulina, an occasion he later recalled in some detail:

> She seemed very focused and spoke softly as if the walls had ears. I realized then that composers suspected they were being bugged. Schnittke, for example, was terrified and always unplugged the phone when he had visitors. Sofia also seemed anxious. She lived in a small, modest apartment of about 400 square feet that looked out over a cemetery. Modern paintings decorated the walls. She talked about a private gallery in her building where one could get pictures on loan and for sale. In later years she also put up art prints with Christian motifs and an icon. I had brought her some sheet music and records, and she was very pleased. I noticed how isolated she felt. Of course, all the composers—Schnittke, Denisov, and Suslin—were in need; but Sofia was introverted and shy, and that contributed to her isolation. Her compositions—almost exclusively chamber music and small ensemble pieces—impressed me as bearing a strong personal stamp: unusual instrumentation and sounds, a strong emphasis on dynamics, and the use of unconventional percussion. As a publisher, I was mostly interested in pioneering orchestral and chamber works with feasible instrumentations, but hers were unusual and problematic. I advised her to write more orchestral compositions, as they were necessary for establishing a composer's reputation and for getting the attention of reviewers. Within the Composers Union she was not taken seriously at that time and was subjected to harsh criticism for her "Western compositional techniques." She had practically no chance of having her works purchased by the culture bureaucracy or to get any commissions.[32]

A few months later Köchel could see for himself what the leading composers in Moscow thought of Gubaidulina. He accompanied a delegation of Soviet musicians on a tour of Germany in October 1970; among them were Khrennikov, Karen Khachaturian, Eshpai, Shchedrin, and a few instrumentalists. "These gentlemen would roar with laughter every now and then, and when I asked the interpreter, he said: 'This was just another dubious Gubaidulina joke.' Intellectually she was head and shoulders above these men, but they found her art a source of nothing but ridicule."[33] To meet someone like Köchel, who took an interest in her work and, as a publisher, would champion her cause, greatly strengthened Gubaidulina's position at that period. Köchel began to travel to Moscow regularly, soon directed the publishing company with energy and commitment, and took significant risks in his support for Soviet composers by smuggling payments in his right shoe for Shostakovich and secretly importing and exporting scores and books. Over the years he developed close friendships with some of the composers, especially Schnittke and Gubaidulina.

Sofia's circle of friends at that time included Olga Stupakova, the pianist, Oxana Leontieva, the musicologist who had written a book on Orff, and her husband, Daniel Zhitomirsky; the latter two later lost interest in contemporary music. As for composers, she felt intellectually closest to Denisov and particularly Schnittke; Elizaveta Tumanian was primarily a personal friend. As summers were usually a time for relaxation, in 1969 Gubaidulina rented a room on a hill above the Bay of Koktebel for herself, Kolya, and his mother; however, she pitched a tent for herself to enjoy the natural scenery of the Crimea and the Black Sea coast. In the summer of 1970 she and Kolya drove together with Liza (E. Tumanian), Oxana, and Daniel to the Karelian town of Sortavala, where they stayed at the creative retreat of the Composers Union. Tumanian later recalled the weeks they spent there:

> Sonia had a little hill that she considered her sacred retreat for peace and quiet and did not reveal to anyone. We gathered berries and mushrooms and went skinny-dipping. The weather was glorious, and I proposed an excursion by boat for several days. We took off in two boats filled with provisions and blankets and rowed for three days among the islands of Lake Ladoga. At night we slept under the stars and saw the northern lights. Kolya and Dima, Oxana's son, went fishing; and Sonia prepared our meals over an open fire.[34]

A Trip to Warsaw and a Radio Recording of *Night in Memphis*

Since its beginning in 1956, the Warsaw Autumn Music Festival provided the most important annual venue where noncomformist Soviet composers could listen to music from the West, and meet their colleagues and performers from outside the Iron Curtain. Denisov was the first to be given permission to travel to Warsaw in the 1960s, and a few years later Gubaidulina submitted her application to the Composers Union. After been turned down, she received a private invitation from a friend in Warsaw and later recalled what happened then:

> For any personal travel, the applicant was always required to submit a letter of recommendation from his employer, and in this case the employer was the Composers Union. I was asked to appear before a commission of the Composers Union, and they were supposed to pass judgment on me. Vano Ilich Muradeli, the head of the Moscow chapter [i.e., the Moscow Composers Union], and Yury Abramovich Levitin headed this commission, and a few other Party members sat on it. The conversation was really interesting and went something like this:

> V.M.: Unfortunately we cannot arrive at a judgment about you because you are pursuing a wrong artistic direction.
> S.G.: Do you know any of my works?
> V.M.: (somewhat hesitant) Well, yes . . .
> S.G.: Which one do you know?
> V.M.: I have heard your Violin Sonata.
> S.G.: I never wrote one!

V.M.:   Well, perhaps it was a String Trio.
S.G.:   I'm completely innocent; I never wrote one either.
And so it went until Muradeli said:
V.M.:   Don't make me look ridiculous!
S.G.:   Don't you see that *I* am the one who is offended! One can arrive at a
        positive or a negative judgment, but you refuse to make any judgment at
        all. Does this mean I don't even exist? And am I prevented from visiting
        my friend in Warsaw because I write bad music?
I just started laughing out loud because I realized that somewhere higher up it
had already been decided that I would not be allowed to travel.

A few years later, in September 1970, Gubaidulina finally received permission and traveled by train to Warsaw as part of a small group, including Alfred Schnittke, Nikolai Sidelnikov, Valentina Kholopova, and Boris Getselev and his wife, the music scholar Tamara Levaya from Gorky. She met Lutosławski and other Poles as well as Stockhausen, who had also come to Warsaw that year, declaring his turnaround as a composer: "At first I was as hard as Socialism, then as free as the West."[35] Stockhausen supervised the sound mixer for his live electronic orchestral work, *Mixtur,* that was directed by Michael Gielen. Siegfried Palm, the cello virtuoso for contemporary music from Cologne, played Ligeti's Cello Concerto and, together with Aloys Kontarsky, Denisov's Three Pieces for Cello and Piano. Gubaidulina was very much impressed by the trombonists in a group of instrumentalists conducted by Tom Prehn, "who moved the bells of their instruments in different directions as if 'talking' to each other, or searching for something lost on the floor, or doing a 'dance.'"[36]

Back in Moscow, Gubaidulina began with preparations for a piece that had been commissioned by letter for the new music ensemble Musica Viva Pragensis by the Prague composer Marek Kopelent. As the artistic director of the ensemble, which was conducted by his friend, the composer Zbynek Vostrak, Kopelent was putting together a program for the tenth anniversary tour of the group. Within the Eastern block, it had established a strong reputation as a first-rate ensemble for contemporary music, but this was to be almost its last tour before further travel was prohibited.

At the same time that Gubaidulina started to work on the piece for the Prague group, preparations were made in the Czech capital for a radio recording of *Night in Memphis.* Václav Kučera had maintained his contacts with Gubaidulina on his regular visits to Moscow, always inquiring about new compositions. When she told him of the hopelessness of having her cantatas performed, he was able to enlist the interest of the conductor František Veiner at Radio Praha [Radio Prague] for *Night in Memphis.* The cantata was recorded in Studio 1 of Radio Praha between December 1 and 4, and then broadcast with a brief introduction by Kučera. Jaromír Stransý had translated the text into Czech, and Kučera later reported having received numerous letters from listeners expressing appreciation for the performance. Evidently the work had symbolic value in a city where the spring of 1968 had come to a violent end. A few months later *Night in Memphis* had its premiere at the Zagreb Biennial [*Muzički biennale Zagreb*], and on May 13, 1971, Igor Gjadrov conducted the Symphony Orchestra of Radio Zagreb, featuring the mezzo-soprano Eva Novšak-Houška; on the program were also Lutosławski's *Jeux venitiens* and works by Henze and Reimann.

An attempt to stage a Moscow performance of *Night in Memphis* was doomed from the start, because the soloist, Emma Gorelova, did not attend rehearsals regularly. For this performance Gubaidulina had prepared a tape recording of the male chorus. Kolya and his friend, Yury Shershnov, had put the spoken passages on tape at Elizaveta Tumanian's, and Sofia had prepared a usable recording in Murzin's studio. Kolya's friend lived in Gubaidulina's apartment at that time, as he was in desperate straits. He had leukemia and was expected to live only a few weeks. Also, the KGB was after him; he had been interrogated and lost his job as a lawyer. Because he was not permitted to live in Moscow without work, he married his girlfriend in the fall of 1970. Sofia and Kolya were invited to the wedding and took the inner urban to Elektrostal, the home of the bride's parents. "It must have been a grotesque situation for Sonia," Kolya later remembered,

> What with the different types who had gathered there—an uncle of the bride, a prison guard with a broken nose; the bride's mother, who expected that everyone would stay for the night and drink; and many other relatives. But Yury was not allowed to drink because of his medications, and we drank so little ourselves that the other guests were taken aback. Nobody knew about Yury's illness. Because he had to be back in Moscow the following morning, we left the wedding that evening and the festivities continued like the usual drunken debauchery but without the bride and groom. Only a few weeks later, Yury checked into a Moscow hospital and died within a short time. Sofia was fond of him as a human being and suffered with him through the last weeks of his life.

7 | Finding the Legato in the Staccato of Life, 1970–1975

A United Community: Composers, Performers, Audience

The invasion of Czechoslovakia by Soviet troops in August 1968 precipitated a new political and cultural ice age in the Soviet Union. One of its manifestations was the election of Serafim Tulikov as head of the Moscow Composers Union. Born in 1914, Tulikov succeeded Vano Muradeli, who had died in the summer of 1970. Tulikov, a Party loyalist and composer of rather limited musical taste and accomplishment who counted among his works such popular songs as *March of the Soviet Youth* [*Marsh sovetskoi molodëzhi*] and *Song of the Volga* [*Pesnia o Volge*], was a thorn in the side of the small group of nonconformist Moscow composers. They made a virtue out of necessity, closed ranks, and built a network of mutual support. Whereas radio stations in the West with their new-music series and festivals with their requests for well-paid commissioned works were supporting contemporary music, composers in Moscow had to rely entirely on the personal initiative and courage of individuals. The history of unofficial Soviet music from the mid-1960s to perestroika is, in fact, the history of mutual support and assistance among composers, performers, and the public that sympathized with them. Among the performers, as among the composers, a small group was actively engaged in furthering the cause of contemporary music by commissioning works from the composers. Money was a secondary issue for the performers, for, in contrast to the composers, they usually had a steady income; it was not always easy, however, to find an organizer or a concert hall. Within the Composers Union, it was primarily Grigory Frid, with his Moscow Youth Musical Club, and Edison Denisov, with a series of performances he directed under the title "New Works by Moscow Composers" ["Novye proizvedeniia kompozitorov Moskvy"] who had the diplomatic skill and persistence to keep up a schedule of performances. Also of great importance was the commitment shown by a number of instrumentalists who arranged semi-official concerts in various venues—the Physics Institute of the Academy of Sciences [Fizicheskii institut Akademii nauk (FIAN)] and other scientific institutes, or in the House of Folk Arts [Dom narodnogo tvorchestva]—advertising them only by word of mouth. Alexander Rabinovich, as early as the 1960s, had performed Messiaen's *Vingt regards sur l'enfant Jésus,* Stockhausen's *Klavierstück X,* and other works in such places and under such conditions. And Alexei Liubimov, the ever energetic pianist, had presented an evening with Terry Riley's *In C* and John Cage's *Amores, Water Music, Variations II,* and *Fontana Mix.* Liubimov became the center of a circle of musicians who had committed themselves to modern music, among them Lydia Davydova (soprano), Mark Pekarsky (percussion), Tatiana Grindenko (violin), Boris Berman (piano) and, somewhat later, Anatoly Grindenko (bass). Together they formed the ensemble Music of the Twentieth Century [Muzyka dvadtsatogo veka] and gave performances in Tallinn (Estonia) and in Soviet Georgia; only in Moscow did they remain nameless, as all names had to be officially approved. Somewhat later, in the first half of the 1970s, Pyotr Meshchaninov arranged chamber concerts with players from the State Symphony Orchestra. He liked to offer mixed programs of classical composers combined with music by Stravinsky, Messiaen, and Gubaidulina. To obtain permission for such performances, Meshchaninov had to take his applications from pillar to post, usually with the result that nine out of ten were rejected. In 1974, to everyone's surprise, Evgeny Svetlanov, the conductor of the State Symphony Orchestra, consented to a performance of Gubaidulina's *Rubaiyat* and Denisov's *Sun of the Incas.* He normally would have adhered to his motto, "Chamber music is sloppiness," but when Meshchaninov took the paperwork to the Party representative at the Moscow Philharmonic, the latter crossed out the names with two large X's and grandly pointed to the *vertushka* (hotline telephone to the Kremlin) on his desk, indicating his own line of responsibility. Finally, there was Gennady Rozhdestvensky, the principal conductor at the Bolshoi Theater and of the Large Symphony Orchestra of the All-Union Radio and Television Network of the USSR [Bol'shoi simfonicheskii orkestr Vsesoiuznogo radio i televedeniia, SSSR]. In the 1970s he gained international stature in a succession of appointments as principal conductor: at the Royal Philharmonic [Kungliga Filharmonikerna] in Stockholm, at the BBC Symphony Orchestra in London, and at the Vienna Symphony [Wiener Symphoniker]. Many Soviet composers were indebted to him for his courage and persistence in dealing with the fears of organizers and the pressures exerted by bureaucrats who tried to discourage performances of their works. He often used his prestige to their advantage. However, staging performances of works by these composers in Moscow was only one problem; another set of difficulties emerged when it came to giving concerts abroad—especially in the West—but occasionally good luck was on their side.

Two Works Performed at the International Festival in Royan

Claude Samuel, an influential organizer and publicist, had been the artistic director of the Eighth International Festival of Contemporary Art in Royan [Festival international d'art contemporain de Royan] in April 1971. In his introductory remarks for the festival program, he asked about the identity of those who were hiding behind such unknown names as Gubaidulina and others. But less than three decades later he invited the now widely acclaimed composer to his famous Centre Acanthes near Avignon. At that time Royan in France—like Donaueschingen and Darmstadt in Germany—was an annual gathering place for the musical avant-garde, attracting critics and audiences from all over Europe. The 1971 festival focused on East European composers, and Gubaidulina was fortunate enough to have two of her works on the program. The Armenian pianist Irina Yermakova played Gubaidulina's Piano Sonata on the morning of April 4; that same afternoon the ensemble Musica Viva Pragensis presented the premiere of her *Concordanza*. Irina Yermakova had studied with Samuil Feinberg and Lev Oborin and was married to the French Slavicist Alain Préchac; they lived in Paris and often traveled to Moscow together. Préchac was then writing a book on Soviet literature, in a series published by the Sorbonne, and he had asked Kolya Bokov for information on some of the unofficial writers. Having been invited to give a piano recital at Royan, Irina Yermakova—whose friendship with Victor Suslin had begun in their student days—put together a program of "Soviet Piano Music" consisting of Schnittke's *Variations on a Single Chord* [*Variatsii na odin akkord*] and piano sonatas by Alexander Rabinovich (his Second), Victor Suslin, and Sofia Gubaidulina. It is interesting to note, in retrospect, the particular slant with which Gubaidulina was introduced to audiences in the West that had probably never heard of her. "Sofia Gubajdulina [*sic*]," so the festival program reads, "is the central figure in a small group doing music research within the Composers Union that works on rather significant pieces of electronic music."[1] Compositions with synthesized sounds and live electronic music were quite the rage at that time, especially in France. Of the six works performed by the ensemble from Prague, three combined tape-recorded sounds with instruments. The audience heard *Concordanza* together with works by Isang Yun, Włodzimierz Kotoński (from Poland), Marek Kopelent, Zbynek Vostrak, and the French composer Solange Ancona—the last three with tape recorder.

Concordanza stands at the beginning of a new chapter in Gubaidulina's creative work, regarding both technique (it is the first work in which she uses quarter tones) and her general religious and spiritual attitude toward her work as a composer. In later years Gubaidulina often said that art has a religious function, that in the "staccato" of life it must restore the "legato." Art is the *re-ligio* (connection) to God in our fragmented, quotidian life. The religious intensity and drama that had found direct expression through the existential situation in her earlier cantatas now began to shape the music itself, which in all its dimensions suggests religious feeling and religious intention. Titles like *Concordanza* and notations such as *staccato* and *legato* took on connotations suggesting the religious dimension. The following comment by Dorothea Redepenning, the most respected German authority on Gubaidulina's work, underscores this point:

> The basic meaning of *Concordanza* is derived from "concordare"—to sound together, to harmonize—and it is realized in the modes of articulation: in the legato flow of voices without intervening rests and—as a subtle climax at the center of the work—in the dialog between the double bass and the violin's soft harmonics. The opposite, "Discordanza," is represented by the staccato of the winds, the pizzicato of the strings, and such "scatty" passages as that of the double bass solo after its first legato section. It also presents itself in marching rhythms, trills, tremolos, and the hissing sounds produced by the players. As the two opposite elements interpenetrate they gradually change. The chromatic runs return near the end, at first in the tremolos of the strings and the staccato of the winds; only at the very end do the winds achieve a final legato.[2]

Gubaidulina's new treatment of her musical materials began with something of a crisis. After stripping everything down to essentials in the Five Etudes, after her critical engagement with twelve-tone technique, and after her work at the electronic studio (including experiments in microtonality), she always returned to the same fundamental question: What possibilities lie beyond the twelve notes of the tempered scale?

"In conversations with Pyotr Meshchaninov," she later said, "the question of new musical possibilities kept recurring. He argued that the twelve tones of the tempered scale establish boundaries too rigidly, allowing for no free, unoccupied space—tonal space that corresponds in a sense with the subconscious realm, the lunar side of a living organism. But it is precisely this subconscious tonal space, so to speak, that allows a composer the possibility of shaping the distinctive profile of a work with the help of strongly functional, out-of-the-ordinary intervals."[3]

Meshchaninov believed that the seventy-two-fold division of the octave by the ANS tone synthesizer provided such an expansion of the tonal system. However, because the synthesizer had turned out to be useless in practical application, the problem remained unsolved.

Preoccupied with these questions, Gubaidulina returned to Sortavala in September 1971. The summer season was over, most of the guests had departed, and Gubaidulina occupied the last of the cabins at the retreat that lay scattered among granite blocks on a bay of Lake Ladoga. The woods on the opposite shore had already turned color and the temperatures at night dipped below freezing, but that did not deter her from taking moonlight swims. In a euphoria of creativity brought about by her peaceful solitude, she wrote a string quartet to test the limits of musical possibilities—a piece, as Gubaidulina later suggested, that in some ways can be seen as a counterpart to *Concordanza:*

> The idea of disintegration, dissociation, lies at the heart of the First [String] Quartet. I have to say that there is a certain amount of pessimism in it, a metaphor for the impossibility of togetherness, of understanding one's neighbor, a metaphor for the utter deafness of humanity (life itself in those years was so dark, so sad and hopeless . . .). The work grows out of a single pitch, from a common point. But various aspects of the musical material—the rhythmic and melodic successions, the types of articulation, and the dynamics—gradually begin to contradict one another. This dissention within the tonal material is emphasized visually as well. At the beginning the four instrumentalists are in center stage, grouped all together. Then the musical events drive them apart, in ever increasing distance from each other, to the four corners of the stage, where each player concentrates only on his/her own playing, already entirely unable to hear the others. Utter isolation to the point of madness.[4]

In early 1972 Boris Berman commissioned Gubaidulina to compose a work for harpsichord and percussion. He had performed Berio's *Sequenza IV* in Moscow as early as the late 1960s and wanted to enlarge his repertoire for harpsichord; also, he was eager to include Mark Pekarsky, with whom he liked to perform. "Sofia was a friend," Berman later commented; "with her tremendous interest in unusual sounds, she took a special interest in Mark's collection of instruments, and he liked to demonstrate his more exotic pieces."[5] When Gubaidulina looked at the collection, Pekarsky suggested that she select three instruments for which no one in Russia had ever composed a piece: *chang,* a dulcimer-like instrument from Central Asia; *byan chung* (Chinese bells); and Chinese cymbals. Gubaidulina added to these *cymbales antiques* and began to work on her composition. During rehearsals she advised Berman on the registration of the harpsichord and then traveled with the performers to Leningrad; the premiere took place on April 5, 1972, in the October Concert Hall [Oktiabr'skii kontsernyi zal] near the Finland Railroad Station [Finliandskii vokzal]. In the silence that followed the last note, the musicians spoke the words, "Ite, missa est"—the closing formula of the Roman Catholic Mass, meaning "Go, the Mass is ended." The words were later stricken from the score.

The premiere performance was an enormous success, and the audience repeatedly applauded the composer. Gubaidulina soon changed the title, *Logogriph,* to

Music for Harpsichord and Percussion Instruments from Mark Pekarsky's Collection [*Muzyka dlia klavesina i udarnykh instrumentov iz kollektsii Marka Pekarskogo*]. The work combines harpsichord with a variety of Asian percussion instruments, and the similarity between the sound of the *chang* and the harpsichord builds a bridge, in a sense, between East and West. The carefully worked out structure of the work reflects its original title: in a logograph a word takes on ever new meanings as the first letter is successively omitted, a process suggested musically by expanding and contracting melodic and rhythmic figures.

The first half of the 1970s saw the Third Wave of emigration from the Soviet Union. In 1973, the year after the premiere of *Music for Harpsichord and Percussion*, Boris Berman was among the Moscow musicians who escaped the Party's and the bureaucracy's repressive regime. He joined that large group of individuals who either left voluntarily or were forced into exile: among musicians and conductors this included Rostropovich, Volkonsky, Alexander Rabinovich, Rudolf Barshai, and Kirill Kondrashin; among writers, Maximov, Siniavsky, and Solzhenitsyn, to name three of the best known. Each departure weighed heavily on those who stayed behind.

Gennady Aigi: The Genesis of the Five Romances, *Roses*

Sofia Gubaidulina got to know the poet Gennady Aigi at about the time *Logograph* had its premiere. Having come to Moscow from his native Chuvashia in 1953 to study at the Moscow Institute of Literature, he had found lodgings at a student residence in Peredelkino. In her first year as a student, Sofia had met him there when she and a group of music students, including Mikhail Marutaev, had been invited by the literature students for a visit to Peredelkino. "[Marutaev] performed his Piano Sonata," Gubaidulina later said, "and I sat quietly in a corner. That was the first time I saw Gennady Aigi." The Chuvash had shown some of his poems to Pasternak, who liked what he saw and encouraged Aigi to write in Russian. When the campaign of defamation set in after Pasternak had been awarded the Nobel Prize, Aigi spoke out in support of his mentor—with predictable consequences: not a single volume of his poetry was printed in the Soviet Union. Alain Préchac's request for information prompted Kolya Bokov to suggest several unofficial writers (among them Aigi) and to invite them to his apartment near Preobrazhenskaya ploshchad'. Aigi recalled the occasion in the memoir he wrote specifically for this biography:

> In the spring, my friend Sergei Bychkov informed me that Kolya Bokov, Sonia's second husband, wanted to get to know me. He invited a group of artists—musicians, writers—to his apartment (a kind of salon), including myself. When I

arrived, there was a group of young people sitting around drinking and talking about poetry. Vsevolod Nekrasov was one of them. I was in a lousy mood and didn't really want to get into the conversation. But then I got to talk with Sevakh [Vsevolod] because he asked interesting questions. Sonia was somewhere in the kitchen or at her desk and didn't participate in the conversation. I liked Kolya. We kept on drinking and I started to talk more and more. But the thing that surprised me was that the kitchen didn't show a woman's hand. The flowers, the table setting—it was all Bokov's doing. The hallway was lined with shelves of good books—it was all very attractive. Then I left, and that was all for that evening. A week later the phone rang. Sergei Bychkov said, "We want to come over to see you, Sonia, Kolya, and I." The men were in a cheerful mood—Sonia was quiet. She was usually quiet when there was company, but it didn't spoil anyone's mood—it seemed natural. They arrived with bottles and then got some more. We all sat around the table, including Sonia, but she seemed reserved, even a little lost. It is possible that she did not drink at all because her behavior never changed; but that didn't bother the others. Perhaps she nursed a single glass of wine all evening—but the others drank, and all of that seemed quite normal. When I drink, I become braver and braver, talk a lot, and say some things straight out—and I had a lot to drink. Not in an arrogant way but straight out I said to her: "Sonia, I think it's sort of funny. These contemporary composers should really take an interest in contemporary poets, but then they use ancient texts from Egypt. . . . We're part of the same life and share the same problems. I think we modern artists need to support each other. Using these ancient poets doesn't give us any support." Sonia remained silent. The week before at Sonia's, we were all supposed to read our poems. I don't like that very much, but I had read some of mine. When Sonia left my apartment that evening, she asked for some of my texts, and I gave her a few poems without having any expectations. A week or so later Sonia called me and said: "You know, Gena, I am working on a song cycle based on your poems and I have selected the following. . . . What do you think?" Of course I agreed and told her how pleased I was. She asked about some matters of language, like accents. I had given her manuscripts. Among them was an old version and it bothered me a little because I had already done a revision. Sonia asked me to dictate it to her over the phone; she could take the time, her work was moving along great. Our first conversation was probably at the end of April or the beginning of May. Early that summer she finally called me again to tell me that she had completed her cycle, *Roses* [*Rozy*].[6]

On March 1, 1973, *Roses* had its premiere in a concert of Grigory Frid's Moscow Youth Musical Club at the Moscow Composers Union.

We had a discussion after the concert, and Frid said: "Let's ask Aigi what he thinks about this music." I was in a good mood and didn't want to hold back. "It used to be that music took poetry for a ride, that poetry was secondary to music. From now on we don't want to forget Webern. This concert shows that poetry and music have equal rights, it proves the unity of music and poetry." Then we all drove over to Sonia's: Kostia [Konstantin] Bogatyryov, a few other friends, Lydia Davydova (the soloist that evening), and her husband, Leonard. We drank and were in a festive mood. Kostia was the first to leave—at 6:00 AM. It was daylight when we woke up in the apartment, just Leonard and I, nobody else. We sold the empty bottles and bought a new one. Toward evening, Sonia came back and we met her with our bottle. In the months leading up to the concert I had not seen Sonia. When I went to see Kolya, she was not present even though she was at home. On a few occasions, Kolya and Seryozha [Sergei Bychkov] came to see me. We had become good friends. Kolya was a brilliant Voltairian—sharp, ironic, sarcastic—who wrote excellent parodies and made and sold books of collage from newspaper articles. He wrote fine prose. ... Victor Bokov, the well-known Soviet poet, is his uncle. Without intending to, I became a witness to the separation between Sonia and Kolya. Many young people came to their apartment, among them a very beautiful young woman—mysterious, quiet, and attractive. We're all together—when suddenly Sonia storms out of the room into the kitchen, where Kolya and this girl were sitting and talking on the window seat. Sonia exploded—but it wasn't just jealousy. She was very angry and determined—but not hysterical. "It's all over between us! You'll have to pack up and leave this very day!" I was astonished. I realized that it wasn't a simple outburst of jealousy and anger but a determined separation from Kolya, and the outburst lasted just a few minutes. A few weeks later I saw Sonia and said to her: "I know that girl—I've been courting her myself. She's a strange girl, silent and attractive. And I know the relationship that could have developed between her and Kolya. It's nothing that would have hurt you." "It doesn't matter even if that's the case. I have my reasons for doing what I did," Sonia replied quietly. I was very impressed by Sonia's determination, her strength, and her calmness. It was the act of a very courageous, calm person.[7]

The scene in the kitchen was only the straw that broke the camel's back. Her work was her highest commitment, and for that she needed peace and solitude. At the end of his memoir, Aigi makes a poignant comment that drives this point home: "When I think about Sonia, I always see the same image: I am at her place and am about to leave and say good-bye. I say: 'Do we want to get together next week?' Sonia touches my hand softly: 'Gena, we—you and I—first want to do more work, and then our next meeting will happen all by itself. Work—that's the most important thing.'"[8]

A Blocked Performance at Warsaw Autumn 1972

Even though the Polish Composers Union [Związek Kompozytorów Polskich] was officially in charge of arranging the Warsaw Autumn Music Festival, the Soviet Composers Union—that is, Tikhon Khrennikov—had control over their people. The year 1972 proved to be no exception, as Moscow did not hesitate to interfere in planning the program. The official program prospectus listed a concert by the Moscow-based Prokofiev String Quartet [Gosudarstvennyi strunnyi kvartet imeni S. S. Prokof'eva] for September 19, with works by Sofia Gubaidulina, Vitaly Geviksman, and Roman Ledenyov, and the Brussels Radio Symphony Orchestra [Orchestre Symphonique de la Radiodiffusion Nationale Belge, Bruxelles] was scheduled to play Denisov's *Peinture* [*Zhivopis'*]. These works, however, did not appear on the final program, much to the consternation of Detlef Gojowy upon his arrival in Warsaw. He was an expert on early Soviet music who later did much to support the Soviet avant-garde in his capacity as music editor at the Westdeutscher Rundfunk (West German Radio). Right then and there, he tried get to the bottom of the omission and later gave the following account:

> That same year, Warsaw Autumn was the venue for a highly official guest performance by the elite of the Soviet Composers Union. In fact, its eminently powerful General Secretary, Tikhon Khrennikov, headed the delegation and used this opportunity to perform his Second Piano Concerto. Naturally, the delegation was not eager to have any undesirable competition, and a diplomatic protest by the Soviet Embassy succeeded in eliminating the four composers from the program. A simple order from above was enough to strike the Prokofiev String Quartet, but eventually even the Brussels Radio Orchestra had to bow to the edict from Moscow. . . . Asked for an explanation at a press conference, the Soviet representative referred the questioner to the Moscow Composers Union because it had sole responsibility for its composers and the performance of their works abroad.[9]

It is entirely possible that the real reason why Khrennikov and his delegation traveled to Warsaw was to abort the festival, but the Poles were wary. Suspecting that something was in the offing, a group of composers, among them Lutosławski, Penderecki, and Krzysztof Meyer, drove out to Jabłonna after Khrennikov's speech at the Warsaw Academy of Music [Akademia Muzyczna w Warszawie]. An elegant reception was planned at the palace, located about fourteen miles outside Warsaw, and the Russians had every intention to deal with the termination of the festival on that occasion. The Poles, however, fully understood their guests' psychology and were determined to fill the time with distractions before the concluding two o'clock banquet. They claimed that the Russian interpreter was not sufficiently familiar with musical terminology to handle a discussion among experts and that a different interpreter would have to be brought in. Many of the Polish composers were, of course, completely fluent in Russian, but it took an hour before the new interpreter was ready and available. An array of inconsequential questions filled the time before the beginning of the banquet, and when it was finally served the festival had been saved. For the next several years the Moscow Composers Union boycotted Warsaw Autumn.

Detlef Gojowy found out that the long arm of Soviet cultural politics reached all the way into West German editorial offices when he submitted the names of several composers, Gubaidulina's among them, for inclusion in two supplementary volumes of *Riemann's Musik-Lexikon.* As an expert on Soviet music, he had been asked by the editor to name important composers, musicians, and music scholars, and he put together a list with the help of Alfred Schnittke and Yury Kholopov before sending it to the publisher. He never received a response until the publication of the first supplement in 1972, which failed to include Gubaidulina and others whose names he had submitted. As a result of a "consultation" with Soviet authorities, everything that did not conform to the Party line was deleted, a step that prompted Gojowy to withdraw his name from the second supplement.

During the second half of the concert on September 19, 1972, from which Gubaidulina's First String Quartet had been eliminated under pressure from Khrennikov, the Polish harpsichordist Elżbieta Chojnacka played contemporary pieces for the harpsichord. Exactly twenty-five years later, also at the Warsaw Autumn festival, she would perform a work she had commissioned from Gubaidulina. What goes around comes around.

An Evening of Musical Improvisation

On March 1, 1973, at his Moscow Youth Musical Club, Grigory Frid had arranged a "meet-the-composer concert" dedicated to Sofia Gubaidulina. The program consisted of the song cycle *Roses;* the cycle of piano pieces *Musical Toys,* played by the composer; *Logogriph,* since then re-titled *Music for Harpsichord and Percussion Instruments from Mark Pekarsky's Collection*; and *Night in Memphis,* as recorded in Prague. Gubaidulina chose that evening to dedicate the cantata to Andrei Volkonsky, an artist who in many ways was the leader of her generation of composers. This dedication was also a courageous gesture of farewell, as Volkonsky had applied for an emigration permit. Every attempt at performing his music in public had been blocked since the mid-sixties, making his life all but intolerable. In May he left Moscow, never to return. During his last weeks there, Gubaidulina and Pyotr Meshchaninov came to say good-bye and found a deeply distressed man who had already taken his emotional leave from Moscow.

The day after the Youth Club concert of March 2, 1973, dedicated to Gubaidulina, she was back on the same stage for the Club's 214th event: an evening of improvisation. Improvisations were all the rage in the West, with ensembles and composers getting together from Paris to Cologne and from Rome to the hippie commune in San Francisco. In those years of change and unrest, improvising may sometimes have been a bit of shock therapy for the bourgeois establishment of the West; but in Moscow during the Brezhnev era it was politically dangerous, as improvising by its very nature is unpredictable. As a precaution, Frid had been called in to see the top Moscow *partorg* (party organizer), who had been informed that a subversive evening concert was being planned at the Youth Club. "What do you mean by improvisation?" he was asked. "Are you sure you know what the musicians will play and what the audience will say about it? Perhaps there will be comments critical of the regime."[10] The concert took place as scheduled, Frid having given the program a broad historical dimension: a continuo realization based on a classical keyboard progression; a demonstration, by Alexei Liubimov, of the possibilities for ornamenting a Mozart sonata; and a "collective improvisation" under Gubaidulina's direction. Also onstage were Grigory Frid with his collaborators and discussion partners: Grigory Golovinsky, the music scholars Nelli Shakhnazarova and David Rabinovich, and the literary critic Dmitri Sezemann. Gubaidulina gave the musicians only a brief sketch of the formal structure, leaving the improvised rendition to Lydia Davydova, Mark Perkarsky, and Lev Mikhailov (clarinet). "We were tossing coins in Frid's Club at that time," she later recalled. "I was interested to see what would happen if the instrumentalists were given absolute freedom of invention, with only a pre-scribed basic form. I always agonized over the discrepancy between my imagination, the written score, and the players' interpretation. The results that evening were not necessarily great—the whole thing was too playfully extravagant. Some in the audience applauded but others yelled 'Awful! Hooligans! That's impossible! That's indecent!'"[11]

After the concert, Grigory Frid also had to accept his share of criticism. Members of the Youth Club's Artistic Council (Khudozhestvennyi sovet) complained: "This is cacophony and sickness, not art."[12] Nevertheless improvisations of all stripes soon continued in Moscow. A year later Alexei Liubimov and his ensemble played passages from Stockhausen's *Aus den sieben Tagen*, first in Tallinn and Riga and later in Moscow and Leningrad. And the Moscow Jazz Club [Moskovskii dzhaz-klub], founded by Alexei Batashov in 1971, issued invitations every year for a spring festival and played experimental jazz, improvisations, and contemporary music in its quarters on Kashirskoe Shosse. The Moscow Composers Union took a dim view of this kind of music.

Steps, a *Graduale* for Orchestra

The same year in which she completed *Music for Harpsichord and Percussion* and *Roses,* Gubaidulina wrote her first work for large orchestra, *Steps* [*Stupeni*]. In it the composer gave fuller expression to an intention she had only suggested by the words "Ite, missa est" in *Music for Harpsichord and Percussion.* The work is composed in the form of seven descending steps: the orchestral timbre and tone color undergo gradual transformation, moving downward from high to low register. A moment of stasis and rest marks the end of each episode. The descending motion is enhanced by a continual expansion of the sound spectrum: from the cold, impersonal sonority of the instruments at the beginning to the rich sound palette of a thirty-part string section at the climax, and, finally, all the way to the dark, chaotically vibrant whisper of the human voice at the seventh step. At this point each member of the orchestra speaks the opening lines of "Vom Tode Mariae," from Rilke's poetic cycle *Das Marienleben:*

> Derselbe grosse Engel, welcher einst
> Ihr der Gebärung Botschaft niederbrachte,
> Stand da, abwartend, dass sie ihn beachte,
> Und sprach: "Jetzt wird es Zeit, dass du erscheinst."[13]
> The same great angel, who once
> Brought to her tidings of her birth,
> Stood there, waiting for her attention,
> And said: "Now is the time for you to appear."

The seven-step descent into death—that is, the end of man's mortal life on earth—is at the same time the beginning of a new life, a birth in the realm of the eternal, proclaimed by the Angel of the Annunciation.

The title *Steps (Stupeni)* associates the work with the *Graduale* of the Catholic Mass. Although in Orthodox liturgy gradual psalms (*Stepennye psalmy*)—Psalms 120–134—can be part of the service, Gubaidulina did not write this work specifically for use in the Church but in the spirit of the Orthodox liturgical tradition. Since its earliest beginnings, Orthodox Church music has permitted only the use of the human voice. The sound of the choir is considered to be an echo of the celestial song of the angels, just as icons are physical representations of a non-physical essence.[14] Gubaidulina's innovative and individualistic departure from Orthodox tradition in this piece made her a heretic in the eyes of the Church. Her baptism, however, had not simply been an act of meaningless formality; she saw it as conferring responsibilities of faith on her. Troubled by this discrepancy, she talked with Father Vladimir, whom she respected as a liberal-minded and un-dogmatic priest. He did not reveal his personal opinion in this conversation but proved to be tolerant: "Be at peace within yourself; continue to be active and write your music."

Nikolai Berdyaev:
A Christian Liberation Philosophy of Creativity

Besides poetry and prose, philosophical and religious writings were an important source of reading for Sofia Gubaidulina: Meister Eckhart, Florensky, later Hegel, but particularly Nikolai Berdyaev. Berdyaev's works had been suppressed during the Soviet era, but they enjoyed a great renaissance in the 1990s, largely because many of his ideas express the religious mentality of Russian culture. Though strongly influenced by Orthodox Christianity, he was not reluctant to attack the highest dignitaries of the Church as enemies of freedom. Of greatest importance for Gubaidulina, however, were his thoughts on the Christian commitment to artistic creativity which he based on the biblical story of Genesis. As man was created in God's image and God created the world out of the freedom that already existed in the void, so the creative human being continues the process. For Berdyaev, God is a continuously evolving entity and in this process of evolution is dependent on man. "True creativity is theurgy, divine agency, collaboration with God."[15] Hence man is a "theurg," a divinely inspired being who actively participates in the ongoing process of creation. Man's specifically creative process takes place in two realms: an inner, spiritual realm, where the artist and creative individual receive inspiration, and an external, lower realm, where inspiration is embodied and materialized in an actual work of art. According to Berdyaev, a tragic discrepancy defines the relationship "between the flame of the creator's initial vision and its ultimate rule-bound realization: every creative act aims at achieving eternity but ends in a traitorous compromise with time. It is this compromise that fills the whole realm of culture with a great sadness and leaves an insurmountable bitterness in the heart of every creative being."[16] Gubaidulina recognized the connection between her own experience of the creative process and this articulation of it.

She realized that there was no possibility of performing a work like *Steps* in Moscow; its instrumentation alone—twenty-eight winds, sixty strings, keyboard instruments, and five percussionists—posed enormous difficulties. On one of his regular visits to Moscow, Jürgen Köchel had taken the score with him to Germany, but it would be seventeen years before *Steps* was to have its premiere. Together with several other compositions of the 1960s and 1970s, it belongs to Gubaidulina's so-called pieces for the drawer.

In April 1974, out of the blue, Gubaidulina received a letter written in English and sent from Rome, informing her that *Steps* had received an honorary mention in the category of orchestral music at the Seventh International Composers Competition of the Italian Society for Contemporary Music [VII Concorso internazionale di composizione della Società Italiana Musica Contemporanea]. Her publisher in Hamburg, having tried to get the work performed in West Germany, had also sent a copy of the score to Rome. The jury, under Ligeti's presidency,[17] gave first prize to Morton Feldman's *Chorus and Orchestra II*, but in addition to the prize money for first place, the jury also awarded three honorable mentions—and among the 207 submissions in the orchestral category, Gubaidulina's work stood in first place.[18] The award letter probably gave the erroneous impression in Moscow that Gubaidulina had been awarded first prize for *Steps* in the Italian competition, and to this day one can still find that assertion in several texts about the composer.

Detto II: A Commission from Natalia Shakhovskaya

At a chance meeting on the street in the early 1970s, the cellist Natalia Shakhovskaya (the wife of Boris Artemiev) asked Gubaidulina for a cello piece. Although the cellist did not have much experience with contemporary music, she was intrigued by the spirit of Gubaidulina's music. A prominent cellist in those days, Shakhovskaya had won the first prize in cello at the 1962 International Tchaikovsky Competition. After her period of candidacy with Rostropovich, he had praised her for her unusual and original talent as well as for her thoughtful, but always interesting and refreshing, performance style. She became Rostropovich's successor as a professor of cello and double bass at the conservatory after his emigration in 1974.

As soon as she had completed *Steps*, Gubaidulina turned to the composition for Shakhovskaya, a piece she called *Detto II*.[19] The composer's intention, in this work for cello and chamber, was "to penetrate into the depths of a tone in order to live mentally inside its microscopic spaces. . . . The cello is especially able to speak with great expressive force within a subchromatic space. Starting with microintervals, the tonal field expands and ever larger intervals emerge. A reverse process occurs in the recapitulation."[20] Because the language of this work was entirely unfamiliar to both the cellist and the ensemble, they had to try a number of experiments. In Shakhovskaya's own words:

> When the pizzicati of the violin did not stand out sufficiently, I suggested that the instrument be placed on the knees like a cello—and right away the sound was louder, clearer, and more assertive. The beginning of the second part was technically extremely difficult—virtually unplayable. Gubaidulina confirmed my suspicion that this had been done on purpose, and she said: "Do as much as you can with it." She looked at this difficult passage in terms of color—it was the expression that mattered to her, the intonation was secondary.[21]

On May 5, 1973, under the auspices of the "Moscow Stars" [Moskovskie zvëzdy] Festival, Shakhovskaya performed in the Small Hall of the Conservatory. Following sonatas for cello and piano by Valentini and Brahms, as well as Benjamin Britten's Suite No. 1 for Cello Op. 72, Konstantin Kremets conducted the premiere of *Detto II* with an ad hoc ensemble paid for by Shakhovskaya. Because conservatory students and instrumentalists from several other orchestras with different work schedules made up the ensemble, somebody was always absent during rehearsals. The French horn player from the Radio Orchestra, for instance, appeared only for the last rehearsal, so that the performance was less than polished.[22] Shakhovskaya later remembered that evening:

> The Small Hall was a traditional academic center for academic chamber music in Moscow and therefore of course not the usual site for Sofia's music. The audience was rather conventional—several older ladies and gentlemen. At the end of the first movement, with its suspended, cosmic atmosphere, an old man in the first row got up, spat in my general direction, and left the hall.[23] It was all a bit comical. Mstislav Rostropovich was also in the audience that evening. Enthusiastic and happy that the work had seen the light of day, he spontaneously invited us all to his home after the concert. The party was the usual affair following a successful performance—good food, vodka, and many toasts.[24]

In the late 1970s Ivan Monighetti performed this piece again under the direction of Yury Nikolaevsky.

In 1973 Gubaidulina celebrated her forty-second birthday. She has commented that every seven years she goes through a deep personal crisis that is precipitated by the tensions between the spiritual-intuitive and the rational-intellectual sides of her personality. These crises always result in strengthening her soul and spirit and diminishing her intellectuality. The abyss of darkness—the "dark night of the soul"—has always fascinated her, and there she experiences divinely constructive forces as well as the destructive powers of the Adversary, never knowing what they have in store. Earlier crises had always been dominated by destructive forces: her severe illness at age fourteen, or her dark, suicidal thoughts at twenty-eight. "But in that year [of 1973]," she later recalled, "I found peace as I experienced a whole new state of being: deep within my soul I opened a door to God. Perhaps I had reached the middle of my life. Seven years later I expected another crisis and prepared myself for it, but nothing happened."

A Search by the KGB

As the KGB was preparing Solzhenitsyn's arrest and deportation to the West in late January 1974, a potentially disastrous event that could have interrupted her work for some time also took place in Gubaidulina's life. One day the doorbell rang at about 9:00 AM, and the composer got up from the piano, calling "Who is it?" Hearing the reply, "A telegram," she opened the door to face six unfamiliar people: a KGB officer, three KGB officials (one of them a woman), and two "witnesses off the street"; behind them Kolya Bokov. The KGB officer explained the reason for the surprise visit, showing a search warrant. She was disgusted and nauseated but realized she couldn't refuse: "All right, do what you have to do," she told them. The KGB officer and officials spread out among the rooms and for the next six hours turned everything upside down: scores, books, art volumes, every closet and cabinet in the kitchen and hallway, even flower pots on the window sill. One official worked his way through her desk. As if having anticipated this search, Gubaidulina had recently put things in order and removed all *samizdat* publications, except for an excerpt from one of Avtorkhanov's books that was in the lower right desk drawer. The KGB man started at the upper left, taking his time looking at clippings from several Soviet dailies. Not seeing a thematic connection among them, he asked about it, and she replied: "I'm a composer and am interested in everything." He studied at length a few slips of paper relating to Pyotr Meshchaninov's theory, with rows of numbers, symbols, and incomprehensible spaces (for pasting future musical notations)—all of which seemed highly suspicious. After finishing with the upper right drawer, he stopped searching the desk, and Sofia was saved by his fatigue and carelessness. The discovery of the Avtorkhanov text would have inevitably resulted in both a trial and a prison term. For Gubaidulina this search and its violation of her privacy felt like rape. But it was not her only encounter with the KGB. Only a few weeks later, another KGB officer came to ask her in detail about Kolya, and then said: "I suggest you don't talk about this meeting, or you'll be in trouble." Sofia did not reply but quickly informed Kolya. Later, in exile in Paris, he talked about these events:

In the fall of 1973 the KGB had arrested three *samizdat* workers in Kiev. I knew one of them and had met with him once in Sonia's apartment. When they interrogated him he told them about my microfilms, and now the KGB went after me and my films. But I had secured them with a friend who was above all suspicion. That morning they came at eight o'clock straight to Olga Stupakova and her husband's apartment, where I often stayed after our separation, even though my official residence was at Sonia's apartment. All ten of them fanned out over the rooms and then half of them took me over to Sonia's. On that same day they also searched Mark Liando's house in Tomilino and two other Moscow apartments. When we arrived at Sonia's door, rang the bell, and Sonia responded from inside, I was supposed to say "Kolya," but I remained silent. During those months I had to appear before the KGB on several occasions and had to deal with the same officer who had also interrogated Sonia. Afraid that they would use Sonia as an informer, I asked: "You went to see my former wife, Sofia Gubaidulina. Don't you know that Soviet law doesn't permit this?" The officer got all excited and threatened me: "Just calm down. There's a lot we can do to you and your friends."[25]

The following event, which occurred at about the same time, was quite possibly related to the KGB visits. One evening, when Sofia stepped into the elevator, she encountered a strange man. On the seventh floor he blocked her exit, and the two rode up and down together. "A man perhaps twenty-five years old," she recalled later, "with cold, evil eyes. He grabbed my throat and slowly squeezed it. My thoughts were racing: it's all over now—too bad I can't write my bassoon concerto anymore—I'm not afraid of death but of violence. And then I told him: 'Why so slowly?' That may have bothered him, but I was able to trick him into leaving me alone." At the militia, the Soviet police station, they gave the usual explanation: "It must have been a sex maniac." In the next few days no sex maniac showed up in the neighborhood, nor did the KGB appear again.

The situation was much more precarious for Kolya Bokov. During his interrogations the KGB threatened him first with imprisonment and then with commitment to the infamous psychiatric hospital in Kazan. Finally they let him emigrate, and in April 1975 he left for Paris via Vienna; well into the 1980s he and Sofia maintained an amicable correspondence.

Marina Tsvetaeva: A Musical Portrait

The beginning of 1974 was also an exciting time for another Moscow composer. On February 6, Gennady Rozhdestvensky conducted Alfred Schnittke's First Symphony in Gorky, which now again goes by its former name, Nizhny Novgorod. The conductor had retreated to Gorky—at that time a city closed to foreigners—as a Moscow performance would have been blocked by the established composers. Schnittke's work, reflecting contemporary culture with its episodes and imitations of avant-garde and classical music, of jazz and rock, had already caused excitement and passionate debate in advance of the concert. A large audience from many different places descended on Gorky and gave the work an enthusiastic reception, making the performance one of the key events of Soviet musical history in the 1970s. It must have been a time of particularly sharp controversy, as only three weeks later, when Schnittke's symphony was discussed in the Commission for Chamber and Symphonic Music, Sofia Gubaidulina was the first to speak out.[26] She stood firmly by her colleague and expressed what many in the audience must have felt: "This work made one of the strongest impressions we, musicians and audiences alike, have experienced in the past decade. The work is so grand in scale, as well as in power of conception, that it stands, I think, among the most important works in music history."[27] With its borrowings from a variety of styles, periods, and genres, the symphony laid the foundation of Schnittke's "polystylistic" idiom and was a thorn in the side of the regime. With but a single exception, all performances, both in the Soviet Union and abroad, were therefore blocked for the next fifteen years. The symphony's powerful impact on Gubaidulina can be detected in one of her own works of that time, *Hour of the Soul*.

In the early 1970s the Ministry of Culture asked the conductor Vitaly Kataev to put together a large wind ensemble that would perform serious music. Wind bands had until then been units of the Red Army, playing marches, anthems, and fanfares on parades and in public parks. In order to develop a repertoire for this new orchestra, Kataev commissioned works from several composers, Gubaidulina among them. She jumped at the idea and chose an unusual instrumentation for her new piece: with more than fifty wind instruments, she used twelve B♭ clarinets, six French horns, and five tubas; for a smaller combo-like group within the ensemble, she chose percussion, celesta/piano, two harps, four cornets, tenor and a baritone saxophone, and two double basses. The work concludes with a cantilena on a poem by Marina Tsvetaeva from her cycle *Hour of the Soul* [*Chas dushi*], which Gubaidulina then chose as the title for her own work. In 1976 she reworked it for symphony orchestra, percussion solo, and mezzo-soprano, and re-titled it *Percussio di Pekarski;* a final revision of the percussion part was undertaken in 1987, and the work's title reverted to *Hour of the Soul*.

Hour of the Soul is a musical portrait of Marina Tsvetaeva as an artist, her strength and greatness, and her fight against the trivialities of a life that ended in suicide. Two musical realms stand in juxtaposition: percussion (or, in the first version, the small combo-like ensemble) and the full ensemble. Tsvetaeva was fond of percussive sounds, and it is said that the drum was her favorite instrument. When she was only twenty-one years old, she wrote in a poem: "The place of women does not appeal to me! Boredom is what I fear, not wounds! To be a drummer! Ahead of all others! Everything else is vanity!"[28] The conflict begins to develop at the beginning of the work, becomes more pointed in the confrontation with an aggressive and hectic external world, and finally reaches a climax in a "passage of quotations" that defines the aggressive and hectic external world as oppressive. The ensemble as a whole and several instruments separately allude to pop songs and mass songs—genres the composer dislikes: a street song from the civil war, drinking songs, a popular film score from the 1930s, and the theme of the weekly newsreel of those years. These are musical quotations immediately recognizable to all who grew up during that era in the Soviet Union. A *fortissimo*-passage by the full ensemble is followed by a shorter, free reprise of the first part. "This entire section," in the words of Dorothea Redepenning, "is soft and restrained; it seems scattered, almost confused, like a resolution that collapses into an extended fermata on D that is held until the very end, with a solo voice rising above the single note."[29] The lyrics follow:

> At the inmost hour of the soul,
> In the depths of night . . .
> (A gigantic stride of the soul,
> Of the soul in the night.)
> At that hour, O Soul, hold sway over
> The worlds where'er Thou desirest
> To reign—the soul's domain;
> O Soul, hold sway.
> Rust the lips, powder
> The eyelashes with snow.
> (The Atlantic sigh of the soul,
> The soul in the night . . .)
> At that hour, O Soul, darken
> Thine eyes, where'er like Vega
> Thou risest. . . . The sweetest fruit,
> O Soul, make bitter.
> Make bitter and darken:
> Grow: hold sway.[30]

By the time Gubaidulina completed her orchestral portrait of Marina Tsvetaeva, Vitaly Kataev's project had already been abandoned. Prohibited from performing the works he had chosen, the conductor had resigned from his post. Thus another of Gubaidulina's compositions was put away in "the drawer" and stayed there for thirty years. This 1974 version for winds finally had its premiere at the Transart Festival in Bolzano, Italy, on September 11, 2004. In the presence of the composer, the Dutch conductor Kasper de Roo directed the wind ensemble Windkraft Tirol and the mezzo-soprano Nathalie Stutzmann. The following day a repeat performance was given as part of the Klangspuren Festival in Innsbruck, Austria. Both performances were excellent, but the enormous production costs may well limit it to these two occasions.

In June 1974 Nadia left Kazan to move in with her mother in Moscow. The Soviet capital offered the best educational opportunities, and after passing the requisite entrance examinations Nadia enrolled in a special high school emphasizing science and mathematics. Although there was never any question that Nadia deserved an excellent education, the family's limited finances were pushed to the limit, forcing Sofia to take out loans. As Nadia prepared for her entrance examination, memorizing the *History of the Communist Party of the Soviet Union* [*Istoriia komunisticheskoi partii Sovetskogo Soiuza*], her mother gave her Avtokhanov's book to read.

From the very start, Gubaidulina had told her daughter: "I have no pedagogical talent, and I can't and won't try to teach you." Nadia was treated like an adult, and there never was any "you must ..." but only "would you perhaps ..." And it seems that at times she was even asked for advice. Nadia lived with her mother until she began her studies at the university in the summer of 1979.

A year earlier Sofia Gubaidulina's personal life underwent an important change, which had long-lasting effects. The stimulating professional work with her colleague Pyotr Meshchaninov had led to a deeper personal relationship; however, as each a musician and committed to a rather reclusive life focused on work, they decided to maintain separate apartments. Meshchaninov lived on the southwestern outskirts of Moscow, at 125 Prospekt Vernadskogo; Sofia's apartment was located in the northeastern section. The metro stations Yugo-Zapadnaya and Preobrazhenskaya ploshchad' were the two end points of the Sokolnicheskaya Liniya on which one could cross the city in forty minutes. On long walks and many vacations, they discussed musical and compositional problems. Meshchaninov was the only person with whom Gubaidulina exchanged ideas about her evolving compositions, and she is indebted to him for many small but important suggestions. Openness and receptiveness in this regard have been an important feminine aspect of Gubaidulina's personality. Every viable suggestion undergoes a period of gestation to test its merit; then it is reformed in the overall process of creation, transformed, and finally carried out. In the early 1990s, after Gubaidulina had bought a house in Germany, she and Meshchaninov officially registered as a married couple in Moscow. This step made it possible for Meshchaninov to escape the chaotic and precarious conditions in Moscow and follow his wife to Germany.

After the failed performance of *Hour of the Soul,* Gubaidulina had better luck with a new work for winds during the second half of 1974. The young composer Dmitri Smirnov, who worked as an editor of compositions for winds at "Sovetskii Kompozitor," stopped to talk with her one day after a concert. A few pages were still available in a forthcoming volume, and it was common practice in such a case to ask a friend or a composer of interest for a contribution, which would then have to be written on very short notice. A few rubles would be the only remuneration. Smirnov also successfully recommended Gubaidulina for a seat on the editorial board, where, in collaboration with other composers, they made selections among the submitted scores. Probably about the same time when Smirnov asked for Gubaidulina's contribution, Leonid Chumov, a trumpet teacher and Grigory Orvid's assistant at the conservatory, also requested a work for winds from her. He wanted to perform it with his students, and within a short time Gubaidulina wrote *Quattro* for two trumpets and two trombones. But it turned out to be an unexpected challenge for Chumov, because the piece—especially the trombone cadenza—was much too difficult for his students, and he had to find more qualified musicians for the performance.[31] Hence, instead of being first performed at the conservatory, the work had its premiere in the Concert Hall of the Composers Union. At this performance, on November 22, 1974, Leonid Chumov played with Fyodor Grigin, the solo trumpeter at the Bolshoi Theater; Anatoly Skobelev, professor of trombone and now a member of Pletnyov's National Symphony Orchestra [Rossiiskii natsional'nyi simfonicheskii orkestr]; and Anatoly Nesterenko, a trombonist with the Bolshoi Theater. Even these experienced musicians were struggling with this piece at their first meeting, but they reached a professional level of performance after two or three rehearsals.[32] The rhythmic character and entertaining performative style of this work—trumpets and trombones play together in the same direction and in opposition, the trumpets turn to the right and to the left or up or down—all has enormous appeal, and the performance was a huge success. However, the tragic and religious dimensions of this piece were clearly not evident in this rendition, and it seems that the audience was largely treated to rather buffoonish theatricality.[33] Shostakovich was in the audience and rose for a standing ovation, so that the musicians felt obliged to present a part of the work as an encore.[34] Among the young composers in the audience was Alexander Vustin, for whom this was the first encounter with Gubaidulina's music. A year later he composed *Slovo* (*The Word*) for winds and percussion, a piece that was clearly inspired by the profound experience of that evening. When Chumov later had four of his students play *Quattro* for a degree recital, Orvid reprimanded him severely: "If anything like this ever happens again, you'll be fired."[35]

The French pianist and music organizer Jean-Pierre Armengaud arrived in Moscow in the winter of 1974–75 to study with Heinrich Neuhaus. A cultural agreement between Moscow and Paris had made it possible for him to spend several months in the Soviet Union. He brought with him the beginnings of his doctoral dissertation on Prokofiev and on the Third Piano Sonata by Boulez, which he later played for Neuhaus's students. Armengaud, who was acquainted with Denisov, had organized his own music festival, Fêtes Musicales de la Sainte Baume, near Aix-en-Provence, and he was scouting for composers and new works in Moscow.

"When I called a composer," Armengaud said,

> the usual answer was, "Let's meet at the Composers Union." Contacts with foreigners were frowned upon. But Sofia said right away, "Come and see me at my place," and we spent a whole day together talking and listening to recordings of music on tape of Soviet quality. She told me then: "I write for myself and have no prospects of having my works performed." She was full of ideas and spoke with passion, and I sensed that she wanted to distance herself from the other

composers—she didn't want to belong to any group. Sofia was free—free from the political and economic system, free like a bird. Of that triad—Denisov, Schnittke, Gubaidulina—she is the most "Russian" as far as I am concerned; that is, envisioning eternity without an eye to material goals. Her music has something archetypal: instead of making statements, it impresses. The person sitting before me was an artist, not a composer. What I see in Russia is a certain syncretism of the arts—everything is one: poetry, painting, philosophy, music. It is the essential character of Russian art. In France art always passes through rationality, through the medium of language. When I spoke with her about playing her music at Fêtes de la Sainte Baume, all she said was "Well, if you think so."[36]

Armengaud scheduled two concerts for August 3 and 4, 1975, in Sainte Baume under the title *La nouvelle musique soviétique,* and after his return to France he sent invitations to Denisov, Schnittke, and Gubaidulina. When his letters arrived at the Composers Union, Khrennikov was furious and ordered all three to appear before the Presiding Council [Predsedatel'skii sovet], a body he himself had created. He charged them with "separatism," as Soviet music could not be allowed to be represented by only these three composers. Their travel permits were denied[37]—but their music was nonetheless performed.[38]

A Trip to Prague and a Concerto for Bassoon and Low Strings

Earlier that year, in January 1975, Sofia Gubaidulina had been allowed to go on a twelve-day trip to Prague to see Marek Kopelent, with whom she had remained in contact since *Concordanza.* She had succeeded in getting her travel permit only by circuitous means, a typical case of the chicanery and harassment to which Moscow composers were then subjected. During a conversation with his colleague, Paul-Heinz Dittrich, at Warsaw Autumn in 1973, Marek Kopelent had conceived the idea to prepare a communal composition that would demonstrate the friendships among composers from different socialist countries. He was friendly with three composers living in the Eastern bloc: Dittrich in East Germany, Tiberiu Olah in Romania, and Sofia Gubaidulina. They all lived and suffered under similar circumstances. Kopelent wrote to both Olah and Gubaidulina, explained his project, and requested their collaboration. Because Olah never replied (perhaps the letter never reached him), the joint project was launched from Prague, East Berlin, and Moscow. The work was supposed to be an oratorio, and Kopelent and Dittrich at first thought of using texts from either the Bible or the Koran. They soon rejected this idea, however, as it obviously would not pass censorship. They finally agreed to use the writings of the Czech humanist scholar and teacher Amon Comenius. With assistance from the Comenius Pedagogical Institute [Pedagogický ústav J.A. Komenského] in Prague, Kopelent put together a Latin libretto on the themes of tolerance, peace, and cooperation among peoples. The nine parts of the oratorio were to alternate between instrumental music, vocal music, and vocal-instrumental passages, and each composer was to write three of the various parts. Given his preference for wind instruments, Kopelent had been planning a chamber piece for winds, but Dittrich insisted on a "large work," and the score that finally emerged was composed for solo voice, speakers, large chorus, chamber chorus, and an orchestra without string instruments. After all three composers had received their assignments (Gubaidulina wrote parts 4, 6, and 8), Dittrich and Gubaidulina prepared graphic sketches of their parts and sent them to Prague, where Kopelent pasted them together with his own drafts and sent them back to Berlin and Moscow. The individual parts still had to be forged together, and the composers had agreed to meet in Moscow for that purpose. However, the visa applications for the two men were rejected with the following remark: "It is not permitted that two married men visit a divorced woman." After considerable effort, Gubaidulina succeeded in getting a visa for a trip to Prague with the help of an invitation from Marek Kopelent's wife. It was the first time in five years of isolation that she could travel abroad.

Paul-Heinz Dittrich arrived from East Berlin during Sofia's first weekend in Prague, and the three collaborators produced a coherent score after a period of hard and intensive work. Each composer finished his or her own individual parts after returning home, and in July 1975 the oratorio was completed and given the title *Laudatio Pacis*. At that time Dittrich wrote in a letter from East Berlin to Prague: "Our work is finished and it will be played!! Somewhere in this world. . . ."[39] This "somewhere"—eighteen years later, after many futile efforts—turned out to be Berlin, which after the fall of the Wall had again become a place of cultural interchange between East and West. But long before this, Kopelent and Dittrich had tried at first to make arrangements for a performance in Paris as part of the celebration of the thirtieth anniversary of the United Nations Educational, Scientific, and Cultural Organization (UNESCO) in 1975. *Laudatio Pacis* was dedicated to UNESCO, and the composers prepared an accompanying text in four languages explaining the genesis of their work. However, the plan foundered on infighting among several bureaucracies, intrigues, and finally the rejection of the dedication by UNESCO's president M'Bow. At the time any performance in East Germany was conditional on the approval of Moscow and Prague, and although the former remained noncommittal, Prague issued a definitive no, as Kopelent was persona non grata in his own hometown. Even Westdeutscher Rundfunk (West German Radio) in Cologne, often willing to fund and produce experiments in contemporary music, refused to commit itself—partly because of problems of instrumentation and organization, and partly because of political difficulties.[40] The composers eagerly anticipated the premiere during the Berliner

Festwochen 1993, with Daniel Nazareth conducting the chorus and orchestra of the Mitteldeutscher Rundfunk, Leipzig. Although it was not easy to coordinate the complicated and extensive apparatus of the production and to forge the nine parts from three different composers into a coherent whole, the performance was a success.

While working on *Laudatio Pacis* with its large, world-embracing theme, Gubaidulina was also preparing a very different piece that focused on juxtaposing a single solo instrument and an ensemble of four cellos and three double basses—her Concerto for Bassoon and Low Strings. Valery Popov, an extraordinarily gifted bassoonist, had provided the impetus for this work. He was a member of the State Symphony Orchestra, taught at the conservatory, and also belonged to a group within the orchestra that occasionally gave chamber performances with Pyotr Meshchaninov. He had heard the Russian premiere of *Concordanza* on January 15, 1974, and subsequently asked Gubaidulina for a composition for bassoon.[41] Out of his wish to extend the repertoire for bassoon, he requested works from several other composers at about the same time.

For Gubaidulina, this meant the beginning of a work routine that would repeat itself again and again in her life whenever she wrote for an outstanding musician whose identity had virtually become one with his or her instrument. It is sparked by enthusiasm and, in an act of feminine devotion, leads to a total immersion into the nature of the instrument and the personality of the performer: How does he handle his instrument? How does he produce its particular sound? How does he relate to his environment? What is his posture? These questions are essential, because, for Gubaidulina, performer and composer are completely equal. They can result in an idea or an important impulse for a new work. In one way or another, performer and instrument always participate in the process of composition.

"I had never heard a bassoon with such a voice," she later said,

> and was literally bewitched by the musician's artistry. I attended all his concerts and class lessons at the Moscow Conservatory, where he taught. Gradually I began to penetrate into the essence of the instrument itself, to understand it like some character in a play. It was then that the idea came to me to surround the "personality" of the bassoon with low-register strings—double basses and cellos. The interactions between the soloist and the surrounding instruments are complex, contradictory, as in a dramatic scene full of action. The concerto includes moments of reconciliation and hostility, tragedy, and loneliness.[42]

In Valery Popov's words: "Sonia came three or four times to my lessons and afterward asked me some questions. Then I received the score. From a technical point of view, the piece with its variety of sounds, double notes, trills, and glissandi, was a sensational expansion of the bassoon's possibilities—something entirely new for Moscow."[43]

But Gubaidulina's work prickled some of the composers of the *nomenklatura*. When the Bassoon Concerto was presented to the Commission for Chamber and Symphonic Music, there was a clash of objections and praise, with Victor Peiko supporting his former student. In the early fall of 1975 the Composers Union considered a performance of the work in planning for the annual congress of the Moscow affiliate. However, Serafim Tulikov, president of the Moscow Composers Union, objected strenuously, and Evgeny Makarov, who presided over its Artistic Council, became known for his comment, "This branch [meaning Gubaidulina] must be hacked off!" On other occasions he had praised her: "I'm enthralled by your scores!" He had even requested copies—only to quash performances.

It is surprising, in retrospect, that Pyotr Meshchaninov actually directed the premiere of this controversial piece only eight months later, on May 6, 1975, in the Hall of the Composers Union. Over the next few years Edison Denisov made seven futile attempts to include it in the programs of his series "New Works by Moscow Composers"; only on the eighth try was he successful.[44] This "life drama" of the bassoon, which—like a Chaplinesque representative of the simple people—is exposed to the aggressions of the "low" strings (*nizkii*, the Russian word for "low," can refer to both a low register of sound and a low level of morality), may have been the cause of a scene in the restaurant of the Composers Union following the performance. As was common practice, Gubaidulina had invited musicians and friends for a party after the premiere, when Nikolai Budashkin, a highly decorated composer of popular songs and music for folk instruments, stepped up to her table rather drunk. It was the first time he had met her, and, given her powerful, explosive music, he probably expected a physically imposing monster of a composer. He mumbled something about "This Gubaidulina person, so thin and fragile," as if she could be snuffed out by an effortless breeze.[45]

Shortly before the controversies erupted over the Bassoon Concerto, a truly shattering event disrupted Soviet musical life: Dmitri Shostakovich died on August 9, 1975. As he lay in state in the Great Hall of the Conservatory, countless people passed by the open coffin, an honor guard on both sides, while the militia blocked off the street outside. At the burial his grave overflowed with floral arrangements; even the Party and the KGB sent contributions. Tikhon Khrennikov and other dignitaries read eulogies, and a military brass band played Schubert, Chopin's *Funeral March,* and the Soviet National Anthem. Dmitri Dmitrievich—like Messiaen in Paris and Cage in New York—was not only an important catalyst and inspiration for a new generation of Russian composers; he was a symbolic figure for an entire era of Soviet music. Nine months before his death, Gubaidulina had seen the sensational new staging of his early opera, *The Nose* [*Nos*], at the Moscow Chamber Theater [Moskovskii muzykal'nyi kamernyi teatr], the first Moscow performance in more than forty years. She later recalled that evening as "one of the most powerful impressions in my life."[46] The works Shostakovich had composed in the period after Gubaidulina completed her studies did not affect her; but the ascetic simplicity of his very latest string quartets and his Sonata for Viola, written as he was approaching death, moved her deeply. "The late quartets are probably the most precious of Shostakovich's works for me. ... Fear of death terrorized Shostakovich, tormented him. And you can hear it in his music. One perceives the boundary between earthly life and the preparations for the world to come. The tension between the one and the other generates some invisible current, and the music is transformed into an utterly overt confession."[47] Shostakovich's death marked the end of a defining period of Soviet music.

8 | Composing and Improvising, 1975–1979

A Collection of Folk Instruments at
Viacheslav Artyomov's Apartment

A small group of Moscow composers gradually emerged in the 1970s with whom Sofia Gubaidulina eventually became quite friendly. This postwar generation consisted of Elena Firsova, her husband Dmitri Smirnov, Alexander Raskatov, Vladislav Shoot, Victor Ekimovsky, and some who were a few years older: Alexander Vustin, Viatcheslav Artyomov, and Victor Suslin. She was already well acquainted with Artyomov and Suslin and saw them often. Artyomov, an enthusiastic drummer, went on a number of folkloristic excursions to Central Asia and the Transcaucasus and always returned with a small collection of folk instruments. A visit to his studio apartment in Fili, at the southwestern outskirts of the city, was therefore always delightful. Besides a variety of drums and a few "civilized" instruments, Artyomov owned an Uzbek-Tadzhik *dutár* (a two-string instrument with a pear-shaped body and a long neck made of mulberry wood), a *pandúri* and a *chongúri* (plucked instruments from Gruziia [the Republic of Soviet Georgia]), an Armenian *kanón* (a large, zither-like instrument), as well as a few *salmúri* (whistle flutes from Gruziia). It was fascinating to touch or blow these instruments ever so softly, to hear their strange sounds, and to sense their fine acoustic qualities. One fall day in 1975 Artyomov, Gubaidulina, and Victor Suslin happened to sit on the floor improvising together, but within the next few months this casual event turned into a serious improvisation and research project—and not just by chance. Many works in those years, in both East and West, were sober, rather dry compositions lacking in spontaneity and vitality. These three composers longed for something closer to life and played with instruments not commonly used in traditional orchestras. Artyomov explained his improvisations twenty-five years later: "Our improvising was actually based on a common motivation. The seventies were difficult years, and we had to stick together and work together to fight our political environment. We met quite often, sometimes with Schnittke and other composers. And at one of these meetings we began our improvisations."[1] Their enthusiasm was sparked at their very first meeting, and soon they met regularly at Artyomov's apartment to work on their improvisations. Playing these instruments confronted them with an unfamiliar world of music that demanded patient exploration. They were inspired by the natural spontaneity of folk musicians, but they wanted to go beyond mere imitation or re-creation of musical folk traditions. Trained as pianists, they each had a particular talent for another instrument: Artyomov was a skilled string player, Victor Suslin excelled on the recorder, and Gubaidulina was a whiz as a percussionist.[2] As a warm-up, they would play a few simple exercises, and then the pieces would grow longer, with twenty to twenty-five minutes as an upper limit. What happened afterward was mostly repetitious and clichés. Their meetings often lasted five to six hours, after which they would launch into a relentless critique of their performance during the session.

They discovered a whole new world of sound, and in the years to come they would seize every opportunity to use new and different instruments. At first they included bright red zithers of varying sizes—well-crafted instruments of East German manufacture—which Victor Suslin had discovered in a toy store. Later, in Riga, they bought East German recorders, and they added cymbals and gongs to the drums as well as tubular bells, metal plates, and numerous chimes and jingles. They would buy toy instruments because of the special sound quality, and they experimented with every conceivable part of each instrument—pounding the bodies of string instruments and blowing recorders upside down. Then they added unconventional contraptions of their own making, such as the "friction rods" (India rubber balls wired to a metal rod) later used in Gubaidulina's String Quartet No. 4. They each made recordings of special sounds, transitions, and combinations, as well as of melodic and rhythmic inventions, but considered them communal property. They used these recordings not only in their joint improvisations but also in each individual's own compositions.

Feeling somewhat unsettled at first by the freedom of improvisation, the three composers initially tried to establish defining frameworks. They devised sketched outlines and graphic scores for some of their public performances. Gubaidulina wrote three scores of this kind, one of them for percussion instruments titled *Lines, Curves, and Dots* [*Linii, izgiby i tochki*], which was the title given in the program of the premiere though the work was later renamed *Dots, Lines, and Zigzags* [*Tochki, linii i zigzagi*].) Eventually they found, however, that performances without any type of script or score were much livelier and more interesting, and that the pieces did not lack logical development and structure. But these spontaneous *"compositions à trois"* demanded a high degree of attentiveness to each of the other players and to the organic whole—not an easy task for these three idiosyncratic personalities. The two men especially had to go through a difficult learning process. "It is easier for a camel to pass through the eye of a needle," Victor Suslin once said.

> Whenever our composer egos got us moving off in different directions, you could instantly hear the result: the musical material fell apart, proportions were destroyed, and it became especially evident that this material is organic, not mechanical. It is so easy to kill an organism! Just a few egotistical impulses, a few careless motions, and it's all over, the organism is dead. Whenever there were any signs of ego tensions between me and Artyomov, Gubaidulina became our referee, and we had complete trust in her judgment. Sonia's special gift in joint performances was to create musical situations of fruitful conflict, to elicit tensions, and to insist on moving beyond them. She often was the "fuel" for our combined engine, and occasionally she would project an amazing kind of demonic energy when she went into something of a trance during our playing, not hearing us but subjecting herself wholly to her inner voice and forcing us to follow her. It had nothing to do with the willfulness of a self-important composer—no, it was more like an inner "demon" implacably demanding: "Only this, and no other way."[3]

But Gubaidulina could also be a strong force for bringing together extreme opposites.

Improvising Onstage

Concert programs in the West often state that Gubaidulina, Artyomov, and Suslin founded the improvisation group Astraea in 1975. This is somewhat misleading, and Gubaidulina has specifically commented that "we didn't come together as a concert group but only as a composition laboratory among ourselves."[4] She has even admitted that their occasional stage performances were not among their better moments.[5] The first appearance of the group—it still had no name—took place on March 28, 1976, in the Concert Hall of the House of Scientists [Kontsertnyi zal Doma uchënykh], where Alexei Liubimov had organized a concert of vocal and instrumental music of the thirteenth and fourteenth centuries. Gubaidulina, Artyomov, and Suslin, dressed in black minstrel costumes, played their red zithers and Soviet Georgian *samúri* pipes during interludes between the main program pieces, which included old Italian dances and works by Francesco Landini and Adam de la Halle performed by three other musicians using historical instruments.[6]

Artyomov chose the name S-M (Stabile-Mobile [*Stabil'-mobil'*]) for the ensemble, and he later talked about its first appearance in the Moscow Jazz Club on October 24, 1977 (Gubaidulina's birthday!):

> We had rolled up our instruments in a carpet and arrived by taxi. During the first part of the program a big band had played in the style of Glenn Miller. Then it was our turn, and we unrolled our carpet on stage. There were as many as eight hundred people in the audience. The lights were turned down so that we could concentrate. We played without warming up. Our music was light and soft in contrast to the big band. We had a few girls who were singing without text in the background, and I had given an Indian text to a journalist friend to read aloud. We were well received, and the concert was a big success. Afterwards, a strange man took us home—probably a KGB agent. He gave us his phone number and said: "If you ever have any problems or want to exchange some currency or want to leave the country. . . . just give me a call." We joked around and told him we wanted to travel to China. That obviously puzzled him. These people [KGB agents] don't have individual faces; they all look the same, like trees in the forest.[7]

The KGB seemed to take an interest in this threesome who played a kind of uncontrollable music. At a performance in someone's private apartment, attended by many foreigners and several nonconformist painters, they were introduced to a "colleague" at the Serbskii Institut, one of Moscow's notorious psychiatric hospitals. He asked them a few questions: "What are your names? Where do you come from? What did you study?" But he was most interested in asking: "Where did you get to know one another?"[8] But it never came to anything.

The evening at the Jazz Club, however, was not the only concert they gave with other musicians. Another time they were joined by girls on zithers from Dmitri Pokrovsky's folk group. They entered the hall through different doors, opened the evening with a prelude, and concluded with a postlude. The six-part main program in between was conceived by Artyomov:

Prelude
    Mantra (all three)
    1. *Vision of Markandeia*. Prologue (Artyomov)
    2. Percussion Intermezzo (all three)
    3. *Personal Song on the Theme of a Chuckchee Bear Incantation* (Suslin)
    4. *Lines, Curves, and Dots* (Gubaidulina)
    5. *Supernova of the Year 1054*—dedicated to I. S. Shklovsky (Artyomov)

Artyomov had written a short text for distribution at this performance. He wanted to encourage audience participation at the end, and it worked. "Everybody play," it read.

Play, and you'll have new ears, new eyes, and a new life. Today, let's take the first step toward this goal: we ask that at the end of the performance you support us with applause and then with bells (everyone who has one). The whole thing will take only an hour and a half, as we play without intermission. Relax. Let your guard down, and let the sound move freely through your body. Try to sense and soak up every moment of the sound. Whatever happens cannot be repeated. Realize that you are part of the universe of sound. Let's get started.

Because S-M soon struck the three musicians as too academic—it smacked of Boulez and his school—Artyomov came up with a new suggestion: Astraea, the name of an early-nineteenth-century Freemason lodge in Russia. Astraea gave a few more performances—a second appearance in the Jazz Club, an evening in the studio of the Scriabin Museum, and one in Baku in response to an invitation. A performance was also held in the Small Hall of the Moscow Composers Union but was open only to members. This free and uncontrollable music was too dangerous in the eyes of the official music establishment. Astraea's weekly sessions between 1975 and 1981 were like a subtle but essential keynote underlying the individual creations of the three composers during those years and leaving its traces even in some of their later works.

Financial Strains and a Commission for a "Music Hall"

During the last week of December 1975 Sofia Gubaidulina, Pyotr Meshchaninov, and Victor Suslin and his wife traveled to Tallinn, the capital of Estonia, for the second performance on Christmas Day of Schnittke's First Symphony. As Estonia had its own well-established musical life, and Moscow's long arm of control did not always extend to the border republics, one could take advantage of a certain degree of freedom. Gubaidulina stayed with the family of her colleague, Arvo Pärt, whom she knew from his concerts and visits to Moscow; her travel companions returned home on the overnight train. Pärt, having returned to an active musical life after a professional crisis and several years of seclusion in the countryside, had undergone a remarkable change. His new faithful commitment to simplicity and quiet contemplation brought him closer to Gubaidulina's own concept of music and commanded her particular admiration.

Gubaidulina's trip to Tallinn had unexpected consequences for her at home. The same evening that Schnittke's symphony was played in Tallinn, Nikolai Peiko, Gubaidulina's former teacher, gave a concert in Moscow. Apparently he was deeply disappointed that his ever faithful student preferred to attend the performance of Schnittke's controversial composition. Peiko's personal support and interest in her work noticeably diminished from this point on. When they happened to meet not long afterward, his behavior toward his former student was so offensive that, twenty years later, anger and outrage welled up in her as she spoke of it. And even though he had once come to the defense of her Bassoon Concerto, he disparaged it with a tactless pun after its premiere.

But life in Moscow, together with Nadia, continued—and that meant composing, improvising, and earning a living through music. The years 1976 through 1978 were particularly difficult financially, as Gubaidulina was not commissioned for any film scores. She tried everything else: writing stage music for a play by the Belorussian dramatist Vasil Bykau; composing small pieces for collections of music for wind instruments that Dmitri Smirnov and Leonid Chumov had been able to obtain for her; and even peddling her compositions from one place to another. A committee in the Ministry of Culture had the authority to pay composers substantial amounts for their works, and Gubaidulina took the score and the Prague recording of *Night in Memphis* to its chairman, a composer and Party functionary by the name of Anatoly Ushkaryov. He took a quick look at the score, then praised the music but criticized the text: nobody would be interested in that sort of thing. Sofia protested, pointing out the importance and high cultural value of the old Egyptian inscriptions. "You've got to find texts that celebrate Soviet life," he replied. And on her insistence that the whole committee should listen to the piece, he simply said: "Even if they all vote for it, I'm the chairman, and I've got the final say." In the end the committee did hear the recording, and Sofia actually received a modest payment which she used to pay off half her debts.

During these difficult months the conductor Alexander Mikhailov, also the ballet master who had started "Ballet on Ice" ["Balet na l'du"], came to see Gubaidulina. They were planning a "Music Hall" [*Miuzik-Kholl*] in Moscow with official funding. Such theaters had been built in the Soviet Union in the 1930s for the productions of light music, dance shows, and circus acts—following the American model. Gubaidulina's visitors wanted a composition that would combine popular and serious music, and Sofia, having no other commissions pending, agreed and received a substantial honorarium. Setting immediately to work, she conceived *Concerto Grosso*, a piece later renamed Concerto for Symphony Orchestra and Jazz Band [*Kontsert dlia dvukh orkestrov, estradnogo i simfonicheskogo*].

Although the music-hall project came to nothing, this time her work did not end up in a drawer. First performed on January 16, 1978, by the Symphonic Pops Orchestra of the State Radio and Television Network of the USSR [Estradno-simfonicheskii orkestr Gosteleradio SSSR] under the direction of Alexander Mikhailov, it was recorded later that year, on September 23, in Studio GDR 3 [Gosudarstvennyi Dom Radioveshchania (i Zvukozapisi) = State House of Radio

Transmission (and Sound Recording)]. As a popular ballet piece, it actually had two ballet performances: Vakil Usmanov choreographed for the Stanislavsky Nemirovich-Danchenko Music Theater [Muzykal'nyi teatr imeni K.S. Stanislavskogo i Vl. I. Nemirovicha-Danchenko] in Moscow, and Yury Puzakov for a performance in Tartu, Estonia. The choreographers asked Gubaidulina to add a slow movement, and she obliged with a symphonic adagio. Later, in 1978, Sergei Mikhailov also commissioned a capriccio for his pop orchestra, and eventually it turned into *Te salutant.*

It is astonishing, in hindsight, that despite Gubaidulina's strained financial circumstances, despite all the difficulties and disappointments, she always found the strength to continue with her work as a composer. Surely it is an indication of her inner strength, her rich reserve of ideas, and of the fact that she rarely lacked commissions, albeit for unremunerated work. In 1976, besides completing *Concerto grosso,* she wrote a Trio for Three Trumpets, *Dots, Lines, and Zigzags* (for bass clarinet and piano, written for Due Boemi di Praga), as well as the organ work *Light and Darkness* [*Svetloe i tëmnoe*] (for Alexei Liubimov). The last two were soon to be performed. Wanting to reach beyond the confines of the piano, Liubimov had begun to play the organ and performed *Light and Darkness* on May 25, 1979, in the Concert Hall of the Capella [Kontsertnyi Zal Gosudarstvennoi akademicheskoi kapelly] in Leningrad, together with works by Victor Suslin, Pärt, Schnittke, and others. More than ten years later the German organist Friedemann Herz performed the same piece in the same hall, with its excellent acoustics and location on the banks of the Moika Canal. He did much to develop an audience for the organ music of Gubaidulina and other Soviet composers in Germany.

At that time Gubaidulina received yet another request for a composition from Alexei Liubimov. Together with the conductor of the Ural State Academic Philharmonic Orchestra [Ural'skii gosudartsvennyi akademicheskii filarmonicheskii orkestr] in Sverdlovsk, Liubimov was planning a music festival in that city on the edge of the Urals, and they wanted to perform a work for symphony orchestra and percussion, with Mark Pekarsky as soloist. Gubaidulina took her earlier piece for winds, *Hour of the Soul,* and rewrote it as the previously mentioned *Percussio di Pekarski,* a concerto for percussion, soprano solo, and large orchestra. This turned out to be another festival that never made it beyond the planning stage, and Gubaidulina's new version was another work that ended up in the drawer.

Besides having her circle of friends among composers in Moscow and Estonia, Gubaidulina maintained friendly relations with Leonid Hrabovsky and Valentin Silvestrov in Kiev. The story of her first meeting with Silvestrov was later told by Gennady Aigi, whom Silvestrov always visited on his trips to Moscow:

We talked about Sonia because he liked her music, but it turned out that they had never met. We went to see her—she lived by herself and wasn't busy—and we spent the whole day together. It was an instant friendship. That day we listened to a lot of recordings of her music. When asked how she was doing, she replied: "Recently I have not been doing so well creatively because I have too many requests—from a music school, and a performance center has asked for some jazz." Valya [Valentin Silvestrov] asked if there were any recordings of her jazz music, and that's what we then listened to. He liked everything. Sonia had also heard some of Valya's work—but she only knew the title of *Quiet Songs* [*Tikhie pesni*], with texts by classical Russian poets. So Valya sang for us—he liked to do that. He sang everything, and he liked to dedicate his songs to his friends. He dedicated Pushkin's "Winter Pathway" ["Zimniaia doroga"] to me. When he sang a song with words by Lermontov, he stopped in the middle and asked Sonia: "Do you like it?" "Yes, very much!" "Then I'll dedicate it to you." And he immediately went to the piano and wrote a dedication on the music. When we left her apartment, Valya said to me: "Did you notice that Sonia looked quite depressed when we arrived? But when I sang of Lermontov's lily of the valley [who nods her silver head]—'I see God in the heavens . . . [lines from Lermontov's 1837 poem, "When the yellowing wheat field ripples . . ." ("Kogda volnuetsia zhelteiushchaia niva . . .")]—I noticed that she relaxed her frown, and that's why I dedicated my song to her." Later Sonia told me about Silvestrov's songs: "It will be said about this music that its language is too simple. But this simplicity is deceptive. It has a wonderful depth. And this simplicity is something entirely new—it is a new musical language." In 1993 Sonia and I listened to Valya's music in a concert, and she said: "It is quite amazing how quickly Valya's music has become classical."[9]

After a Seven-Year Delay: The Premiere of *Rubaiyat*

After a long period of sustained effort, the premiere of *Rubaiyat* was finally scheduled to take place in the Hall of the Composers Union on December 24, 1976. Pyotr Meshchaninov, together with some musicians of the State Symphony Orchestra, had put together a program (it also included Denisov's Concerto for Flute and Orchestra and Geviksman's Third Symphony) and he also conducted the rehearsals. The conductor of the actual premiere, the busy and ever peripatetic Gennady Rozhdestvensky, appeared only on the day before the performance. He suggested that Meshchaninov, having conducted the rehearsals, also conduct the performance. However, it was self-evident that Rozhdestvensky's name and fame were essential to gain recognition for the composer, and Meshchaninov, who also performed on the piano, declined the offer. He had marked the score carefully,[10] and Rozhdestvensky, who always prepared himself thoroughly, conducted both the final rehearsal and the premiere. The singer Sergei Yakovenko, for whom Gubaidulina had written *Rubaiyat*, later recalled his impressions of the evening that had been seven years in the making:

While rehearsing the *Rubaiyat,* and even on December 24 [1976] when we assembled in the Hall of the Composers Union, we weren't at all certain that the premiere would take place. Unless I'm remembering wrong, this was Gubaidulina's first full-length composer's concert in the traditional two parts with an intermission, and rumors were flying all the while about a "general opinion" that it would be prohibited. I had barely arrived backstage when Robert Simonov, a Party organizer in the Composers Union, pounced on me and in a quiet, ingratiating voice asked, "May I please take a look at your music?"[11] After handing him the score, I nervously watched his reaction. The censor thoughtfully turned page after page . . . I don't know how well he read music, although he supposedly had training as a composer and wrote marches for military band; anyway, he very carefully read the poetic text. There was an ideological cliché at that time about "uncontrollable associations" [*nekontroliruemye assotsiatsii*]. This formula was invoked to cancel many a classical performance. On reaching the words,

O, Fate! Thou thyself affirmest authority over all things!
Thy might is boundless when obsessed by gloom, thou
Bestowest blessings on base hearts and blight on noble ones!
Art thou barren of good or merely mad?

the Party censor knitted his brows and questioned, "Who's being referred to here, what's the implication?" I replied that obviously the medieval poet had in mind the despotic and cruel Oriental overlords. Smirking and muttering something about my perverse taste, that I'm always singing, they say, any sort of abomination, Robert Alexandrovich proceeded into the crowded auditorium. This "mischief," by the way, was not without consequences for me.

At that time Yakovenko also performed works by Denisov, Schnittke, Frid, and Lutosławski, as well as various musical renditions of Pasternak's poetry. His narrative continues:

When the question was raised about awarding me the honorary title "Merited Artist [of the USSR]" [*Zasluzhennyi artist SSSR*], Robert Simonov, whose signature on the document was required, killed it: "Over my dead body." . . . But at concerts during the 1970s and 1980s I performed the *Rubaiyat* many times, and not only in Moscow—where, besides Rozhdestvensky, both Yury Nikolaevsky and Pyotr Meshchaninov conducted—but also in Nizhny Novgorod (conducted by Alexander Skulsky), Novosibirsk (conducted by Arnold Katz), Omsk (conducted by Victor Tietz, a German national). . . . And everywhere listeners enthusiastically greeted the music. I don't remember a single unsuccessful concert when the performing musicians or the public seemed to react indifferently. Despite its essentially avant-garde style, which was packed with unfamiliar techniques, the work did not seem hard to understand; it captivated the audience with its unique charm, magical timbral combinations, and explosive power. Still, the performance with Rozhdestvensky on that December evening was the high point. Even the rehearsals were festive occasions. I remember how Gennady Nikolaevich explained to the musicians that, after an aleatoric episode, each of them in turn had to enter precisely at his signal in intervals of a few seconds. Ten instrumentalists had to remember which finger of his left or right hand he would use to give them their cue. As he did not have enough fingers for the two additional players, he cued them with a wave of his elbows. Everyone seemed satisfied, but it turned out that I, as the soloist, also needed to be cued. Now what? Roshdestvensky thought for a moment and suggested, with a smile: "What about winking at you with my left eye, Sergei Borisovich?" The success of the concert was ear-shattering, the enthusiasm of the audience boundless, and the cantata's finale had to be repeated. That night, despite her modest resources, Sonia borrowed money somewhere, reserved the restaurant at the Composers Union, and threw a banquet for all the participants in the concert. It was a moving and noble gesture honoring her colleagues and comrades-in-arms.[12]

A Performance in East Berlin and a Flute Quartet for Paris

Two months later, on February 22, 1977, Due Boemi di Praga presented the premiere of *Dots, Lines, and Zigzags* at the Information Center of the Czech Socialist Republic in East Berlin, with additional performances in Bernburg and Greifswald. The ensemble and the composer were not personally acquainted, and the performance had come about in circuitous ways. Sofia Gubaidulina had heard about Josef Horák, the "Paganini of the bass clarinet," and his piano accompanist Emma Kovárnová from her Prague composer friend Ivana Loudová. In 1955 Horák had staged the world's first recital for bass clarinet and since then had elevated it to the level of a solo instrument by playing numerous works by Hába, Hindemith, Jolivet, and the serialists. (Stockhausen invited Horák to Darmstadt in 1968 to be among the soloists for his *Musik für ein Haus*.) Horák's mellow, singing tone and his extension of the pitch and dynamic range and the expressive possibilities of the bass clarinet have had a worldwide impact.

Because so many of her scores were gathering dust in a drawer, and so many performances were denied official permission, Gubaidulina decided to risk letting these works be smuggled abroad. Horák, stopping over in Belgrade on one of his trips, was handed the score that had been dedicated to "Due Boemi di Praga." The "Two Bohemians from Prague" made several recordings for radio and performed it on their tours. But it took all five years, until November 22, 1982, for the duet to come to Moscow, and for Gubaidulina to hear her own work in the Small Hall of the Moscow Conservatory. Following a late-evening seminar on the bass clarinet, which was also attended by Lev Mikhailov and his students, the Due Boemi and a group of Moscow composers and musicians gathered at Sofia's apartment for an all-night party of celebration and good conversation.

In April 1977, six weeks after the Berlin premiere of *Dots, Lines, and Zigzags*, Gubaidulina completed a new composition with unusual instrumentation—a quartet for four flutes. It had been commissioned by Pierre-Yves Artaud in Paris, the founder of the flute quartet Arcadie. Gubaidulina had been recommended to Artaud by Jean-Pierre Armengaud, and Artaud had also witnessed the debacle of the derailed invitation to the Sainte Baume music festival. Arcadie was one of the first quartets of its kind and had begun giving concerts in the mid-1960s. The group worked very hard and achieved its major phase in the 1970s, performing about eighty concerts per year. Artaud had been a student in composition classes given by Messiaen and Jolivet and then became France's leading interpreter of contemporary flute music; Arcadie was therefore always on the lookout for new compositions. The other three flutists had classical backgrounds. As early as 1975, the French composer Michel Karsky (his mother was a well-known Russian emigrant painter) had taken the request to Gubaidulina on a trip to Moscow. At his suggestion, Artaud wrote a letter to Tikhon Khrennikov, the head of the Soviet Composers Union, requesting permission for Gubaidulina to write the piece for the Parisian quartet. The letter remained unanswered until one day, surprisingly, a telegram arrived from the Composers Union noting that the application file was still incomplete: the title of the work, its length, and the date of its performance were missing. Artaud never responded.

The first French performance, on February 25, 1979, was part of a concert in the church of St. Denis in Athis-Mons on the outskirts of Paris. To protect the composer from possible danger, Gubaidulina's name was not listed in the program. In the next few years, however, Arcadie performed the Flute Quartet at least fifty times, and even the three classical musicians of the group, after some initial reservations, soon came to accept it.

Gubaidulina wrote the Quartet—which had been performed earlier by Irina Loben, Alexander Korneyev, Alexander Munshin, and Oleg Cherniavsky in the Hall of the Composers Union—in fairly short breaks between composing two other works focusing on a single instrumental family. One was the previously mentioned Trio for Three Trumpets, the other was the *Duo Sonata* for two bassoons (written for Valery Popov), composed in the same year but after the Flute Quartet.

A Trip to Baku and New Instruments for Astraea

The premiere of Vasil Bykau's play, *The Crossroad* (*Perekrëstok*), took place at the Taganka Theater in Moscow on October 6, 1977; Yury Liubimov and Boris Glagolin directed the play, and Gubaidulina wrote the music. Artyomov, Victor Suslin, and Gubaidulina had made arrangements for the following day to travel together to Baku, the capital of Azerbaijan, but Gubaidulina was not at the airport to meet them. Suslin called Moscow from Baku. Gubaidulina was feeling depressed and told him they could take the trip without her. She had arrived early at the airport and had stood in line for two hours. When it was finally her turn, the female official who had taken her ticket told her, "You're too late." But, in fact, the plane stood on the tarmac for another two hours, and it appeared likely that the official simply had sold her ticket "under the table." Suslin cheered her up and persuaded her to take the trip the following day.

The three visitors to Baku stayed with the music scholar and organist Yury Gabai, and the Azerbaijan composer Frangis Ali-Sade, who had performed in piano concerts of Western and Soviet music, later described this visit:

> The Society of Students and Scholars had invited Astraea, and they gave two concerts, one in the Small Hall of the State Conservatory [Azerbaidzhanskaia konservatoriia imeni Uz. Gadzhibekova] and the other in the Academy of Sciences. It was standing room only in the hall at the conservatory, and after the concert the students asked many questions, eliciting interesting answers from the three performers. At Yury Gabai's, we listened to Schnittke's First Symphony. I showed them around Baku, and they stopped by my place. Those were unforgettable days for me. From then on, every time I traveled to Moscow I looked up Sofia; later I saw her on various occasions, the last time at the performance of her *St. John Passion* [*Johannes-Passion*] in Berlin.[13]

Two days of leisure on the beach of the Caspian Sea with one of Artyomov's friends provided some welcome relaxation. The vacation home was located near a large shifting sand dune that was enclosed by a stone wall. The sand had covered several fig trees, and a peculiar odor of fruit, salt water, and oil hung in the air. Evenings along the shore stirred the imagination, and the three musicians played their instruments on top of the dune under an open sky.[14]

On the return trip, they brought with them a small collection of new instruments: two *tars*, a *kemancha*,[15] and several Azerbaijan drums. From then on, Gubaidulina liked to play her *tar* during improvisations, and for a while it was her favorite instrument. Originally a Persian instrument, the *tar* has a body shaped like a figure eight, made of mulberry wood, and covered with a sound board made of a bull's bladder or fish skin. It has somewhere between nine and eleven metal strings, of which two pairs are used for playing the melody and the rest for a drone accompaniment. Held almost horizontally across the chest, it is played with a plectrum. "It would seem to speak all the time, all by itself," Gubaidulina later commented, "as if I had nothing to do with it. I'd have the urge to sing, and it would answer me. It had the timbral characteristic of being able *to respond*."[16]

The discovery of new sounds on folk instruments was not the only inspiration derived from the realm of folk art. Although as pianists these three musicians had been trained in the tempered tuning of the piano, they tuned their zithers in four different ways—diatonic, chromatic, pentatonic, and in quarter tones—and began to experiment. Formal aspects of folk music also inspired them: the structure of the traditional Azerbaijan *mugám* or the Soviet Georgian *krimanchúli* choruses, whose heterophonic voices could be easily rendered by a variety of recorders. At that time Gubaidulina began to take an interest in various folk cultures independently of her work with Astraea. In the early 1970s she had met the Dutchman Erich van der Vossen at a concert. As the director of Philips-Polygram, he frequently traveled in Eastern bloc countries, bringing along records, including the extensive Archiv series of ethnic music produced by Philips. In an interview during the 1990s Gubaidulina spoke about her particular interest in this music, emphasizing its universally human elements and calling it the basis of her own self-realization:

> I would not want to limit my consciousness by either a Russian or a Tatar national perspective. I have always wanted to be receptive to the much wider spiritual world of the entire earth. This is why I have closely studied the folklore of various countries. I am familiar with Russian folklore and it is very important to me. ... But my "assignment" [*zadannost'*] was to broaden my perspective on folklore. I want to tune myself as much as possible to this wavelength, and so I have studied Armenian and Georgian folklore, Yakutian folklore, African art, and the art of Bali, of the East Indians, of Tibet, and so on. I have strived to absorb into myself as many varied national cultures as possible in order to fertilize the soil in which I myself, my unique individuality, could thrive. Then, to penetrate as honestly and deeply as possible into that individuality: who exactly am I in reality? And to reveal in music, in sound, the Truth that I discovered deep down in myself.[17]

When Sofia's brother-in-law died in November 1977, she immediately traveled to Nikolaev in Ukraine to be with her sister during this difficult time. Gubaidulina has often talked about death in interviews and always said that she is not so much afraid of death as of life and violence. She once said to Enzo Restagno:

> [My sister] had to make arrangements for the funeral and was a bit anxious that I would have to stay at the house with the dead body. But for me these hours I spent with death turned out to be of great importance. I began to understand myself better. I could physically feel the presence of death; I was focused and very much at peace. My inner being was not affected by emotions, because emotions are based on sorrow and pain; but I was beyond the sensation of emotions. It seemed to me as if I had entered a space outside of life, a space that I experienced as filled with absolute solemnity. It was a wonderful experience of a meeting in absolute silence.[18]

Ten years later this experience became the inspiration for a new work. Vera Gubaidulina, who had earned a good living for many years as a physician on

Sakhalin Island, had helped to support her sister with a substantial sum at a time when Sofia was having great financial difficulties. Vera asked her sister for a requiem without, however, setting a deadline. She hoped that the composition would grow out of a genuine creative desire. Because Gubaidulina always conceived of death as a boundary-crossing event—or, as in *Steps*, the entry into an eternal world—the requiem became an *Alleluia* [*Alliluiia*] in the late 1980s, "a hymn of praise to death" as the beginning of a new life.

Collaboration with Vladimir Tonkha and Friedrich Lips

Gubaidulina began working together with the cellist Vladimir Tonkha and the bayan artist Friedrich Lips in the second half of the 1970s. Although these two working relationships were at first independent of each other, she eventually dedicated her *Seven Words* [*of Jesus Christ on the Cross*] [*Sem' slov (Iisusa na kreste)*] to both artists, and they both appeared as soloists in its premiere. Besides *Offertorium* (her Concerto for Violin), *Seven Words* has been the most widely performed of her works and has earned high critical praise. But it was not until several years after her first meeting with Tonkha and her introduction to the bayan by Lips that Gubaidulina completed *Seven Words* and the work had its first performance (more on this later).

In the early 1970s the cellist Grigory Pekker, professor at the Novosibirsk Conservatory, asked Gubaidulina for some cello etudes. He was planning to issue a collection of etudes for his students, and since few were available, he got in touch with several composers. Pekker must have been considerably puzzled when he first looked at Gubaidulina's etudes in 1974. She had used these ten pieces to explore different kinds of musical expression through different kinds of sound production on the cello. They were artful miniatures that did not resemble traditional etudes but had been written as compositional exercises. It was quite appropriate that Vladimir Tonkha later called this cycle Ten Preludes for Violoncello in his concert programs. Because Pekker had never studied contemporary music, he did not know what to do with the score he had been sent and simply ignored it. Three years later, as Gubaidulina thought about who might perform these artistically and technically demanding pieces, she decided on Vladimir Tonkha, an artist of exquisite technique and great musical sensibility. She had met him as early as 1967 in Kazan, where he taught at the conservatory and, on one occasion, performed a sonata for cello and piano by her former teacher Albert Leman. She now called to ask him tactfully if he were interested in performing her etudes. "There is only one problem," Tonkha replied, "I don't have the music." But on December 12, 1977, he gave the first performance of Ten Etudes for Solo Cello[19] at the Moscow Composers Union and later played them again and again—under the title Preludes—on concert tours throughout Europe, the United States, and Japan.

In contrast to the revered, classical status of the cello, the accordion—and its Russian version, the *bayan,* which is played with buttons rather than keys—has a somewhat questionable reputation:

> The *bayan* is a button-accordion named after a legendary ancient Russian fairytale. Its development from the standard accordion, which is broadly represented in Russian folk music, goes back to the early part of the twentieth century. The right side has fifty-two buttons arranged in three rows so that three adjacent steps of the chromatic scale lie diagonally next to each other. The left side with five rows of twenty buttons each provides for simple bass accompaniment and additional bass notes as well as major and minor chord formations. Some bayans for advanced players are equipped with a single bass extension capable of producing chords in various registers as well as polyphonic runs in the bass.[20]

The bayan was enormously popular in the countryside and was a part of every village wedding and festival from Belarus to Siberia. Although a lot of pseudo-folk music and kitsch was written during the Soviet era, one outstanding artist made a name for himself: Vladimir Zolotaryov from Magadan, a good friend of Friedrich Lips. Despite his considerable talent as a composer, Zolotaryov had not passed the entrance examination for the Moscow Conservatory, as he was unable to play his music on the piano. Khrennikov, however, accepted him into his composition class despite Zolotaryov's failure to complete the examination. But a year later he quit his studies. He was thin-skinned and resented everything related to the Soviet system. In those years he gave *samizdat* editions of Solzhenitsyn and Nietzsche's *Zarathustra* to his friend Lips, and on one occasion told him: "You have to make sure that our dream of having Denisov, Schnittke, and Gubaidulina write something for the bayan will come true." In the winter of 1974–75 he tried to gain admission into the Composers Union and asked Friedrich Lips to play his Third Sonata for Bayan at a crucial meeting of the Composers Union of the Russian Federation [Soiuz kompozitorov Rossiiskoi Federatsii]. A month earlier the Moscow chapter had been unable to arrive at a decision about his membership. Grigory Frid presided over the meeting of the Russian Union, which was attended by about thirty members, including Artyomov and Gubaidulina. Zolotaryov's piece made a strong impression and proved his personal—though not strictly academic—talent. Most of those present spoke in his favor, as did Artyomov and Gubaidulina, who stood up at the end to congratulate him and to thank Lips. But his story finally ended in tragedy: a few months after this meeting, in May 1975, Zolotaryov committed suicide at the young age of thirty-three. It has remained unclear to this day whether he ever succeeded in gaining admission to the Composers Union.

At that same meeting Lips asked Gubaidulina what she thought about the bayan and whether she would write a piece for it. "I would gladly write a work for the bayan," she replied, "but I must familiarize myself with this instrument, that is to say, I do not know it at all."[21] As Lips later recalled, their collaboration began soon thereafter:

> She came to see me at the [Gnesin] Institute, in the classroom, and at home. I naturally explained to her all the possibilities of the instrument. ... However, I was astonished how pedantically she asked about all the details, how meticulously she probed every detail which seemed of little importance to us bayan players. She was striving, one can say, to penetrate under the hide of this monster (as she subsequently called the bayan) and to get to know it from inside.[22]

After Gubaidulina had completed her first composition for bayan, *De profundis*, in 1978, she took the score to Lips at the Gnesin Institute and played it for him on the piano. Lips later recalled:

> I was enchanted not only with the music, but also how well she used the reeds of the bayan which showed the acoustic potential of the instrument in a fresh new way. At my request she introduced for the first time into Russian musical literature the tonal *glissando* [for the bayan]. Of course I had to make some editorial corrections, when working on this piece, to ... make the notation more comfortable for bayan players, but this was not work, but a pleasure.[23]

Since the early 1980s Lips has played this piece, which was dedicated to him, "hundreds of times in the USSR and other countries."[24] Accordionists and bayanists of many different countries have played it as well, among them Elsbeth Moser (Switzerland), Teodoro Anzellotti (Italy), Stefan Hussong (Germany), and Mie Miki (Japan). Gubaidulina's second piece for bayan, *Et exspecto* [*resurrectionem mortuorum*], a sonata in five movements also written for Friedrich Lips, was composed in 1985. When she met with him at that time to discuss various aspects of the new work, she pointed to the instrument and said: "Do you know why I love this monster so much? Because it breathes."[25]

Mie Miki gave an account in 1994 of how she experienced the quasi-religious music of *Et exspecto* from the perspective of her own different cultural background. She spoke at a concert discussion in Krefeld, Germany, in response to a question from the audience as to whether she tried to give this work her own interpretation or sought to convey the composer's interpretation. She, too, spoke about the bayan as a breathing instrument:

> This piece spoke to me because I sense three elements. First, something beautiful, something good, even something sacred. Second, something dark and disturbing. These opposite characteristics are always within us, within society, in our life as a whole, and these two elements are here juxtaposed. For me, it

means something like heaven and earth. The third element is breath—the wind that connects heaven and earth. The music begins in a very high, bright register and descends down to earth as with the wind. And when it lands on earth, that's the beginning of the drama. . . . The contrasts become sharper and sharper from one movement to the next until blocks of chords appear in the fourth movement. The chords are played in different ways, and I see them as columns, columns connecting heaven and earth. At times they are beautiful, sacred tonal columns and sometimes they are dissonant clusters. And then they appear like columns at a great distance. The actual distance does not change, but we experience the soft tones as far away, the loud ones as nearby. So there are many perspectives in these columns of sound that are placed into space, and this solid material always has a tendency to become fluid. At the end, the clusters sound like streaming lava. . . . I am particularly fascinated by the last movement. The three levels have been completely dissolved here, and the tones are actually floating through space. The right and the left hands are playing entirely different tempi. If you play the same tempo on both sides, you can stand firmly on the earth, but with two different tempi it all dissolves. Playing this, I have thought of landscapes in deep snow. Snowflakes fall, but when the wind blows, they also fly crisscross. Here everything goes down, deeper and deeper, and finally disappears as it returns into the earth. These mental images have been a strong inspiration for me and have given me the strength to express myself through this instrument. These buttons are so tiny, they are nothing . . . but when the music pours forth I feel such a cosmic grandeur that I feel I am touching something infinite, reaching infinity itself. That's why I like to play this piece so much.[26]

Introitus: The Beginning of a New Cycle of Works

When Pyotr Meshchaninov returned from concert tours with the State Symphony Orchestra of the USSR, he often brought forbidden books with him: Berdyaev, Avtorkhanov, and Solzhenitsyn in Russian-language editions, or music literature, such as Stockhausen's commentaries on music. Among these, in the early 1970s, was a volume on the music of the Middle Ages, part of an East German music encyclopedia,[27] which he showed to Gubaidulina some time after the performance of the Bassoon Concerto. "This might interest you," he said, and called her attention to the Proper of the Catholic Mass, which consists of four parts with changing texts appropriate to the time of the liturgical year: Introit, Offertory, Gradual, and Communion. About a year later, when Alexander Bakhchiev asked Gubaidulina for a work for piano and chamber orchestra, she decided to try her hand at the first part of the Proper.

In 1977 the conductor Yury Nikolaevsky founded the chamber ensemble Ricercar, and they performed a number of works by Bach and his sons, with Alexander Bakhchiev and his wife, Elena Sorokina, as piano soloists. Bakhchiev had heard Gubaidulina a few years earlier when she played her *Musical Toys* in Frid's club. "That evening," he later commented,

> Alexei Liubimov played a piece by Cage, Victoria Ivanova sang Debussy, and I played something by Mozart. Sofia's performance and the special expression on her face, reflecting both the composer and the interpreter, left a strong impression on me. She was completely natural and so was the music, and her playing revealed her exquisite sense of tone. She gave each passage the same attention regardless of whether it was fast or slow. Later I heard some of her other works, but I did not have a clear sense of her as a composer. When I asked her for a composition in 1977—Yury Nikolaevsky and I thought of it at the same time—I had no great hopes. But only a short while later Sonia informed me that she had completed *Introitus*.[28]

With this work for piano and chamber orchestra, Gubaidulina returned for the first time since 1965 to the piano as the featured instrument. For several years she had concentrated on unusual instruments that had rarely been used by soloists—percussion, string bass, trombone, bassoon, and bass clarinet. Furthermore, this attempt at finding a musical rendition for the spiritual meaning of the opening Introit of the Mass represents the beginning of an important cycle of compositions, for *De profundis, In croce, Offertorium, Descensio,* and *Seven Words* were soon to follow. The religious content—always present, even if not explicitly stated—manifests itself in the titles as well as in the complex use of instrumental and compositional symbols. In *Introitus*, Gubaidulina worked with two themes. The first of these consists of three adjacent tones in each of four different pitch realms: microchromatic (quarter tones), chromatic, diatonic, and pentatonic. By establishing different motifs, these tones create different acoustic spaces or types of experience, ranging from the microchromatic as the most sensuous to the pentatonic as the most spiritual. The last part of this work achieves a unification of these pitch realms. The second theme consists of minor and major thirds. A trill extending over several measures at the end embodies Gubaidulina's memory of the mullah's recitative in a Leningrad mosque; it focuses the mind in contemplation and prepares it for the spirit of the Mass.

Bakhchiev's response to this new work was like that of so many other interpreters of her music of the 1970s and later: they had to deal with an entirely new type of music and instrumental playing. "We went through many rehearsals with Sonia, because" he later said,

> *Introitus* is not a common piece of piano music. It requires exceptionally airy, immaterial playing, which she showed me because it came quite naturally to her. But I had to learn it and get used to it, and at the first performance I succeeded only partially. An Introit is the beginning, the introductory item, of the Mass,

but the Mass, of course, does not take place in the work itself; and it is difficult to move toward something that does not actually occur but must be prepared for spiritually. This preparation has to take shape in the course of about twenty minutes, and the audience expects something, but nothing tangible happens. I've played this concerto on several occasions and in each instance, no matter whether the audience was made up of professional musicians or the general public, the long trill at the end would be followed by a long silence. The audience was as under a spell . . . and then they burst out in applause.[29]

The premiere of *Introitus* on the evening of February 22, 1978, in the Hall of the Composers Union was an important event. Part of Denisov's series of "New Works by Moscow Composers," the program also comprised three other premieres: Elena Firsova's *Postludium* for harp and orchestra, Victor Suslin's Violin Concerto, and Viacheslav Artyomov's *Elegies I–III,* as well as the Russian premiere of Denisov's *Aquarelle* for strings. With the hall filled to the last seat and virtually the entire phalanx of unofficial composers present, Alexander Ivashkin gave the introduction. At the celebration after the performance in the restaurant of the Composers Union, Vladislav Shoot stepped up to the table and rather crudely expressed the significance of the occasion by saying, "If a bomb were to go off in here, it would be the end of Russian music."

A Visitor from East Berlin and *Bacchanal,* a Work after a Poem by Boris Pasternak

Things seemed to move along nicely for Gubaidulina in 1978. In September the official state recording company Melodya, issued *Detto II,* with Ivan Monighetti and Yury Nikolaevsky.[30] After the premiere of *Introitus,* several others followed during the fall and winter. Gubaidulina greatly appreciated Denisov's willingness to include nonconformist composers in his series "New Works by Moscow Composers," even though these performances were ostensibly open only to members of the Composers Union. But anyone with enough determination and skill usually succeeded in being admitted—although these special admissions always remained exceptions. On October 11, as previously noted, Gubaidulina's Flute Quartet had its first performance in Denisov's series; and on November 27 Valery Popov and his student, Alexander Kochetkov, performed her *Duo-sonata* for two bassoons.[31]

Less than a week later, on December 3, 1978, the musicologist Hannelore Gerlach came to visit Gubaidulina from East Berlin. She was on one of her visits to Moscow to conduct interviews and collect material for her book *Fünfzig sowjetische Komponisten der Gegenwart: Fakten und Reflexionen: eine Dokumentation*

(1984). Gerlach worked on this volume for many years, eventually producing the only detailed and reliable source of information about both establishment and nonconformist composers of the Soviet Union. (The chapter on Arvo Pärt had to be removed later, after the composer had emigrated to West Germany in 1980.) Gerlach's visit on December 3, 1978, in the apartment at No. 2 Pugachovskaya ulitsa, was to be the only meeting between Gerlach and Gubaidulina; but Gerlach's notebook, in which she recorded many of her other interviews and conversations in the Soviet Union, contains no extant notes of this meeting. At the end of the interview Gubaidulina requested the opportunity to think more carefully about Gerlach's questions and to prepare written answers, which Gerlach later received. They are a succinct and clear expression of Gubaidulina's views as a composer, and two passages in particular have to this day been quoted in countless articles and program notes:

> In my opinion, the ideal relationship between traditional and modern compositional techniques is for the composer to be in complete command of all methods—new as well as traditional—but in such a way as not to emphasize either one over the other. There are composers who construct their works very consciously; but I belong to those who are more inclined to let their works "grow." That is why the entire world I apprehend is like the roots of a tree, and the work growing from them its branches and leaves. You can see them as something new, but they are still leaves, and from this perspective they are always old and traditional.
>
> Do I wish to influence the business of the world through art? I am more concerned with affecting the spiritual element in our lives. But this element constantly and at all times demands concrete representation, materialization. Imagine a cessation of this representation at some time or some place. It would be the instant cessation of a natural life process.
>
> The new interest in tonality and thematic development has led to the use of simpler forms (stanzaic form, rondo, and the ostinato principle), to contemplation and meditation (in contrast to the expressivity of the preceding period), and finally to a fondness for retrospection. I believe there are two reasons for this: (1) a certain fatigue of thought, the need to pause before great eruptions; (2) the search for a sharp contrast with traditional materials. Retrospection and simpler forms have the effect of the unexpected.
>
> Dmitri Shostakovich and Anton Webern had the greatest influence on my work. Although their influence has left no obvious traces in my music, these two composers have taught me what is most important of all: to be myself.[32]

The winter of 1978–79 was extremely harsh, the coldest winter in many years, and in the second half of December the temperature plunged to minus forty Celsius. During this cold spell, on December 10, another work by Gubaidulina had its premiere at the Gnesin Institute: *Bacchanal,* for soprano voice, saxophone quartet (with passages for clarinets), bayan, and percussion. The musicians were Anna Soboleva (soprano); the Lev Mikhailov saxophone quartet; Vladimir Dolgopolov, a student of Lips (bayan); and Mark Pekarsky (percussion). Lips himself was on a concert tour and therefore unavailable. *Bacchanal* stands at the beginning of a group of works that coincide in time with works bearing religious titles. In this second group Gubaidulina turned to poems by Pasternak, Francisco Tanzer, Marina Tsvetaeva, and T. S. Eliot. She was drawn to some of these texts because of personal acquaintance with the authors, to others because of their inherently compelling themes.

Pasternak's *Bacchanal* [*Vakkhanaliia*] opens with an evening candlelight service in the Boris and Gleb Church while a furious blizzard is blowing outside. It is a wintry bacchanal that is enacted also on two other levels: at a performance of Schiller's heroic tragedy, *Maria Stuart,* at the theater and at a grand evening gala, where a gray-haired ladies' man meets a dancing girl and spends the night with her. The poem ends with a coda: the scent of roses supersedes the human passions of the night.

The evening's performance, however, turned into a minor disaster. The conductor, Konstantin Kremets, had come down with the flu and asked Pyotr Meshchaninov at the beginning of dress rehearsal to take his place only briefly. But Kremets never returned, and Meshchaninov was forced to plunge cold into the performance. During the snowstorm the saxophones were supposed to play airy, whirling, effervescent passages, but the musicians were used to traditional instrumental performance styles and therefore hardly able to render this atmosphere of attenuated overtones—it was more like rocks being hurled. To make matters worse, the soprano's overly dramatic style was entirely inappropriate. In some passages her voice was to be amplified by microphone so as not to be drowned out by the saxophones, and Gubaidulina had hired a technician to handle the controls. Having spent his wages on vodka in advance, he showed up drunk for the performance and forgot to switch on the microphone. Pasternak's poem consists of fifty-one quatrains (of which Gubaidulina deleted two) and a coda, which—in its musical rendition—effectively resolves the dramatic snowstorm in an atmosphere of quiet transfiguration. However, the excessive length of the work, combined with all the other problems of the performance, doomed its success. The experience was so painful for Gubaidulina that she struck *Bacchanal* from her list of works, never to be reminded of it again.

Music and Symbol:
A Higher World in Images of the Material World

Late in February 1979 Vladimir Tonkha phoned Gubaidulina with a request: "A month from now I am giving a concert in Kazan and I would like to play a piece by you for cello and organ. Could you write one for me?" The idea of writing a piece for Tonkha inspired her, and having no other obligations at the moment she immediately went to work and completed the new piece in twenty-six days. Carrying the score with her, she traveled to Kazan two days before the concert, and Tonkha and the Tatar organist Rubin Abdullin performed the work in the Hall of the Conservatory on March 27. The program consisted of other works, original or arrangements, for cello and organ by Bach, Isaac, Respighi and Marais—and, of course, the premiere of Gubaidulina's *In croce*. Abdullin, who later became the director of the Kazan Conservatory, commented on the rehearsals:

> When Sofia arrived she was a little worried and quite nervous, as the piece was something radically new for Kazan. Her position in Kazan was not exactly very solid. Vladimir Tonkha and I thoroughly discussed the work with her, and each of us spoke out on behalf of "his instrument." In only two words Sofia explained her composition to us: *In croce!* We rehearsed for the better part of two nights leading up to the concert, and we developed a highly creative and interesting working relationship. Then came the performance. It was—contrary to all expectations—a great success.[33]

The clear and simple form as well as the emotional power of the new work directly affected the audience. Sofia's parents had come to the performance accompanied by one her father's sisters, who wept as she thanked Sofia afterward. The juxtaposition of the two "instrumental personalities," the cello and the organ, is a model of the musical symbolism that characterizes the new creative phase that began with *Introitus*.

"In that particular combination I imagined the organ as a mighty spirit that sometimes descends to earth to vent its wrath," Gubaidulina tells us.

> The cello, on the other hand, with its sensitively responsive strings is a completely human spirit. The contrast between these two opposite natures is resolved spontaneously in the symbol of the cross. I accomplished this first of all by crisscrossing the registers (the organ takes the line downward, the cello upward); secondly, by juxtaposing the bright major sonorities of natural harmonics, played *glissando,* and expressive chromatic inflections. At the beginning of the piece, the bright sonorities are entrusted to the organ. The line moves from the higher register downward, while the cello concentrates on expressive chromatics, moving from the lower register upward. At the end of the piece, the instruments

change roles: the cello arrives at the bright natural harmonics in its highest register, while the organ, in contrast, descends into its nether regions with the lowest possible tone clusters.[34]

For Gubaidulina, the symbol is not simply an expedient compositional tactic but an essential element of her philosophy. In music, it can become the meeting point between this world and the transcendent world, thereby enabling "the comprehension of a higher reality in images of the physical, material world."[35] The symbol as intersection between spiritual life and earthly life permeates Russian artistic expression in many different forms, from the world of icons to Malevich's *Black Square* [*Chërnyi kvadrat*], and it becomes a philosophical issue in Florensky and Berdyaev. The religious aura that had begun to infuse Gubaidulina's musical material, starting with *Concordanza* in 1971, now evolved into consciously constructed symbols through the rendition of form and the use of unconventional performance techniques.

Less than six months after the premiere in Kazan, a second organ work by Gubaidulina had its first performance in the Small Hall of the Moscow Conservatory. Encouraged by her success in the Tatar capital, Gubaidulina phoned the organist and composer Tatiana Sergeeva to ask if she would like to perform *Detto I*, her 1969 piece for organ to which she had meanwhile added a percussion part. As Sergeeva later recalled:

> Sofia Gubaidulina came with her score to Rozhdestvensky's conducting class, where I was working as a pianist. In reference to the beginning of the work, she said: "Play it very freely, like improvisation." Yet there is no *rubato* indication in this score, and the end is very rhythmic. For the performance, the percussionist Victor Grishin was missing the oriental *byan chung*, an instrument Sofia owned, but it was always very difficult to reach her by phone.[36]

On October 14, 1979, Tatiana Sergeeva and Victor Grishin performed *Detto II*, for percussion and organ, as part of the first International Festival of Contemporary Music, "Moscow Autumn" [Mezhdunarodnyi festival' sovremennoi muzyki, "Moskovskaia osen'"]. Whereas cello and organ had been used as contrasting instruments in *In croce*, percussion and organ were now complementing each other, as the composer later explained: "The organ harbors within itself the sounds of an entire orchestra, except for the timbre of the percussion. . . . For me, the organ is an instrument that is above earthly life, whereas the percussion instruments are the Great Mystery of the Earth and . . . perhaps of the Underworld. The organ along with percussion somehow connect Heaven and Earth."[37]

A New Acquaintance: Francisco Tanzer

During March 23–25, 1979, Westdeutscher Rundfunk Köln (West German Radio Cologne) had organized a weekend "Begegnung mit der Sowjetunion"; the program was arranged by Detlef Gojowy, with Jürgen Köchel as an adviser. Except for Shostakovich, most of the composers named in the program were familiar only to specialists. The music of the early Soviet era and the two generations that followed had yet to be discovered in the West. The first concert in the series presented works with percussion and began with Gubaidulina's Five Etudes for Harp, Double Bass, and Percussion. The next day the Arcis Quartet played the premiere of Gubaidulina's as yet unnumbered String Quartet of 1971, and it was during that afternoon dedicated to string quartets that the foundation was laid for an inspiring new relationship in the composer's life. It so happened that Edison Denisov, waiting for the performance of his own Double Concerto for Flute and Oboe that same evening, was in the afternoon audience together with Francisco Tanzer, a poet from Düsseldorf. Tanzer had met Denisov and Schnittke on one of their visits to Germany and had discussed his poetry with the two composers. In fact, the previous year Denisov had written a song cycle using Tanzer's poems.[38] Attracted by the seriousness of these two composers who did their creative work under such trying conditions, Tanzer was planning to take his first trip to Moscow in the summer. Gubaidulina's String Quartet impressed him as a powerful and independent work, and when he asked Denisov whether it would be possible to meet the composer in Moscow and talk with him, Denisov replied: "This composer is a she, not a he."

Alfred Schnittke made the introduction in Moscow, and this meeting with the German poet was the beginning of Gubaidulina's intensive study of Tanzer's texts and eventually led to two new compositions. Born in Vienna and raised in Budapest, Tanzer had the proverbial charm of the Austrians. In 1941, after Hitler's troops had marched into Austria, his family left for Paris and eventually landed in New York via Portugal. His parents knew Bruno Walter, and Tanzer read Proust, Joyce, and Musil, besides being fond of music. A year later he enlisted in the U.S. Army, worked as a translator in a German POW camp, and at the end of war served as an officer of the U.S. occupation forces in Germany. After his return to the United States, he enrolled as a student of literature at Columbia University and began work on a novel about his experiences between two cultures and two military fronts. In 1956 he settled in Düsseldorf, writing novellas and poems, in which he reflects upon his life experiences in a deeply humanistic spirit from many different perspectives. His plays for television and radio as well as the stage versions of some of his prose writings were later followed by music for ballets written in collaboration with Manfred Niehaus and Klaus Ager. Tanzer died in October 2003.

Tanzer saw Gubaidulina as a person who had remained unsullied by ideological pressures, someone who had suffered under imposed isolation. She played for him from Bach's *Kunst der Fuge* and was delighted to receive as a present his recently published volume, *Stimmen*—the first collection of his diaries, prose writings, and poetry. Tanzer also brought with him a commission for a piece of chamber music that Klaus Ager, the artistic director of the Salzburg Neue-Musik-Festival "Aspekte Salzburg," wanted to include in the next year's program. Gubaidulina asked Tanzer for an appropriate text for this work and, after his return to Germany, received from him three miniatures: a short passage about music by Robert Musil; his own words, *Anwesende Abwesenheit—abwesende Anwesenheit* (Present absence—absent presence); and a two-line text from his *Journal,* which he had written in September 1943 in response to looking at a watch tower. Gubaidulina later chose these two lines for a spoken ad-lib coda for the new piece. All this set in motion an exchange of letters between Moscow and Düsseldorf that was carried on for years.

A Season of Soviet Music in Paris

In 1979 Gubaidulina established a new and closer relationship with Germany, and she enjoyed her first major success abroad at an important concert in Paris. During the second phase of an ambitiously conceived cultural exchange program between the Soviet Union and France, Paris became a center for Soviet painting and music between the end of May and the beginning of November. The Pushkin Museum of Fine Arts [Gosudarstvennyi muzei izobrazitel'nykh iskusstv imeni A. S. Pushkina] and the Centre Pompidou had jointly arranged "Paris-Moscou," a large exhibition of French and Soviet art during the first third of the twentieth century. It had first been shown in Moscow and then moved to Paris. A concert series under the direction of Pierre Boulez and IRCAM (Institut de Recherche et Coordination Acoustique/Musique) was part of the events in Paris. However, frictions soon developed with Moscow, as Boulez refused to have the Composers Union have any say in the program, and in the end the program became IRCAM's sole responsibility. A musical high point of these months was the much anticipated concert of contemporary Soviet orchestral music on October 22, 1979. IRCAM and Radio-Télévision Française had invited the Kölner Rundfunksymphonieorchester directed by Antoni Witt to play the French premieres of Silvestrov's Second Symphony, Schnittke's *Pianissimo,* and Denisov's Violin Concerto (with Gidon Kremer) as well as the world premiere of Gubaidulina's *Percussio di Pekarski.*

The score of Gubaidulina's work had reached her Hamburg publisher quite miraculously. One of the women working for VAAP [Vsesoiuznoe agenstvo avtorskikh prav (Soviet Agency for Foreign Copyrights)] had taken her aside and whispered in her ear, "Sidnikov would like to take some scores with him to the West," and then asked for the score of *Percussio di Pekarski* (her 1976 first reworking of *Hour of the Soul* for symphony orchestra, percussion solo, and mezzo-soprano). Vasily Sidnikov, then the director of VAAP, was a person of exceptional culture and education. He spoke excellent German and was known for his witty toasts at dinners and his ability to quote works of literature. He was accepting of modern artistic trends perhaps because his son was a nonconformist painter.[39] Besides, VAAP and the Composers Union competed with each other in the collection of foreign currencies: VAAP was always interested in having Soviet works performed abroad because it received royalties. Actual performance permissions, however, were issued by the Composers Union—and the latter was interested in promoting only performances of works by loyal functionaries, who were of no great interest to Western concert organizers. Gubaidulina's mood in those days was so dejected, however, that she was ready for any risk and therefore delivered her score to VAAP. Jürgen Köchel later talked about how the score finally reached the publisher:

> Our publishing company had ordered a number of works from VAAP for performances at festivals in both Cologne and Paris. But our request was denied. About two weeks later Sidnikov called us. He was planning a trip to Hamburg and asked for a hotel reservation and an appointment with the Rowohlt Publishing Company, which handled his German-Russian translation of Rolf Hochhuth. I picked him up at the airport, loaded his suitcases into the car, and took him to his hotel after a meal and his appointment with Rowohlt. At the hotel, Sidnikov looked surprised when he saw a second suitcase, and said: "This doesn't belong to me"—winking at me as he spoke. When I opened the suitcase in my office, I found all the music that we had unsuccessfully requested from VAAP.[40]

The Cologne Radio people had not dared to ask Mark Pekarsky (to whom the piece was dedicated) to be the percussionist because Boulez had warned them: "Don't touch it. You'll first get their consent, but a day before the performance they'll send a telegram that the soloist is indisposed."[41] Thus it was Christoph Caskel, a well-known percussionist and specialist in postwar music from Cologne, who played in the premiere; the soprano part was sung by Marie-Louise Gilles. The audience for that evening's performance filled the large auditorium of Radio France [Radiodiffusion Française] to the last seat, including IRCAM's officials as well as numerous composers, all expecting to be introduced to the contemporary school of Soviet serialism. But it was a great disappointment, as these Russian avant-gardists, compared to their Western counterparts, "looked more like arrière-gardists—and entirely to their honor," in the words of André Lischke, a reviewer of the evening's performance.

> Her [Gubaidulina's] work suggests none of that craving for originality, particularly none of that strange mixture of cynicism and confusion that is evident in the works of some of her Western contemporaries. There is also no dogmatism—twelve-tone technique is a means, not an end in itself. Her efforts are aimed not at making strenuous new demands on our ears but at achieving a self-contained beauty of sound. Listening to her works, one can feel a vibrant, rich compositional spirit that is based on a solid and entirely traditional foundation of the composer's craft, particularly a sensitive and thorough knowledge of instrumentation. That, by the way, has always been a peculiar attribute of the Russian school, from Glinka to Stravinsky, and beyond.[42]

Lischke later said that *Percussio di Pekarski* was the main reason for the evening's success, possibly because it was written by a woman.[43] The reviewer for *Le Monde,* Gérard Condé, also had a favorable opinion of Gubaidulina's work: "Although the beginning offers little expectation of a virtuoso concert, one gradually discovers an inspired composition that does not content itself with simply stringing together notes for better or for worse, but infuses them with meaning."[44] Kolya Bokov was also in the audience that evening and later reported to Gubaidulina in Moscow on the successful performance of her work.

After this promising event in Paris, the pendulum of fate swung in the opposite direction, when the Sixth All-Union Congress of the Composers Union met in the Kremlin Palace of Congresses [Kremlëvskii Dvorets s"ezda] on November 10–16, 1979. For some time Gubaidulina had paid no attention to such official Party events, but this congress had unexpected consequences for her and six other composers. At the opening of these congresses in Brezhnev's presence, Tikhon Khrennikov, the head of the Union, normally read a long report, and every name he mentioned was calculated either for praise or for reprimand. This particular year he attacked the "bad habit" that was spreading in the West of performing the works of nonconformist composers under the rubric of Soviet music. He scolded critics who were sitting idly by, fulminated against the Cologne program "Begegnung mit der Sowjetunion," and then mentioned the names of seven composers, "on whom the organizers bestowed the honor of calling them the Soviet avant-garde: Elena Firsova, Dmitri Smirnov, Alexander Knaifel, Victor Suslin, Viacheslav Artyomov, Sofia Gubaidulina, and Edison Denisov. This constellation is a bit one-sided, is it not?"[45] Published excerpts of Khrennikov's speech in all important newspapers publicized the names of the seven composers, who were privately referred to as the "Khrennikov Seven." The publicity campaign had its desired effect; in Kazan neighbors spoke to Sofia's parents about "this disgrace." Her father said that he was "ashamed of his daughter," and the daughter replied that "an artist's position is not a bed of roses." It was not until the early 1990s that Asgad Gubaidullin gained the necessary distance to look at the situation objectively: "I realize now that I toed the line during the communist period. I was then of the opinion that if everyone thought her music was bad, why should I think she wrote good music? I was a Party loyalist. In those days that wasn't just a question of music, because naturally I know little about music. But I refused to be loyal to my daughter. Today I see my mistake."[46] The blacklisting, however, had not nearly the same dramatic impact as in 1948; in fact, Leonid Hrabovsky, a friend and fellow composer from Kiev, went so far as to say, "I envy you all this publicity." As for Gubaidulina, Khrennikov's speech affected her only in one specific way: she lost her position on the Advisory Council of the state publishing house, "Sovetskii Kompozitor." Permissions for travel and performances were also noticeably harder to obtain for the next two years.

In retrospect, it is difficult to understand why Khrennikov chose precisely these seven names. The works of other, equally nonconformist composers such as Pärt, Schnittke, and Silvestrov had also been performed, and one has to assume that Khrennikov was either completely or largely unfamiliar with the works of the seven he named. Perhaps his ghostwriter simply liked the number seven, or perhaps it is mere coincidence that the list includes all six composers on the program of the first concert in Cologne as well as Edison Denisov, whom Khrennikov suspected of having conveyed the scores to the West.[47] Envy and competitiveness aside, this had nothing to do with music. It was all a matter of communist ideology: any act of personal freedom was seen as an affront to the system.

For Gubaidulina, this speech was the beginning of two particularly difficult years, and, for Victor Suslin, it was the beginning of the end. He applied for permission to emigrate, as he was no longer willing to suffer further humiliation, harassment, and censorship. As he later stated: "Khrennikov said in his speech that our compositions were being performed too often. But I had only one or two performances a year. If that was too many, it probably meant that I shouldn't be played at all."[48] As a postlude to the "Paris-Moscou" festival, and only three days after the All-Union Congress, on November 19, 1979, the French Ensemble 2e2m gave a concert in Moscow. In France it was second only to the Ensemble InterContemporain as the most distinguished group performing contemporary music. The Moscow performance presented an all-French program under the direction of the composer Paul Méfano, the ensemble's artistic director.[49] With Denisov as translator, the Composers Union had a grand reception for the French artists, and a small group—Gubaidulina, Schnittke, Yury Kasparov, and a few other composers—continued the celebration at Denisov's apartment well into the night. It was on this occasion that Gubaidulina personally met the man who had commissioned her Flute Quartet: Pierre-Yves Artaud played flute for 2e2m, and he remembered Gubaidulina from that evening as a "dynamic and courageous woman." The events of the preceding day had left no visible marks on her. For Gubaidulina, the meeting with Paul Méfano on that same evening resulted in a commissioned work for 2e2m.

During the last week of the year, on December 24, 1979, Soviet troops invaded Afghanistan, setting off a debilitating war. The Brezhnev government and the Communist Party adhered to the political status quo with unyielding tenacity, pushing their ideology with undiminished ferocity. Khrennikov's speech with its attack on the nonconformists was part of the political atmosphere in which Gubaidulina wrote her next work.

9 | *Offertorium*—A Musical Offering, 1979–1981

A Forgotten Commission

The year from late spring 1979 to March 1980 was a crucial period and a high point in Sofia Gubaidulina's life. All the recent events previously described—the meeting with Francisco Tanzer, the commission for Salzburg, the first success abroad in Paris, and the condemnation by Tikhon Khrennikov—form the background to the composition of an outstanding work that was to make the composer famous far beyond the borders of the Soviet Union. In October 1980 Gubaidulina would be forty-nine years old, at the end of another seven-year life cycle, and therefore in a phase that heretofore would have pointed to another critical conflict between the verticality of her emotional life and the horizontality of her intellect. Instead, both intuition and reason came together in *Offertorium*, a violin concerto she wrote twenty-one years after graduating from the Moscow Conservatory. The story of how this work came into being begins with a brief prelude.

Probably in the winter of 1977–78 (the participants' memories are somewhat vague as to the precise date), Gubaidulina and Gidon Kremer happened to share a taxi after a concert. It may have been after a performance at Grigory Frid's Moscow Youth Musical Club when the violinist, just on the verge of gaining worldwide renown, said to the composer: "Wouldn't you like to write a violin concerto?" Being a friend of Schnittke and always interested in new pieces, he had performed works by both Schnittke and Denisov, but he was hardly familiar with Gubaidulina's music. Among the few, albeit memorable, impressions he had was the performance of her Sonata for Double Bass and Piano played by Anatoly Grindenko and Gubaidulina at the Composers Union in 1975. Being a string player, he had been impressed by this piece, as "it brought out entirely new sounds and explored the possibilities of the string bass in remarkably original

148

ways."[1] By the end of 1977 Kremer had finally achieved sufficient status—partly based on Herbert von Karajan's comment after Kremer's first London performance that Kremer was "the world's greatest violinist"—to obtain official Soviet approval to concertize freely in the East and West for two years. He gave more than two hundred performances in twenty-five countries, several of them in Moscow and throughout the Soviet Union.[2]

The spontaneous request in the taxicab was a significant event for Gubaidulina, although Kremer soon forgot it in the whirl of his many concert and recording obligations. She greatly admired Kremer both as an artist and as a person, and used every possible opportunity to attend his performances so that she could study "his musical signature." One of the first things she noticed was how Kremer handled extreme opposites and the transitions between them: "From the most delicate, barely audible heartfelt emotion to virtuosic, almost ecstatic playfulness, from dramatic expressivity and sorrowful lamentation to light-hearted dance, from demonic aggressiveness to profound prayerful contemplation."[3] She thought that the most impressive aspect of his playing was his tone. When his finger touched the string she could sense that his entire life energy was focused on this single point: "In this union of the tip of the finger and the resonating string lies the total surrender of the self to the tone. And I began to understand that Kremer's theme is sacrifice—the musician's sacrifice of himself in self-surrender to the tone."[4] The impression Kremer's performances made in the West can be gleaned from a review by Joachim Kaiser, who described an experience similar to Gubaulina's in somewhat different words: "Since my first encounter with Fischer-Dieskau or Maurizio Pollini I have not experienced anything like it. ... It was almost as if this violinist, instead of playing on strings, was making music on his nerves. There wasn't a single note that was all puffed up with that boring yet enviable self-confidence that we know from young Russian prize-winning musicians. Every note vibrated with originality, tenderness, and breathtaking finesse."[5]

Within a single minute, literally, when everything came together, this experience of "the musician's sacrifice of himself in self-surrender to the tone" spawned an idea in Gubaidulina's "vertical" consciousness for a new work. It combined the complex concept of sacrifice as well as the entire composition: "The sacrificial offering of Christ's crucifixion. ... God's offering as He created the world. ... The offering of the artist, the performing violinist. ... The composer's offering,"[6] and, finally (on the level of the music itself), the manner in which the theme offers itself sacrificially. When Gubaidulina told Pyotr Meshchaninov about the central idea of "offering" for her violin concerto, he suggested that she use the "royal theme" of Bach's *Das musikalische Opfer* and transform it.[7]

The violin concerto consists of three continuous movements. In the first movement the theme disintegrates step by step in a succession of variations; in each instance, one single note of the theme is omitted at both the beginning and the end, until, in the second movement, which is not thematically related, only the pitch E remains. "You cannot be reborn until you have died." In the third movement, in the "Chorale," a seemingly new theme emerges one note at a time in the bass line of the harp and the piano, which eventually—in the closing violin passage—turns out to be the original theme in retrograde. "The first shall be last, and the last shall be first."

The work had been completed in outline when Meshchaninov and Gubaidulina talked about it again in Vishnyovka near the town of Tuapse on the Black Sea in the summer of 1979. Meshchaninov suggested that the ascending melody of the solo violin at the end of the deeply devotional "Chorale" be set against descending motion in the piano. Having been named *Offertorium,* the concerto became the second of Gubaidulina's works, after *Introitus,* to make reference to the Proper of the Roman Mass. With the choice of Bach's "royal theme," Gubaidulina paid her respects not only to her great model, Bach, but also to Webern. Inspired by Webern's orchestration of the Ricercar from the *Musical Offering,* Bach's "royal theme" is stated in the opening bars of *Offertorium* by winds in succession, most playing but a single note.

After months of hard work, Gubaidulina completed the score in March 1980. Henrietta Mirvis later remembered meeting the exhausted composer at the conservatory, looking as if she had just returned from another sphere, telling her that she had finished the work, remarking: "I carried this world within me for a long time."

A Garden of Western and Eastern Poetry

During periods of intensive work, Gubaidulina could not be distracted by anything or anyone; her only form of relaxation was to take long walks. In times of less pressure, she devoted the first half of each day to composing or playing the piano and the second half to reading. After Franscisco Tanzer's departure, she read his *Stimmen* (Voices) and then turned to *The Revelation of the Rose* [*Otkrovenie rozy*], a prose poem by the Moscow author Ivan Oganov. This historical novel tells the story of the turbulent life of Sayat-Nova, an Armenian lyric poet and folk singer of the eighteenth century who later became a monk. His poetry strongly influenced the literature of the Transcaucasus. Originally from Tblisi, Oganov translated from Spanish and other languages but wrote his own books without any hope of publication. "He loved the arts just as I do," Gubaidulina later commented, "earned a meager living as a teacher, and said to Nadia and me: 'You are the only readers I have.' He would sit for days in the Lenin Library and other places collecting materials for poetic-historical novels."

One day, during the first half of September 1979, while Gubaidulina was reading in Oganov's book about a flowering garden, the telephone rang. Irina Kotkina, the harpist who had founded a trio for flute, harp, and violin, asked whether Gubaidulina would write a trio piece for a concert that would also include trios by Debussy and Denisov. The timing of this request, just between reading Tanzer and the book on Sayat Nova, was perfect. Gubaidulina asked for a brief period to think it over, sketched a compositional concept during the next few hours, and then accepted. "I . . . realized very quickly that the piece was basically ready. It arose from the impression of two poetic worlds that had coalesced within me into the unified image of an Eastern garden where everything lives in the stillness and pain of Francisco Tanzer's Western poems. Thus the opposing elemental essences of East and West quite naturally became one in me."[8]

In a letter of mid-September 1979 Gubaidulina thanked Tanzer for his book, with "whose very thoughtful and delicate sense of life and contemplation" she "felt a certain kinship. Besides, it suggests a beautiful structure of shifting moods."[9] She also inquired whether the work commissioned for Salzburg could be written for flute, viola, and harp [and speaker, *ad libitum*], as she had decided to use the trio requested by Irina Kotkina for Salzburg and to dedicate it to Tanzer. When the trio *Garden of Joy and Sorrow* [*Sad radosti i pechali/Garten von Freuden und Traurigkeiten*] was finished in May 1980, two months after the completion of *Offertorium,* the consequences of Khrennikov's speech played themselves out. As early as January, the Composers Union had insisted that any performance in Salzburg would have to be made conditional on a performance and review in Moscow, and in May Gubaidulina wrote to Tanzer regarding her request for permission to travel to Salzburg: "Unfortunately I will not be able to be at the premiere because my situation is really terrible and there is no chance of getting a travel permit."[10] As a Moscow performance of *Garden of Joy and Sorrow* could not be arranged before "Aspekte Salzburg," Klaus Ager decided to include Gubaidulina's String Quartet in the festival program. Meanwhile, Tanzer's friends in the world of music had officially submitted to VAAP a request for permission to perform the trio abroad; however, in the summer of 1980 the Moscow Composers Union quashed it, causing Gubaidulina to write to Tanzer on August 4:

> It is a pity that our *Garden* is getting into all these difficulties. The problem is that the Agency for Authors' Rights is not permitted to send unperformed works abroad. The proper agency to turn to is the Composers Union. But at that session of the Secretariat twenty requests from abroad were turned down, our *Garden* among them. Perhaps I will be successful in getting the *Garden* performed here in the fall. Then everything will be legal.[11]

But another six months would go by before the trio would perform in Moscow—on February 9, 1981—in the Hall of the Composers Union. As part of

Denisov's series, "New Works by Moscow Composers," the BSO Trio (Bol'shoi [Theater] Symphony Orchestra= Simfonicheskii orkestr Bol'shogo Teatra, the name adopted by Irina Kotkina [harp], Sergei Bubnov [flute], and Mikhail Goudimov [viola]) played works by Valery Kikta, Efrem Podgaits, Moisei Vainberg, and Gubaidulina's *Garden of Joy and Sorrow* during the first half of the program. Kotkina later recalled that the three musicians were surprised by the unexpected explanations Gubaidulina gave when she first came to one of their rehearsals:

> She was friendly and said with a smile that the piece has five waves. The first wave—as she made an accompanying gesture—the second and the third; then she became more intense until she exploded dramatically at the fifth wave, almost shouting to demonstrate the intensification. We were surprised, because she is such a calm and friendly person, but we really got the point. The viola is at the center of the first wave, the flute of the second, the harp of the third—this segment lies at the golden mean. The fourth wave is a major flute cadenza of great expressivity, and the fifth returns to the beginning, to the viola. We had two possible choices for the ending—a flute coda or a German text by Francisco Tanzer. Our first performance ended with the flute coda. Later we also played the piece with the flutist Irina Loben at various unofficial occasions and exhibitions. Her German is very good, and on these occasions she also spoke the German text.[12]

In its modest compositional simplicity, *Garden of Joy and Sorrow* is defined by two elements—chromatic motion in the flute and harmonics in the viola. The work's quasi-Oriental, poetic charm is fresh and natural, a quality that is partly the result of Gubaidulina's work with Astraea. At Francisco Tanzer's initiative, the work had its premiere in Düsseldorf in October 1980.

An Evening at the Youth Club, Film Music, and Skovoroda's Philosophy

Although Khrennikov's speech made life difficult in 1980, some good things were also happening: a concert in Grigory Frid's club, new acquaintances in the world of film, and the beginnings of several new works. On April 8 the Moscow Youth Musical Club dedicated another meet-the-composer evening to Gubaidulina, featuring the premiere of *De profundis,* with Friedrich Lips. Other works on the program were *In croce,* with Vladimir Tonkha and Tatiana Sergeeva (electric organ); *Rumore e silenzio,* with Alexei Liubimov and Mark Pekarsky; and tape recordings of *Vivente—non vivente* and the *Concerto grosso* (Concerto for Symphony Orchestra and Jazz-Band). It was a very successful evening with a standing-room-only audience that received *In croce* with particularly enthusiastic applause.

Some bread-and-butter work for an animated puppet film, *The Puppet Show* (*Balagan,* after Frederico Garcia Lorca's *El Retabillo de Don Cristóbal*), led to a friendship with the film director Ida Garanina, and Gubaidulina soon took a "working vacation" at Garanina's dacha in Korolyovo, a village on the upper Volga. During production, Sofia also got to know the actor and director Rolan Bykov, who spoke the part of the clown (a few years later he asked Gubaidulina to write the score for his feature film *The Scarecrow* [*Chuchelo*]). *The Puppet Show* was a film with and about music in which all characters at some point had to sing. Bykov, who did not read music, sat in a tiny recording studio with a gypsy singer, Valentina Ponomaryova, trying his best. "I was unable to sing the last piece," he later commented, "which required a particular dynamic, and it really bothered me. But Sonia said, 'No need to; just speak it and it'll be fine; that's how we will do it.' But I still know that if I could have sung it, it would have been better. Garanina's film with Gubaidulina's magnificently picturesque music turned out to be excellent. That's probably why it was withheld from the Soviet public and sold to the English—only we got to see it here."[13]

Oleg Kagan and Natalia Gutman, who were married and performed together as a duo, had asked Gubaidulina to write a work for violin and cello that they could perform on their next concert tour. After the strenuous deadline work for *The Puppet Show,* Sofia spent the summer with her sister, Vera, in Ukraine, using her time there to study the writings of Hryhorii Skovoroda (1722–1794), a folksy but highly educated Ukrainian religious philosopher. After completing his studies at the Kiev Academy, he had traveled on foot through large parts of Southeast and Central Europe, eventually realizing that human happiness can be found only through introspection and self-discovery. To find God within himself, he concluded, man needs neither wealth nor fame nor social status. So this "wandering philosopher," as the people called him, made it his motto "To be content with little." Skovoroda was close to the peasants, loved nature and music, and always carried his flute with him. Gubaidulina, while reading his texts and letters, had an idea for the work requested by Natalia Gutman and Oleg Kagan: *Mysterium,* in five movements, each with a title from one of Skovoroda's aphorisms about joy:

> Your joy no man taketh from you
> Rejoice with them that do rejoice
> Rejoice, Rabbi!
> Now he returned into his house
> Listen to the still small voice within

For both Gubaidulina and Skovoroda, joy is not simply a happy feeling or an everyday mood of gladness; it is a matter of inner joy as an idea and a sense of certainty about God's existence.

To express this realm of joy, Gubaidulina used a musical-instrumental symbol that, when she first discovered it, had filled her with enthusiasm. By slightly altering the pressure of one's finger on the string, one can transform the expressive-sensuous tone of the instrument into the ethereal sound of natural harmonics, suggesting a transition from this world to the world above; the performance then becomes a metaphor for Skovoroda's aphorisms. At the same time the five movements of *Mysterium* also subtly suggest an instrumental Mass: Kyrie, Gloria, Credo, Agnus dei, and Gratias.

A year later Gubaidulina was able to present Oleg Kagan and Natalia Gutman with another work for violin and cello, entitled *Rejoice* [*Raduisia*]. Both musicians were then at the beginning of a difficult phase in their lives: their child was suffering from a serious, long-time illness and was in urgent need of surgery, yet the family was not allowed to travel to the West. Gubaidulina's score, therefore, was put on the shelf for a number of years. Not until 1988 did the Kagan/Gutman duo present a sparkling and successful premiere of the work in Kuhmo, Finland—a performance that was widely reviewed in the Finnish press.

The fall of 1980 was a busy and intense period. The music for the animated puppet film was being recorded, and rehearsals of *In croce* with Vladimir Tonkha and Tatiana Sergeeva were proceeding in the Great Hall of the conservatory for a performance at the second Moscow Autumn festival. The days of the festival were especially intense, as friends, acquaintances, and publishers came to visit Moscow. Moreover, Gubaidulina had begun to work on *Rejoice*.

The winter of 1980–81 kept her occupied with a new film score (more about this later in connection with *Offertorium*) and the completion of the piece for Paul Méfano and the Ensemble 2e2m. At the same time Gubaidulina was beginning to think about a new composition using Francisco Tanzer's poetry. On an earlier visit to Moscow, Tanzer had brought a tape recording of his poems and asked Gubaidulina whether she would like to use them for a composition. He had in mind a dialogue between "the poet in Düsseldorf" and "the composer in Moscow"—short piano pieces interspersed among the poems. It was to be a present for his mother in New York. But in February 1981 Gubaidulina selected ten instruments that would respond to the poems in different combinations: flute, harp, harpsichord, two percussionists, and a string quintet.

After completing her piece for 2e2m, she sent that score to Paris, and on April 30 Paul Méfano conducted the premiere of *Descensio,* written for three trombones, three percussionists, piano, celesta, and harp, in a concert by 2e2m at the Centre Pompidou. The program also presented works by Georges Aperghis, Franco Donatoni, Schönberg, and Webern.

Descensio is part of the group of spiritual works ranging from *Introitus* to *Et exspecto,* and on a subliminal level it deals with the experience of Pentacost, the "descent" of the Dove representing the Holy Ghost. As usual, Gubaidulina had followed her own intuition and did not write the new piece specifically for the instrumentation of Méfano's ensemble, and when it came to rehearsals she was not there to explain her intentions. Thus the French ensemble probably counted *Descensio* among the many works of contemporary music requiring more elaborate instrumentation than they normally provided, and Méfano never performed it again. It was not until November 12, 1997, in a performance by the Schönberg Ensemble under the direction of Reinbert de Leeuw in Amsterdam, that Gubaidulina heard her own work for the first time.

Vienna Festwochen 1981: The Premiere of *Offertorium*

The time between writing the final note of the violin concerto, *Offertorium*, and the first performance by Gidon Kremer was a period of great anxiety for Gubaidulina. In the early months of 1980 the Moscow regime had insisted that Kremer return at the end of his two years abroad to subject himself again to the usual conditions of work in the Soviet Union. His refusal and decision to stay in the West caused a major row. For a while Gubaidulina was in a panic, seeing no possibility of getting the score to Kremer and fearing that a performance by the very person to whom she had dedicated her work would prove impossible. Her friends shared her anxiety. On one of his visits to Moscow at that time, Francisco Tanzer spent an evening with Alfred Schnittke, and all they talked about was Gubaidulina's violin concerto and the problem of having it performed, with Schnittke saying: "*Offertorium* is probably the most important violin concerto of this century, but I am afraid it will never be performed."[14] In the ideologically dogmatic Brezhnev era, Gubaidulina's strongly spiritual work, dedicated as it was to Kremer, was a potential powder keg. In one of his reports to the Composers Union at that time, Tikhon Khrennikov criticized the excessive enthusiasm with which some composers resorted to religious themes—and everyone there knew that his remarks were aimed at Gubaidulina.[15] Seeing no other way out, she decided to give the score to Jürgen Köchel, her publisher, to smuggle it out of the country on his return from the second "Moscow Autumn" festival. Already aware of the highly charged situation and seeking to minimize potential problems for both the composer and his publishing company, he began negotiations with VAAP while still in Moscow for the right to perform the work in the West.

Gubaidulina was then also working on the music for Arkady Kordon's film *The Great Samoyed* (*Velikii samoed*) about the life of the noted painter Tyko Vylka of the Uralic Samoyed peoples. At the beginning of a promising career, he had to return from Paris to his native village to marry the widow of his recently deceased brother, in accordance with the custom of his people. Gubaidulin, fearing that her violin concerto would not be performed anytime soon and feeling desperate about it, suggested using the chorale from *Offertorium* for the funeral scene at the end of the film; this would at least allow her to hear part of her work. As she emerged from the control booth after the recording session, the orchestra applauded, but Kordon came up to her and said: "No! This music is disappointing and inappropriate." His refusal was hurtful, and even a renewed plea, outside in the courtyard, to accept at least a part of the chorale was met with Kordon's brusque refusal: "No, this music isn't beautiful."

As soon as the score reached the West, everything happened in quick order.[16] In late November 1980 Sikorski sent a copy of the work to Gidon Kremer, who immediately tried to find a venue for its performance. He was able to get it accepted for the Wiener Festwochen in May 1981. In April the Österreichischer Rundfunk Orchester received the instrumental parts—in those days it took several months to produce all the materials for a forty-minute-long work for large orchestra. Finally, on May 30, the Finnish conductor Leif Segerstam, a musician of considerable experience with modern music, conducted the premiere at the Wiener Konzerthaus. The soloist, to whom the work was dedicated, spiked a fever on the evening of the performance and later commented:

> The piece was given an unfortunate place in the program, and I was the one who had placed it there, having been given *carte blanche* that evening for my own performance. The concert consisted of three premiered pieces in the first part, all winners of a competition. I think the audience would then have preferred to hear something other than one more premiere, but I recall that they received it very respectfully. For some reason, after that performance, Gubaidulina decided to make certain cuts in the work. Perhaps it was the clumsiness of the first performance—which is always a severe test of both the work and its performer. . . . Perhaps it was the fatigue of the orchestra and its inability to be at its best after many hours of rehearsing the other three works—I just don't know.[17]

Two days after the performance Hans Heinz Stuckenschmidt wrote in the *Frankfurter Allgemeine Zeitung* about the bold and strict movements (reminiscent of Webern) and the great beauty of *Offertorium*, but he suggested, "with all due respect for the composer's skill and spirit," that the work "be cut by half."[18] It is not clear whether Stuckenschmidt would have made this suggestion had the work been performed under optimal conditions and with adequate rehearsal time. All too often the problems of an inadequately prepared performance are laid at the door of the composer. The Finnish composer Kalevi Aho, for example, who has often discussed *Offertorium* in his analytical seminars, has always favored its original version. But the cuts Gubaidulina made have not necessarily been detrimental; to the contrary, a year later the work was performed by the Junge Deutsche Philharmonie under the direction of Charles Dutoit at the

Gustav Mahler-Fest in Berlin and, from there, swept the entire world. Among the outstanding performances featuring Gidon Kremer was the American premiere by the New York Philharmonic Orchestra under Zubin Mehta and later performances by the Boston Symphony Orchestra, the Montreal Symphony, and the Tonhallen-Orchester Zürich, all under Charles Dutoit with Kremer as soloist. Other performances were of equal quality: Gennady Rozhdestvensky conducting the Orchestra of the Ministry of Culture in Moscow and the radio recording of the third and final version by the BBC Symphony Orchestra, as well as Christoph Eschenbach conducting the Norddeutscher Rundfunk Symphonie-Orchester, Hamburg. However, Simon Rattle's performances with the City of Birmingham Symphony Orchestra in many different countries must surely have been high points because of the unusual combination of Rattle's personal artistic commitment and fully adequate rehearsal time—a rarity in today's concert business. Together with Alban Berg's Concerto for Violin, *Offertorium* stands among the great violin concertos of the twentieth century and is performed by a growing number of male and female violinists.

Victor Suslin's Emigration and the End of Astraea

Astraea dissolved in 1981, the year Victor Suslin emigrated and settled in West Germany. A few weeks before Suslin's departure, Alfred Schnittke had been able to obtain one more assignment for Astraea. Having composed the music for Elem Klimov's film, *Farewell to Matyora* [*Proshchanie s Matëroi*], based on Vladimir Rasputin's Siberian novella, Schnittke suggested the inclusion of improvised music to be played by Astraea. After many rehearsals, the trio made two recordings at the Mosfilm studio. Their performance was particularly brisk and inspired, as here they did not have to worry about matters of recording technology, as they had when playing and recording at Artyomov's apartment. Klimov's film is well crafted and successful, despite some interventions by the censors, but it contains only a few short passages of music by Astraea, and even those are barely audible.

Toward the end of June, ten days before Suslin's departure, the trio met at Artyomov's for a final session of improvisation that lasted into the early morning hours, and their playing was inspired by the impending separation. It was the end of nearly six years of playing and experimenting together, a period Gubaidulina summarized five years later:

> Our get-togethers as a group and our improvising contributed enormously to my sound world [*Klangwelt*] and my intellectual development. Listening and reacting to one another was a very important sonic experience. And one thing in particular was very special: As I bowed a string I suddenly felt that I was sounding

my soul. My soul and the sound were identical, one and the same identity. This identity of soul and sound, as well as a second phenomenon—the seeming emergence of a fourth sonic entity in our midst—were really significant. There we are—the three of us sitting on the floor playing and listening, and a fourth sonic personality appears among us. It was a psychological phenomenon: a creating, a giving birth to something new. Astraea was therefore important for me in three respects: expanding my imaginative range in the realm of sound, developing spontaneity, and learning from purely psychological experiences. Such moments were few and far between, but they did happen—and they were the high points for us.[19]

Suslin's departure was hard on Gubaidulina, for they did not know if they would ever see each other again. But what appeared at first to be a loss eventually turned into a gain: beginning with his appointment as editor at Sikorski Publishers in 1985, Victor Suslin was in a position to call attention to Gubaidulina's work in the West.

Sofia speaking at a concert by Grigory Frid's Moscow Youth Musical Club (1969).

A page from *Vivente—non vivente* (1970).

Astraea with their instruments: Viacheslav Artyomov (*Tār*),
Sofia Gubaidulina (Georgian hunting horn), Victor Suslin (*Pandura*).

Astraea improvising at the Moscow Jazz Club (1977).

Sofia with Pyotr Meshchaninov in her house in Appen. Archive Michael Kurtz.

Sofia in Vienna on trip from Lockenhaus (1986).

Sofia, Laurel Fay, and John Cage (Leningrad, 1988). Copyright Monroe Warshaw.

Sofia with Alfred Schnittke and Güntner Bialas (Munich, 1991).

Portrait of Sofia Gubaidulina.

10 | The Rhythm of Musical Form, 1981–1985

A Fiftieth Birthday Concert with Obstacles

With several months lead time Francisco Tanzer made arrangements for a concert in Düsseldorf in late October 1981 to celebrate Gubaidulina's fiftieth birthday. An invitation for the composer to attend in person had been duly submitted to the Composers Union. Unfortunately a discreet suggestion from Soviet diplomats in West Germany that a submission to the Ministry of Culture might be more appropriate came too late. Toward the end of the previous June Gubaidulina was ordered to appear before the Composers Union, and a few days later she reported to Tanzer: "Having been kept waiting for two and a half months, I had a very unpleasant session at the Secretariat. I fully expected to be refused. . . . Now I know their argument: 'No one has ever been permitted such a trip on the occasion of a fiftieth birthday.' . . . The way they treat you is humiliating. Their eyes exude hatred! And their hearts, too. Of course, I'm not going to die because of this refusal, but it is a terrible pity."[1]

Travel restrictions were not the only obstacles. When Moscow musicians gave guest performances in the West, Gubaidulina's works were routinely eliminated from the program. This happened, for example, with *Concordanza* at a concert of the Soloists Ensemble of the Bolshoi Theater [Ansambl' solistov Bol'shogo teatra] during the "Steirischer Herbst" festival in Graz in the fall of 1981, and again occurred with *De profundis* on Friedrich Lips's concert tour of Scandinavia. It took Lips's personal appearance at the Ministry of Culture, with score in hand, to save the integrity of his program.

A few days after her unsuccessful June appearance before the Composers Union, Gubaidulina traveled to the Union's creative retreat at Sortovala for a stay of several weeks. She took long walks in the woods to restore her health and distance herself from the humiliations; she renewed her study of Tanzer's poems, expecting to hand Tanzer a partial score of *Perception* for the planned program in Düsseldorf on his anticipated visit to Moscow in September. That was the title Tanzer had suggested for their collaborative work.

The festive anniversary concert took place on October 31, 1981, in the packed chamber music hall of the Tonhalle in Düsseldorf—without the composer. The occasion was officially organized by the Musikwissenschaftliches Institut of the Robert-Schumann Hochschule and Westdeutscher Rundfunk (WDR); Detlef Gojowy gave the introduction. The program consisted of Gubaidulina's Bassoon Concerto and the official premiere of *Garden of Joy and Sorrow*; Schnittke's *Three Madrigals* [*Tri madrigala*] (with texts by Tanzer), which the composer had dedicated to Gubaidulina for her fiftieth birthday and to Tanzer for his sixtieth; and one work each by the Düsseldorf composer Günther Becker and the American composer Marga Richter. Richter, on her first visit to Germany, was present at the concert and also substituted for Gubaidulina in a composition workshop at the Robert-Schumann Hochschule. The young musicians of the Düsseldorfer Ensemble had been carefully and thoroughly prepared by Wolfgang Trommer, and they performed "at a high level," according to a review in the Rheinische Post.[2]

Two weeks earlier, on October 16, 1981, *Percussio di Pekarski* had its Soviet premiere at the third Moscow Autumn festival. Veronika Dudarova conducted the Moscow Symphony Orchestra with Mark Pekarsky (percussion) and Natalia Rozanova (voice). Placing this performance on the program had also run into obstacles, and Yury Nikolaevsky later recalled playing the piece during the selection process for the program in front of a small audience at the Moscow Philharmonic: "At that time I was one of the few admirers of this work. I later recommended to Sofia to look for a better singer, and we found Elena Dolgova from Rostov on Don. Together with her and the dedicatee of the work, I performed it about ten times during the next few years, from Kishinyov in Moldavia all the way to Siberia."[3]

Shortly after the performance of *Percussio di Pekarski* (originally, *Hour of the Soul,* her portrait of Tsvetaeva), Gubaidulina traveled from Moscow to Gagra, a resort city in Gruziia, and from there wrote to Tanzer:

> Today is the day of our concert. I am afraid—but I am also hopeful that all will go well because the conductor and the players are so good. I'm not in Moscow at the moment but in the south, by the Black Sea. (I decided to take a month's vacation as a birthday present!) All day long I'm swimming and playing tennis. Fantastic! . . . And then we'll make a new start with *Perception.*[4]

The first part of *Perception* was not completed for the Düsseldorf event, as the composition turned out to be more complicated than expected. Gubaidulina set it aside for a while after an unsuccessful performance of the first part—titled *Five Miniatures for Baritone and Seven String Instruments on Poems of F. Tanzer* [*Piat' miniatiur dlia baritona i semi strunnykh instrumentov na stikhi F. Tantsera*]—in the Hall of the Composers Union on February 1, 1982.[5] She was under no deadline, and another assignment needed her attention.

Seven Words of Christ on the Cross for Cello, Bayan, and Strings

In early December 1981, not long after her return from Gagra, Gubaidulina wrote in a letter to Kolya Bokov in France: "I am about to write a piece with the title *7* [*sic*] *Words*, having in mind Jesus on the cross. Do you suppose that something will turn out, that somehow I'll manage?"[6] Vladimir Tonkha had prompted this work and its subject matter. A year earlier, on December 27, 1980, at the Gnesin Institute, he had played a few movements from Haydn's *Musica instrumentale sopra le 7 ultime parole del nostro Redentor in croce* (*The Seven Last Words of Our Redeemer on the Cross*) in his own arrangement for cello and string ensemble. Gubaidulina had been in the audience, and when she came backstage to thank him after the performance, Tonkha said: "Both Schütz and Haydn have written *Seven Words;* why don't you do it, too?" He was thinking of a piece for cello and strings, but it was not to be. At that time Friedrich Lips had also asked the composer for a new work, and as Tonkha and Lips got along well with each other (they both taught at the Gnesin Institute), Gubaidulina decided to write a piece for cello and *bayan.* Her choice of the words of Christ on the cross as recounted in the Gospels meant that she had focused on a Christian theme of central importance. The deeper she delved into the work itself, the more she became convinced that the tonal resources of the two soloists were too limited to do full justice to the material. The cello, which she associated with Christ on the cross, and the *bayan,* representing the realm of God the Father, needed to be augmented by a string orchestra—the "Evangelist," giving voice to the Holy Spirit. Gubaidulina's *Seven Words* is linked not so much to Haydn's as to Schütz's work, especially the recurring passage "I thirst," which appears in her composition at several points. The chromatic and microchromatic material presented by the two soloists, as well as the diatonic material heard in the strings, grow out of this recurring thematic motif as if from a seed, reaching ever higher levels of intensification until the work climaxes in the sixth movement: "It is finished." After a fortissimo passage on the cello's lowest string at the moment of death, the bow slides across the bridge, suggesting transcendence beyond the physical realm. The seventh movement progresses into the spiritual world of the string orchestra—"Father, into thy hands I commend my spirit."

A major musical event was scheduled at the Great Hall of the Moscow Conservatory for April 15, 1982: the debut of Gennady Rozhdestvensky's Orchestra of the Ministry of Culture of the USSR [Simfonicheskii orkestr Ministerstva kul'tury SSSR] performing works by Denisov, Gubaidulina, and Schnittke. The formation of this orchestra had been a combination of coincidence and adventure. The year before, while on tour in West Germany, the Symphony Ochestra of Central Television and All-Union Radio [Simfonicheskii orkestr Tsentral'nogo televideniia i Vsesoiuznogo radio] had lost two of its members within one week: first a harpist, and then Maxim Shostakovich, the conductor, had asked for political asylum. After returning to Moscow, the remaining members of the orchestra were penalized by having their salaries withheld for three months. Rozhdestvensky capitalized on this crisis, using his own position of strength to form a new orchestra with the stranded musicians and naming it the Orchestra of the Ministry of Culture of the USSR. Their first performance, expected with great anticipation, was advertised with the usual small number of posters, but a few days before the performance all posters were either torn down or pasted over. It looked like censorship. Rozhdestvensky called the appropriate state agencies to explain that this action punished the performers, not the composers, and that the former, having invested a lot of work, were now being deprived of their just pay. In the end the bureaucracy yielded to this argument, and the concert—which was dedicated to the three most prominent, officially discountenanced composers—went forward as scheduled. It was a significant event, a watershed for contemporary music in the Soviet Union, for which people came to Moscow from as far away as Soviet Georgia. Rozhdestvensky, who has always liked to speak at his concerts, gave the introduction and began the evening's program with a march jointly composed by Denisov, Gubaidulina, and Schnittke. This opening piece was followed by Denisov's *Peinture,* Gubaidulina's *Offertorium*—"in a fantastic performance by Oleg Kagan"[7]—and Schnittke's *Gogol Suite for Orchestra* [*Gogol'-Siuita*]. The evening had particular significance for Gubaidulina and her *Offertorium,* "even if some comments expressed reservations or opposition,"[8] as the audience was not used to programs consisting entirely of avant-garde works. In the 1960s the focus had been on Denisov and his *Sun of the Incas;* in the 1970s Schnittke had moved to the center of attention with his First Symphony; but now, at the beginning of the 1980s, it was Gubaidulina who stepped out of the shadows into the public limelight within her own country.

On October 20, 1982, as part of the fourth "Moscow Autumn" festival, *Seven Words* had its premiere in the Small Hall of the Conservatory, with Yury Nikolaevsky conducting the chamber orchestra "Ricercar" ["Richerkar"] with Tonkha and Lips as soloists. But things for that evening did not augur well.

To begin with, the censors had disallowed the "Christian" title of the work in the program, substituting for it "Partita" for cello, bayan, and string orchestra. Worse, however, was that the evening's program was too crowded. Gubaidulina's "Partita" was listed at the end of the first half, following two mediocre pieces lasting forty minutes.[9] At that point the overtaxed audience was supposed to take in yet another new work, and one that surely was not easy to comprehend on first listening; three more choral pieces followed the intermission. At the end of the performance even some sympathetic friends were critical of *Seven Words*: Denisov's wife at the time, the musicologist Galina Grigorieva, and the composer Roman Ledenyov thought the work was "downright disappointing."[10] To make up for this failure, Tonkha and Lips insisted on another performance as soon as possible; it took place on April 5, 1983, at an evening of works by Gubaidulina in the House of the Artist [Tsentral'nyi dom khudozhnika]. The estimable revision of *Seven Words* was heard on this occasion together with the Flute Quartet, *De profundis*, and *Introitus*. Like *Offertorium*, the revised *Seven Words* then stood at the beginning of a series of successful performances in the USSR and, beginning in 1986, in the West. Its triumphal march led from Tokyo to New York to Europe, where it was performed on about sixty occasions with Elsbeth Moser (bayan) and many different cellists. A work of sacred music that breaks new ground in its combination of tonality, chromatics, and microchromatics, *Seven Words* has become part of the concert repertoire of symphonic orchestras and has gained broad and positive acceptance by the public.

A "Conspiratorial" Meeting of Composers in Moscow

On October 18, 1982, only two days before that ill-fated premiere of *Seven Words*, German and Russian composers had a secret meeting that had been arranged behind the back of the official Moscow music establishment. On his flight to the fourth "Moscow Autumn" festival Jürgen Köchel had noticed among the passengers the well-known journalist and Soviet specialist Gerd Ruge. Talking to him in the bus from the tarmac to the arrival building, it turned out that a group of five West German composers—Hans-Jürgen von Bose, Peter Michael Hamel, Wilhelm Killmayer, Alfred Koerppen, and Helmut Lachenmann—had also been on the plane and, as guests of the Composers Union of the USSR, would stay at the same hotel as Köchel. He inquired into their plans and duties while in Moscow and spontaneously suggested a secret get-together with some avant-garde Moscow composers. As soon as he had checked in at the hotel, he called his composer friends. Gubaidulina, Schnittke, and Denisov were delighted with the idea, and Denisov, whose apartment had served for many years as the meeting place with foreigners, immediately started beating the Moscow signal drums. The gathering was arranged for October 18, after the evening concert, in Denisov's apartment on Studencheskaia ulitsa, an easy walk from the Hotel Ukraina. The Russian participants included, besides the host himself, Viacheslav Artyomov, Leonid Hrabovsky, Sofia Gubaidulina, Alfred Schnittke, Alexander Vustin, and the couple Elena Firsova and Dmitri Smirnov.[11] Everybody had brought along cassette tapes, records, and scores, and they all listened, asked questions, and commented. Lachenmann played his *Wiegenmusik* on Denisov's concert piano, Hamel his *Schwarz-weiss* piece for piano, and Killmayer excerpts from his *Paradies* cycle. But the evening was far more than a mere exchange of music. It turned into a memorable and deeply moving human encounter that lasted till the early morning hours. Helmut Lachenmann later referred to it as "perhaps the most important part of our visit to Moscow."[12] He was "humbled" by Schnittke's clear and nonconfrontational articulation of the profound musical differences between them, and by his way of always looking for and expressing the things people have in common that help them to transcend their differences. Usually shy and reticent on such occasions, Gubaidulina that evening became engaged in a conversation with Peter Michael Hamel, who had done a lot of improvising with his group, Between. He later wrote the following comments as a special contribution to this biography:

> After all the diplomatic receptions, the personal, "conspiratorial" invitation to Edison Denisov's apartment, arranged by the tireless director of Sikorski Publishers, Jürgen Köchel, was an unforgettable event for all of us in the West German delegation of composers. We—that is, Bose, Killmayer, Koerppen, Lachenmann, and Hamel—met not only Alfred Schnittke, Alexander Knaifel, Mrs. [Elena] Firsova, and the internationally "versed" Denisov, but also Mrs. Sofia Gubaidulina—who was someone very special for me. The art historian Oxana Leontieva had introduced "Sonia" to excerpts from my book, *Durch Musik zum Selbst,* which existed in a Russian manuscript translation. In those days of the Andropov era the Iron Curtain was still impenetrable. It was unbelievable: Mrs. Gubaidulina had only a single performance that year. . . . Her improvisational group "Astraea" was unacceptable in the Composers Union. Who would have thought at the time that she and Alfred would live in northern Germany and become world famous just a few years later?
>
> For me, Gubaidulina's most important thought at that time had to do with Moscow's "gray on gray" and West Berlin's "colorful, dazzling" appearance. She felt that "Russia was perhaps much more colorful inside, whereas West Germany's inside was rather gray on gray." . . . The Persian-Oriental origins along the edges of the USSR were much too vibrant for any state directive to suppress.
>
> Since I have been on the faculty of the Hamburger Hochschule für Musik und Theater, I have had the opportunity to invite Sofia Gubaidulina on several occasions with the support of its former president, Professor Hermann Rauhe, and our Dean of Women's Affairs, Professor Krista Warnke. Together with Victor and

Alexander Suslin, "Astraea" played at the nearby Johanniskirche in April 2000; our Studio 21 for contemporary music played her chamber music based on Bach, *Meditation über den Choral "Vor deinen Thron tret ich hiermit" von J. S. Bach;* and she gave an impressive presentation in Mendelssohn Hall of her *St. John Passion [Johannes-Passion]*, which was followed on March 16, 2002, by a wonderful performance of its second part in Hamburg's St. Michael's Cathedral.

The Scarecrow: A Film by Rolan Bykov

Only a few weeks after that all-Gubaidulina program at the House of the Artist on April 5, 1983, another all-Gubaidulina concert was presented on April 20, 1983, in the October Hall of the House of Unions [Oktaibr'skii zal Doma soiuzov]. Following the performance of *Garden of Joy and Sorrow* and *Quattro,* Gubaidulina decided to "play the hooligan."[13] The last item on the program was *Heads or Tails [Orël ili reshka]*, a work of improvised aleatoric music.[14] Lev Mikhailov played various clarinets; Valentina Ponomaryova, a gypsy-style singer, produced spectacular vocal sound effects; and a group of amateur musicians, led by Sergei Letov on saxophone, joined the performance. Each participant's part in this new work was to be determined by the oracular Chinese book of changes, *I Ching.* Valentina Ponomaryova later described her preparatory visit to the composer's apartment near Preobrazhenskaya ploshchad':

> It was in Sonia's apartment that I heard for the first time about the existence of this book (and now I own it myself). She said: "We will look up what you're supposed to sing." Then she opened the book and said: "I won't say anything now. You go home, and in a few days you'll find out what you will sing. I'm going to study this book." I was completely baffled how this was going to work—to look into the book of changes and to find out what I was supposed to sing. ... As we entered the concert hall on the day of the performance, she told us what we were to do, and that's what we did. She sat in the audience conducting us very subtly, and I thought: I wonder what the ending will be like. At that point she suddenly joined us on the stage and played an intoxicating note using a bow on some child's instrument. It was so fitting, so marvelous, that not only the audience but everyone onstage was completely transfixed. She arrived onstage, and everything that had been transpiring came to a conclusion in that one note....A lot of people remember that concert to this day. I myself often think about it.[15]

Thus ten years after her first act of public "hooliganism" in Frid's club (the evening of improvisation on March 2, 1973), this time no one perceived *Heads or Tails,* with its final flexatone-like note sounded by Gubaidulina, as an undesirable provocation—times were different and change was in the air. But notwithstanding the success of the performance, Gubaidulina was dissatisfied with her experiment in mere chance, and she never included *Heads or Tails* in her list of works.

After finishing *Perception* during the first days of June, she worked on a new film score through the month of July, this time for Rolan Bykov's *The Scarecrow* (*Chuchelo;* 1983). The action concerns a provincial schoolgirl (played by the daughter of the rock singer Alla Pugachova) who is ostracized and abused by her classmates, so that she and her grandfather eventually leave the village. Bykov succeeded not only in presenting a sensitive psychological study with political overtones (Young Pioneers as lazy, brutal, and egotistical monsters); he also created a work of undeniable aesthetic beauty that never indulges in saccharine clichés. Gubaidulina watched the takes repeatedly and developed an intensely serious relationship with the film, much to the surprise of its director:

> She didn't simply compose the music for this film, she participated in it, in its creation. A situation, by the way, that's not at all typical. Nowadays many a composer writes music for a film without so much as a glance at it. In fact, leading composers treat it as not all that serious. Listening to Sonia's music, I realized it was magnificent—each excerpt was better than the one before. But even more astonishing—when water trickled in the film, water trickled in her music. When fire burned in a scene, fire burned in her music. It was no simplistic musical depiction of fire or water, but an artistic musical image. I was astounded, even shocked. . . . "Sonia, do you comprehend how my paltry film relates to your splendid music?" She got very upset: "You mean it doesn't fit? No, no, just try it, try it in the film. You'll see." But when I simply added Sonia's music to the film, it first seemed to be a foreign tissue. The music went through an entire process of implantation in the body of the film. But once it was implanted, it became clear that the music was the very blood flowing through the veins of the film. From the first, Sonia strengthened the fundamentally contemplative, religious resonance of the film. She is, you know, a believer, which one can hear in her music.[16]

The Scarecrow is certainly the most successful film with a Gubaidulina score; it ran in Soviet cinemas during the mid-1980s and eventually became what one would nowadays call a cult movie. Even the German newspaper *Die Welt*, reporting on the pre-Christmas season in Moscow, mentioned it: "The film is currently a huge success in Moscow, stirring emotions and leaving young and old in tears. . . . A . . . film full of exquisitely poetic images. And the response has been enormous."[17] Andrei Sakharov and Elena Bonner saw the film in their exile in Gorky and were moved to tears.[18]

Gubaidulina, however, was excluded from the success of the film. During the first private screening at the House of Cinema [Dom kino] no one paid particular attention to her. Having received a general invitation without a reserved seat, she refused to get involved in the rude scuffle for places and listened to Bykov's introduction standing onstage between two members of the production staff. During the showing of the film she was relegated to standing in the second screening room. When, in 1986, *The Scarecrow* and several of its creators received a Soviet State Prize, Gubaidulina's name was nowhere to be seen. Bykov had stood up for her in the nominating process but had to pull his punches, because, as secretary of the board of the Union of Film Makers of the USSR [sekretar' pravlenia Soiuza kinematografistov SSSR], he could not go all out doing battle for his own film. Three of the names he submitted, including Gubaidulina's, were not considered and disappeared from the list. It had evidently been decided to pay as little attention as possible to the film and probably also to its composer.

At about this time the painter Igor Ganikovsky inquired through a friend of Nadia's whether he would be allowed to do a portrait of Sofia, and she consented. Ganikovsky was then thirty-three years old, had completed his studies as a mining engineer, and had turned to painting only in the mid-1970s. Among the unofficial painters of that time, he loved contemporary music, and many of his later paintings relate to composers and their works. "On my first visit with Gubaidulina," he later said,

> she was in the midst of copying sheet music to earn a little money, as she told me. She sat still for a while, then I asked her to play the piano. I stayed several hours but was very unhappy with the result. During the next few months I came for two more sessions, but the portrait got worse and worse. My fingers trembled, and I felt nervous. Sofia comforted me and said: "It will turn out all right." Then one night I woke up with the feeling, "Now!" I went straight to my easel and within fifteen minutes I painted a new portrait. It was the only time I ever worked at night.[19]

In the 1990s Ganikovsky produced an oil painting, *Garden of Joy and Sorrow,* a series of collages titled *Now Always Snow* [*Teper' vsegda snega*], and a cycle of paper works dedicated to Gubaidulina with the title *The Birth of Music* [*Rozhdenie muzyki*].

Perception: A Conversation about Art between Man and Woman

By the time Gubaidulina finished the score for *Perception* in the fall of 1983, the short piano pieces Tanzer had originally asked for had turned into a fifty-minute composition for soprano, baritone, and seven string instruments. The work, which has often been described as an artistic dialogue between the Düsseldorf poet and the Moscow composer, was written in complete isolation and without any contact with Tanzer. In thirteen movements—only four are purely instrumental—Gubaidulina develops a dialogue articulating opposite male and female concepts of art. The dialogue concerns beauty, the creative process, the creation, and—Gubaidulina's central theme—the relationship between human beings and God. In her dark, vertical world, the woman hears the phrase "Voices at night! Voices again and again," which keeps returning as a motif. For the man, beauty has the clear transparency of a crystal: "Winter / speaks / through you / even / in / summer- /nights / its / clear / language / December / wrought / your / crystal." The woman cares about "giving the crystal a soul." In addition to using eight poems and a brief passage from a letter by Tanzer, as well as a few lines from the Psalms, Gubaidulina herself (at Tanzer's suggestion) also wrote part of the text for the tenth movemenht, "Ich und Du," the dialogue between man and God. She remarked, in a letter of December 1983 to Victor Suslin, "[I] myself wrote the completely crazy, absurd text. You're not going to laugh, are you? It comprises phonetic modulations from sense to nonsense, which is after all the ultimate truth. Imagine moving along vertical lines, from the brain into the depths of the soul, where special senses are found, beyond which lies the infinite. And exactly there [lies] the only thing possible: absurdity."[20] "Ich und Du" appears just before the work's climax in the twelfth movement, where up to six additional layers are introduced, with the help of tape recordings, and function as a retrospective overlay to Tanzer's poem "Montys Tod" (about the death of a race horse) by creating a panorama of perceived simultaneity. On one of their walks, Meshchaninov criticized the piece after a thorough study of its score, giving voice to his own sense of harmonic proportions: "The twelfth movement is too long. But you have to make it even longer so as to avoid giving the impression of it being too long." The ascending motion in the strings is often interrupted with static interludes filled with recorded fragments from the earlier movements. Gubaidulina reworked the movement and lengthened the duration of these interludes. The thirteenth movement, a coda, ends with the soprano's sung words, "Voices fall silent" ("Stimmen verstummen"), and the baritone's spoken lines, "Between suffering and pity stands a cross" ("Zwischen Leid und Mitleid steht ein Kreuz").

A while after completing the score, Gubaidulina happened to meet a Sikorski staff member at a concert. The conversation revealed that *Perception* would probably not be published. The work, so the argument went, was too long and complicated, and the text of the twelfth movement—the combination of Tanzer's poem about the death of a racehorse and the Psalms—was troublesome and likely to be misunderstood by the public. After two years of hard work on *Perception,* with many highs and lows along the way, this came as a bitter disappointment. In eighteen years Gubaidulina had had barely half a dozen of her works publicly performed, and not all these performances were successful. *Offertorium,* her most important composition, was less than a complete success in the West, with experts considering it too long. Now it turned out that another major work, *Perception,* was also too long and unfit for publication. Moreover, every effort was made to prevent her from traveling to the West and to restrict performances of her music within the Iron Curtain, all this at a time when her closest friend among composers, Victor Suslin, had emigrated. It seemed to Gubaidulina, at age fifty-two, as though she had wasted her life. In the coming months dark thoughts crowded her mind.

"The Transformation of Time" and Meshchaninov's Music Theory

The early 1980s began a new phase in the collaboration between Sofia Gubaidulina and Pyotr Meshchaninov, initially bearing fruit in the twelfth movement of *Perception*. In a series of ten lectures at the Moscow Conservatory in 1980, music theoretician Meshchaninov had demonstrated the development and evolutionary steps leading from the monophony of the Middle Ages to the "sonoristics" of contemporary times. As a result, Gubaidulina now found it possible to arrive at a clearer answer to the questions occupying her since the 1970s, specifically, what steps would she need to take to define her own position in the evolutionary history of music. If this era of sonoristics, like the period immediately preceding it, should last about three hundred years, then the present era, as Meshchaninov saw it, marked a new beginning—its "archaic" and therefore "barbaric" phase. As no laws yet existed to explain the new, sonoristic-microtonal materials, such laws would still have to be discovered or developed on the way to the "classical period" of the era of sonoristics; and Gubaidulina felt unable at first to decide which area of compositional technique she should focus on, because she was searching for "what the material demands, not what my own demands are."

At that time Meshchaninov's elemental evolutionary music theory took a significant turn. Just as his earlier theory had explained that the overtone series functioned like the "ur-noumenon," the foundational source of musical pitch materials and their intervallic relationships, he now proposed that the Fibonacci series and the golden mean served a similar function with regard to rhythm. He thought of rhythm, however, not in terms of a regular, pulsing beat but as a proportion of time on both a large scale (formal sections, individual parts of works) and a small scale (the value of individual notes, particular motifs). He spoke of a "rhythm of musical form." Meshchaninov's concept of the "ur-noumenon" and its elaboration had been significantly influenced by his experience as a conductor, especially of Bach's music, which called for establishing the correct proportional relationship between various meters and tempos among the individual movements or sections and the work as a whole. In those years Meshchaninov performed *Die Kunst der Fuge* in his own instrumentation, as well as other of Bach's works. From the early 1980s on, he increasingly integrated into his theory the numerical regularities of the Fibonacci series, realizing their significance as a fundamental spiritual and formational principle on all levels of the natural world. Within the next decade Meshchaninov fully developed the concept of the rhythm of musical form, suggesting connections with both the pitch and textural fabric of music.

As for Gubaidulina, artistic form is a distillation of spirit—the result of a divine, immaterial force permeating the artistic materials and precipitating the substance of the art form—in her case music. The creation of artistic form and its proportions is for her not an intellectual or architectural method of construction but an organic, living process in a medium which she experiences as fluid and moving. Hence she likes to view music as a tree with roots, trunk, and leaves—the roots providing the foundation of form. In the later 1980s she associated the metaphorical image of a tree with Meshchaninov's theory of the complementary transformations of melody, harmony, and rhythm throughout the historical evolution of music. She did so by suggesting a parallel between root, trunk, and leaves and the three realms of Meshchaninov's "musical fabric."[21]

Gubaidulina later explained to the Moscow musicologist Olga Bugrova how she came to choose rhythm as her area of technical-compositional innovation in sonoristics:

> Mulling over which of the three fundamental elements of musical fabric within the sonorous complex might be seen as the "roots" of the tree, I realized that it was rhythm. All of the harmonic, the mass of the resonance, forms the "trunk," while the contrapuntal lines exemplify the "leaves." Under the conditions of sonoristics, the melody can no longer be conceived, as in the past, as the means for developing, elaborating the material. Instead, it must manifest itself as a transformation of the material itself, and the consequence of growth from the "roots" through the "trunk." ... But with all that, one must not suppress intuition nor lose imaginative spontaneity. But, why rhythm? Because it alone presupposes the agency of laws that do not conflict with a system that embraces all possible sonic and timbral conceptions.[22]

In later years Gubaidulina often spoke about the creation of a work of music and, at the same time, about its opposite, the performance of a work. She calls this entire process "the transformation of time," and differentiates between "vertical" time and "horizontal" time, resorting to her favorite metaphors. Vertical time—sometimes also referred to as essential or sacred time or "time outside of time"—is a metaphor for a deep layer within humans, the realm of the soul, the realm of the eternal, of the divine. Horizontal or astronomical time is the measurable time of the beat and the clock; it is also, for her, an image of physical existence. The transformation of time in a work of art occurs twice. At the start there is an encompassing moment of creative inspiration in vertical time, in which the artist apprehends the idea of a work in its totality. It presents, as it were, a multilayered but as yet undifferentiated "column of sound" that cannot be expressed in musical notation. In rare cases it may be a specific set of sonorities, melodic elements, or chords, but the details of the experience vary each time. The first act of transforming time takes place when the composer transmutes the "column of sound" from vertical to horizontal time. In this process a multiplicity of layers and events are separated out from the vertical totality and are horizontally arranged and coded in the sequential order of the musical score. This act of materialization is painful, and one is reminded of Berdyaev's concept of the creative process when Gubaidulina says: "Each time it feels like a crucifixion when I commit a composition to paper one piece at a time, because the essential musical experience takes place within me." The second act of the transformation of time is enacted by musicians and audiences in performance. But it lies in the realm of the imponderable, as it can only succeed if the interpreters penetrate to the essential depth of the work and the audience is receptive to that depth. If that is the case, the score is, so to speak, released from horizontal time and undergoes a retransformation into vertical time. However, the transformation of time, man's being put in touch with his essential, eternal being, can occur in two additional spheres, as Gubaidulina commented, referring to an experience she had when she was hard at work composing *Perception* in the early 1980s:

> One day as I woke up, I felt as if time had taken a leap. While I was asleep it was vertically oriented, and suddenly it was horizontal. At that moment I thought that this is the essence of art. It was clear to me that art exists precisely because this transformation, this leap in life, exists. While sleeping, we experience time out of time.... It is a special time, our essential being. We experience this time not only while sleeping; there is another moment when it occurs: the Eucharistic experience in religion. There is a moment, the moment of resurrection, when man exists out of time. It is this experience which more than any other represents this "existence out of time." We have three ways of experiencing this essential time: in art, in sleep, and in the Eucharist.[23]

A new phase of composition began for Gubaidulina with the twelfth movement of *Perception,* where she begins to experiment with the rhythm of musical form. According to her, one could define this compositional method as the technique of ordering space-time proportions. It does not employ one or another constellation of pitches as building blocks for the composition but rather the proportional relationships of duration between the individual formal parts of the work. As a consequence, their temporal proportions define these relationships and become the basic concept of the work. The overall unity of form is defined by the "melodies" of particular rhythmic successions. What this means in practice is an ever recurring "dance of numbers," that is, an attempt to imbue this principle with musical life. Elaborate proportional calculations, which always contain some musical sound, are deployed and rejected as the work takes shape, until an organically coherent and artistically satisfying result is achieved. A thorough explanation of this approach, combined with a detailed analysis of several of Gubaidulina's works from the 1990s, can be found in *The Numerical Secrets of Sofia Gubaidulina's Music* by Valeryia Tsenova, a scholar who is well known for her work on Denisov and Soviet "underground" music.[24]

Helsinki Festival Weeks, 1984: The First Trip to the West

Gubaidulina was officially prevented from traveling to the West for many more years than Denisov and Schnittke. One reason for this unequal treatment may have been that her colleagues ranked higher in the hierarchy of the Composers Union. Also, both had enjoyed influential backing for their first trips. As early as 1976 Denisov had been permitted to travel to France on the basis of an invitation from the French composer Dutilleux. A year later Gidon Kremer pushed hard and successfully to gain permission for Schnittke to travel to Germany and Austria—as the irreplaceable harpsichordist for Schnittke's Concerto Grosso No. 1. But the real although unacknowledged opposition to Gubaidulina was the result of her hardheaded unwillingness to compromise: from the very start, she never made even the smallest concession in return for favors. The religious spirit of her works also caused resentment and probably led to difficulties. But in August 1984 she embarked on her first trip to the West.

That year the two weeks of the Helsinki Festival [Helsingin juhlaviikot], an internationally renowned festival of music and culture, had chosen "Soviet and Russian Culture" as its theme. Veijo Varpio, the artistic director of the festival, had heard a performance of *Offertorium* in Berlin in 1982; he was impressed and wanted to perform the work in Helsinki.[25] With the advice of the Finnish composer Kalevi Aho, Varpio made plans for two concerts of works by outstanding contemporary composers from the Soviet Union—Denisov, Gubaidulina, Kancheli, and Schnittke. To assure the most authentic performance, he invited Gennady Rozhdestvensky and his Symphony Orchestra of the Ministry of Culture of the USSR as well as Oleg Kagan, as soloist for *Offertorium*.[26] The only noncommunist European state sharing a long border with the Soviet Union, Finland had extensive cultural relations with its Eastern neighbor. It served as something of a cultural bridge during the cold war for reasons that were not only based on a pragmatic good-neighbor policy. Finland, with its birch and pine forests, has much in common with Russia, despite the differences between the two peoples.

A Soviet delegation of cultural functionaries traveled to Helsinki in the winter of 1983–84 to discuss the program, and both sides appeared to be in agreement. A short while later, however, after the Finns arrived in Moscow to complete the talks, problems began to develop. The Soviets refused to accept the festival program and demanded a week of officially approved music and a concert of works by Tikhon Khrennikov. This demand was not simply an expression of Khrennikov's vanity. He constantly had to prove to the Central Committee that he was a respected composer abroad and that his works were being performed, and to this end he went so far as to pay for positive reviews. In dealing with these difficulties, Varpio proved himself a skillful but also forceful negotiator. A whole series of phone calls followed the failed mission of the Finns to Moscow, and again the Soviets traveled to Helsinki, this time with the distinct possibility that the whole festival would fall apart. At that point Varpio stated: "I see only one possibility. The Symphony Orchestra of the Ministry of Culture should perform twice on the first day—Khrennikov in the afternoon and Gubaidulina at night." This would scarcely have been possible under Western labor-union contracts, but in the Soviet Union it presented no problem. However, Rozhdestvensky's refusal to conduct Khrennikov's music necessitated hiring another conductor. The Soviets were now concerned that the 2:00 PM concert would not attract enough of an audience, but Varpio solved this problem by declaring the concert the official opening performance of the festival and inviting prominent individuals from the world of business and politics, including all members of Parliament and President Mauno Koivisto. Just before the official beginning, the Soviets tried one more gambit by announcing that Gubaidulina would not attend. At this point Varpio put all his eggs in one basket, stating: "If Gubaidulina doesn't come to Helsinki, the whole festival will be canceled." Moscow finally relented.[27] In addition to Gubaidulina, Alfred Schnittke, Tikhon Khrennikov, and Andrei Eshpai had been invited, but only Khrennikov, Schnittke, and Gubaidulina—as official guests of the festival—had been given rooms in one of the best local hotels close to the concert hall. As a guest of the Finnish Composers Union, Eshpai, although a much celebrated and well-known composer at home, had lodgings in a hotel at some distance. He took this as an insult and complained to Gubaidulina, promising never to return to Finland. After their return home, however, he told her (somewhat to her surprise) that she was undervalued in the Soviet Union and that her music was very good and successful.

The first evening concert of the festival opened with the performance of Gubaidulina's *Offertorium*, which was rather symbolic given that after two decades of deprivation and sacrifice this was her first personal appearance in the West. *Offertorium* was followed by Shostakovich's Eighth Symphony, and the evening as a whole turned into an enormous success for Gubaidulina. She suddenly became the cynosure of the festival in constant demand for questions and interviews. Four years later even Tikhon Khrennikov was moved to express his admiration in a conversation with Seppo Heikinheimo, a well-known Finnish music critic: "We have many gifted composers, above all Sofia Gubaidulina. I am happy to confess that Oleg Kagan's performance of her fine Violin Concerto in Helsinki in 1984 really opened my eyes to her talent."[28]

Things began to develop for Gubaidulina as early as January, when the Finnish press published biographical portraits of the composers to be featured at the festival. Vladimir Agopov, who had studied composition under Khachaturian and lived as a Russian émigré in Finland, interviewed her for *Kulttuurivihkot,* a magazine for arts and culture. The issue containing the interview was in great demand and sold out immediately.[29] A few months later Agopov visited Gubaidulina once more, this time accompanied by Leonid Bashmakov (a Russian, born in Finland) and Kalevi Aho.

Kalevi Aho was among the first composers in the West who understood Gubaidulina's personality and treated Russian cultural differences with sensitive understanding.

Kalevi Aho: "My First Meeting with Sofia Gubaidulina"

"I first met Sofia Gubaidulina in Moscow in early April 1984, when Yury Andropov was in power. Cultural relations between Finland and the Soviet Union were very good. Owing to Shostakovich's initiative, the composer unions of both countries had instituted an exchange program in the early 1960s. Each year two Soviet composers came to Finland for a week as guests of the Finnish Composers Union, and the Soviet Composers Union invited two Finnish composers for one or two weeks. I was very interested in their most recent works of music and had already written a substantial essay on Alfred Schnittke and contemporary Soviet music. At my suggestion, 'Soviet Music' was chosen in 1984 as the theme of the Helsinki Festival, the most important music festival in Finland, and as a member of the program committee I could exert considerable influence in the selection of works. Reciprocally the Soviet Composers Union wanted to do its part in support of Finnish music. So that year they invited three composers to Moscow and scheduled a chamber concert of Finnish music for April 5, 1984, in the Hall of the Composers Union. Among other works, the program featured my Third String Quartet.

"If I remember correctly, Agopov, Bashmakov, and I went to see Gubaidulina after the concert in Moscow. She lived in the suburbs not too far from the center of the city. I was very eager to meet her because Agopov had told me so much about her. I didn't speak Russian but was able to converse with her in German—or Bashmakov and Agopov translated whatever she could not express in German. Sofia offered us tea and something to eat, and pretty soon we got into a conversation that I shall never forget. We had brought a few cassettes and records and first listened to Agopov's First String Quartet. Then Sofia played for us recordings of her latest works. She was lively and candid, and we were charmed by her personality—it is rare that one meets a person with such a radiant, invisible aura surrounding her physical presence.

"She said that the Finnish countryside had strongly influenced her because she often spent time at the creative retreat of the Soviet Composers Union on Lake Ladoga in the former Finnish province of Karelia. She loved the solitude of the lake and the Finnish woods so far away from Moscow, and she was fond of wandering in the fall through the Karelian forests of birches to gather mushrooms. She told us about the difficult years of struggle in the 1960s and 1970s when she tried to establish herself as a composer. Even in the spring of 1984 she was not yet officially accepted in the Soviet Union and had never been permitted to be present at performances of her music abroad. Unofficially, however, she had become one of the most respected composers in the Soviet Union, and many of Russia's top musicians liked to perform her works.

"She talked about her mystical—'liminal'—experiences, which sometimes appear to be religious in nature. Her most recent work, *Perception,* was something like a 'telepathic dialogue' between a composer (Gubaidulina) and a foreign poet (Francisco Tanzer). After that, she began to work on a piece based on an idea that aimed beyond physical reality itself. It was to be a dialogue between a living composer (Gubaidulina) and a dead composer (Shostakovich). She said that she was able to establish contact with the deceased in her dreams. This mystical experience was repeated several times, so that a continuous dialogue evolved from one dream to another. It was her desire to express in music the reciprocal discourse between the physical world and another world, but unfortunately I don't know in which of her works she developed these mystical experiences. In later conversations we did not talk about it again.

"Sofia's focused personality, her extremely high artistic standards, and her capacity for complete intellectual concentration impressed us deeply. It was clear that she had extraordinary intellectual powers and a very strong artistic will. Our first meeting was extraordinarily intense—I felt my consciousness expanding. I had suddenly become receptive to very strange worlds within myself and also became conscious of hitherto unknown realities outside myself.

"As we returned to the hotel by taxi I thought to myself that composers like Gubaidulina can only come from Russia. Perhaps it was fortuitous for her development as a composer that she had been confronted by many—albeit not insurmountable—difficulties in the course of her career. Without these struggles she might not have developed her mind as much as she did; if everything had gone smoothly she might not have pushed herself to understand the reasons for being a composer or to think about the higher purpose of her compositions.

In the 1980s her works fulfilled a very important 'social mission' in the Soviet Union: they were seen as symbols of artistic independence, absolute honesty, and freedom.

"I also asked myself whether it wasn't dangerous to move with such determination toward a solitary existence. It is so easy to lose contact with reality in isolation, and if you lose your sense of reality and only work for yourself, art loses its social significance—you're no longer able to communicate through art. But in Gubaidulina's case things were different.

"Daily life in the Soviet Union was so complicated and difficult that it was all but impossible to escape the realities of daily existence. Sofia's works are rooted in Soviet reality; they express the deepest yearnings and Utopian desires of so many Russians; they reflect the hopes for liberation from everyday ugliness and complications. They present a Utopian ideal of inner peace, transfiguration, and light.

"And in the taxicab I silently hoped that she would never emigrate so as not to lose the sensitivity with which she projected the essence of the hopes and Utopian desires of her people. But I can well understand why she decided in 1992 to settle in Germany. The first years of Russian capitalism were even dirtier and more complicated than daily life under the Communists. And I thought about what would happen if she became a world-famous composer. Would she be able to maintain her authentic self, her freedom, and her sense of reality even under entirely different conditions? But I was quite sure at the same time that her mind was so strong and capable that she would be able to resist the superficial lure of fame. It was my hope that she would return again and again to Lake Ladoga, to the forests of Karelia, and to her Russian origins to purify and regenerate herself.

"Some Finnish modernist composers of the 1980s criticized several of Gubaidulina's works for their 'mystical-religious and compositional banality.' For them, composing was primarily a matter of solving complicated musical problems, and the more they were in command of these technical processes, the more they believed music would be infused with content. (In their view, content derived entirely from technique—what a banal idea!) For Sofia, things stood quite differently: the process of composing must begin with a fundamental spiritual-philosophical idea; then and only then will she select the musical material for the work in question and develop the musical technique that is appropriate to the basic concept and capable of best conveying her message to the audience. This expresses my ideas as well, and that's why I feel so close to Sofia Gubaidulina's music—even though we are two such different personalities.

"Earlier I mentioned Sofia's aura. She radiates goodness, tolerance, light. Even though I normally don't consider myself particularly receptive to mysticism or religion, I welcome people who 'radiate,' whose presence is clad in an aura of light. And her best works are, like herself, radiant and profound. That's what I recall of my first meeting with Sofia Gubaidulina."[30]

A Sojourn in the Country and an Orchestral Work for the Berlin Festival

Seven Words and *Perception* were the only two new works written in the three years after 1981, but 1984 saw a burst of creativity. Gubaidulina experimented with "the rhythm of musical form" in four works of fundamentally different character and instrumentation. The first of these was a new commission by Mark Pekarsky's percussion ensemble, and she gave it the programmatic title *In the Beginning There Was Rhythm* [*V nachale byl ritm*]. It was followed by three new compositions: a five-part suite for mixed chorus, *Hommage à Marina Tsvetaeva* [*Posviashchenie Marine Tsvetaevoi*], based on texts by Tsvetaeva; *Quasi hoquetus,* a trio for viola, bassoon, and piano, commissioned by Valery Popov and Alexander Bakhchiev; and a piece for Friedrich Lips, *Et exspecto,* the previously mentioned solo sonata for *bayan.* Even though these compositions required complicated and extensive numerical calculations, Gubaidulina worked on them with great enthusiasm.

At that time Gubaidulina also became involved in writing the score for Ida Garanina's animated film based on Kipling's *The Cat That Walked by Himself* [*Koshka, kotoraia guliala sama o sebe*]. The recording studio had a tape recorder with twenty-two tracks, and Gubaidulina was given free choice of any musician she wanted. She recorded three tracks: Mark Pekarsky and his ensemble; Valentina Ponomaryova's brilliant and varied vocal effects; and an original composition for orchestra. This made it possible for her to combine the tracks together in any way she chose, for example, by taking down Pekarsky, adding the orchestra, and so on. Gubaidulina had thus created an imaginative and inspired score to which a speaker's voice would be added on a fourth track, placing her music in the background. She was allowed to keep the tapes with the recordings and later used parts of the orchestral score in *Pro et Contra.*[31]

Toward the end of her work on the film score, Gubaidulina often sat at her desk around the clock in an effort to meet deadlines. Completely exhausted, she would then seek recuperation on short visits to Sortavala on Lake Ladoga in Karelia or brief sojourns in the countryside. On one of these occasions in late spring, Ida Garanina offered her the use of her dacha on the upper Volga.

The train for Uglich left Moscow close to midnight, and four hours later Gubaidulina arrived at Skniatino, a stop without either station building or platform, nothing but a small wooden shed for the purchase of tickets beside the tracks. She waited for daylight, then shouldered her heavy knapsack and set out on the four-hour hike. The way led alongside the Volnoga, a tributary of the Volga, through an area that has since become conservation land. Except for the birdsong at dawn, there was utter silence. After weeks of intensive work in the city, the solitude and quiet raised her spirits, but at the same time a sense of stark contrast clouded her euphoria. Every few miles her route led her through deserted villages, where windows and doors were nailed shut and some of the wooden houses lay in ruins and the fields fallow. It was depressing to pass through an area where forced collectivization had resulted in this devastation. Only in Korolyovo, the last of the villages, a few inhabitants remained. Most of them were Muscovites who had bought some of the houses as dachas. Gubaidulina waited on a bench in front of Garanina's house for an hour until the owner's mother appeared. After a simple breakfast, she wanted to rest; her sense of euphoria from enjoying the surrounding nature during the early morning hours had made her oblivious to her heavy knapsack and the strain of the long march. "At that moment," she later recalled, "I succumbed to unbearable pains and cramping, and it felt as if my heart was giving out. Ida's mother heard my moaning and immediately came in to see me. Only with the utmost effort was I able to follow her instruction to stand on the cold floor. Then she brought me some milk to drink, and the cramping gradually stopped. The following day was the beginning of a week of heavenly relaxation."

The distressing experience of Soviet agricultural policies was nothing new for Gubaidulina. Earlier, in Tomolino, she had witnessed situations giving her the impression that the peasantry had to endure much greater hardships than the intelligentsia. The kolkhoz people were kept like slaves. They were denied passports, making it impossible for them to travel or seek employment outside of agriculture. Their wages were pitiable. Once, at the mess hall next to the Tomolino station where she often ate, Gubaidulina had fallen into conversation with a beggar buying a plate of soup for a few kopeks. He had left his village, because he was unable to support his family. He earned seven kopeks a day at the kolkhoz—not even enough to buy matches. And now he was begging in the city. "I suffered when I heard about the ongoing problems and the misery of these people," Gubaidulina later said. "And this suffering is reflected in my music. In those days Kabalevsky criticized our music and told our younger generation of composers: 'Why so somber, why so much pain? Life, after all, is beautiful.'"

The period from July 1985 to June 1986 was the calm before the storm in Gubaidulina's life. The election of the fifty-four-year-old Mikhail Gorbachov as Secretary General signaled the end of the regime of the old guard and was the prelude to major upheavals throughout the Soviet Union. For Gubaidulina, the first sign of a major breakthrough came on July 5 and 6, 1985, when West-deutscher Rundfunk, at the behest of Francisco Tanzer and Jürgen Köchel, produced a studio recording of *Perception* for broadcast on January 9, 1986. Victor Suslin traveled to Cologne for rehearsals and recording sessions to help with the interpretation of the score. The soprano soloist, for example, after being informed that *Ich und Du* is not about a man and a woman but about the relationship between man and God, changed her interpretation of this movement altogether. Gubaidulina received a copy of this recording in the early fall of 1985 and was delighted at the quality of the performance—much better than she had dared to hope. She invited her friends Elena Firsova and Dmitri Smirnov as well as Gerard McBurney, an Englishman, to play the recording for them. McBurney, then on a one-year student appointment at the Moscow Conservatory, had for some time wanted to become acquainted with Gubaidulina. On his return to England, he became an important interpreter of Russian culture through television and radio programs as a well as numerous articles. Toward the end of the year Gubaidulina talked with Gidon Kremer about his plan to include *Perception* in the program of the Lockenhauser Kammermusikfest in the summer of 1986. Kremer would later invite Gubaidulina to attend, giving her renewed hope.

Gubaidulina returned to the countryside for the summer of 1985, but this time to Ussolye [Ussol'e], a village northeast of Moscow, where Nadia's mother-in-law owned a dacha. There she began to work on a new piece for orchestra, commissioned a year earlier by the Berliner Festwochen—her first major commission from the West. Initially she had proposed a work for baritone and chorus, but Berlin reiterated its wish for an orchestral piece. At the same time as she made this decision, Gennady Rozhdestvensky proposed that she write something that could be performed at the Berlin festival in unconventional orchestration together with Georgy Dmitriev's *Lëdostav—Lëdokhod* (*Freezing—Thawing*).

Gubaidulina then started a symphonic work, which she titled *Stimmen . . . verstummen . . .* , the last words from *Perception*. A symphony in twelve movements, it develops two ideas that have repeatedly preoccupied the composer: silence and the rhythm of form. The plan was to write a symphony in "consonantal rhythms": as the odd-numbered movements diminish in consonantal proportions, the even-numbered movements increase. The very center of the work—that is, the movement precisely at the golden mean—is a silent solo performance by the conductor, whose gestures define the rhythm of silence. The symphony begins on a bright D-major chord, which vibrates and flickers throughout the first movement and diminishes in length in each succeeding odd-numbered movement. An opposite world of interwoven and variegated microelements gradually emerges in the even-numbered movements. The clash of these two worlds in the eighth movement creates an apocalyptic explosion. Following the conductor's silent solo, the D-major chord resolves into G-major, and after a pealing of bells the whole work fades away in a coda. During the summer weeks in Ussolye, Gubaidulina was working out the numerical proportions of her new composition, starting with its macro-dimensions and finally arriving at each note and rest. By the end of her sojourn, she had completed the conductor's solo and the central ninth movement.

11 | Travels, Travels, and More Travels, 1985–1991

Austria: Chamber Music Festival Lockenhaus,
June 28–July 13, 1986

In mid-May 1986, during the first months of Gorbachov's perestroika, Sofia Gubaidulina wrote with great excitement from Moscow to Victor Suslin: "It is downright fantastic: it looks as if they will let me travel to Lockenhaus for a performance of *Perception*. ... It would be wonderful if we could see each other again!"[1] This second trip to the West was the beginning of a period of considerable turmoil in Gubaidulina's life, and she later told a journalist from Kazan: "These trips came upon me like a whirlwind. I have to confess that I was not prepared for them. I go somewhere, present myself at social events, and end up completely exhausted. All I then wish for is to be at home, to turn off the telephone, and to settle down to work."[2] But the loss of her cherished peace and solitude was compensated for by a wealth of new impressions—in Europe, the United States, Japan, and Australia—by concerts with large orchestras and famous interpreters of her music, and by encounters with composers, musicians, and promoters.

Gidon Kremer's Lockenhauser Kammermusikfest is among the musical highlights of each summer season. Every year he invites friends and musicians for two weeks to the Burgenland southeast of Vienna. At some distance from the major tourist areas they play and rehearse in a relaxed setting but at a high pitch of creative intensity. David Geringas once referred to these weeks as "the high point of the season. Those performances were for me among the very best. But it wasn't just friendship, enthusiasm, and a high level of achievement that marked the entire event, the audience also grew and matured along with us."[3] In 1986 Gubaidulina and Schubert were the focus of the festival, and Sofia eagerly anticipated the premiere of *Perception,* for which Francisco Tanzer had also come to Lockenhaus.

"The weather was fine, the atmosphere relaxed, and the musicians wanted to do their best for her," Hans-Ulrich Duffek, the head of Sikorski Publishers, later remembered. "In terms of its musical substance, *Perception* is a work very typical of Gubaidulina's compositions. With string soloists like Isabelle van Keulen, Kim Kashkashian, and Thomas Demenga we had first-rate musicians, and Dennis Russell Davies is a conductor of great and wide-ranging experience. In order to coordinate the musicians with the recorded passages, he conducted wearing earphones."[4] The vocal soloists were Jutta Geister and Charles Naylor, and the whole work was performed and received with great enthusiasm. Seven months later *Perception* was played for the first time in England, and Paul Griffith, writing for the *Times,* commented on the London performance: *Perception* is "a liturgy, a public meditation on themes of communion between man and woman, words and music, humanity and God."[5]

The Lockenhaus festival led to a number of important relationships in Gubaidulina's life: the brief meetings with Gidon Kremer in Moscow developed into a closer friendship; the reunion with Victor Suslin was an occasion for celebration; and the first meeting with Elsbeth Moser was the beginning of a warm and deep friendship.

The other event of importance was the Western premiere of *Seven Words,* with Mario Venzago conducting the chamber orchestra of the Junge Deutsche Philharmonie, and Elsbeth Moser (bayan) and David Geringas (cello) as soloists. The other, established soloists at first treated Elsbeth Moser with cool disdain, as they considered her instrument not entirely presentable. The audience, however, was fascinated by the use of the popular-music "accordion" in a work of sacred music; David Geringas gave a bravura performance; and Elsbeth Moser, who had burst into tears during dress rehearsal, played her part with utter devotion.

A few days after the end of the Lockenhaus festival, Gidon Kremer summarized the event: "It was the second time that Sofia Gubaidulina was allowed to travel to the West, and she spent two weeks with us. Her radiant personality affected many of us deeply. I am sure that this had much to do with the convincing performances of her works. I often thought how wonderful it would be if we could always be in dialogue with the composer, how each note would then be truly convincing."[6]

During the next few years Gubaidulina was again invited to Lockenhaus: in 1989 with Alfred Schnittke and in 1995 with Victor Suslin, both times for a wide-ranging presentation of each musician's works.

West Berlin: The Premiere of *Stimmen . . . verstummen . . .*

In the 1920s Berlin was an important center for Russians who had fled their homeland during the Russian Revolution. About three hundred thousand Russians then lived in the city with their own Russian-language newspapers and numerous publishing houses. During the cold war, and especially after the construction of the Wall, the city ceased to function as a significant meeting ground between East and West. When Gubaidulina visited Berlin in 1986, its Western half was an island within East Germany that had been given special political status accompanied by generous subsidies to its cultural institutions by the West German government. Ulrich Eckhardt, the artistic director of the Berliner Festspiele, was the right man in the right place who knew how to turn this situation to his advantage. With a keen sense of artistic quality and the ability to talk and listen, he was a key figure in the city's cultural life until the end of the twentieth century. In the early 1980s the festival's focus on the Russian and Soviet avant-garde of the early part of the century had become the basis of good relations with a number of Soviet organizations, and the 1986 festival featured the current Soviet avant-garde. For four weeks new developments in all the arts were presented to the public, with music at the center of attention.

Gubaidulina's trip to Berlin was her first visit to Germany. Since early childhood she had studied German culture and learned the language. After the rural setting of Lockenhaus, she was now at the largest cultural festival in Germany together with Karlheinz Stockhausen, Luigi Nono, and Hans Werner Henze. But at Lockenhaus she had been among friends and supporters, whereas in Berlin she was still largely unknown. Besides the usual crowd of curious journalists requesting interviews, women composers were eager to get to know her.

Gubaidulina's symphony for the Berlin festival had been completed at the very last minute. At the end of June the German Embassy sent the score by diplomatic pouch to Hamburg, where the orchestral parts were prepared under considerable time pressure and then promptly returned to Moscow. In early August, Rozhdestvensky started rehearsals for the Berlin performance. As is so often the case in the world of international music performances, time pressure forced abbreviated rehearsal sessions, because, after ten days of rehearsals in Moscow, Rozhdestvensky and his orchestra set out on a tour of the USSR and a series of guest appearances in East Germany. These concluded only two days before the Berlin performance.[7]

On September 4, 1986, the much-anticipated premiere of *Stimmen . . . verstummen . . .* took place in the Berliner Philharmonie. Although the orchestra and the conductor were entirely up to the task, the lack of adequate rehearsal time made it difficult for them to sustain this symphony, comprised of twelve movements, through to the end, although the reception was generally positive. Rozhdestvensky had never rehearsed the silent cadenza—he had simply told his musicians, "Something else will happen."[8]

Not only the audience but the musicians were riveted on the conductor as he gestured silently at the golden-mean center of the work. His beat of the quadruple meter could easily assume the sign of the cross over the orchestra. Luigi Nono, one of many composers present at the performance, came backstage and silently pressed and held Gubaidulina's hands.

A few days after the concert Nono, Gubaidulina, Denisov, Avet Terterian, Suslin, and many others gathered at the home of Arvo Pärt. The party also included Mark Pekarsky, who had been invited to Berlin with his ensemble to perform Gubaidulina's *Jubilatio* [*Iubiliatsii*], his first concert in Germany. Nono spoke so highly of *Stimmen . . . verstummen . . .* that Victor Suslin asked him for a letter of recommendation for Gubaidulina. Nono obliged with a text—since then often reprinted—that speaks not only of his impressions of this particular work but also of his understanding and love for the Russian avant-garde of the twentieth century.

But Nono's generosity went even further. Having enjoyed the concert by the Mark Pekarsky Ensemble, he approached Pekarsky, asked him about life and the music scene in Moscow, and discussed the problems he himself had observed on his visits there. The following day he bought a number of percussion instruments as gifts for Pekarsky to complete his Moscow collection. After Nono died in 1990, Pekarsky dedicated a memorial concert to him under the title *Signor Luigi's Magical Gift* [*Volshebnyi podarok Sin'ora Nono*]. Performed on November 25, 1991, it featured eight works specially composed for this occasion by several Moscow composers—Victor Ekimovsky, Nikolai Korndorf, Vladimir Martynov, Alexander Raskatov, Vladislav Shoot, Vladimir Tarnopolsky, and Alexander Vustin. Each work focused on one of the instruments Pekarsky had brought back with him from Berlin. The program also included Gubaidulina's *Can You Hear Us, Luigi? Here's a Dance, Which an Ordinary Wooden Rattle Will Dance for You* [*Slyshish' li ty nas, Luidzhi, vot tanets, kotoryi stantsuet dlia tebia obyknovennaia treshchotka*] for six percussionists.

Stimmen . . . verstummen . . . is a work that seemed rather conservative to many who had been conditioned by the serialist mentality of the 1950s. Over the next few years it received both unfavorable and strongly positive reviews, reflecting each critic's personal bias. In March 1988 Gubaidulina traveled to London to be present at the celebrated English premiere with Rozhdestvensky and the BBC Symphony Orchestra at the Royal Festival Hall. Six months later, on September 29, she attended the successful Danish premiere with Michael Schønwandt and the Danish Radio Symphony Orchestra [DR Radiosymfoniorkestret]. Besides

Rozhdestvensky, it was Reinbert de Leeuw, the conductor of the Amsterdam Schönberg Ensemble, who became the major advocate for *Stimmen . . . verstummen . . .*, working with a variety of orchestras in the Netherlands, England, and the United States. When given carte blanche for a concert at the Amsterdam Concertgebouw during the 1996–97 season, he combined various ensembles he had worked with in the Netherlands into one orchestra and chose Stockhausen's *Gruppen* and Gubaidulina's *Stimmen . . . verstummen . . .* for the evening's performance. As he later explained his choices, "Just as *Gruppen* is a masterwork of the 1950s, *Stimmen . . . verstummen . . .* represents for me the best of the 1980s."

> The musicians were highly motivated and the evening was a great success. The D-major triad at the beginning of the work is something really new—I have never heard a triad quite like it. Innovations don't necessarily define the quality of a work. I grew up during the period of serial dogmatism, and it was a revelation for me when I got to know the music of Charles Ives in the 1960s. Earlier, music consisted of a whole range of prohibitions, and even later there were squabbles among the various parties of modernism. But I never got involved in that. Sofia is a composer with her own unique language. She doesn't follow anyone's example and doesn't belong to any school. What matters today are the personalities who create a world of their own—but not disconnected from history, of course. The idea that there's only one way is old-fashioned. Sofia's music clearly comes from another world, from entirely different circumstances of life. It is my impression that her strength and her sense of the times we live in also come from her experience of having to develop her own language in the face of official pressures. People like to refer to the Russian soul. Perhaps that means that each note is filled with meaning and significance like in Shostakovich's last quartets. Perhaps ritual is part of it, the ritual quality of Gubaidulina's music.[9]

England: Huddersfield Contemporary Music Festival, November 17–26, 1986

During the second half of November 1986 Gubaidulina traveled to England for the first time. The Huddersfield Contemporary Music Festival, the most important contemporary music event in the British Isles, had also chosen East European and Russian music as its thematic focus for that year, and Gubaidulina and Lutosławski had been invited for that reason. Richard Steinitz, Hudderfield's artistic director, had not received answers to his letters to Tikhon Khrennikov and Gubaidulina for many months, but then just a week before the opening of the festival word suddenly came from the Composers Union announcing Gubaidulina's impending arrival. For the two weeks of the festival, Gerard McBurney was hired as Gubaidulina's guide and translator. He picked her up at Heathrow and immediately showed her the usual tourist spots—Big Ben, Buckingham Palace, and Piccadilly Circus. After years of isolation, all these places seemed surreal, and on the banks of the Thames Gubaidulina, in her excitement, kept repeating: "That's the Thames—I can hardly believe it." The following day they drove in heavy truck traffic to Yorkshire, deeply engaged in a long conversation about the creative process, sensuality, and sexuality.

Huddersfield, deep in the valleys of the Pennine Chain, is a small industrial town well known for its cultural activities. Several handsome buildings, its concert halls, the festival, and the university's Department of Music have all contributed to its reputation in the world of contemporary music at home and abroad. One afternoon in London at Boosey & Hawkes's, Richard Steinitz made his first discovery of Gubaidulina's music; fired with inspiration, he added five of her works to the program: *Phacelia* (the piano version), *Concordanza, Detto II, De profundis,* and *Garden of Joy and Sorrow.* Performances of two additional works had come to naught in the planning stage. A special commission by the BBC of a string quartet could not be completed,[10] and the performance of *Offertorium* during the closing concert with the BBC Symphony had to be dropped, as this event was primarily dedicated to Lutosławski and the composer conducted only his own works. While in rehearsal, some of the British musicians regarded Gubaidulina as something of an exotic figure, and after experiencing the total commitment of the players at Lockenhaus, she was somewhat disappointed in the rather phlegmatic performance of *Concordanza* by Music Projects/London under Simon Bainbridge. Her pleas to play with more passion and fire were not taken seriously. An entirely different experience was the performance of *Detto II* with the Ensemble Modern, directed by Heinz Holliger, which was then making its British debut in Huddersfield. As early as the 1960s, during repeated visits to Warsaw and Zagreb, Holliger had championed music and composers from the East. On November 23 he and the Ensemble Modern played Friedrich Goldmann, Marek Kopelent, York Höller, and Gubaidulina. The performance of *Detto II* was crisp and lucid but a bit pale, and Gubaidulina would have liked to speak about the meaning and intentions of her music during rehearsals. In Moscow it would have been normal procedure, but here in England and the West it seemed inappropriate—it just wasn't done. However, Gubaidulina came upon first-rate interpreters of her *Garden of Joy and Sorrow:* Ursula Holliger, Aurèle Nicolet, and Jean Sulem, the first violinist of the Ensemble InterContemporain.

It was a pleasure to meet the other, mostly younger composers at the festival—Nigel Osborne and Oliver Knussen from England and York Höller and Helmut Lachenmann from Germany. Only Witold Lutosławski, although perfectly polite when Gerard McBurney introduced him to Gubaidulina at the hotel, gave the impression that he was not interested in striking up a conversation. It may have been a stereotypical case of the "cultivated" Pole meeting the "primitive"

Russian.[11] A number of years later, when Lutosławski attended a rehearsal of *Quasi hoquetus* in London, he said to Gubaidulina: "Your compositions are quite original."

Among all the musicians at Huddersfield, it was the cellist Francis-Marie Uitti (playing with a double-bow) whom Gubaidulina found most interesting; of the works that were new to her she especially liked Lachenmann's *Salut für Caldwell* (for two guitars)—because of the players' silent motions and gestures that "created a space of unheard music."[12] When Helmut Lachenmann was asked in a public discussion to comment on English music, his reply went something like this: "English music always looks backward, it is nostalgic. German music always deals with large, global issues. The French are always in search of the other, perfection, beauty." "And Russian music is always about pain," Gubaidulina added softly, in the course of Gerard McBurney translating Lachenmann's comments for her.[13]

Life in the Soviet Union had taught Gubaidulina to guard herself instinctively; she would never, for instance, discuss anything important in a hotel room. The flood of new impressions at times could overwhelm her, so that Gerard McBurney took her by herself on an excursion to nearby Haworth, the home of the Brontë sisters. On the return trip to London, Sofia spent the night at the home of Susan Bradshaw, the pianist, who had invited a few friends in Gubaidulina's honor. Among them was the composer Peter Maxwell Davies, who gave Gubaidulina a very pretty belt as a present.

During those days Guibaidulina talked a lot about T. S. Eliot's *Four Quartets*, and she was on the lookout for a good recording of it. She spoke about the four seasons and the four string quartets that she wanted to compose for Eliot's poem. Because Eliot's own recording of *Four Quartets* was not immediately available, Gerard spoke the texts on tape, adding also Emily Brontë's poem, "No Coward Soul Is Mine." Gubaidulina gave the tape to Natalia Gutman at a concert in London to take back to Moscow.

Germany: *Hommage à T. S. Eliot* at the Cologne Philharmonie

In March 1987 Gubaidulina's second trip to Germany took her to Cologne. For many years after World War II the city had been a Mecca for contemporary music, and just a year before Gubaidulina's arrival, an arena-shaped concert hall had opened between the cathedral and the Rhine. The Kölner Philharmonie soon became one of the first concert halls in Germany, featuring guest appearances of the top musicians and orchestras of the world, often presenting contemporary music. With Gidon Kremer's support, Gubaidulina had received one of four commissions for the opening season. Kremer was looking for a second work to be played on tour together with Schubert's Octet (string quartet, clarinet, bassoon, and French horn), and he had asked Gubaidulina in Locken-haus for an octet. But even though at first she did not warm to that particular instrumentation, she eventually decided on an octet with soprano in seven movements, changing from *tutti* to strings to winds, with and without voice, as she moved from one movement to another. The text she chose came from Eliot's *Four Quartets*. After a concert in Moscow in 1985 Dmitri Silvestrov, a specialist in English literature, had handed her his translation of *Four Quartets*, knowing of her obsession with the thematic range of Eliot's work. Following her intensive preoccupation with "vertical" and "horizontal" time in the early 1980s, reading Eliot put her into an extraordinary, exuberantly creative mood, so that the resulting work itself is a powerful combination of her fiery Tatar nature, her Russian religiosity, and Eliot's world of thought. The Anglicized American poet—who once referred to himself as a classicist in poetry, a royalist in politics, and an Anglican Catholic by religion—deals in this cycle of poems with the same central questions that forever preoccupied Gubaidulina, only he comes at them from the perspective of the humanist trained in the classics and in philosophy. What was new for Gubaidulina, however, was that Eliot always represents these issues in fours: four elements (earth, water, air, and fire), four seasons, four concepts of God (the Father, the Son, the Holy Spirit, and the Virgin), the four ages of man, and the four dimensions of temporal existence (past, present, future, and the eternal or extra-temporal sphere). She carefully avoided the danger of drowning out the musical quality of Eliot's language by selecting only a few, thematically focused passages from *Four Quartets* and by deploying the soprano voice in no more than three of the seven movements. The original choice of eight movements (twice four) was eventually reduced to seven. The fourth movement is at the center—"the still point of the turning world"; the first, third, fifth, and seventh movements are arranged as a cruciform and relate to the seasons of the year—winter, summer, autumn, and spring; the sixth, chorale-like movement is placed as a prayer in anticipation of spring. Just at the time Gubaidulina was working on Eliot's poetry, two more commissions came in: both the BBC and the Kuhmo (Finland) Chamber Music Festival [Kuhmon Kamarimusiikki] requested string quartets. Elated by her work, she conceptualized a "Chamber Mystery" for four string quartets as a frame for the octet and an overlying chorus.

On March 20 Gubaidulina arrived at the Frankfurt airport and immediately continued on to Düsseldorf, where the musicians were already rehearsing Schubert's Octet. The last sheets of music had again been sent to Hamburg by courier for immediate copying and distribution to the players. It had been Gubaidulina's plan to add further layers of time by inserting into the performance tape recordings of spoken passages from *Four Quartets* and excerpts from rehearsal sessions in Düsseldorf—discussions and musical fragments. On March 25, the very day of the premiere of *Hommage à T. S. Eliot* [*Posviashchenie T. S. Eliotu*], these recorded materials were added for the first time, but they turned out to be too much of a good thing. The quality of the recording did not meet expectations; more important, however, was the concern that the audience was exposed to new impressions between the movements. Hence, with Gubaidulina's consent, the inserted recordings were dropped for the performances that followed—to everyone's satisfaction. During rehearsals the musicians had been looking for a suitable encore, so Gubaidulina, from one day to another, composed *Ein Walzerspass nach Johann Strauss*. The musicians continued to improve the quality of their performance in the course of their subsequent tour of Germany, so that at their tenth and final concert at the Metropolitan Museum in New York they reached a peak even without rehearsal.[14] Looking back twenty years, the names of the musicians who then performed with Gidon Kremer are noteworthy. Today most of them are soloists and teachers of international stature: Christine Whittlesey (soprano), Eduard Brunner (clarinet), Klaus Thunemann (bassoon), Radovan Vlatkovic (French horn), Isabella van Keulen (violin), Tabea Zimmermann (viola), David Geringas (cello), and Alois Posch (double bass).

Two days after the successful premiere in Cologne, Gubaidulina flew back to Moscow to begin work on the new string quartets. But her plans for a "Chamber Mystery" came to naught for the very pragmatic reason that Eliot's works were normally not allowed to be set to music. If Gubaidulina's publisher had tried in advance to obtain the rights to a musical version, it is possible that *Hommage à T. S. Eliot* would never have been written. Only the intensive efforts by Sikorski Publishers (who referred to Gidon Kremer and his ensemble as the performing artists) and after careful review of the score by experts at Eliot's London publisher, Faber & Faber, did Eliot's widow give special permission for Gubaidulina's work. However, "Chamber Mystery" with choral music using Eliot's texts never saw the light of day.

Two months after the premiere in Cologne, Gubaidulina visited England for the second time. The renowned festival in Bath had dedicated one day to Soviet music and, on May 24, under the title "Raising the Curtain," presented Elena Firsova, Denisov, and Gubaidulina in public discussions and two concerts. For the second time the String Quartet No. 3 was to have its premiere, but again it was not finished, and in its place Andrew Ball performed the Piano Sonata. Gubaidulina and Firsova had arrived in London a few days earlier to stay with Elizabeth Wilson, who has welcomed many Soviet artists to her home. Gerard McBurney accompanied them to Covent Garden to see Peter David Maxwell's chamber opera, *The Martyrdom of St. Magnus*, but opera was never Gubaidulina's favorite genre. A visit to Cambridge under McBurney's guidance included a religious service in King's College Chapel (McBurney wearing the scholarly robe belonging to his father who had once been a science instructor there), where they listened to hymns and psalms performed by the King's Singers. The two composers returned to Moscow in early June.

As soon as Gubaidulina had returned to Moscow, Sikorski Publishers called with the news that she had been awarded the "Fondation Prince Pierre de Monaco" prize for her overall work. However, as the invitation to attend the award ceremony came too late for Gubaidulina to make arrangements, she wrote a letter expressing her gratitude and asking for an alternative date.

Finland 1987: A Guest Appearance at the Kuhmo Chamber Music Festival

In 1970 the cellist Seppo Kimanen presented his first chamber music festival in Kuhmo, a small town in central Finland. He had been searching for a quiet location suitable for the development of chamber music. The first concert drew an audience of no more than eight people. That was about to change, however, even if very slowly, in keeping with the timelessness which is the essence of Finnish nature as seen in its forests, lakes, and granite. For ten years Kimanen planned and gathered experience until the one thousand–seat church was filled year after year. Today a few days at Kuhmo are part of a regular summer program for most educated Finns.

Since the mid-1970s Kimanen had taken regular trips to Moscow—for a short period in his role as artistic director of the Helsinki Festival Weeks [Helsingin juhlaviikot]—and had made it a habit to invite Russian musicians to Kuhmo: Alexei Liubimov, the duo Natalia Gutman and Oleg Kagan, Yury Bashmet, and others. Gidon Kremer had been to Kuhmo as well, and Lockenhaus is in many ways indebted to its somewhat older Finnish sibling.

The extent to which Gubaidulina was still subjected to mistreatment in Moscow in the mid-1980s can be measured by the following event. After a meal at the restaurant of the Composers Union, Kimanen stepped with her into the coatroom, when a small, elderly female employee started to yell at her for two or three minutes. "She was actually shouting. A coat check woman considered herself superior, even at the Composers Union, where she should have been respectful. I was amazed, but Sofia simply listened. She was obviously embarrassed because I was there as a foreigner. Then she took her coat and we left. 'What was that?' I asked, and she simply replied: 'It's nothing. That's the kind of stupid people we have here.' It must have been a traumatic experience for a single woman to live under such circumstances. It took a lot of inner strength."[15]

As a founding member and cellist of the Sibelius Quartet, Kimanen had commissioned a string quartet for the summer of 1987 and invited the composer to Kuhmo. In her ten-minute String Quartet No. 2, Gubaidulina contrasts earthly existence (which can be ugly and brutal) with an existence gently spiritual, by alternating the symbolically rich tonal resources of vibrato and natural harmonics. The first part of the work builds on a foundational G; at the midpoint of the second part stands a sonority based on the pitches D, A, E, F♯, and C♯; the underlying generative principle of formal development derives from the Fibonacci series. Like many other musicians before them, the members of the Sibelius Quartet were amazed by how well Gubaidulina explained her musical vision during rehearsals:

> Sofia Gubaidulina is a rare combination of refined sensibility and great inner strength. At Kuhmo, she was always modest and pleasant, but during rehearsals she was very precise about what she expected from us. But she gave us space and did not pressure us, and that is ideal in any kind of rehearsal. When referring to the light world of her quartet she would speak about angels and birds, and her singing for us had an aura of pure soul. That was completely unusual for a contemporary composer from the Soviet Union, as people there were used to being forced to make compromises in order to survive. Of course, we didn't have enough rehearsal time because I was the organizer of the entire festival.[16]

On July 23, 1987, the Sibelius Quartet performed the successful premiere of the String Quartet No. 2. The String Quartet No. 3 had meanwhile been completed, and it had its premiere on August 22, 1987, at the Edinburgh Festival, performed by the Arditti Quartet, the English specialists in contemporary music. The following summer, when Kuhmo focused on Soviet music, Gubaidulina was invited for the premiere of her *Rejoice* [*Raduisia*].

Louisville (USA), Paris, and a Moscow Concert with Art Show

Gubaidulina departed for the United States on September 19, 1987, full of excitement and expectations. Her musician friends had given her mixed reports based on their own visits there—many positive accounts concerning people's friendliness and openness but also unsettling details about widespread crime. During much of her travels through the United States, Gubaidulina was in the company of Laurel Fay, a musicologist specializing in contemporary Soviet music and a consultant to the Schirmer Publishing Company. They had met in Moscow in the early 1980s. After only a day in New York, they were off to Louisville, Kentucky, to meet with the Louisville Orchestra, which was celebrating its fiftieth anniversary with a special festival, "Sound Celebrations." The orchestra had made a name for itself in the field of modern American music, and the invitation from Lawrence Leighton Smith, its music director at the time, had come to Gubaidulina in roundabout ways. In the spring of 1987 the School of Music at the University of Louisville had bestowed the Grawemeyer Award—a prestigious and well-endowed prize for composers—on Harrison Birtwistle. Gubaidulina and Stockhausen had also been finalists. Smith, a member of the jury, had been so impressed with *Stimmen … verstummen …* that he invited the unknown composer to the forthcoming anniversary festival. Nine other countries were represented by thirteen additional composers, among them Harrison Birtwistle, Peter Schat, Vladimir Ussachevsky, and Ellen Taafe Zwilich (the latter two from the United States), as well as many critics who participated in public discussions. Most of the works at the festival were written in the 1980s, and Gubaidulina was represented on the program with her String Quartet No. 3, performed by the Muir Quartet, a young American ensemble that included contemporary music in its repertoire and was soon to repeat Gubaidulina's quartet in New York and Boston.

Before her return to Moscow on October 2, Gubaidulina spent a few days with Laurel Fay in New York. She was no longer a complete stranger as a composer there; the New York Philharmonic and Gidon Kremer had introduced her with *Offertorium* in Alice Tulley Hall in 1985. The two and a half days went by at a pace typical for New York: three radio and newspaper interviews; a photo session with the *New York Times;* a dinner with the Schirmer staff; a party at Laurel Fay's that was attended, among others, by the conductor Joel Sachs and the pianist Cheryl Seltzer (who had performed *Introitus* as early as 1981 in a series devoted to contemporary music). Gubaidulina had a visit with Ussachevsky as well, and also discussed initial plans for a performance of *Offertorium* the following year with the Boston Symphony Orchestra. The view of the Manhattan skyline from the Empire State Building demonstrated the gigantic dimensions of American culture, causing this nature-loving city dweller to think about the transitory nature of the material world. She recalled that somebody once called this urban mass "mould encrusting nature" that would soon drag down the world to perdition, and she said to Laurel Fay: "It is a disgrace. Human beings have exerted themselves to build this—but it is transitory."

In November 1987 Gubaidulina accepted her first invitation to Paris to be present at Gidon Kremer's Radiodiffusion Française performance of *Offertorium.* The artistic aura of the French capital had always attracted many of her countrymen: Diaghilev's Ballet Russe with its composers and dancers, Tsvetaeva, and painters like Chagall and Kandinsky, and also Berdyaev, all had lived for a time in Paris after the Bolshevik Revolution. "Paris is certainly worth a trip," Gubaidulina said a few months later in an interview with a Kazan paper. "When you go for a walk there, it is like being in a fairytale."[17] "But my relationship with France," she added on another occasion, "is, of course, very limited, as I don't speak a word of French. That makes it difficult to be in close touch with another culture." In England and the United States she had friends like Gerard McBurney and Laurel Fay to act as cultural interpreters; in Paris she was on her own. But she returned home with a new commission from Radiodiffusion Française—a string trio that she composed over the next year. She was reading a lot of Pasternak at that time, his works having become available as a result of perestroika, and she dedicated the Trio for Violin, Viola, and Cello to the memory of the great man whose suffering was a subtle bond between them. On March 4, 1989, three members of the Moscow String Quartet played the premiere of the new work at the Salle Gaveau in Paris.[18]

On December 3, soon after her return to Moscow, another all-Gubaidulina concert was given at the House of Architects [Dom arkhitektora]; it took place in combination with an exhibition of twenty-five pastel paintings by Vladimir Yankilevsky in an adjoining room. In the web of relations among unofficial artists in Moscow, Gubaidulina's connections with the painters were rather tenuous, even though a few of their works, on loan from Alexander Gleser, an art collector, hung in her apartment. On September 15, 1974, she had interrupted her own work to see the famous Moscow open-air nonconformist "Bulldozer Exhibition" [Bul'dozernaia vystavka]. Public showings by these artists had been extremely rare before the onset of perestroika. Instead, artists showed their work in private homes, at a concert, or in a scholarly institute—and even then for no more than one evening. Occasionally Gubaidulina visited one of these exhibitions in the company of Pyotr Meshchaninov. In addition to Ilya Kabakov's paintings, she was especially fond of the works of Vladimir Yankilevsky because of their close connection with music. Yankilevsky, who moved to New York in the early 1990s and now lives in Paris, had had no previous contact with Gubaidulina before this concert, although he and Schnittke were friends. "In the late fall of 1987," Yankilevsky later said,

> I received a call from the House of Architects informing me that Sofia Gubaidulina had requested a showing of my paintings in conjunction with her concert. Because it was just a single evening, I chose "The Space of Experience" ["Prostranstvo opyta"], a cycle of pastel paintings I had just finished. It was a theme with various fugal improvisations. Though a painter, I am a composer, a musician, as my paintings are based more on the rules of music than those pertaining to painting—I see and I hear. I hear each color as a sound, a tone. Music, especially Bach and Shostakovich, has had a greater influence on my work than painting, and the laws of musical form are more relevant to my tryptichs than the laws of painting. My pastels were hung in a square room next to the concert hall. They played Sofia's Concerto for Bassoon and Low Strings [and *Garden of*

Joy and Sorrow], and during the second part Mark Pekarsky and the jazz singer Ponomaryova were doing their improvisations. The Bassoon Concerto revealed to me close parallels between it and my pastels—the same structure and tonality. "The Space of Experience" is like a scale model of the universe, with different forces meeting, clashing, and harmonizing. These elements are abstract, but the relationship is anthropomorphic. You can transpose these elements to a musical level, interpret them musically, but they are not musical illustrations but constitute their own parallel world. The same thing that is perceived by the ear is apprehended by the eye, because there are no isolated phenomena, no boundaries—it is all one. Art is the continuously changing world experienced by humans, but as we cannot show this process, we capture it in a single moment of time.[19]

Boston 1988: "Making Music Together"

When Sarah Caldwell, the American conductor, met Rodion Shchedrin on one of her trips to Russia, they conceived the idea of a major cultural exchange program between the Soviet Union and the United States—"Making Music Together." It was started in Boston in March 1988 with three weeks of Soviet music. Almost three hundred Soviet musicians, dancers, poets, and composers made the trip, among them Shchedrin, Schnittke, Gubaidulina, and—representing the younger generation—Korndorf. Because of his respected position in the Soviet music establishment, Shchedrin was able to enlist a number of first-rate artists in the project: the Bolshoi Ballet Ensemble with Maya Plisetskaya (Shchedrin's wife), who danced in three ballets composed by her husband; the Soloist Ensemble of the Bolshoi Theater [Solisty Bol'shogo teatra]; and many other soloists. The whole enterprise, however, was disastrous for its Boston organizers. Because of extremely careless organization, it was "the greatest festival that no one attended."[20] The festival program did not become available until two weeks before the opening, and many of the concerts suffered from general confusion. Sarah Caldwell had not demonstrated great skill in lining up sponsors for an event of that size, and in the end the state governor had to provide public funds to save it from financial collapse. Each composer had a special concert dedicated to his or her works, and Gubaidulina's could feature Tonkha, Lips, the Muir Quartet, and even Gidon Kremer, as the Boston Symphony Orchestra was presenting Schnittke's First Symphony and Gubaidulina's *Offertorium* in concerts running parallel to the festival. This gave Gubaidulina an opportunity to hear a first-rate American orchestra and experience the somewhat conventional taste of an American subscription audience. She expected the worst for the reception of her own work when members of the audience booed and walked out of Schnittke's symphony. But it all went well: Kremer gave a fine performance under the direction of Charles Dutoit and even raised the level of his playing the following day.

Gubaidulina enjoyed the high intellectual level and cosmopolitan atmosphere of New England. The students in Malcolm Peyton's composition class at the New England Conservatory were alert and eager, and her meetings with other American composers went well—with the Korean-American Earl Kim and with Ivan Tcherepnin (Nikolai's grandson and Alexander's son), who directed the electronics studio at Harvard. Several women composers attended her concert and gave a reception in her honor. Wherever she went she was given sheet music and records as gifts, and later described her overall experience at the festival as "the pleasure of new encounters."[21]

Meeting John Cage in Leningrad

In April 1988 Gubaidulina was invited to the Wittener Kammermusiktagen in the town of Witten on the Ruhr to attend a concert in her honor on April 24, featuring *Seven Words* and *Perception*. Afterward she made her first trip to Hamburg and Appen, where, at Victor Suslin's, she started work on two songs that had been commissioned by Roswitha Sperber, the singer and director of the Heidelberg International Festival, "Women Composers, Yesterday—Today" ["Komponistinnen gestern—heute"]. Soon after her return to Moscow, she visited Leningrad for the Third International Music Festival of the USSR [Tretii Mezhdunarodnyi muzykal'nyi festival' SSSR]. The extensive festival program included her Tsvetaeva portrait, *Hour of the Soul* (with revisions in the percussion part), featuring Mark Pekarsky and Lina Mkrtchian as soloists.

That year the festival attracted about 250 visitors from sixty-two countries, among them John Cage, who was on his first and only visit to the Soviet Union. Laurel Fay's special account of the meeting between Cage and Gubaidulina describes the event in detail:

> When I journeyed to the Third International Music Festival in Leningrad in May 1988, it was an unexpected pleasure to discover John Cage among my travel companions. Rather a lot of time on the way there was spent in transit lounges and hotel lobbies, and finding out that I was a specialist in contemporary Soviet music, Cage latched on to me. He was thrilled to be visiting Russia for the first time and fascinated by absolutely everything. He was eager to pick my brains about the most interesting composers, the latest trends in musical and cultural life, what he ought to look at and listen to. His genuine excitement was terribly touching, and I found myself doing whatever I could to try to enrich his visit. Of the Soviet composers I knew who were also in attendance at the festival, Gubaidulina was the one I thought most likely to engage his interest. It struck me that personal contact between them might prove mutually rewarding.

Having ascertained that both composers were responsive to the idea, I took the initiative to try to arrange a meeting. It wasn't easy. The only practicable time and place to get together was at a concert, but there weren't many opportunities. Cage was only there for four days and wherever he went he was surrounded by people wanting to rub elbows, request autographs, and have their photographs taken with him. At a symphonic concert at the Philharmonia's Bolshoi Hall on Sunday evening, May 22, I managed to persuade both of them during intermission to sit out the first piece on the second half of the program. I located an uninhabited lounge backstage where the three of us could sit down, and they could chat without disturbance.

The conversation didn't last very long, five or ten minutes at the most. I was the interpreter. They bypassed small talk. Fresh from hearing the performance of Cage's *Music for Fourteen* the previous day, Sofia had an advantage as Cage had not yet heard any of her music. Mentioning her interest in musical time, she queried Cage about his own [use of timing]. *Music for . . .* is notated with flexible time brackets. In the performance we had heard the day before, each of the musicians of the Bolshoi Theater Soloists Ensemble, who were scattered around the stage and auditorium of the Philharmonia's Maly Hall, had been conspicuously equipped with a watch. Sofia wanted to know why. Ideally, she thought, the performers ought to depend on their own internal clocks. Cage agreed wholeheartedly, but said that in his experience performers couldn't always be trusted to heed their inner clocks. As I recall his explanation, he said they had an unfortunate tendency to rush. Sofia was sympathetic but remained firm in her opinion. Both considered it a critical issue.

My sense as we emerged from the all-too-brief encounter was that both composers were satisfied with their exchange, that they hadn't considered it a waste of time. I had no inkling then how indelible an impression it had made on Cage. He left Leningrad the next day, and thus didn't have the opportunity to hear the moving performance of *Hour of the Soul* later that week, but he asked me to send him tapes of Sofia's music, as well as music by other interesting Soviet composers, a request I fulfilled when I returned to New York. Cage and I stayed in touch. I don't remember that he ever commented to me about his reaction to Sofia's music, but a year later he phoned to tell me he had written a piece inspired by their conversation and he wanted to be sure he was spelling her name correctly. The piece in question was *Two2* for two pianos. Cage read me the inscription that was subsequently inscribed in the published score: "This piece is in response to a conversation in Leningrad with Sofia Gubaidulina. 'There is an inner clock.'"[22]

Gubaidulina later described American culture by comparing it to Russian culture—both relatively young in contrast to "the old Europe" that lies in the center between them. "America is a young country," she said, "that represents youth":

Its culture is still in a tender stage and probably needs some help. There is an abundance of imagination and magnificent talent, but it all seems to be somewhat in floating suspension, like Ives or Cage, whose highly talented and magnificent efforts I have been aware of. If American culture is like a fourteen-year-old youth, Russian culture is a seventeen-year-old boy. At that age one is either a robber or very earnest and full of high ideals. One may be very talented but has hardly yet achieved one's acme. Particularly in music we are still at the beginning—we have not had a Bach or a Beethoven. But there is also no need for us to put on the brakes as in the rest of Europe, where, after reaching the top, the road goes downhill. In India, China, and Japan the cultural acme lies much farther in the past. But I believe that China in particular is experiencing a new wave, that both the Chinese and the Japanese are gaining momentum and have great new opportunities.

An *Answer without Question* for Gennady Rozhdestvensky

Concerts and visits gradually gave Gubaidulina name recognition in the West, and she received an increasing number of commissions. Some she had to decline because of prior commitments; others fell through or resulted in finished pieces only several years later.[23] Besides writing a number of smaller pieces, Gubaidulina worked on two large companion compositions between the summer of 1988 and the summer of 1990; these were works that could also be performed separately. One was a symphonic work recently commissioned for the Louisville Orchestra; the other was *Alleluia* for large chorus and large orchestra, written for the Berliner Festwochen 1990. At that time she gave them the joint provisional title *Mysterium tremendum*. Each part has seven movements and is based on an Old Slavonic Orthodox hymn.

Until October 1988 several trips interrupted Gubaidulina's work on this project. At the end of May she flew to Monaco to receive her own prize and to be part of the jury that selected the winner for 1988.[24] On June 22 she was present when Roswitha Sperber sang her *Two Songs Based on German Folk Lyrics for Mezzo-soprano, Flute, Harpsichord and Cello* at the Heidelberg Festival for Women Composers. Then she took her second trip to the Kuhmo festival for the premiere of *Rejoice!* Two months later she was in Copenhagen for the Danish premiere of *Stimmen . . . verstummen . . .* Finally, on October 2, she was in Dresden at a concert that had been arranged in her honor by Hannelore Gerlach at the second Days of Contemporary Music [Dresdner Tage der zeitgenössischen Musik], with a program consisting of *Perception, Quasi hoquetus,* and *Garden of Joy and Sorrow.* The atmosphere in the city was already fraught with a certain restlessness that would culminate a year later in the fall of the Berlin Wall. The performance of *Garden* concluded with a spoken passage from one of Tanzer's poems:

When is it really over?
What is the true end?
All boundaries are
Drawn in the earth
As with a piece of wood
Or the heel of a shoe.
To this point . . .,
This is the boundary.
Everything is artificial,
Tomorrow we will play
Another game.

The audience was visibly agitated and burst into vigorous applause.

Toward the end of the year Rozhdestvensky asked for an unusual favor from Gubaidulina: a concluding piece for a concert that would also include Prokofiev's Overture for Chamber Orchestra, in B♭ Major Op. 42, Shostakovich's setting of *Eight English and American Folk Songs for Low Voice and Orchestra* [*Vosem' angliiskikh i amerikanskikh narodnyik pesen dlia nizkogo golosa s orkestrom*], and Ives's Fourth Symphony (works that really did not fit together very well, in Gubaidulina's view). Not wanting to turn down the conductor's request, she settled down to four weeks of concentrated work to produce a collage of the other three pieces on the program, giving it the title *Answer without Question* [*Otvet bez voprosa*] (alluding to a work by Ives, *The Unanswered Question*). But because she did not consider this collage as properly her own music, she wrote next to its title "A Composer of the Twentieth Century" ["Kompozitor dvadtsatogo veka"].

At the performance on January 4, at the Moscow Philharmonia, Rozhdesvensky displayed a good sense of humor, according to Gubaidulina's later recollection: "I was hiding in the last row of the balcony waiting to see what would happen. Near the end, just before they played *Answer without Question,* Rozhdestvensky turned to the audience and said: 'You will now hear a work whose composer is a mystery to everyone. All it says here is "A Composer of the Twentieth Century."' At that point the musicians appeared on stage wearing colorful clothing and carrying their instruments ready to begin. After the last note, a man in a typical KGB suit holding a file folder stepped forward as the audience was cheerfully applauding and announced: 'We have just determined the composer of this piece—it is Sofia Gubaidulina.' The audience responded with laughter and enthusiastic applause."

Japan: Kobe and Tokyo—Experiencing a Vertical Culture

In the spring of 1989 Gubaidulina went on two major trips, one to the West and one to the East. Cheryl Seltzer and Joel Sachs introduced her to New York with a concert in their Continuum series on April 22, presenting *Quasi hoquetus, De profundis, Quattro,* and *Perception.* The emotional and dramatic power of the music, "in which textures are neither tonal nor atonal,"[25] captured the New York audience. Besides many emigrants who were present that evening in Alice Tulley Hall, John Cage heard the performance and personally expressed his appreciation to the composer. Only a few weeks later, on May 25, Gubaidulina set out on her first trip to Japan.

When the Japanese composer Yuji Takahashi became the artistic director of the music festival in Kobe, he consulted Gidon Kremer about artists whom he might invite, and Kremer suggested Gubaidulina.[26] Takahashi had lived abroad for many years and did not fully reengage with his own culture until the 1970s. Over the last two decades his compositions have developed unique and innovative combinations of words and music. Poetic texts—by Japanese authors as well as by Mandelstam, Goethe, Kafka, and others—are spoken to improvisations based on a variety of set patterns, with the music flowing from the natural movements of the player's hands and fingers. Takahashi was also active as an organizer, conductor, and publicist of contemporary music—for instance, in Kobe in 1989.

He later commented: "I had written Sofia that I wanted to invite her together with Astraea, but she did not warm to that idea. She was not sure whether improvisation would still work after such a long time, and she said that she would need a travel permit from the Composers Union. So I wrote to Khrennikov."[27] Gubaidulina's experience on her first trip to Japan was much like that of her Western colleagues, Cage, Messiaen, and Stockhausen. Fascinated by the elegant, old culture of Japan and by the courteous manners of its people, she particularly admired the architecture and the artistry of shaping nature on a small scale. A rock garden was a microcosm presenting the vertical world in artistic miniature. A year later, she said to a Russian music journalist in Tokyo: "My relationship to Japanese colleagues and the Japanese public is very close, very friendly. I am half-Russian and half-Tatar, and that's why I am partly Eastern. For me, Japanese culture is not exotic but something that organically relates to my own inner world."[28] Gidon Kremer and his Lockenhaus ensemble performed superbly in Kobe (a city of one million in the southern part of the main island of Honshu), playing *Quasi hoquetus, Rumore e silenzio,* the String Quartet No. 3, and *Hommage à T. S. Eliot.* A second performance was given in Tokyo, where Gubaidulina met the composer Tōru Takemitsu and the young composer Toshio Hosokawa, whose works are frequently performed in the West. Later Hosokawa recalled:

> Shortly before Sofia came to Japan, Toru Takemitsu invited me to his home and played a large orchestral piece for me. But he didn't tell me who had written it. It was very powerful, impressive music and it turned out to be Sofia Gubaidulina's violin concerto, *Offertorium.* Soon thereafter we met in person. I had a composer's concert at Casal Hall at the end of May. She was very busy and came only to the second part when my *gagaku* music, *Mandela,* was being played.[29]

Yuji Takahashi had also made arrangements for Gubaidulina to give a lecture at one of the institutes for higher learning in Tokyo. A number of composers and musicians came to hear her, among them the *sho* player Mayumi Miyata, who had worked together with Cage and often gave concerts in the West, and the great koto master, Kazue Sawai, who together with her husband ran a large koto school. After the lecture the organizer asked Gubaidulina whether she would prefer to spend her free afternoon looking at temples and shrines in Kamakura or visiting a famous koto master. Not knowing anything about the koto, she chose the visit to Kazue Sawai, who later gave the following account:

> The *koto* came to Japan from China in the sixth century together with Buddhism and is of course related to the spirit of Buddhism. I myself am neither a Buddhist nor a Shintoist, but I feel a close relationship because one encounters the influence so often in everyday life. I believe that Sofia is a Christian, but deep inside her she also relates to Buddhism and Shintoism. When I am playing—at a concert or at home—I always feel that I am praying. Nowadays koto music is not for the average citizen. Ever since European musical culture came to Japan, the significance of the koto has been underappreciated and in decline, and over the past thirty years koto music has taken on the status of underground music. That's why I can pray like that. I played three pieces for Sofia. Afterward her cheeks turned pink; she moved her arms in excitement and embraced me. She touched the strings lovingly and kept exclaiming in admiration. Then both of us together played the seventeen-string koto, and I asked her later: "Couldn't you write a piece for the koto?" And she replied: "Yes, I'll write something." I had no idea at that time what kind of a person and how great a composer she was.[30]

This meeting was the beginning of an artistic collaboration that is further discussed below. Following Gubaidulina's visit to Japan, Takahashi and Takemitsu both published supportive articles about her and her music, contributing in no small degree to her growing reputation in Japan.

In Kobe, Takahashi had promised Gubaidulina to invite her again for an orchestral concert with soloists of her own choice. Already in March 1990 this offer became a reality, and Gubaidulina returned to Tokyo accompanied by Lips, Tonkha, and the violinist Vladislav Igolinsky. Takahashi conducted the Shinsei

Nihon Orchestra in a performance of *Offertorium* and *Seven Words* at Suntory Hall. In keeping with the style of his own compositions, he introduced *Seven Words* with a recitation of Christ's words from the Gospels.

Yury Liubimov, the director of the Taganka Theater, was in the audience and said to a Russian journalist after the concert: "Sofia Gubaidulina and I are old friends, and the first thing I did after the concert was to ask her permission to use *Seven Words of Christ on the Cross* in an upcoming production of *The Brothers Karamazov* [*Brat'ia Karamazovy*]. The music is amazing and I am deeply moved."[31] *The Brothers Karamazov* eventually turned out to be *Elektra*. Directed by Yury Liubimov, the premiere of this play in Athens, on May 26, 1992 (as well as additional later performances in Moscow) included *Seven Words* as theater music.

London, Amsterdam, Bad Kissingen: Perestroika and a Summer Full of Festivals

Only eight days after her return from her first visit to Japan Gubaidulina set out on another five-week journey. Gorbachov's perestroika policy had started a tectonic shift not only in the Soviet Union; the West also began to raise the Iron Curtain. Old prejudices began to crumble, and in many places interest and enthusiasm for the neighbor to the East were on the rise, leading to new festivals featuring Russian and Soviet art.

Gubaidulina first set out to revisit London, where the Almeida Festival had arranged a major presentation of Soviet music. She and Silvestrov came as invited guests, but so did a younger generation of composers; Elizabeth Wilson, who was in charge of the program, also had invited a number of outstanding Moscow musicians. On July 14, at a special concert dedicated to Gubaidulina, the Andritti Quartet played her three string quartets and the String Trio in a demanding performance without intermission. Although suffering in stifling heat, the audience gave the performance its full attention, and the *Financial Times* commented two days later: "This concert . . . will undoubtedly count as one of the highlights of the 1989 schedule; for though various aspects of Gubaydulina's [*sic*] singular, independent, and absolutely distinctive compositional personality have already been demonstrated in previous festivals, this was surely her most concentrated, most revealing display so far."[32]

The next day Gubaidulina traveled to Amsterdam to be present at the Holland Festival, the most important cultural festival of the Netherlands, which for the first time introduced its audience to contemporary Soviet music on a large scale. Concerts, operas, and dance performances were scheduled in various locations for a whole month. Elmer Schönberger, in charge of contemporary music at the festival, had prepared himself thoroughly on repeated visits to Moscow. An unfamiliar world had opened up to him, and he was determined to present it in an ambitious program presented by invited Russian players as well as first-rate Dutch musicians. Schönberger commented on the "otherness" of this different musical world in the program brochure: "Russian composers, unlike so many of their Western-European counterparts, prefer to talk about the 'soul' of their music rather than about 'techniques,' 'structures' and 'material.' Their musical attitude has a highly-developed [*sic*] aesthetic and often religious dimension. This also applies for both the female composers who are prominently represented in the programme: Sofia Gubaidulina ... and Galina Ustvolskaya."[33] The nearly thirty concerts at the festival had an impact well beyond Holland itself: some of them were broadcast live on Radio Netherlands [Wereldomroep] accompanied by interviews with composers, musicians, and other music experts. The level of performance was remarkably high, and the concerts featuring Gubaidulina's and Ustvolskaya's works, in particular, turned out to be major triumphs. The three Amsterdam ensembles for contemporary music divided the performances among themselves: Nieuw Ensemble played *Garden of Joy and Sorrow;* Asko Ensemble, under the direction of Lucas Vis, performed *Hommage à T. S. Eliot;* and Reinbert de Leeuw and his Schönberg Ensemble presented *Perception.* De Leeuw continued to promote Gubaidulina's music by commissioning a piece for chamber choir and instrumental ensemble.

Bad Kissingen was the next stop on Gubaidulina's travels, and she was present for the premiere of the orchestral version of *Steps* on June 22, 1989. After the cosmopolitan and relaxed atmosphere at the Dutch festival, Gubaidulina now encountered a festival of the upper bourgeoisie at an elegant spa, where contemporary music was suitably intermingled with the great composers of the past. But in 1989 even Bad Kissingen's festival was dedicated to art and artists from the Soviet Union, and at the opening concert Tchaikovsky's overture-fantasia *Romeo and Juliet* [*Romeo i Dzhul'etta*] and Chopin's First Piano Concerto in E Minor Op. 11 were followed by Gubaidulina's *Steps.* The concert concluded with Scriabin's *Le Poème de l'Extase* [*Poema ektaza*]. Gubaidulina must have found it a moving experience to hear her work for the first time in seventeen years in a regular concert hall. The audience and the reviewers expressed their general satisfaction with *Steps.*

Three days after the premiere Gubaidulina traveled to the resort island of Sylt in the North Sea for two weeks of rest. Gidon Kremer had invited her again to Lockenhaus; the Rev. Joseph Herowitsch (who together with Kremer had organized the festival) had requested from her a composition for a special celebratory religious service on July 9. He had made arrangements to deliver to her in Moscow the full text of the psalm "Jauchzt vor Gott" with the request to set it to music for four-part choir.[34] The Konzertchors Darmstadt, under the direction of Wolfgang Seeliger, was scheduled to sing it at the service. All of this meant that the two-week vacation turned into a period of intensive work resulting in a new score for choir and organ, entitled *Jauchzt vor Gott* [*Likuite pred Gospoda*]. Because the piece grew larger than had been originally planned, Gubaidulina asked for a one-week postponement of the performance, but this proved to be impossible as the choir had to depart immediately after the service.

On the way to Gidon Kremer's festival Gubaidulina stopped again in Bad Kissingen to participate in the First Soviet-German Composers Symposium. But Lockenhaus was a disappointment, for, as it turned out, the performance of her new choral work did not take place. The score had arrived per fax only two days before the scheduled performance, and there were problems with the organ. So Gubaidulina returned to Moscow on July 16, after listening to performances of her String Trio (with Isabelle van Keulen, Veronika Hagen, and David Geringas) and of *Seven Words*. She was not able to accept invitations that summer to any of the Swiss events featuring *Seven Words* and other works: the Junifestwochen Zürich, the Schlosskonzerte in Thun, and the Internationale Musikfestwochen in Lucerne. The dates of these festivals partly overlapped, and Gubaidulina needed to return to her work as a composer.

Pro et Contra in Louisville; "Wien Modern"; and a Festival in Sverdlovsk

Back in Moscow Gubaidulina continued to work on her two large companion compositions, the one for Louisville, the other for Berlin. The first two movements of the first part—already named *Pro et Contra*—had already been sent to the conductor of the Louisville Orchestra earlier that summer. As Gubaidulina flew to the premiere on October 29, 1989, she carried with her the orchestral parts and the score of a third movement, which she handed to Lawrence Leighton Smith at the rehearsal the following day. Most conductors would have rolled their eyes in exasperation and refused to accept the music, but apparently Smith recognized this third movement as the important climax of the work. He and his orchestra, at any rate, accomplished the nearly impossible and in the remaining four days put together a remarkable performance of the forty-five-minute work. For that 1989 season, the annual six-week concert series of the Louisville Orchestra, "Classics in Context," had chosen "The Arts and Russia during the Revolution" for its theme, and the concert on November 3 combined Gubaidulina's work, Prokofiev's Second Piano Concerto, and Scriabin's *Prometheus* in a computer-controlled, technically accomplished performance of the light score. The audience expressed its appreciation of Gubaidulina's work, which to this day has not been extended beyond the three movements. Hubert T. Willis, the sponsor of this commissioned work, invited the composer to his home for a simple and relaxed dinner, and, when asked why he donated funds to support this kind of music, he replied, without affectation, "Because I get a tax write-off."

This performance of Scriabin's color symphony was to have consequences. According to Laurel Fay, "It was as ideal an embodiment of the letter and spirit of Scriabin's score as one could imagine. And yet the result was aesthetically disappointing."[35] After the concert Gubaidulina and Fay tried to analyze the reasons for the disappointment. It seemed to them that light and sound tended to suffocate each other rather than merge in a true synthesis. Yet both were convinced that a more sensitive, artistically accomplished interplay of music and light could be achieved. At that point in their conversation, Fay said: "If *any* composer could write color music in such a way that it would complement the aural experience rather than conflict with it, it would be you." As Fay later commented, "The instant [the words were] out I could see from the expression on her face that . . . the challenge was irresistible."[36]

Gubaidulina had planned to take a break the week after Louisville, visiting with Laurel Fay and sightseeing in New York. Instead, she withdrew to her room to do research on light and color, and to think about their possible use in *Alleluia*. Among the preliminary concepts she contemplated were seven colors for the seven movements; light as an imperceptible existence among us; light as a solo in complete silence, as the rhythmicization of silence; light as a contrasting rhythm against a background of sustained sounds; sound as an extension of a ray of light, coupled with light as an extension of a pattern of sounds; the imitation, or competition, between a rhythmic figure in sound and a rhythmic figure in light; and light as stasis.[37] On the last day in New York Gubaidulina and Fay attended a concert with instruments designed by Harry Partsch; on November 12, Gubaidulina left for Moscow.

After two weeks at home Gubaidulina traveled to Vienna, where she, Friedrich Cerha, Bruno Maderna, and Karlheinz Stockhausen were the featured composers at the festival Wien Modern. For the second time a month of contemporary music, under the artistic direction of Claudio Abbado (then the city's general music director and the music director of the Vienna State Opera), dominated the old historic music capital. Even before Gubaidulina's arrival, the Ensemble Modern had performed *Detto II* and *Quasi hoquetus* at the opening concert; a week later the Arditti Quartet had played her string quartets and her String Trio in three concerts, together with quartets by Webern, Rihm, Maderna, Kurtág, and others. The musicians were all first-rate, and Gubaidulina's two orchestral works were particularly well received. Shortly after her arrival, on November 26, Simon Rattle conducted the City of Birmingham Symphony Orchestra in a performance of Stravinsky's *Sacre du printemps* and *Offertorium*, with Gidon Kremer as soloist. On December 1 Michael Gielen conducted the Radio Symphonieorchester Wien (formerly the ORF-Sinfonieorchester) in a performance of *Stimmen . . . verstummen . . .* as well as works by Cerha and Maderna. At the conclusion of the festival, in a concert of solo pieces by Bach, Oleg Kagan and Natalia Gutman played *Rejoice!* It was one of Kagan's last performances of this work before his tragic death the following year.

In the course of the winter Gubaidulina's home country finally gave her the recognition that had been long overdue: an all-Gubaidulina concert was to be given for her in the Large Hall of the Moscow Conservatory. On December 27, 1989, Gennady Rozhdestvensky conducted the State Orchestra of the Ministry of Culture in *Stimmen . . . verstummen . . .* and *Offertorium*. It was Gidon Kremer's first performance of this work in Moscow. Just a few weeks later, during the second half of January, the first festival entirely dedicated to the works of Gubaidulina in the Soviet Union took place in Ekaterinburg (still called Sverdlovsk at the time).

Gubaidulina decided to go on a quick trip to Rome for a two-day meeting, January 15–16, 1990, devoted to the conditions and problems confronting composers today in Italy and the USSR. It marked the conclusion of a series of concerts throughout Italy, June to November 1989, held under the common theme, Italy's homage to Soviet Composers. Gubaidulina and Perteris Vasks had been invited to represent the Soviet Union, and among the Italian composers were Giacomo Manzoni and Enzo Restagno—the latter an influential musicologist and artistic director of the Torino Settembre Musica, where he had featured Nono, Carter, Henze, and other important contemporaries. Gubaidulina's meeting with Restagno was to have important consequences: he invited her to Turin for 1991 and commissioned a work for Settembre Musica.

During the winter and spring of 1989–90, Gubaidulina gave all her attention to the extensive score for *Alleluia*, which she was expected to complete by May. As travel had to be reduced to a minimum, she hesitated to accept an invitation to Sverdlovsk, where Vladimir Tonkha and Yury Nikolaevsky (then the conductor of the Symphony Orchestra of the Sverdlovsk State Academic Philharmonia [Sverdlovskaia gosudarstvennaia akademicheskaia filharmoniii]) were making plans for a Gubaidulina festival. However, Alexander Gazerelidi, the administrative director, who had done excellent preparatory work, was able to persuade her to interrupt her work once again for ten days. Yury Noklaevsky had always been a loyal supporter of Gubaidulina's work in the Soviet Union, having conducted more than fifty performances since the end of the 1970s—not only the already mentioned chamber music pieces but *Night in Memphis* and *Perception* as well as most of her orchestral works and a variety of solo concerts.[38] Tonkha once referred to him as a conductor with the precision of a Swiss watch. His calm demeanor and solid dependability were also essential qualities in the often fluid and unpredictable conditions of the Soviet music world. The intensity of the Sverdlovsk festival grew with every passing day: each of the four concerts raised Gubaidulina's stature in the city, so that at the concluding concert—presenting *Stimmen . . . verstummen . . .* and *Offertorium* (with Vladislav Igolinsky as soloist)—it was standing room only. In the atmosphere of restlessness and looming change that was sweeping the country, the Sverdlovsk festival was not only an enormous success for the composer and the performers; it also offered the public an experience of unprecedented artistic freedom in program selection and uninhibited conversations with the composer.

The Last Year in Moscow

The intelligentsia in the Soviet Union experienced the first years of perestroika as a period of great liberation and vibrant cultural activity. Manuscripts that had been suppressed for decades were being printed; silenced composers were again being heard; and any topic under the sun could be freely discussed. Various artists' associations elected as their new leaders people who had distinguished themselves as nonconformists during the Brezhnev era—only the Composers Union took its time, leading Edison Denisov to remark sadly, "Perestroika applies to writers, painters, film makers, and everyone else, except musicians."[39] Tikhon Khrennikov remained as chairman. When he resigned in April 1992, he had been in his post for forty-four years.

The period from February 1990, four years after the beginning of perestroika, until December 1991, with its many unsettling events and ever more difficult living conditions, marked the end of the communist regime in the Soviet Union. In February 1990 Lithuania was the first Soviet Republic demanding independence, prompting immediate Soviet intervention in Vilna. In March the Third Congress of People's Deputies dissolved the authority of the Communist Party, thereby opening the way to a multiparty system. At the beginning of August, with the termination of censorship, freedom of the press became a reality. Finally, an operational stock exchange in Moscow began to appear in the fall of 1990. Basic social and political structures were revamped, and members of the intelligentsia became *biznessmeny* (businessmen), bankers, or even politicians in one of the newly emerging parties.

Before long, however, the other side of the coin came into view. Conmen and speculators ruthlessly exploited the unstable conditions, and the crime rate intensified. By the fall of 1990 a major crisis in the availability of consumer goods spread throughout the land: milk, bread, and eggs were often not to be found, and matches and laundry detergents were in short supply. Sugar could be bought only with rationing coupons. Was perestroika being actively sabotaged by elements of the economic mafia? All sorts of rumors made the rounds, and many a member of the intelligentsia was haunted by apocalyptic thoughts of a general catastrophe.

Until the mid-1980s Gubaidulina had been able to enjoy her regular walks in Losinyi Ostrov Park, a necessary part of her life as a professional composer, but then things gradually changed. As she later commented:

> I lost my connection to the earth and stayed at home at my desk. When I was out, I constantly had to be on the alert, driven by the common daily fear that someone might come from behind and hit you over the head. A person who writes music cannot live with that level of anxiety. Besides being in contact with nature, with the stars, with the earth, and with the leaves on the trees, I have to feel free.[40]

And some traumatic incidents actually did occur. In the mid-1980s, while walking home late at night to his dacha from the suburban railroad station at Abramtsevo, Pyotr Meshchaninov was attacked and robbed. Gubaidulina herself was threatened two or three years later while trying to vacation again in Ussolye. Even this small village could not escape the chaotic effects of the great social and political changes. "Even in the afternoon in broad daylight," she recalled,

> there were disturbances and I heard the voices of some young men shouting, "Let's surround him!" Around midnight several people showed up at my quarters, walked around the house, knocked and pounded on the door and walls. They sounded very threatening but then withdrew. I was afraid and could not go back to sleep. Two hours later a man appeared at the door trying to force it open ... perhaps drunk, I don't know. As I was by myself—there was neither a phone nor a neighbor—I yelled in the worst possible peasant language: "If you come in, I'll kill you!" I had a rake with iron tines in my hand and was desperate enough for anything—it was a horrible situation. But my words seemed to have scared him, and he went away. I spent the second half of the night by the door holding the bolt. The next day I packed my knapsack and returned to Moscow.

Despite all this chaos and sense of danger, Gubaidulina continued with her travels. After her second trip to Japan in March 1990, she spent two weeks in Germany in April, attending concerts in Hanover and Cologne. Having completed the score for *Alleluia*, she went on her second trip to Finland toward the end of July to participate in the Scandinavian Anthroposophist Congress ("Taite 2000") in Tampere, the second largest city in Finland. The concluding concert in the cathedral, with her own performers from Moscow, was entirely dedicated to her work. Two of its high points were an especially successful performance of *In croce*—Vladimir Tonkha playing in front of the altar and Tatiana Sergeeva from the organ loft in the rear (an arrangement that gave spatial emphasis to the crossing effect)—as well as an improvisation that for the first time presented Manfred Bleffert in collaboration with Sofia Gubaidulina. Bleffert, who does not write his music in score but lets it take shape by way of improvising within pre-established scales and sonority fields, had arranged his specially constructed instruments on one side; Mark Pekarsky's percussion instruments were set up on the other side. As both artists played without either paying attention to the other at first, two separate worlds encountered each other. Gubaidulina, seated between them, joined and unified their playing with the soft resonant chiming of the celesta, until all three, with Bleffert's blocks of sound, ended the improvisation in total concentration on barely audible, fading notes. The reviewer for *Aamulehti* considered the evening's performance "one of the most elegant concerts of new music in Tampere in years." She then continued: "It was so much in a class by itself that I might go so far as to say that only once in a decade someone comes along who shows how it should be done."[41]

Ten days later Gubaidulina embarked on her first flight to Australia. Together with the American composers John Corigliano and David del Tredici, as well as the Viennese composer Kurt Schwertsik, she had been invited to the Musica Nova festival in Brisbane. It was "the longest, largest, loudest and liveliest festival of contemporary music to be unleashed in Australia."[42] *Hommage à T. S. Eliot, Introitus,* and other chamber works were part of the program, and the Queensland Symphony Orchestra, under the direction of the Dutchman David Porcelijn, performed *Offertorium* with Charmain Gadd as soloist. Whereas the nine invited Australian composers were engaged in open disagreement regarding new directions in tonality, materials, and complexity, *Offertorium* occupied a special position—partly because of its "rugged individualism"[43]—that fit none of the other tendencies. In reply to the organizer's question as to what had prompted her to take this long trip, Gubaidulina replied: "I wanted to look at the sky of the southern hemisphere."

Two weeks after her return from Australia, on September 11, *Alleluia* had its premiere at the Berliner Philharmonie. In a letter to Laurel Fay from Brisbane, Gubaidulina had commented on the combination of sound and light in this work: "I must say that the composition of this piece was a great experience and pleasure for me. Our idea to employ a color scale proved very beneficial. Once again, just as in *Stimmen . . . verstummen . . .,* a protagonist emerged who provides the piece with a canon (in the former it was the gestures and rhythm of the conductor, here it is the rhythm and symbolism of the beam of color.)" After mentioning a book on color theory that explained the perception of colors, she continued: "Can you imagine what a wonderful metaphor this is for the idea of sacrifice? We perceive the world in color only as a consequence of the sacrifice of white light."[44]

As Laurel Fay commented in a subsequent lecture, "The perception of color as the consequence of the 'sacrifice' of white light. Goethe's famous line from the preface to *Theory of Color* [*Zur Farbenlehrer*] sounds remarkably prescient here: 'Colors are the deeds of light, what it does and what it suffers.'"[45]

Ulrich Eckardt always assembled the best musical talent for the Berliner Festwochen, and *Alleluia* was performed by the Berliner Philharmoniker and the Choir of the Mitteldeutscher Rundfunk, Leipzig, under the direction of Simon Rattle. The conductor, who had made a name for himself partly because of his exceedingly high rehearsal standards, fully plumbed and developed the score in the available five rehearsal sessions, and in the end achieved an overwhelming success. The Berlin audience greeted the composer with ecstatic cheers and applause. During his years as general manager in Berlin, Eckardt had invited and met all the major musicians and composers of the postwar period; he later commented on Gubaidulina's success:

> Sofia Gubaidulina does not follow any trends; she creates art out of an original force deep within her, a force that is in some ways metaphysical. The source of her strength is more encompassing, deeper, but also darker than that of other great artists. In her work, emotion and sound as well as craftsmanship and structure are a single coherent unity. I consider her the most significant and original composer of our time—taking into account all her male colleagues.[46]

The first performance that attempted to incorporate the light score took place on February 18, 1994, at Avery Fisher Hall in New York. Leon Botstein conducted the American Symphony Orchestra together with the Concert Chorale of New York and the American Boy Choir. But on this occasion only the stage was suffused in light, and a proper performance of the work still remains to be done.

Enzo Restagno: "Discovering Sofia Gubaidulina"

In Janury 1991 Enzo Restagno planned to spend two weeks in Moscow to prepare a book on Gubaidulina. He made it a practice at the beginning of each of his music festivals to introduce a book on the composer he had invited. At the time of his Moscow trip consumer goods were scarce, and Gubaidulina was hard-pressed to find enough supplies on empty store shelves to entertain her visitor during the extensive daily interview sessions. Restagno's book—the first solid study of Gubaidulina—consists of two parts: "Life" (interviews conducted by the author) and "Work" (introductory analyses ranging from the Five Etudes to *Alleluia*, written by Valentina Kholopova). In response to a special request for inclusion in this biography, Restagno later wrote down his recollections of those days in Moscow:

It was Luigi Nono who first drew my attention to the music of Sofia Gubaidulina many years ago—I don't exactly remember when. He told me that she had suffered incredibly in her life and that she had great talent. I trusted Nono's judgment implicitly, which is not a matter of course, since those who really know something about music are quite aware that the judgments of composers are rarely objective. They are capable of maintaining the most paradoxical things with the deepest conviction in accordance with their taste and aesthetic sense. Nono, however, was incredibly liberal in his judgments: he pursued a logic that was purely musical and was based solely on intuition, and for him the things not expressed were far more important in music than those stressed explicitly. From the way he talked to me about Sofia Gubaidulina's music, which was then completely unknown here, I found myself strongly attracted by the silences, the suffering, the loneliness. What I was searching for in those years, when the idea of perestroika first appeared on the horizon, was something comparable to a kind of *Notes from the Underground,* and I was convinced that Sofia Gubaidulina could be an eloquent narrator for these memories. After preliminary contacts and a meeting in Rome, we agreed to get together in Moscow in January 1991. Consequently I went to her house every day for a couple of weeks that winter to hold long conversations, which were taped and later provided the basis for my book. These conversations took place on two levels and in two different languages: in Italian with the help of an intelligent and sensitive interpreter, Vera Kramskaya, and in German. Sofia Gubaidulina spoke German fairly well at that time but not sufficiently well to deal with more sophisticated arguments, and so we availed ourselves of the help of our interpreter. But when the work was done and we talked freely, we spoke directly in German. It was a pity to have to resort to the mediation of an interpreter—even though ours was very good—because Sofia sometimes had an incredibly inspired tone in her voice and words, and even if I could not understand them perfectly, they affected me intensely. I was exhilarated by this almost metaphysical and paramusical comprehension, also because I often realized that it was mutual. We communicated with looks: we heard the other speak in his unknown language of which we, nevertheless, guessed a great deal, and then we waited for the moment when the words of the interpreter would reveal to us what we had been so eager to understand. At that moment a light of satisfaction gleamed in her eyes and in mine, because we had received confirmation of the flash of intuition we had experienced a moment earlier.

Italian and Russian are two very different languages, but they possess a special musical charm which we discovered by turns during those long conversations. But it was not only a matter of the charm of voice and language—those were just a starting point of a deeper understanding of the horizons of her music, which I had diligently analyzed for a few months before visiting her. I told her at length about the impressions that reading her scores had left in me, and to make myself understood, I talked less of counterpoints and chords but rather of Gogol, Anna Akhmatova, Maria Tsvetaeva, Mandelshtam, Stravinsky and his

Symphony of the Psalms [*Simfoniia psalmov*], Russian churches, icons, of Pushkin and the endless suffering which has always marked the history of the Russian people. We got along so well—she understood me at once—and when I showed her that I had discovered in some passage of her music the most decisive turning points in the history of her country, she was very pleased and praised me in such a way that still makes me very proud today. One day I asked her whether she would like to go to Zagorsk [Sergiev Posad] with me the next day, and she very kindly accepted. I had also visited that holy city, which is part of the mythical "Golden Ring," in early summer a few years earlier. It was on a Sunday full of sunshine, the sky was the deepest blue, and a great crowd of believers was entering and leaving the various churches. I saw an old man with a long beard, wearing a visor, boots, and an old knapsack on his back. I looked up and saw the blue of the sky mirrored in the intense blue of the onion domes of the church crowned with their golden crosses: my heart nearly stopped, because here was one of the most beautiful Chagall paintings come to life! I returned to Moscow in the firm belief that Zagorsk was one of the most extraordinary places on earth, and that is why I asked Sofia Gubaidulina to come with me to this town eighty kilometers outside Moscow. This time it was a winter morning, frightfully cold, and there was hardly anybody there. However, in one of the churches a few poor old women were attending an endless religious ceremony. I looked on from a corner and did not bother Sofia even with a word. Only a few hours later did we resume our conversation in front of the icons. I am still grateful to her for having explained to me that, in these icons, the baby Jesus in the arms of the Madonna often has wrinkles around his eyes like an old man. These wrinkles, explained Sofia, express the painful history of mankind and should therefore inspire us to understanding and compassion. She told me all this very calmly and naturally, as if it were the simplest thing in the world; and I must agree that in a certain sense it really is, but at that moment I experienced an insight which proved to be of great benefit. In this, as on many other occasions, Sofia Gubaidulina enabled me to rise above my nature in the humane and intellectual sphere. The same happened with all the other great musicians I have written about in my books. I am very grateful to her for those great moments.[47]

Beginning in the fall of 1990 Gubaidulina's living conditions became increasingly difficult. Often the stores were empty, and she had to stand in line for hours to obtain the most essential goods. Her fellow citizens were full of anger, aggression, and nastiness. The situation reached a critical point in January 1991, when Red Army soldiers aimed their weapons at the inhabitants of Vilna and Riga. Many people feared the onset of civil war or the outbreak of widespread violence. "It really got to me," she later commented, "and I was unable to write music. It was an either-or proposition for me: either leave Moscow or death—that is, the death of my work and with that the death of my existence."

When Victor Suslin phoned Gubaidulina at that time, he found her in a mixed state of pent-up fierceness and deep despair—nothing he had ever encountered before. It struck him that something urgently needed to be done, and he immediately contacted Elsbeth Moser, who had many contacts through her position as a professor in Hanover. What could be done to help Sofia out of the worst of her dilemma, at least temporarily? On a two-hour walk Moser thought of everyone she knew and finally decided to call the Ministry of Culture of Lower Saxony. After two more hours her call was returned—with a solution to the problem. During the last week of February Gubaidulina left Moscow with only two suitcases to participate (together with Schnittke) in a concert and a panel discussion conducted by Günther Bialas at the Münchner Akademie der bildenden Künste on February 28. The next day she left for Vancouver to be present at a number of concert performances of her music. Shortly before her departure from Moscow, Pyotr Meshchaninov had returned to Leningrad from a concert tour in the United States; he called Gubaidulina and was stunned to learn that she had left Moscow to start a new life in Germany.

12 | Worldwide Fame, Worldwide Demand, 1991–1996

Workshop in Worpswede and Schreyahn;
Sixtieth Birthday Concerts

By the time Gubaidulina returned to Germany from Canada on March 11, 1991, she, too, had joined the ranks of Soviet emigrants of the third generation. It was the price that had to be paid for getting away from the unpredictable and difficult living conditions of these years of upheaval. Elena Firsova and Dmitri Smirnov had moved to England; Denisov had an apartment in Paris; and Schnittke had accepted a professorship at the Musikhochschule in Hamburg the previous year. Gubaidulina was offered a faculty position at the Sibelius Academy [Sibelius-Akatemia] in Helsinki but declined, as she wanted to compose rather than teach and was also not ready to leave her native country.

While Gubaidulina was still in Moscow, she had begun work on a concerto for cello, male chorus, female speaker, and orchestra that Veijo Varpio had commissioned for the 1991 Helsinki festival. Similar to her 1972 orchestral work, *Steps,* its theme is a gradual approach to God. Gubaidulina began her new composition under the chaotic living conditions of her last few weeks in Moscow, but the main portion of the labor was accomplished in Germany, where favorable circumstances happened to fall her way. The centerpiece of this work is the "Buch vom mönchischen Leben" (Book of monkish life) from Rilke's *Stundenbuch,* which the poet wrote in response to his travels in Russia at the beginning of the twentieth century. As a result of Elsbeth Moser's helpful intervention, Gubaidulina—having just returned from Canada in mid-March 1991—was able to move into an apartment in Heinrich Vogeler's "Barkenhof" in the artist colony of Worpswede. Rilke himself had lived there during his Worpswede years in the early 1900s, and this historical coincidence gave wings to her creative energy. For the next three and a half months she was able to recuperate in rural peace from the strains of life in Moscow and dedicate herself to her new composition without worries. Full of happiness and gratitude, she later commented on the theme of her work in a conversation with the music journalist Lutz Lesle: "The poems, the prayers of the 'Book of Monkish Life' are very close to me. This longing for God! This aching for God! That is what people are in search of nowadays. Never has the apocalypse been so near, the end of the world such a real possibility, and the possibility that the just shall be saved so unlikely."[1] Gubaidulina anticipated the rehearsals in Helsinki with some anxiety because of the attempt to combine the cello with sung and spoken word, but it turned out to her satisfaction. *Aus dem Stundenbuch* joins Rilke's poems with music in variously nuanced shades, "from emphatic singing to vocalized recitation all the way to the profoundly felt spoken word—a stepwise ascent to an 'intimacy with God.'"[2] As the work unfolds, a two-fold development takes place in the exchanges between male chorus and orchestra, the passages for solo cello, and the ensemble passages for cello and orchestra together. While the chorus and the orchestra descend to ever lower regions, the tessitura of the cello ascends into its higher and brighter regions—a polarity that, for Gubaidulina, makes a coherent whole: only in the dark depths of the soul can God's light be found. What Rilke had expressed through the persona of a Russian monk was close to Gubaidulina's own world, and one critic was completely on the mark with the observation that the cello concerto was Gubaidulina's "own book of prayers written in musical notation."[3] On August 27, 1991, Eri Klas conducted the City Orchestra of Helsinki [Helsingin kaupunginorkesteri] and the Estonian Men's Chorus [Eesti Rahvusmeeskoor], with Vladimir Tonkha as soloist; he had requested a cello concerto, and Gubaidulina had dedicated it to him. Since then, *Aus dem Stundenbuch* has been performed several times in both Russia (St. Petersburg, Moscow, and Ekaterinburg with Tonkha as soloist) and Tallinn, Estonia (with Ivan Monighetti).

The visit to Helsinki for the premiere of her cello concerto was not Gubaidulina's first trip in the year of her sixtieth birthday. In the second half of July 1991 she had visited Switzerland to be present at the performance of seven of her chamber music works at the Sixth Internationales Musik Festival Davos.[4] Michael Haeflinger, the artistic director in Davos, having chosen "improvisation" as a new theme for his festival, had also arranged for two performances by Astraea in the Church of St. Johann. For the first time, after ten years of involuntary interruption, Sofia Gubaidulina and Victor Suslin gave a joint concert of improvisations. Because professional connections with Viacheslav Artyomov had been severed, Gubaidulina suggested Mark Pekarsky and Valentina Ponomaryova as replacements. The Japanese *sho*-player Mayumi Miyata, whom Gubaidulina knew from her visit to Tokyo, had also been invited to Davos that year. As Miyata was a skilled improviser, Gubaidulina and Suslin spontaneously invited her to play with Astraea as a fifth addition to the quartet. Haeflinger arranged for a meeting in Davos with the Japanese jazz enthusiast and music manager Masanobu Araya, who invited Astraea to give a concert of improvisations in Japan that same year. Other invitations followed for 1993 and 1997.

On her way from Davos to Helsinki, Gubaidulina stopped in Basel on August 16, 1991, to talk with representatives of the Paul Sacher Stiftung about a possible acquisition of her scores. A few years earlier, Paul Sacher—one of the great twentieth-century patrons of music—had opened his large private collection of original scores, sketches, and letters by many modern composers to research. He now wanted to add the works of other composers to his archive. Gidon Kremer, who had been helpful in arranging this meeting, later commented: "I knew that when Alfred Schnittke and Sofia wanted to settle here [in the West], they would find it difficult to earn a living. It seemed appropriate for me to get in touch with the archive through Reinhard Paulsen, my very active assistant and manager in Hamburg. I asked him to discuss matters with Sacher and his representative, and in Gubaidulina's case it actually resulted in a contract."[5]

Gubaidulina left Helsinki for a few days in Moscow and then flew to Turin on September 13, where the "Settembre Musica" Festival was to present an "Omaggio a Sofia Gubaidulina" in five concerts. Among the birthday celebrations of that year, the Turin event was the most significant, offering performances of four large works: *Offertorium, Stimmen . . . verstummen . . ., Alleluia,* and *Hour of the Soul.* Tonkha, Lips, and the Arditti Quartet also played a number of chamber works. Yet another concert—premiering *Even and Uneven* [*Chët i nechët*] (commissioned by the festival) with Gubaidulina at the harpsichord and the celesta—was dedicated to Mark Pekarsky's percussion ensemble. When the composer met Patricia Adkins Chiti, the English vocalist of *Hour of the Soul,* in Turin, it turned out that they had corresponded many years before. In 1978 Adkins Chiti, president of the Fondazione Adkins Chiti: Donne in Musica and accomplished musicologist, had programmed a performance of Quattro at the Palazzo Braschi in Rome, during the "Donne in Musica" Festival. After her stay in Turin, Gubaidulina vacationed for ten days in Porto Maurizio on the Ligurian Sea and returned to Germany on September 30, 1991. She had been awarded a stipend and the use of a house for nine months in the artist's colony Schreyahn in the Wendland region.

During the first weeks at Shreyahn she focused almost exclusively on finishing *Silenzio,* a trio for bayan, violin, and cello that had been commissioned by the Hannoversche Gesellschaft für Neue Musik and was dedicated to Elsbeth Moser. Then Gubaidulina traveled to several concerts and birthday celebrations. At the end of October she visited Heidelberg to receive the "Heidelberger Künstlerinnenpreis." Following a concert in her honor on November 2, Astraea—with

Gubaidulina, Victor Suslin, and his son, Alexander (double bass)—improvised late into the night. Only a few days later Astraea performed again, for the appearance arranged earlier by Masanobu Araya, an event that Victor Suslin later described:

> We flew to Tokyo on November 3 and arrived in a euphoric mood. It was like being on another planet. Unable to sleep, we took a walk and planned to rehearse later at the hotel. But all we did was talk. The next day we were determined to rehearse thoroughly, but we never got beyond checking the microphones. Eventually we played without any rehearsal. It was a successful twenty-five-minute improvisation that was issued on a CD.
>
> Masanobu Araya had invited us for only one concert, but we had to stay for a whole week because the hotel rate was less than the cost of an immediate return flight. So we toured Kyoto and Tokyo with Ken Ito, a young composer, as our guide. He finally took us to some dive at the edge of the city, but it turned out to be a treasure trove. They had all sorts of Asian and Pacific instruments there. Sofia bought a sitar and I a Chinese violin, and the dealer gave us a child's koto as a present. On the return flight, our Astraea instruments and all these new purchases caused a problem. Because the size of the sitar would surely have required an extra ticket, as any cellist has to pay for his instrument, we simply took the sound box off and stowed it in our luggage. Sofia clutched the neck of the instrument between her legs on the flight and put her hat over it, and that's how we got home without a second ticket.

On November 16, 1991, *Silenzio* was performed for the first time during the sixtieth-birthday concerts and festivities in Hanover, with Elsbeth Moser, Kathrin Rabus (violin), and Christoph Marks (cello). Then Gubaidulina traveled to Bochum for a reunion with Gennady Aigi. On his first trip to the Bundesrepublik Deutschland, he read from his poems in her honor.

Prayer for the Age of Aquarius: Oratorio-Teatro-Balletto in Genoa

After three weeks of work in Shreyahn, Gubaidulina returned to Italy to receive the Premio Franco Abbiati in Varese, near Milano, on December 18, and then on to Genoa by chauffeured car. A few months earlier Genoa's postmodern opera house, Teatro Carlo Felice on Piazza de Ferrari, had had its grand opening. As part of "Old and New Indian Ways," a grand Italian-American festival celebrating the five-hundredth anniversary of Columbus's western voyage, a performance of Gubaidulina's *Prayer for the Age of Aquarius* took place on December 27, 1991. It was billed as an "oratorio-teatro-balletto." The artistic director of the festival, Valentin Proczynski, with the help of Enzo Restagno, had been able to enlist Gubaidulina's interest in this large-scale project. Normally she was reluctant when it came to requests for operas or works of ballet. The libretto for *Prayer* spans the entire myth from the fall of man in the Old Testament all the way to the life and work of Christ and a foreshadowing of Columbus. The music for this magnum opus consisted of the new cycle of works, *Pro et Contra,* as well as *Alleluia* and *Lauda* for alto, tenor, baritone, speaker, mixed chorus, and large orchestra. It had been composed specifically for the Genoa festival and is based on texts from the Apocalypse in various languages. The performers included many well-known names: the ballet ensemble of the St. Petersburg Mariinsky Theater (then still known as the Kirov Theater) was choreographed by Georgy Alexidze; Galina Vishnevskaya was the speaker in *Lauda;* and Rostropovich conducted the Latvian State Chorus [Valsts Akadĕmiskais koris Latvija] and the orchestra of the Teatro Carlo Felice. It was the first collaboration between Rostropovich and Gubaidulina. She came to admire him as a conductor and was satisfied with his chosen tempo in the rehearsal of *Pro et Contra.* Then the ballet master requested that the tempo be reduced for the sake of the dancers. "In one of the first rehearsals," Rostropovich later recalled,

> After we had played the beginning, she [Gubaidulina] said to me: "Everything is fine, the tempo is correct, and everything is well balanced." A little while later, a flutist from the orchestra asked her: "Please, is this an F or an F♯?" Without thinking much about it, she simply said: "F♯!" She knows the difference between what's important and what isn't. But I have also seen her in tears. At a performance of this work in Seville, annoying street noises intruded and the sound system was rather poor. We talked with the manager, but there wasn't much he could do, and Sofia had tears in her eyes.[6]

A Country House of Her Own

Gubaidulina spent the first half of 1992 in Schreyahn. She was hard at work to complete a number of commissions from Western organizers and musicians for early performances. During the first week of March she had to interrupt her work for another visit to Basel to finalize the contract with the Paul Sacher Stiftung.[7] The sale of the manuscripts made it possible for her to plan the purchase of a house. Things went well: a for-sale sign hung in the window of a house next to Victor Suslin's in Appen-Unterglinde, and it was just what she was looking for. The closing took place in June 1992, and Gubaidulina moved in shortly thereafter. The little yard was ideal: a small lawn, a miniature pond, and a large stone brought back memories of Japan. The first piece of furniture was the sitar from Tokyo.

One of Gubaidulina's first visitors was Mstislav Rostropovich. On July 19, 1992, he was to conduct the *Aquarius-Ballet* from Genoa at the Schleswig-Holstein

Musik Festival in Neumünster.[8] Missing a grand piano at Sofia's new and mostly empty house, Rostropovich went to Steinway in Hamburg to acquire an addition to its furnishings.

Koto Lessons with Kazue Sawai in Tokyo

Gubaidulina's fourth visit to Japan in September 1992 began in Yatsugatake, a spa with warm thermal waters in the mountains of Honshu. For some years, Tōru Takemitsu and Sviatoslav Richter had organized an annual fall music festival there. In 1992 they introduced a number of women composers under the theme "From the Late Nineteenth Century to the Present," and the concert on September 21 was dedicated to Gubaidulina; it featured her Quartet for Four Flutes, *Garden of Joys and Sorrows,* and *Rejoice!*

Gubaidulina returned to Tokyo the day after the concert. Kazue Sawai had not forgotten that she had asked the composer in 1989 to write a work for the koto and now invited her for a week. Gubaidulina lived and worked without interruptions in a room provided only with a standard thirteen-string koto and seventeen-string bass koto. The only interruptions came at meal times when a student would knock on the door and bring a tray of food. In the course of the week, Gubaidulina heard four performances by Kazue Sawai: a traditional koto concert; a concert of contemporary koto music; a work by Ichirō Higo for koto and orchestra; and a jazz improvisation together with Budgie Morris (saxophone) and Motoharu Yoshizawa (double bass) in a club crowded with young listeners. She was impressed with the koto's range of performance styles but decided not to use any of what she had heard during the four performances in her own composition, saying to her hostess: "This instrument is full of unrealized possibilities, and I want to bring them out." Kazue Sawai gave the following account of Gubaidulina's week-long visit and her composition for the koto:

> In the middle of the night I heard the sound of a koto from the room where Sofia was supposed to be sleeping. The sound continued for several hours and was joined by Sofia's voice singing in accompaniment. When I called out, "Let's have breakfast" the following morning, she exclaimed "Listen! This instrument produces such beautiful sounds. What a wonderful instrument this is!" and played for me for the next two hours. I was surprised by the multiple shades of tones that she drew out of the koto. The sounds brought back a memory.
>
> One hot summer day I was practicing in an open, airy space. Tired of playing, I left my instrument and went into the next room. The breeze that had been blowing grew stronger and suddenly I heard a faint and unfamiliar sound. It grew louder and stronger and soon I was captivated in an aura of innumerable gold and silver threads flowing down from heaven. I could not move. Then, like the tide ebbing, the sound slowly faded away. The wind had played with the

strings, making the koto sing as though it were alive. Since that day I have come to believe that musical instruments have many sounds that they intrinsically possess and want to express, beyond the sounds that human beings produce through their control and performance. All the same, human arrogance makes us continue the routine of forcing instruments to play according to our scores and we forget to draw out the sounds the instruments really want to play.

Throughout the week that Sofia spent in the room in our modest home, she slept next to the instruments, the mattress and bedclothes right beside the koto and seventeen-string koto on the floor, the strings at eye level. Every day of that week was filled with excitement as fragments of what would become the piece, ... *Early in the Morning, Right Before Waking* ... [... *Rano utrom pered probuzhdeniem* ...], gave us hope that we could re-create with our own hands that moment when the wind wove a gold and silver aurora. (The evening of that [earlier hot summer] day I had tried to repeat the experience using an electric fan—it produced sounds but not the sensation of being enveloped in an aura.) Sofia would look at the instruments with the most gentle gaze; she would listen to their sounds with an indescribably beautiful expression of joy on her childlike face. When the time came to return to Germany, she lovingly caressed the koto with her cheek and carried it home.[9]

Gubaidulina completed the work for four standard kotos and three seventeen-string kotos (bass kotos) in Appen. On her next visit to Japan ... *Early in the Morning, Right before Waking* ... was performed on June 4, 1994, by the Koto Ensemble Kazue Sawai in a rock garden in Tokyo together with works by Yuji Takahashi, Tadao Sawai, and others.

Paying the Price of Fame

The move to the new country home came just at the right time. The months leading up to the spring of 1994 were a period of unprecedented hard and concentrated work in Gubaidulina's life. In 1993 she wrote seven important compositions which were performed in quick succession: *Dancer on a Tightrope* [*Tantsovshchik na kanate*], *Now Always Snow* [*Teper' vsegda snega*], *Meditation über den Choral "Vor deinen Thron tret ich hiermit" von J. S. Bach*, ... *Early in the Morning, Right before Waking* ... [... *Rano utrom pered probuzhdeniem* ...], *Und: Das Fest is in vollem Gang*, the String Quartet No. 4, and *In Erwartung*. Production schedules such as this one, as well as trips at home and abroad, were the price of fame, and Gubaidulina was willing to pay it. March 11, 1994, was the date for the 250th anniversary celebration of Leipzig's Gewandhaus Orchester, one of Germany's oldest and most renowned symphony orchestras with close connections to Arthur Nikisch, Bruno Walter, and Wilhelm Furtwängler. German president Richard von Weizsäcker honored the event with an appropriate speech, and Kurt Masur, having chosen *Offertorium* for the program, had invited Gubaidulina.

Another important event at that time was the premiere of *Now Always Snow* by the Schönberg Ensemble and the Nederlands Kamerkoor under the direction of Reinbert de Leeuw. Gubaidulina has considered this piece, in which she used texts by Gennady Aigy for the second time, one of her more accomplished compositions, and the premiere on June 12, 1993, at the Holland Festival in Amsterdam, had been carefully prepared. De Leeuw performed it later with great success in both the United States and the Netherlands.

Gubaidulina and Victor Suslin were also invited to concerts by the summer academy of the Salzburg Mozarteum in August, and, during November 20–24, 1993, Sofia was in St. Petersburg participating in a new international festival of contemporary music, the programs of which were presented under the title "Sofia Gubaidulina and Her Friends" [*Sofiia Gubaidulina i eë druz'ia*]. The "friends" included not only composers Suslin and Silvestrov but performers Gidon Kremer, Mark Pekarsky and his ensemble, Vladimir Tonkha, Tatiana Sergeeva, and others. Tickets were extremely expensive, it was freezing cold, and public transportation was scarce. Still, for most concerts the hall was three-quarters full (Kremer's performance actually sold out), a remarkable achievement considering that in the relentless struggle for survival in noncommunist Russia, art and culture had become unaffordable or at best of secondary importance among the intelligentsia.[10]

Gubaidulina left St. Petersburg and traveled via Moscow to Kazan for an early December festival with two concerts, a reception by the prime minister, and several other honors bestowed on her as a famous Tatar composer. When a group of young people without tickets forced their way into the hall for a performance of *Alleluia*, damaging a wall in the process, the Minister of Culture of the Republic of Tatarstan smiled and said to Gubaidulina, as she later recalled: "What a wonderful bunch of youngsters we have here! They crash the hall not for a rock concert but for your music. It will be a pleasure to repair the damage."

After the last-minute completion of the score for *In Erwartung* at the end of December 1993 for its first performance in Stockholm, Gubaidulina set out on a five-week marathon trip on January 18, to be present at four separate premieres. Her first stop was New York, and then Las Palmas in the Canary Islands, Stockholm, again New York, and finally Washington, D.C. The first premiere, on January 20, 1994, featured the Kronos Quartet in her String Quartet No. 4. Because this California ensemble often works together with folk artists and weaves elements of pop and jazz into its performances, it always travels with a sound and light technician. Each performance is a show, although some of the crossover pieces do not remain in the repertoire for long.

The Americans had performed Gubaidulina's String Quartet No. 2 many times, issued it on a CD, and then commissioned another string quartet from her. The composer chose three sound layers for this work, indicated in the score as A, B, and C. Sound layer A is a prerecorded tape with the instruments tuned a quarter-tone higher. Layer B is also a prerecorded tape of extended ricochets produced by a springy steel string (e.g., a piano string), attached to a small solid rubber or plastic ball, being bounced across the string players' instruments. Layer C is the live quartet playing on stage. Layer B is heard first, and then layer A is added to the texture. Finally, the live quartet enters with layer C. A colored-light projection is coordinated with the three sound layers.

With this superimposition of different timbral layers, Gubaidulina reestablished connections with the basic concept of her 1987 quartet cycle and T. S. Eliot's philosophy of time. The concert at Carnegie Hall was well attended, and Gubaidulina's work was given an advantageous position as the last piece on the first half of the program. Lee Hyla's *Howl*, with the nearly seventy-year-old Allen Ginsberg reading from his famous poem, followed the intermission. Gubaidulina did not know who Ginsberg was, and she was probably unknown to him as well. Every work played that evening was accompanied by special lighting effects; only Gubaidulina's quartet came with a complete lighting score.

The Quartet No. 4 was perfect for these four players from California. Over the next six months they performed it fifteen times in the United States, and then in Canada, Germany, Switzerland, the Netherlands, France, Finland, Estonia, Italy, and Israel. As early as the fall of that same year, the Kronos CD, *Nightprayers* (including the String Quartet No. 4), made the classical hit parade of *Billboard Magazine* and remained on it for eleven weeks, reaching seventh place—all in all, a successful record for a piece of contemporary music presented in the American style.

After the New York premiere, Gubaidulina flew to the Canary Islands on January 27, 1994, to be present at the premiere of her second cello concerto, *Und: Das Fest ist in vollem Gang* on February 1. Because the organizer's original invitation to Simon Rattle and the City of Birmingham Orchestra had failed because of logistical problems,[11] the Finnish Radio Orchestra [Radion sinfoniaorkesteri], directed by Jukka-Pekka Saraste, was invited in their place. After only two rehearsals back home, the Finns arrived with David Geringas (the soloist to whom Gubaidulina had dedicated her work) in Las Palmas for their performance at the Music Festival of the Canary Islands. It was only a moderately successful event, largely because Saraste, a serious professional, focused his attention on the first part of the program, Stravinsky's *Sacre du printemps*. David Geringas—a Rostropovich student and winner of the International Tchaikovsky

Competition in the same year that Gidon Kremer won First Prize—proved to be an excellent and highly motivated soloist; in the course of the next few years he played Gubaidulina's work almost forty times on three continents.

Gubaidulina traveled from the southern sunshine of the Canary Islands to the cold winter of Stockholm to attend the premiere of her latest composition, *In Erwartung,* played by the Raschèr Saxophone Quartet and the Kroumata Percussion Ensemble. Since the Raschèr Quartet's first inquiry about a work for saxophone quartet and orchestra in 1988, the project had remained dormant until Gubaidulina decided on a piece for saxophone quartet and percussion ensemble in May 1992. As usual, she came to the rehearsals feeling anxious, but the American saxophone quartet and the Swedish percussion sextet had prepared themselves so well that they needed no additional advice. After the brilliant premiere on February 12, 1994, the musicians continued to play the piece on a tour of several Swedish cities and were consistently rewarded with standing ovations.[12]

Gubaidulina's second trip to New York started in Stockholm on February 14. In New York she was met at the airport by Laurel Fay and stayed with her for a few days. The day after her arrival she heard a performance of Schnittke's Seventh Symphony with the New York Philharmonic Orchestra under Kurt Masur. After the concert Gubaidulina, Masur, and Fay accompanied Schnittke—Sofia's friend and colleague of many years—back to his hotel. In alarmingly poor health, Schnittke had to return to Germany in a wheelchair the next day. It was his last visit to the United States. As previously mentioned, *Alleluia* was performed with a completely realized light score on February 18, 1994.

Only a few days later, on February 24, Gubaidulina was in Washington for the premiere of *Dancer on a Tightrope,* a piece commissioned by the Library of Congress. The score is now in its distinguished and extensive collection that also includes works by Bartók and Stravinsky. The instigation of this composition had come from a plan initiated by the Library of Congress to honor Robert Mann, the senior member and first violinist of the Juilliard Quartet, one of the premier U.S. ensembles. After a long and distinguished career, Mann was about to retire from the Quartet, and it had been his wish to play a Gubaidulina composition together with the pianist Ursula Oppens. When Gubaidulina and Laurel Fay delivered the score to the Library of Congress, they had a conversation in Russian with James Billington, the Librarian of Congress and author of *The Icon and the Ax: An Interpretive History of Russian Culture* (New York: Random House, 1966), who was eager to get to know the composer. After three days in Washington visiting with her daughter Nadia, who now lived there with her family and was working as a biochemist, Gubaidulina returned to Germany on February 27.

Simon Rattle: "I would call her a flying hermit . . ."

The premiere of *Figures of Time* [*Figury vremeni*] had been planned for the 1993–94 season at Birmingham's new Symphony Hall but had to be postponed because of Gubaidulina's heavy work schedule. It finally took place on November 29, 1994, and followed Haydn's Symphony No. 22 (*The Philosopher*) on the program. Anne-Sophie Mutter played Beethoven's Violin Concerto after the intermission. With many interruptions, Gubaidulina had been working for a long time on this piece, again and again rejecting her "number games" but finally completing a composition for large orchestra in four movements. Simon Rattle's performances of *Offertorium* and *Alleluia* had impressed her deeply, and she told a Birmingham journalist on the day preceding the concert: "I was absolutely enchanted by his forcefulness, his energy, his depth and his sophisticated musical talent. So I felt a strong desire to create some work jointly with him. When you have a particular performer in mind, your work has something unique and individual, you see them as you're doing the composition. You gauge how exotic can be the musical task you propose."[13]

The meeting between Sofia Gubaidulina and Simon Rattle was an encounter between two very different worlds and cultural backgrounds, which Rattle described with typical English humor—at the same time, however, commenting incisively on Gubaidulina's music and artistic intentions:

> To this day I often conduct Russian composers, even though Tchaikovsky has been a large blind spot for me. What I like about many of these works is the powerful atmosphere, the depth, the darkness, and the willingness to go beyond the usual. And that is exactly what has attracted me to Sofia's music—there are no limits set by nature. . . .
>
> I have some very funny memories of the Birmingham performance of *Figures of Time*—it was quite wonderful. When I got to know Sofia, I spoke no German and she no English. But we had to communicate somehow, either with signs or the help of others. I always had the impression that whatever she said in German sounded somehow crazy—even though I didn't understand it. When I began to understand German a little better, I noticed that indeed it *was* crazy. . . . She is a really crazy woman, of course in a completely positive way, like my first view of a Russian icon with Judy Garland's hairdo—which was along the same lines. *Figures of Time* brought us closer together, and I recognized her high idealism—an idealism regarding certain tonalities of this work. Toward the end there are the sounds of the flexatone. I suppose she was able to produce some special sounds on it at home. And now she expected the lead violinist and the percussionists—who played the four flexatones—to produce the same sounds at the same volume in a large concert hall. Then her flexatone broke and was com-

pletely out of commission. Because the flexatones in the orchestra were not being used just then, she got up on stage, took the instrument of one of the musicians, played it, and then repaired her own with the parts of the other one. Naturally, the Birmingham percussionists went nuts, and every time she approached the stage they scrambled to pack up their instruments, and said: "My God, that's awfully nice. What do you suppose she's trying to do now?" All this was rather interesting. At any rate, she has very precise ideas about sound, and you have to somehow manage to produce these sounds. She's a great idealist.

She often told me, "Simon, I always look up." She does always look up at the sky, the way she did when she was young. And sometimes I think I should also look up occasionally and take her down a notch. All this looking up may be something very Russian . . . but I am sure it means something. Her piece was tremendously successful in Birmingham and also when we played it in Holland, in Amsterdam and Rotterdam. But like many of her works it is not easy to rehearse because it depends on a very special kind of connection with the audience. One ought to have the audience at the rehearsals so as to understand the silence, the fullness of the required time. Much of what seems pointless in an empty concert hall makes perfectly good sense in the presence of the audience. That's one of the reasons why I like her—she is a true "communicator" who will take any risk and is somehow convinced that it will grab the audience. It is quite wonderful what she told me about the last movement, which I found very confusing. Because I could not at all see what she intended with it, I said to her: "Sofia, I need your help." To which she replied: "Imagine you are living in a large apartment complex filled with the horrible noise of electric guitars. Naturally you aren't going to get any sympathy from any of these people. Finally you tear open the floor boards to see what is beneath you. And then you notice it is really and truly hell itself. That's what I wanted to convey in the last movement." The piece then comes to a radiantly melodic ending, as is so often the case with her. In East-European music, starting with Modest Musorgsky, it is always helpful to know what it is about—to be familiar with the *story,* so to speak. Sometimes it is quite obvious but not always, as for instance in [György] Kurtág's music. With him, you have to invent your own subtext. But Sofia doesn't keep her secrets to herself as Kurtág does. She answers questions that are put to her, even though her answers sometimes take you to a place you didn't expect. She is a person full of surprises.

I would call her a "flying hermit," because she is constantly in orbit, only occasionally touching terra firma. She is not the sort of hermit who lives in a cage. It is more important for her to look at the light, and every now and then she comes down to earth to bring us light before she is off in orbit again. She is much more interesting than someone who has committed himself to this world down here. She does not give me the impression of being someone who deals very practically or effectively with worldly matters. Rather, she seems like someone who filters an unendurable spiritual ecstasy into her music. Perhaps it is because of the language barrier between us, because we cannot communicate very easily. But I have the impression that she is mostly preoccupied with trying to capture these things. Although her palette of colors is very dark, very Russian, she is preoccupied with light. After all, you need dark glasses when you look at the sun during a solar eclipse.

I am very interested in what she will do over the next few years, what new paths she will be seeking. She is much too extraordinary to keep working the same gold mines. Also, she has a wonderful sense of humor, and I'm curious how it will continue to show itself in her music. But it is difficult to say anything about a composer before one has a chance to look at her complete "*oeuvre*"—thank God, she is still a young woman with much to look forward to.[14]

The "Présences" Festival in Paris

The fifth "Présences" festival of contemporary music, organized by Radiodiffusion Française, took place in Paris, January 28–February 19, 1995. It focused on Sofia Gubaidulina and on music with "unconventional instruments," and its almost thirty concerts presented forty premieres. Begun in the early 1990s by Jean-Pierre Armengaud and Yves Prin, "Présences—Festival de création musicale" was to be a venue for the performance and discussion of contemporary music. Until that time, the Parisian world of music had been largely defined by Boulez and his IRCAM school. Armengaud, who had been active for more than twenty years developing Russian music in France, later talked about how the plans for "Présences 1995" had evolved in the context of the contemporary music scene in Paris:

> In 1992 our theme had been "Young European Composers" [L'Europe des jeunes compositeurs] and the following year it was "Russia" [Russe]. Denisov had helped me to put the program together, and we presented several generations of Russian and Soviet composers together with a number of French composers. It was a good thing that Boulez had a high regard for Denisov—because Denisov represented a bridge to postserial music—and suddenly one could notice the beginnings of a new, contemporary music in France. The Paris reviews of our concerts were terrible; they considered this music a kind of outdated modernism. *Le Monde* wrote that some of the compositions were flat and not very professional. It may be true that some of them were a bit naïve—but a few years later this musical language became dominant, even in France—tonality and repetitions in the style of Arvo Pärt and others. At that time I wanted to show that the world of music was undergoing a transformation with a change of generations and that this process needed some fresh air. In 1993 our success was only so-so. . . . Then things developed quickly, and postmodernism took a leap forward by 1995. People came and urged me: "Play something by John Adams!" I was pushing to invite Sofia to Paris and had visited her in Germany to discuss the program. I think the success of "Présences 1995" was greater than that of our Russian project two years earlier. Russian music has two currents: one leads to

Germany and that is Schnittke, the other to France and that is Denisov. Sofia's music also has something French, perhaps an element of impressionism, but she needs Germany and is now connected to that country by living there.[15]

In the nineteenth century French and Russian culture existed in fruitful symbiosis. Gubaidulina herself experienced the spirit of French culture and its people as, on the one hand, jovial and playful and, on the other, rational and formal. As she later said: "Perhaps they are too much enamored of surface glitter. Within IRCAM, a new generation seems to be freeing itself from Boulez and his school. I am particularly impressed with Kaija Saariaho, the Finnish composer; her music is special, very beautiful and elegant."

Gubaidulina was introduced to the Paris audience on February 18, 1995, with four large orchestral works, *Perception,* and eight chamber music works. The high point of the program was the premiere of her flute concerto, *Music for Flute, Strings, and Percussion* [*Muzyka dlia fleity, strunnykh i udarnykh*] that was performed together with *Khôra,* a new piece by Pascal Dusapin, and John Adams's *El Dorado.* With the experience of an earlier performance of *Offertorium,* Charles Dutoit conducted the Orchestre National de France, and Pierre-Yves Artaud performed on four different flutes—bass, alto, grande, and piccolo.

As early as 1979, after playing Gubaidulina's Flute Quartet, Artaud considered asking Gubaidulina for a flute concerto, but he realized his request only now, with the support of Armengaud and Radio-Télévision Française. He played the Flute Quartet once again in the afternoon before the premiere of *Music for Flute, Strings, and Percussion,* this time with the Quatuor Arcadie flute-quartet ensemble, of which Artaud himself is a member. Just as the United States produces outstanding brass players and Russia first-rate string players, one can speak of France as the country with a distinct, if diverse, flute tradition. The French were acclaimed flute players even in the Renaissance, and there may be some connection between the special articulation of the French language and the flute. When asked about Gubaidulina's flute concerto and her composing for the flute in general, Artaud later commented:

> Gubaidulina's music leaves the performer a large "space." The musical text strongly demands the player's physical and mental involvement because the final result is largely left to the artist's personality and imagination. As with the sphinx, her text poses more questions for the artist than can be answered. Like Sherlock Holmes, every performer must assemble the clues, the evidence, or the embryonic evidence that, if put together properly, will reveal the puzzle and release the deeper meaning that is hidden to the eye in the score. Each mystery, however, contains within itself its answer or answers.
>
> One could say that Sofia Gubaidulina's music makes total demands on the performer's personality; the performer, in return, has the responsibility of

performing an act of creation. In this regard, one can contrast her music with Stockhausen's or—somewhat provocatively—even Mozart's; in their scores the interpretive artist feels "uncomfortably" sandwiched between "doing too much" (vulgarity) and "doing nothing" (platitude). It is exceedingly difficult to achieve the right expression because it must be a perfect balance impossibly positioned between total, subjective involvement and objectivity.[16]

In *Music for Flute, Strings, and Percussion*, Gubaidulina continued to work with the musical symbolism that she had begun to use two years earlier in her String Quartet No. 4. The musicians are divided into two groups, with the instruments of one group tuned a quarter-tone higher than those of the other. Making the symbolic intentions palpable, this arrangement creates two musical worlds—the world of light and the world of shadows, set off by the quarter-tone difference. Gubaidulina continued these experiments in some of her later works: *Quaternion* for four cellos (1996), Concerto for Viola and Orchestra (1996), *In the Shadow of the Tree* [*V teni dereva*] for koto, bass koto, *zheng* (a Chinese version of the koto with steel strings), and orchestra (1998), and *Risonanza* for three tumpets, four trombones, organ, and six string instruments (2001).

Outside the festival itself, an opportunity came about for a special musical improvisation in a recording studio in Paris. Mitsu Ishii, the producer of Kyoto Records in Japan, was looking for another piece by Gubaidulina for a CD publication of ... *Early in the Morning, Right before Waking* ... When he suggested a recording of an improvisation with Kazue Sawai, Gubaidulina proposed that they invite Mayumi Miyata as a third performer. Thus the two Japanese artists arrived in Paris in early February 1995 to join Gubaidulina at the recording studio for their improvisations.

A few years later Mayumi Miyata gave the following account:

> Sofia had arrived with a large satchel full of instruments, an old violin and a number of folk instruments. We didn't talk much before doing the first recording session, and I think the results were quite good. The second session was too long and got a bit boring. Then we agreed on the basic structure, and when we played for the third time the music grew and developed its own direction away from our predetermined structure. The three of us have very different personalities. Kazue is always in a high state of excitement and plays with utmost concentration, like in a dream, easily forgetting the other players. I myself am quite calm, perhaps a little cold. Sofia is also energized by excitement but differently from Kazue. She is vibrantly alive and full of youthful and childlike energy, like a young girl. She surprises by always bringing something new, and she delights in the sound. We had great fun with our improvisations.[17]

The product of these two days in the recording studio was a Japanese CD with the title, *Three Strangers in Paris*.

Nono's *La lontananza nostalgica utopica futura*
with Sofia Gubaidulina

From June 26 to July 9, 1995, Gubaidulina visited Gidon Kremer's Lockenhauser Kammermusikfest in Austria for the second time. Her own compositions and Victor Suslin's works, together with an appearance by the Astraea ensemble, were given center stage. In each of the twenty concerts of the festival, the audience could hear one work by these two composers. The festival program also included "Hommage à Luigi Nono," in which the Ensemble Mark Pekarsky performed Gubaidulina's *Can You Hear Us, Luigi? Here's a Dance, Which an Ordinary Wooden Rattle Will Dance for You* for six percussionists. Kremer had met Nono three years before his death, and in 1988 the composer wrote a piece for solo violin and eight-track audio tape with the title, *La lontananza nostalgica utopica futura. Madrigale per piu "camiantes" con Gidon Kremer* (*The Nostalgic Utopian Future Distance. Madrigal for More "Wanderers" with Gidon Kremer*). Kremer was aware of Gubaidulina's admiration for Nono and her sense of gratitude for his friendship. In fact, Kremer had been able to enlist her assistance in the fall of 1991 when recording a CD of Nono's piece at the Experimental Studio of the Heinrich-Strobel-Stiftung of Südwestrundfunk in Freiburg, Germany (October 28–30, 1991). In February 1988, preparing his new composition, Nono had recorded several hours of Kremer's improvisations on the violin, together with passages from Bach, Beethoven, Schumann, and Brahms, as well as single notes or fifths, voices, noises of doors and chairs, and so on. That same autumn he manipulated these sounds in the studio to prepare eight separate audio tracks. The violin score in six parts is arranged on music stands throughout the room, with the violinist wandering from one to the next during the performance. Nono had conceived *La lontananza* . . . not as a work for solo violin and accompaniment but as an artistic interaction between the violin and a one-hour, eight-track audio tape. As neither the entrances of the violin at the beginning of each of the six parts, nor the length of the various fermatas and rests, nor the selection from the eight audio tracks are specified in the score, each performance creates a new work of music.

A little more than a month after Lockenhaus, on August 16, 1995, Gubaidulina and Kremer got together again for a concert at the Kollegienkirche in Salzburg, where Sofia worked the control desk for the audio tape in *La lontananza* . . . The driver taking her to the rehearsal had been late, and she tried to prepare herself as best she could in the time that was left. She wanted to play down passages of extremely loud noise, such as banging doors and fragments of speech, as Nono's use of unpredictable and surprising material was rather alien to her own aesthetics. André Richard, the director of the experimental studio in Freiburg, who knew Nono's work well, had set up the electronic equipment for Gubaidulina and assisted with everything ahead of time. After discussing matters with him, Gubaidulina found herself in a dilemma. In retrospect, she felt that the performance that evening was not satisfactory, possibly because the interaction of audio tape and violin did not succeed—at least not according to Luigi Nono's preferences.

The concert with Kremer's solo performance was part of the Salzburg Festival series "Musik Unserer Zeit." He had put together a program that began with the chaconne from Bach's D-minor Partita; then led into Schnittke's *Preludium in memoriam Dmitri Shostakovich* [*Preliudiia pamiati D. Shostakovicha*] (for violin and audio tape), four melodies from Stockhausen's *Tierkreis,* and Eugène Ysaÿe's Violin Sonata in D-minor; and Nono's work came after the intermission. Kremer had already played this program in about twenty cities around the world and, in his introductory remarks to the audience, called the concert his "musical legacy." The Salzburg performance left a deep impression on many listeners, not least as a result of the architectural features and acoustics of the Kollegienkirche, which turned out to be perfect for Nono's spatial sound projections, but probably also because of the participation of a distinguished composer at the sound desk.

Concerts and Events Celebrating the Composer's Sixty-Fifth Birthday

The next twelve months were a period of relatively slow compositional output, but they required several trips in connection with concerts honoring Gubaidulina's sixty-fifth birthday. Concerts and workshops in San José, California, were followed by the Third Festival of Contemporary Music in Moscow (Tretii festival' sovremennoi muzyki), April 7–12, 1996, organized by the producer Vadim Dubrovitsky. This concert presented works not only by Gubaidulina but also by Giya Kancheli, Tatiana Sergeeva, Sergei Berinsky, and Alexander Vustin. Vladimir Tonkha, with his cello ensemble Si-ENS, performed the premiere of *Quaternion* for four cellos on April 11, 1996.

At Marek Kopelent's invitation, Sofia Gubaidulina and Victor Suslin spent the first ten days of September at a Baroque palace in Česky Krumlov (Czech Republic) to teach a master class in composition for young composers from various East European countries. It was one of the rare occasions when Gubaidulina let herself be persuaded to teach composition.

"It seems to me," she commented later,

It is fashionable these days to keep coming up with ever new musical material. It always has to be new, something must be done that has never been done before, or else it is of no interest to the jury or the person who commissioned it. A young Lithuanian composer who was criticized by her colleagues because she still used bar divisions in her compositions once asked me: "Should we compose with or without bar divisions?" It depends on what you are writing. In a work for just two players you can do without, but not in an orchestral work with a conductor.

In 1998, when again asked to teach composition, at the Centre Acanthes (under the presidency of Claude Samuel), she declined and explained her reasons: "Today, when everyone must invent his own sound world, the craft itself is no longer what is basically at stake. One can therefore transmit only purely theoretical or mechanical aspects. In the end, it is less a matter of teaching composition than of helping young composers to realize themselves."[18]

On November 16 Gubaidulina was again in England to attend a splendid portrait concert dedicated to her by the London Sinfonietta. She also accepted an anniversary invitation to the long-standing Huddersfield Festival of Contemporary Music in Great Britain, for the premiere, on November 25, 1998, of the first version of *Galgenlieder* for mezzo-soprano, percussion, and string bass, with Patricia Adkins Chiti (mezzo-soprano), Marta Ptaszynska (percussion), and Alexander Suslin (double bass). Adkins Chiti had commissioned this song cycle in fifteen parts based on the poems of Christian Morgenstern (in German). The work was dedicated to Adkins Chiti who, in that period, was the only European singer performing Gubaidulina's works. The composer pays her musical tribute to Morgenstern—a German poet of the early twentieth century—in short theatrical scenes, which render the intriguing relationship between the poet's complex humor and his love for the creatures of this earth.

In December 1996, Michael Haeflinger introduced Gubaidulina to the audience at the Tonhalle in Zurich with performances of five chamber concerts by the Collegium Novum Zürich, Gidon Kremer, and several of Kremer's colleagues. This series included a rare performance of the cycle for *domra* and piano, *On Tatar Folk Themes* [*Po motivam tatarskogo fol'klora*]. In January 1997 concerts in Bochum presented the German premiere of the first version of *Galgenlieder* and of *Quaternion,* and in March Gubaidulina revisited Switzerland for an exhausting bus tour of several cities with the Collegium Novum Zürich, under the auspices of the Credit Suisse "Rendez-Vous" series, featuring the composer in residence.

In December, at Gidon Kremer's request, Gubaidulina completed a work for the Schubert Anniversary Year 1997, at the same time fulfilling a wish by Irena Grafenauer to compose a work for flute. The premiere of *Impromptu* for flute/alto flute, violin, and strings—a work dedicated to Irena Grafenauer and Gidon Kremer—took place on January 16, 1997, in the Kölner Philharmonie concert hall. It stood at the beginning of a year that would take Gubaidulina on two important trips to the United States.

USA Again: Chicago and Tanglewood

Gubaidulina now had enough commissions to keep her busy well into the new century. They had been initiated by renowned soloists, orchestras, and institutions. The media sometimes referred to her as "the most important living composer." To conserve her energy and to avoid letting the quality of her work deteriorate under too much pressure she forced herself on occasion to decline a request or at least to postpone it.

One of the more prestigious commissions of the 1990s was the Concerto for Viola and Orchestra requested by the Chicago Symphony Orchestra. Famous for its outstanding brass section, the Chicago Symphony has always competed with the New York Philharmonic for the number-one ranking in the United States. At a pre-concert talk, Gubaidulina said that she had been quite aware of writing this work for an orchestra renowned for its brass players and for that reason had taken the risk of adding Wagner tubas to the instrumentation. On April 17, 1997, Kent Nagano conducted the premiere with Yury Bashmet as soloist in a program that also included one of Stravinsky's concert suites from *Firebird* [*Zhar-Ptitsa*] following the intermission. Nagano was new to Chicago, and Bashmet was playing the new piece for the first time; but the audience received it well, and management, sponsor, and orchestra players were all equally enthusiastic. A few years later Bashmet—one of the great modern violists—gave the following account of what had led up to the concerto dedicated to him:

> I was quite shocked by my first encounter with Gubaidulina's music. It happened at Oleg Kagan's house as he played for me his recording of *Offertorium*. I had previously heard things about her but didn't know any of her music. It wasn't beauty, ugliness, or any particular ideas that attracted me to this violin concerto; it was the whole atmosphere, the great intensity of feeling, so that I decided to ask her for a work. Years went by, however. . . . At the end of the 1980s I heard that the Italian music publisher Ricordi had commissioned a viola concerto from Gubaidulina for me. That came as a surprise, and when I saw her later in Russia and asked her when she would write the piece, she said: "Oh, I can't tell yet, I'm very busy. But you can rest assured—I want to write something for you."
>
> Again, a number of years passed, and then I received the score just a few weeks before the premiere.[19] That's not so bad for me, because then I'm forced to learn the piece in a very short time. But that only works if the music grabs me in some way. As soon as I received Gubaidulina's score it caught my interest. She is really a creative and strong personality who doesn't simply experiment but has a clear sense of direction. The Viola Concerto is without a doubt a great piece of contemporary music, and when a musician plays her works he is influenced by them. I am not just talking about new technical performance possibilities—although in this regard, her work has a few things to offer, and the

timbral language is quite original. She always goes beyond mere performance techniques to express universally human themes; this is what makes her music so powerful. It deals with life and death, love and hate, good and evil. She does it in a very particular way—partly because she is a woman, something that one should never forget.

The middle of the Viola Concerto is very powerful and wild, a bit like the steppe and wild horses—one can sense her Tatar temperament. But her music is not only like the steppe—mostly it is like the vision of a story, and she knows exactly how to tell the story of her hero from the very start: now this is what is happening; now this is what I am feeling. And at the same time she looks at everything from a great distance, a cosmic distance. When I play, I feel like both an individualized hero and a representative of what is common to all mankind. It is, of course, easier for a composer to tell the story of a single individual, but all great works go beyond that. Sofia talks about the great issues in her own language, and the original instrumental effects she invents are never there for originality's own sake but because she uses them to penetrate to a more profound level, because she has something to communicate. In her art she is unique, like Schnittke, like Shostakovich; and during the Soviet era many tried to emulate Shostakovich, but few succeeded. . . .

I have often played her Viola Concerto. Schnittke used to occupy first place in my repertoire of twentieth-century works, as far as number of performances was concerned. Then Sonia took over first place, and now the demand for each of them is about even. Bartók's Viola Concerto stands in third place. I like to play Sonia's Concerto with Valery Gergiev, because he has the same fire, the same "wild" temperament, but every good conductor finds something unusual in her music that he or she likes to bring out.[20]

After the Chicago performances Gubaidulina and Bashmet traveled to Boston, where the Viola Concerto was presented a few days later with the Boston Symphony Orchestra under the baton of Bernard Haitink. There she saw Ivan Tcherepnin again and also held preliminary discussions about her upcoming summer at the Tanglewood Music Center, the summer residence of the Boston Symphony Orchestra in western Massachusetts.

Besides offering concerts of the Boston Symphony Orchestra, in August Tanglewood presents a five-day Festival of Contemporary Music as part of its summer music academy for young instrumentalists, vocalists, conductors, and composers who can sharpen their skills under the tutelage of the Boston Symphony Orchestra musicians and other world-class artists, while having the resources of a great symphony orchestra at their disposal. The Festival of Contemporary Music always features a composer in residence and a visiting composer from abroad. An important event on the American contemporary music scene, the performances take place in a newly built concert hall with excellent acoustics. In 1995 Reinbert de Leeuw, then the festival's artistic director, had presented a very successful performance of

Stimmen . . . verstummen . . . and now, in 1997, Gubaidulina was to be the visiting composer. She came directly from the European premiere of her Viola Concerto in London, and she brought with her the nearly completed score of a new work that was to have its premiere at the end of October in Paris. Thus she spent the last few days before the start of the festival working on the new work's completion and only then started rehearsals with the Tanglewood Fellows, young professionals from all over the world who made up the orchestra. Besides a chamber concert with *In the Beginning There Was Rhythm,* the program also included the Flute Quartet, the String Quartet No. 3, *Quattro,* and *Rubaiyat,* as well as a performance of *Now Always Snow* (carefully prepared by Reinbert de Leeuw), which the *Boston Globe* described as "the artistic and emotional high point" of the festival.[21] The atmosphere in Florence Gould Auditorium—which was only half full for most of the performances—was one of excitement and enthusiasm. Meanwhile, the Boston Symphony Orchestra played its usual fare of symphonic medleys for a chatting audience of picnickers spread out on the lawn.

The colorful program of the "Tanglewood-on-Parade Day" included a balloon ride to which Gubaidulina had been invited. The altitude of the chestnut-colored balloon could be controlled from the gondola, but the direction it took depended on the wind. For safety reasons, a number of cars with radio transmitters followed the balloon, which landed shortly before dusk near a monastery several miles from its planned destination. Everyone had become visibly anxious, but Gubaidulina enjoyed the quiet and the special quality of the light on high.

Shortly after her return from Tanglewood, Gubaidulina took a two-day trip to Turin. Enzo Restagno, celebrating a retrospective of his Settembre Musica festival, had invited all the composers he had introduced over many years, and Gubaidulina was pleased that after the performance of her *Hommage à T. S. Eliot* Luciano Berio came up to her to express his gratitude. From Turin, she went on to Fiuggi Città, a small medieval village to the South of Rome in the Lazio Region, where Patricia Adkins Chiti, as president of the Fondazione Adkins Chiti: Donne in Musica was artistic director of the International Festival "Donne in Musica—Gli Incontri al Borgo," September 8–14. The Fondazione's guest list also included Elena Firsova, Frangis Ali-Sade, Tatiana Sergeeva, and many other women composers from different parts of the world. At a special September 12 concert, "Omaggio a Sofia Gubaidulina," at the Collegiata di San Pietro Church, a variety of Italian musicians played together with Tatiana Sergeeva, Vladimir Tonkha, and Alexander Suslin. The program included *Garden of Joy and Sorrow, Light and Darkness,* seven of the Ten Etudes for cello, *Ein Engel, In croce,* and *Quattro.* This concert was broadcast live by the Radio Audizioni Italia (RAI) RADIO 3. Of the four brass players performing *Quattro,* Massimo Bartoletti had already participated in its Rome performance presented by "Donne in Musica" in the Palazzo Braschi in March 1980, twenty-eight years earlier.

Together with Pyotr Meshchaninov, Gubaidulina traveled from Fuggi via Venice and Padua to a hotel in Merano (South Tyrol), where for two weeks she could enjoy the sun, mountain walks, and swimming. Then she returned to Appen to work on two large orchestral pieces and to prepare for an important premiere in February 1998.

Canticle of the Sun:
A Work for Rostropovich's Seventieth Birthday

In the early 1990s Mstislav Rostropovich had asked Gubaidulina for a cello composition, but this suggestion did not evolve into a specific project until a few years later. During the 1995 Festival Présences, as Gubaidulina, Jean-Pierre Armengaud, and Hans-Ulrich Duffek were visiting Rostropovich at his Paris home, he repeated his request, which then evolved into a commission by Radio-Télévision Française for a work for cello and chamber choir. Once Gubaidulina had decided that *Canticle of the Sun* [*Sonnengesang*] would be based on the original Old Italian texts by St. Francis of Assisi, she set to work in her usual fashion. She studied his life and works, and began to compose the music after listening to tape recordings of the Old Italian texts provided by friends. The premiere was originally scheduled for the end of October 1997, with Paris as the chosen location. But as Gubaidulina did not finish the score until August in Tanglewood, Radio France was unable to adhere to this plan and gave Rostropovich permission to premiere the work in another country. Efforts to do so in Tokyo and Amsterdam, however, remained unsuccessful. Eventually Rostropovich presented the premiere of *Canticle of the Sun* on February 9, 1998, in the Old Opera in Frankfurt am Main (Alte Oper Frankfurt, Opernplatz, Frankfurt am Main), on the first stop of his tour of Germany with the percussionists from the Lithuanian National Symphony Orchestra [Lietuvos Nacionalinis Simfoninis Orkestras] and the Kaunas State Chorus (Robertas Šervenikas, conductor).

Gubaidulina wanted not so much to intensify the power of St. Francis's words with her music as to set them straightforwardly, in a manner similar to what she had done in her *Hommage à T. S. Eliot.* To give the work expressive force would be the responsibility of the two percussionists and especially the cello soloist, the latter being the central dramatic figure in the piece. After sections glorifying the sun and the moon, the four elements, and life itself, the work reaches its climax as the soloist leaves the cello step by step, walks over to beat on a large drum, and then invokes the response of the chorus with flexatone glissandi. After this episode—designated by the composer, "Responsorium"—the soloist returns to the cello and moves into its highest register for the "Glorification of Death."

Gubaidulina dedicated *Canticle of the Sun* to Mstislav Rostropovich for his seventieth birthday and wrote in the program brochure that the content and nature of the work were, of course, related to Rostropovich's personality, which she always imagined as being illuminated by the sun and charged by its light and energy. "The extraordinary sonorous depth of his instrument has inspired me to a very important musical gesture and made me take the risk to choose as its text St. Francis's *Hymn to the Sun*. This was, of course, a rash thing to do. But it was also important to bring out the sun-like qualities of the brilliant musician that Rostropovich is."[22] The *Frankfurter Rundschau* considered it more than just an act of rashness. The reviewer's sarcasm was perfectly evident in the headline: "Like a Sun God—Pure Glorification: Mstislav Rostropovich Embalmed by Gubaidulina." Appreciation had turned into cult, he wrote; the soloist had become a master of ceremonies.[23] Different standards prevail in Moscow, however, and one should refrain from applying an alien yardstick.

Visiting the Centre Acanthes and a Prize in Tokyo

Three large orchestral pieces made up the work schedule for 1998: a concerto for koto, bass koto, and zheng; a concerto for two violas; and a concerto for bayan (requested by Friedrich Lips and scheduled for the ceremony of the Léonie Sonning Prize [Léonie Sonnings Musikpris] in Copenhagen, May 1999). Gubaidulina decided, around the New Year of 1999, to cancel the bayan piece because of her heavy workload.

In July 1991 she traveled to Villeneuve-lez-Avignon in southern France. For many summers Claude Samuel has organized the activities of the Centre Acanthes in an old charterhouse, inviting a distinguished composer along with musicians and musicologists. The composer's work is then presented to an international audience (including many students) in concerts, analytical discussions, and instrumental workshops. As Gubaidulina had expressly asked not to be obliged to teach, Victor Suslin and Sylvio Gualda, the percussionist, handled the composition classes. Instrumental lessons were offered by Alexei Liubimov (keyboard), Mark Lubotsky (violin), Elsbeth Moser (accordian and bayan), Valery Popov (bassoon), and Vladimir Tonkha (cello). Detlef Gojowy discussed the works in his analysis course.

Even before her departure for southern France, former West German Chancellor Helmut Schmidt had announced at a press conference that Sofia Gubaidulina was the recipient of the music prize of the Japanese "Praemium Imperiale." Its endowment makes it the "Nobel Prize of the arts," and it is considered the highest ranking prize in the eastern hemisphere. Comprising its selection committee are distinguished individuals from the world of politics and business; in 1998 the committee included Helmut Schmidt, Edward Heath, David Rockefeller Jr., and Umberto Agnelli. Gubaidulina received the prize at a ceremony in Tokyo at the end of October, and in the afternoon of October 31, 1998, in the chamber auditorium of Santori Hall, Mie Miki (accordion), Katsuya Matsubara (violin), Kenichiro Yasuda (cello), and Georg Friedrich Schenck (piano) played three works selected by the composer: *De Profundis, Dancer on a Tightrope,* and *Silenzio.* Sofia Gubaidulina was now counted among the best-known composers in the world.

West and East, Light and Shadow

In April 1999, within a two-week period, two works Gubaidulina had composed the previous year premiered, one in the East, the other in the West. Gubaidulina flew to Tokyo for the April 14 performance of her concerto for koto, bass koto, zheng, and orchestra, *In the Shadow of the Tree.* Charles Dutoit conducted the Japan Broadcasting Corporation Symphony Orchestra (Nippon Hōsō Kyōkai [NHK] Symphony Orchestra), perhaps the best of Japan's three hundred orchestras and among the best in all of Asia. Kazue Sawai performed as soloist on all three instruments.

Ever since Tōru Takemitsu's *November Steps* for *biwa* (Japanese lute), *shakuhachi* (five-hole bamboo clarinet), and orchestra, many attempts have been made to join East and West by using classical Japanese instruments together with Western orchestral instruments. As is true of many of her earlier works, Gubaidulina wrote *In the Shadow of the Tree* for a particular artist: she was thinking of Kazue Sawai, the master of the koto. She was not so much concerned about traditional sounds but rather, as in . . . *Early in the Morning, Right before Waking . . .,* she cared more about the new sound possibilities of the koto. It turned out to be a work about the encounter between East and West, its title pointing to the symbolism with which Gubaidulina had experimented in a number of different works since her String Quartet No. 4. The string players are divided into two groups, and one group tunes its instruments a quarter-tone lower than the other to suggest the relationship between light and shadow, between a normal tone and one lowered by a quarter tone. Light and shadow primarily represent West and East: the light of day and the sun symbolize the clarity of the West; the shadow of the night and moon represent the East—Gubaidulina's "dark night of the soul." Of the solo instruments in this particular work, the zheng is tuned a quarter-tone lower than the koto and the bass koto.

It was Charles Dutoit who had commissioned and conducted *In the Shadow of the Tree* after earlier performances of *Offertorium* and *Music for Flute, Strings, and Percussion.* The energetic and accomplished Franco-Swiss maestro had regular professional responsibilities as chief conductor of three major orchestras on three continents: the Orchestre Symphonique de Montréal, his chief residence since 1977; the Orchestre National de France in Paris;, and, since 1996, the Japanese NHK Symphony Orchestra.

"When I became the director of the NHK Orchestra in Tokyo in 1996," Dutoit later commented,

> We decided to commission compositions. The Japanese Broadcasting Corporation NHK is an enormous organization, about as large as the BBC and Radiodiffusion Télévision Française combined. I was particularly interested in commissioning works by international composers, not only Japanese. The first commission went to Sofia because I knew her quite well. Then it was Tan Dun's turn, as we also wanted some Asian composers, and then came Penderecki. After Gubaidulina had decided on a work for koto and orchestra, we met with Kazue Sawai, the koto player during the preceding season in Tokyo. The two women seemed to get along very well, although, having no language in common, communication was a huge problem. Gubaidulina thought that the soft sound of the koto, which sometimes can be strong and aggressive, would cause a problem in conjunction with a large orchestra. So she decided to use a large orchestra, such as a chamber orchestra, so as to be able to draw on the entire range of instrumental possibilities but not let them play at full volume. Koto and orchestra are a most interesting combination, and it was fascinating for me to see how she composed for the koto in a way that is quite different from the usual use of the instrument. Rarely surprised, I am an experienced reader of scores and usually can see what a piece will sound like. But in this instance I found it difficult, and until I arrived for rehearsals in Tokyo, I could not quite imagine how it would all sound together, especially some particular sounds played in an unconventional manner on the koto. The piece turned out to be longer than she had told us, and that posed a problem on our subsequent tour of the United States. Her music is very adaptable, however, and with every night on the tour things became more comfortable.
>
> Just as in her Flute Concerto, here the string players are divided into two groups, with one group playing a quarter-tone lower. That works when you tune the instruments, because you have strings in isolation. But in a concert it becomes difficult, as the players tend to adapt to one another's intonation. A quarter-tone is not much, and, playing vibrato, a large group encounters problems. The players hear something different here and there, and, unless they exaggerate, they will adapt. To sit close together and not to play *unisono* is not easy. Gubaidulina's philosophy underlies everything in *In the Shadow of the Tree.* But given the characteristic Japanese tendency to perform with perfection, we succeeded in creating two different sound colorations between the string groups. The questioning of one group and the response of the other turned out to be quite effective, and all was well. At the premiere in Santor Hall, I was surrounded

by the three solo instruments, with the koto player moving like lightning from one to the other.[24]

Kazue Sawai provided a different but complementary account of the rehearsal sessions and performances of the work:

When we were listening to the recordings of our improvisations in the Paris sound studio [for the CD entitled *Three Strangers in Paris*], Sofia whispered in my ear in "our English": "I received a commission for a concerto—could I write a koto concerto?" I didn't know where the commission had come from, but two years after she whispered to me I got a call from NHK: "Sofia Gubaidulina is composing a koto concerto. Would you be willing to be the soloist?" I suspect that NHK was a little shocked that she would write something for the koto. They had asked for a work of contemporary music, but the koto is an old, classical instrument. I had already played three Japanese koto concertos—by Takashi Kako, Maki Ishi, and Ichirō Higo—all in the conventional style. From Sofia, I hoped to get something with new koto sounds, but at the same time I was dying to see what would happen with a large orchestra behind me. When I saw the score, I first thought: I can't do this. . . . If I could read this score I would be a conductor. Three days before the premiere I asked Sofia over for a rehearsal, but she said: "You're quite a genius. Play it as you're able to. Your solo part comes first, and when you're done you give Dutoit a signal." I played and then looked at him, and he began. . . . In the middle part I had to play a few quarter notes, and as that seemed too slow for the score, Dutoit said: "You're playing too slow." Sofia came over and said: "No, Kazue's breathing is correct," and then changed the score. At one point I had to play with a violin bow and was very nervous because just behind me sat a group of professional string players. "Sofia, can't I leave this out?"—"No, that's the way it has to be." But after the violin-bow cadenza at the first rehearsal the string players applauded. We rehearsed three times, an hour and a half each time, which was neither too little nor too much. The premiere still lacked good breathing between the koto and the orchestra, and it developed only toward the end of our tour. The whole thing was special: the small country of Japan, the small koto instrument; but it all came together—the NHK Orchestra, a Swiss conductor, and a Russian composer.[25]

Two weeks later, on April 29, 1999, Kurt Masur conducted the New York Philharmonic Orchestra at Lincoln Center's Avery Fisher Hall in a performance of Gubaidulina's *Two Paths (A Dedication to Mary and Martha)* [*Dva puti (Posviashchenie Marii i Marfe)*] for two viola soloists and orchestra. The former music director of Leipzig's Gewandhausorchester, now the music director of the New York Philharmonic, later related what had led up to commissioning the new concerto:

For a long time we had been trying to improve the viola section of the Philharmonic to bring it up to the level of the orchestra. In our search for leading instrumentalists for the viola section we were fortunate to engage Cynthia Phelps and Rebecca Young as our premier violists. It was quite extraordinary that someone who heard Cynthia Phelps for the first time in our viola section wanted to commission a work that would feature her as a soloist. But as we were unable to agree on the style of the new work, the sponsor withdrew his support for it as well as his money, which infuriated my wife. I got to know my wife in Rio de Janeiro when she herself was playing in the viola section. She was so angry that we discussed the situation at home. Suddenly she said: "I want to commission this work," and I answered: "Why not?" She insisted on using her own money, not mine; that's how the commission didn't come from me but from my wife. As we went along talking about how the commission should be arranged, it occurred to us that Alfred Schnittke had just written a viola concerto for Bashmet, and we said, how about a double concerto? We realized that there is only one other, Bach's Brandenburg Concerto No. 6, and suddenly an idea struck me: ... if Gubaidulina were to write this, it would be by the woman who is closest to Bach in spirit, and we could perform both works, separated by three hundred years, on the same evening. And that is exactly what happened. And that was the hour of the concerto's birth in our home.

The resulting piece is remarkable in the way it intuitively takes into account the two people for whom it was written—even though Gubaidulina knew neither of them. She worked from the basic idea we had conveyed to her: that these two violists are not only competitors but—and this is unusual in any orchestra—truly close friends. With her broad grasp of literature and the Bible, she thought of the story of Mary and Martha, and tried to give it passionate expression in her basic concept. And now I have to say something that has deeply impressed me: the listener is never made aware of the simplicity and at the same time the harmonic complexity of this music. Quite intuitively, the listener grasps the musical language that, in this particular form, has never been heard before; and intuitively he senses the conflict between the two violas as well as the different character of the two instruments that give expression to human thought and emotion. What happens in the orchestra is so moving, so masterful and yet of such great simplicity, that I always have to say—something always true of Gubaidulina—we had to search for the sound that she imagined and that seemed to us an adequate rendering of her conception of the work. In this context, I said to her that the low notes in the orchestra strongly reminded me of a unique experience a year earlier when I was for the first time in Tokyo on New Year's Eve. I experienced a city of several million inhabitants where the New Year is not greeted with screaming and fireworks at midnight but with utter silence. All one can hear in this huge city is the deep sound of the bells of Buddhist monasteries. That is exactly what Martha wanted to express: basically the stalking approach of death. It is not a matter of mourning or sorrow but a reminder: You have only one life; use it wisely. I believe that all religions try to help us overcome our fear of dying, of our own death, but also to use the knowledge of our inevitable mortality to make us aware: Be glad for every morning when you wake up, for every day that has been given to you. Gubaidulina moves each listener to these boundaries.[26]

It rarely happens that two important new works by a single composer are performed on the same day in the music capital of any country—but that is what happened on April 29, 1999, in New York. By happenstance Charles Dutoit had been scheduled a year earlier to conduct the American premiere of the koto concerto in Carnegie Hall on the very same evening. The managers of the two venues solved the problem of such a spectacular double feature by having Dutoit perform Gubaidulina's work before intermission and Masur take his turn after intermission. During intermission, the composer was whisked by car from Carnegie Hall to Lincoln Center. The following year the New York Philharmonic took the piece on tour to Europe and played it fourteen times—in Spain and Portugal in January, then, in June, in Germany, Austria, the Netherlands, France, the Czech Republic, and Poland.

Referring to another New York performance of this work a few years later, Cynthia Phelps, one of the two viola soloists, recalled almost four years after this occasion:

> It was a fantastic experience to play it in May 2001 in the Cathedral of St. John the Divine in New York on Memorial Day. When I first saw the score, I was struck by two impressions: I could not believe the range of coloration in the two solo viola parts, and I was quite taken aback by how very high the first viola part (my part) lay. Also, I was worried about the difficulty of making all the harmonics speak properly. Of course, the beauty and success of this music is indeed due in some part to the fact that two instruments of the same timbre could have such a different and incredible assortment of colors. Gubaidulina knew exactly what she wanted. The piece strikes me spiritually with such feelings of compassion, commitment, and magnanimity. And I feel a deep connection with the beauty of this work—more so as the years have passed. I must admit, it is due in part to the wonderful performing circumstances I was lucky enough to have—all my colleagues in the Philharmonic, Rebecca Young as my partner, and, of course, Kurt Masur conducting. I have nothing but wonderful associations.[27]

13 | The Center of Life
St. John Passion and St. John Easter, 1996–2004

A Commission from the International Bach Academy, Stuttgart

In November 1995 the International Bach Academy in Stuttgart [Internationale Bachakademie Stuttgart] began to think about possible events for the 250th anniversary of Bach's death to be observed in the year 2000. The idea soon emerged to request four new compositions based on the story of Christ's Passion as told in the Gospels of Matthew, Mark, Luke, and John. These new works would relate to a central preoccupation in Bach's work and were to be written by four major contemporary composers representing German, Russian, Anglo-American, and Hispanic culture. The project manager was Christian Eisert, who later commented: "The decision to ask Sofia Gubaidulina for the Russian Passion was self-evident because she is preoccupied with questions of religion and theology, and Bach is an important figure in her life as a composer."[1] The German composer Wolfgang Rihm was also an easy choice, but a long and difficult search was conducted for the remaining two. When, in February 1996, Gubaidulina received the Bach Academy's invitation to contribute a composition, two things were immediately clear to her. First, the request was a perfect fit for a lifelong, not fully articulated desire at the center of her being as well as a tremendous challenge to bring together all her religious and musical aspirations in one great work. Second, the Gospel of John was most particularly *her* Gospel, and his account of Christ's Passion *her* passion. She accepted Eisert's invitation within days, writing him that she considered the project very interesting, attractive, and culturally significant, and that, without exaggeration, it would be of central importance in her life; she was also aware of the great difficulty and enormous responsibility it would present for her.[2]

Gubaidulina's choice came as no surprise, as the Gospel of John, with its central concept of the *logos* and its emphasis on pity and love, is closer than the other three Gospels to the heart of the Orthodox Church. When the musicologist Dorothea Redepenning asked the composer at a discussion session on the eve of the premiere why she had chosen the Gospel of John, Gubaidulina's modest and seemingly simple answer probably surprised the audience: "I love Jesus as He is presented by John." Whereas the other Gospels emphasize the relationship between Jesus and mankind, so Gubaidulina would argue, John's narrative presents Christ as the Son of God, as an embodiment of the *logos*. Its central message is expressed in the repeated phrase, "I am in the Father, and the Father is in me."

In an interview at the time of the premiere, Gubaidulina once again stressed the importance of religion in her life: "[The Gospel of John] encompasses all human existence. For me, this is extremely important, especially now in this era bordering on two millennia. . . . Mankind has lost its connection to religion. There is widespread skepticism toward everything having to do with religion. I believe that people no longer have a sense of the true meaning of life. For me personally, life without religion is meaningless."[3] *St. John Passion* would therefore also be a profession of Gubaidulina's personal faith.

Preliminary Thoughts and Ideas

Immediately after receiving the first letter from the Bach Academy in February 1996, Gubaidulina began to think seriously about a Russian-language Passion— particularly considering that such a concept is not part of Orthodox tradition and actually goes against it. Although she had no intention of writing a work to be used in church services (an impossibility, given the prohibition against instrumental music), she wanted to draw on the spirit of Orthodox Christianity and Orthodox liturgical traditions, as they were at the root of her personal experience. The Eucharist—the communion of the believing Christian with Christ resurrected—is the central event of that liturgy. In an interview for a book by Enzo Restagno during the weeks of political turmoil in January 1991, Gubaidulina explained this particular aspect of the Orthodox Church, the possible realization of an actual "binding" (a *legato*, in the original sense of the word) in the Eucharistic sacrament:

> Whereas in the Catholic and Protestant churches the believing Christian participates in the ritual only in *remembrance* of the sacrificial act, in the Orthodox Church the believer, in enacting the *epiklesis*, invokes the Holy Spirit to come and to transform *in actuality* the bread and the wine into Christ's blood and body.[4] He truly experiences the encounter with Christ, the living Son of God, when the priest proclaims: "Christ is among us." And at the moment when the bread is broken, he *actually* experiences Christ's death as if it were his own death,

in order then to undergo true resurrection, the transformation of his human essence. And this transformation is in truth the immortality of his soul, the unspeakable joy that is impossible to experience if it is only a matter of remembering or glorifying a great event. The Russian Orthodox believer experiences the process of renewal as an actual fact that has taken place in the real world.[5]

Thinking about a Russian-language Passion after lively discussions with Pyotr Meshchaninov, Gubaidulina soon arrived at a concept that turned a difficult assignment into a creative opportunity. In Orthodox tradition, the "art of experience" is more important than the "art of representation," as expressed in instrumental music or in theatrical and oratorical speech and action, all of which are excluded from Orthodox liturgy. There is even an aspiration to transcend everything temporal and material in order to achieve a "superior plane of stasis"[6] that triumphs utterly over time and matter. In this sense the Passion was to be static and not dramatic. But by connecting the Passion—the story of Christ's earthly, "horizontal" experience of suffering—with material that is related in spirit and its equal artistically, the possibility exists to create a balance necessary for both the composition and the performance. Such a connection is achieved by joining together the temporal-earthly "horizontal" events of the Passion with the supratemporal "vertical" realm of the Apocalypse of St. John. When Gubaidulina met with Helmuth Rilling, the director of the Bach Academy, on March 18, 1996, in Hamburg, she discussed with him her particular concept and explained her motives and intentions for it. That same evening Rilling conducted Bach's *Johannes-Passion.*

One thing had been self-evident to Gubaidulina from the start regarding this commission, even though it remained unspoken: Christ's Passion and Crucifixion were inconceivable without His victory over death in His Resurrection. Good Friday is always followed by Easter, the highest and holiest holiday of the Orthodox Church, celebrated with joyous passion in a midnight service on the eve of the Day of Resurrection. Before midnight, the church is only sparsely lit and the choir sings in a minor mode ending in total silence. Then, at midnight, every church bell begins ringing, and the priests carrying sacred banners, followed by the congregation holding burning candles, leave through the portals for a walk around the church. On their return, they find the door locked, as the church has become Christ's tomb. The priest's knocking elicits the response from within, "Christ is risen," which the choir then intones in a hymn: "With His death He hath conquered death, and given life to those who are in their graves." Then the doors are flung open, and all enter the brightly lit church, kissing each other thrice on alternate cheeks, pronouncing the Easter greeting, "Christ is risen," and receiving the reply, "Truly, He is risen." The priest then opens all the doors of the iconostasis to signify that the heavenly kingdom is now accessible.[7]

The Cross:
First Preparations in the Spirit of Architecture and Painting

Gubaidulina's joining of Christ's Passion and the Apocalypse is unusual and possibly unique in the history of music, but not in the history of art. Something similar exists in the early-fourteenth-century frescoes of the Arena Chapel in Padua and in the sixteenth-century frescoes of the Sistine Chapel. When Gubaidulina stayed with Pyotr Meshchaninov in Fuggi in September 1997, she traveled to Rome with him to prepare herself for her new composition by viewing the Sistine Chapel—a task that required much concentration in the throng of other visitors. The western wall of the chapel shows the life of Jesus from His baptism in the river Jordan to the Last Supper as painted by four early Renaissance artists: Pietro Perugino, Sandro Botticelli, Domenico Ghirlandaio, and Cosimo Rosselli. Then Michelangelo, after completing the ceiling frescoes with scenes from the Old Testament, painted the Last Judgment in the apse.

Before leaving Italy, Gubaidulina and Meshchaninov spent four days in Venice, where they studied the architecture and mosaics of the Cathedral of San Marco. They also stopped in Padua to see Giotto's frescoes at the Arena Chapel (Capella degli Scrovegni). This single-nave structure is decorated mostly with scenes from the Gospels along its sides and in the front, and with Giotto's depiction of the Last Judgment on the back wall where the entrance is located. The cruciform shape of most churches—with their intersection of the nave by the transept—symbolizes for Gubaidulina the meeting of the "vertical" heavenly realm with the "horizontal" earthly world, as does the liturgy and the sacrament of the Eucharist. "All I had to do in music," she later wrote in a program brochure, "was what had been done often and long before me in architecture and fresco painting. In my own work I have also tried to join those two texts in such a way that the two accounts, while always retaining their identity, cross each other—events on earth that take place in time (the Passion) and events in heaven that unfold out of time (the Apocalypse)."[8]

Composing the Passion and the Resurrection
according to St. John

In May 1999, after her return from the premiere in New York of *Two Paths*, Gubaidulina returned to her preparations and seriously delved into the composition of her new work for the next eleven months. In some ways she had already probed the theme, as *Two Paths* was "a dedication to Mary and Martha," the sisters of Lazarus (the disciple "whom Jesus loved")[9] who are described in the Gospel of John as, respectively, representatives of the *vita activa* and the *vita contemplativa.* The process of composition, however, was interrupted on several occasions by trips to performances and two important prize ceremonies: on May 6, 1999, Gubaidulina received the Léonie Sonning Music Prize, a distinguished award that had also been given to Shostakovich; and on October 24, 1999, the President of the Federal Republic of Germany, Johannes Rau, presented her with the Preis der Stiftung Bibel und Kultur.

What Gubaidulina had already presented in *Offertorium* as the central issues of Christianity—sacrifice; submission of individual will and ego to a higher purpose; a life of suffering and pain—was to be rendered more completely in her new composition based on the Passion and Resurrection. The Orthodox Church's celebration of the mercy and joy of the Resurrection vanquishing death contrasts rather sharply with the Western (especially Protestant) emphasis on suffering, sacrifice, and death. For Gubaidulina, both traditions are of great importance, with sacrifice and suffering possibly placed more in the foreground. Her balanced approach made it impossible for her to compose a work of dogmatic Orthodoxy. As she later explained: "The chasm between the two systems of faith saddens me deeply. The early Christians did not have such a chasm in mind. Jesus lives in our hearts, not in dogmatic systems. That's why I decided to write a work that transcends divisions over dogma. As an artist, because I am responsible only to myself, all that matters is that I am true to myself."

In this state of mind, Gubaidulina sat down to work and to raise her idea of musical verticality and horizontality to a higher level. The vertical realm of the Divine Father, which conventional Christian dogma considers perfect and omnipotent, exists beyond time and is for that very reason incomplete. The horizontal world of physical creation, on the other hand, is mortal. God sent His Son so that He would save mankind from eternal death through the sacrifice of His own death on the cross. In this act of self-sacrifice the two worlds intersect—the divine, eternal vertical and the human, mortal horizontal. The "superior plane of stasis" in the vertical realm, however, is devoid of motion; it lacks the force of the Holy Spirit, which becomes actively effective only in the form of the cross, the intersection of the vertical and the horizontal (as in the Orthodox liturgy).

As was her habit with any new score, Gubaidulina did much preliminary reading and research. She wrestled with conflicting interpretations of John's Gospel and the Apocalypse, with traditional Christian concepts of the Trinity, and with many other problems. Then she proceeded to lay out the conceptual plan and prepare the texts for *St. John Passion* [*Strasti po Ioanu*] and *St. John Easter* [*Paskha po Ioanu*]. Finally, beginning with the end (as has always been her preferred mode), Gubaidulina composed *St. John Easter* in the summer of 1999 and then proceeded to complete *St. John Passion* (the "horizontalizing" of the score), which occupied her from the autumn of 1999 until April 2000.

St. John Passion, as a separate and independent work, has eleven parts (crossing the horizontal world of the Passion and the vertical world of the Apocalypse) that can be divided into two main sections: The Preparation (Nos. 1–7) and The Central Event (Nos. 8–11). The individual parts have the following titles: 1. "The Word"; 2. "The Washing of Feet"; 3. "The Commandment of Faith"; 4. "The Commandment of Love"; 5. "Hope"; 6. "Liturgy in Heaven"; 7. "Treason, Betrayal, Flagellation, and Judgment"; 8. "The Road to Golgotha"; 9. "A Woman Clothed in Sunlight"; 10. "Entombment"; 11. "The Seven Vessels of Wrath." Events in heaven are told in parts 1, 6, 9, and 11; events on earth in parts 2–5, 7, and 10; part 8, "The Road to Golgotha," is at the center, where the events of the Passion and the Apocalypse intersect polyphonically. With this "cross" as a background, the "double spiral" of the entire process unfolds: "walking the road" and the feuding among the people. "The Road to Golgotha" leads up to the decisive formal moment: "The Death of Jesus" and "A Woman Clothed in Sunlight," which are followed by "Entombment" and—like a summation of the entire work—"The Seven Vessels of Wrath."[10]

In April 2000 Gubaidulina completed her work connecting the Passion and the Apocalypse of St. John. (She had sketched out *St. John Easter,* but it would take another four months to finish it.) Completely exhausted, she spent a two-week vacation on Crete with Pyotr Meshchaninov; for the first few days she could do little more than lie down and rest.

Passion 2000, Stuttgart, August 26–September 10, 2000: The Performance

Passion 2000, the two-week festival arranged by the Bach Academy, linked different cultures and cultural periods. Its guiding principle was that nothing modern can exist without the past, and the past takes on many different forms when viewed from the present. The festival opened with a performance of Bach's *Johannes-Passion* and closed with his *Matthäus-Passion.* The program also listed daily concerts not limited to Bach's music: an ambitious symposium on the performance practices of Bach's church music, lectures, discussions following concerts, and religious services.

Besides Gubaidulina's *St. John Passion* and Wolfgang Rihm's *Deus Passus* (according to St. Luke), an Argentinian of Jewish-Russian origin then living in New York, Osvaldo Golijov, composed *La Pasión según San Marcos* (The Passion according to St. Mark), and Tan Dun, the Chinese composer also living in New York, added an English-language *Water Passion after St. Matthew.* The significance and elaborate nature of the entire festival were reflected in the approved budget, which came to 5.2 million Deutsche Marks. First-rate musicians from each composer's home country performed the four modern Passion works, and the public turned out in large numbers. For the Passions themselves, as well as for the discussions, all twenty-three hundred seats of the Beethovensaal in the Stuttgart Liederhalle were completely sold out a day before the actual performances (which included introductions of the composers and the conductors). The Passions were broadcast live on television and radio, and critics and music enthusiasts had arrived from all corners of the globe. Even though the reviewers might be of very different minds about the four compositions, it soon became clear that a true meeting of cultures in the spirit of Bach had been successfully arranged.

Following Wolfgang Rihm's *Deus Passus*, Gubaidulina's *St. John Passion* was scheduled for performance on September 1, 2000. Expectations ran high. Having given much thought to the choice of the right Russian conductor with a well-trained ensemble of first-rate soloists, choir, and orchestra, Gubaidulina decided in November 1998 to ask Valery Gergiev, the young, charismatic music director of the Maryinsky Theater in St. Petersburg, who had also established an excellent reputation in the West. Gergiev accepted. With a heavy schedule of commitments in the West, he worked tirelessly without regard to his health and accomplished enormous tasks that sometimes required him to take unexpected breaks. In the summer of 2000 his schedule was particularly crowded, as he had agreed on short notice to substitute for Claudio Abbado at the Salzburg Festival. Thus the rehearsal with the conductor, the soloists, the choir, and the orchestra could not be scheduled any earlier than two days before the performance. Gubaidulina and Pyotr Meshchaninov had traveled to St. Petersburg as early as August to assist with ensemble and choir rehearsals. But at 2:00 PM on August 30, Gergiev failed to show up. Meshchaninov began to rehearse with some of the performers as the television crews became more and more impatient. After a while word came that the conductor would arrive shortly, but the waiting continued. Gergiev finally appeared and the rehearsal could begin—four hours behind schedule. The conductor worked the musicians with his typical passion and energy until 11:30 PM. Dress rehearsal on the following day served also as a recording session for a CD to be published by the Bach Academy. Gubaidulina and Gergiev discussed some last-minute changes in the tempi as well as a few additional corrections, all of which were to become part of the performance, except that the central eighth part was still too fast. Nevertheless the premiere on the evening of September 1 turned out to be a huge success. The audience applauded for twenty minutes, celebrating the composer, the conductor, and the musicians alike. Among all the requests for audiocassettes, CDs, and scores that the Bach Academy received over the next several months, those for Gubaidulina's *St. John Passion* stood in first place.[11] Additional performances with Gergiev conducting the performers from

St. Petersburg were given in Berlin (September 3, 2000), St. Petersburg (November 1, 2000, and June 21, 2001), Paris (September 26, 2001), Amsterdam (April 4, 2002), and Rotterdam (April 5, 2002). On September 27, 2003, Antoni Wit directed the Orchestra of the National Philharmonia in Warsaw (Filharmonia Narodowa w Warszawie) with its chorus in yet another performance that was the concluding concert of the Warsaw Autumn festival. Gubaidulina had anticipated the first St. Petersburg performance with some trepidation, as she was aware of the extremely Orthodox Christian views of some of her colleagues, who were quite familiar with the Orthodox Church's dogma regarding music. On the whole, however, the public response was enthusiastically positive.

Since the 1980s the Royal Stockholm Philharmonic Orchestra [Kungliga Filharmonikerna] has organized an annual composer's festival in Stockholm, which in alternate years has celebrated a Swedish and a foreign composer. In 1989 and 1995, respectively, Alfred Schnittke and Arvo Pärt had been honored at this one-week celebration—a central event in the cultural life of the Swedish capital. The fifteenth festival, November 9–16, 2000, was dedicated to Sofia Gubaidulina, the largest event to date featuring her music. Ten of her large orchestral compositions as well as seven chamber works were performed that year.[12] With the exceptions of Yury Bashmet, Elsbeth Moser, Oleg Krysa (violin), and the conductor Andrei Boreiko, only Swedish performers were invited, all of them first-rate. Although Gubaidulina had arrived just a few days earlier to participate in the rehearsals, she had to cancel because of attacks of vertigo and severe headache that required hospitalization. Fortunately the test results were encouraging and pointed to nothing worse than acute exhaustion, a result of her long and intensive work on the St. John Passion. After two days of bed rest at her hotel, she was able to attend all concerts. For an entire week Stockholm's musical life focused on Gubaidulina's compositions, which large audiences rewarded with generous and lively applause. On the last day of the festival the composer was awarded the Honorary Gold Medal of the Stockholm Concert Hall Foundation (Stockholms Konserthusstiftelse).

A Work for the Schönberg Ensemble and Seventieth-Anniversary Concerts

Sofia Gubaidulina's seventieth birthday occasioned many concerts in 2001 and the spring of 2002, mostly in Europe but also in the United States and even in Tongyong (South Korea) and Kuala Lumpur (Malaysia).[13] The composer's central preoccupation, however, was the completion of St. John Easter, as the entire Passion-Resurrection cycle was to be performed in Hamburg in March 2002. The succession of events began with a weekend of concerts (February 25–26), organized by Alexander Ivashkin, at the Purcell Room in London along with a symposium at Goldsmith College, but Gubaidulina was unable to attend because of other obligations.

Gubaidulina had begun work on a piece commissioned by Reinbert de Leeuw and the Schönberg Ensemble in late fall of 2000, but she had had to put it aside to complete the *St. John Passion*. The initial "numbers games" turned out to be difficult, and she was unable to come up with an acceptable solution before the end of that year. Early in 2001, however, things began to fall into place, and in February Gubaidulina completed *Risonanza* [*Rezonans*], a work for three trumpets, four trombones, organ, and six string instruments. On April 18, 2001, Reinbert de Leeuw conducted its premiere with the Schönberg Ensemble in the hall of the Concertgebouw in Amsterdam. In *Risonanza*, Gubaidulina used brass instruments for the first time to explore the light-and-shadow symbolism that she had developed in her earlier works for strings, again tuning one group of brass players a quarter tone higher than the other group. At the premiere, the musicians were well prepared, and the audience applauded generously.

Even before the Amsterdam concert, Gubaidulina had traveled to the United States to attend a series of concerts (April 10–11, 2001) that the Lyric Chamber Music Society of New York had dedicated to her. Besides works by Mozart, the program featured Gubaidulina's string quartets and her String Trio, with Evgeniya Alikhanova and the Moscow String Quartet. After several months of intensive work in Appen, the composer left on September 14, for a weekend of concerts and discussion in Düsseldorf arranged by Francisco Tanzer. From there she went on a trip to Lake St. Moritz in the Swiss Alps to participate in a workshop dedicated to her chamber music (September 19–23) at the "Chesa da Cultura" of the Swiss Stiftung Pro Musica e Cultura, with Elsbeth Moser and Vladimir Tonkha as the guest lecturers. This was followed by a brief visit to Paris, where Gergiev conducted *St. John Passion* at the Théâtre du Châtelet on September 26. Sikorski, her publisher in Hamburg, and Cecilia Cartellieri had made arrangements for a chamber concert in her honor, which took place on December 9, in the Rolf-Liebermann-Studio of North German Radio (Norddeutscher Rundfunk [NDR]). Reinhard Flender and Peter Michael Hamel had composed special birthday tributes for this occasion.[14]

In January 2002 Gubaidulina came for her third visit to Bochum for the weekend of January 18–20, and soon thereafter (February 28–March 3) attended the East-West Music and Cultural Festival at the Goetheanum in Dornach, near Basel, Switzerland, an event that was dedicated to her and Toshio Hosokawa. The Swiss program included chamber music, an East-West symposium on religion and culture, a performance by Astrea, and a humorous-satyrical improvisation by Gubaidulina, Mayumi Miyata, and Kazue Sawai. It served as a delightful balance to the seriousness of the concluding concert, in which Robin Engelen conducted the Junge Kammerphilharmonie Klangwerk, a young ensemble, in an excellent presentation of Gubaidulina's *Seven Words* and Hosokawa's *Into the Depth of Time* that moved the audience to tears. Vladimir Tonkha and Mie Miki played exceptionally well, but in the end one had to conclude that Tonkha was truly at home in the world of Gubaidulina's music, and Miki in Hosokawa's.

During the birthday year, however, Russia was the venue of the most elaborate festivities: the International Festival Sofia Gubaidulina (Mezhdunarodnyi festival' muzyki Sofii Gubaidulinoi) was staged as an intercity event in both Kazan (October 20–22, 2001) and Moscow (October 23–31, 2001). The Tatar Ministry of Culture together with the Kazan Conservatory initiated the festivities in Kazan, where Rubin Abdullin, the organist for the premiere of *In croce,* had meanwhile assumed the directorship of the conservatory. In Moscow it was Vladimir Tonkha who took the initiative, became the artistic director of the festival, and requested and staged original birthday compositions for the occasion from Dmitri Smirnov, Victor Suslin, Yuji Takahashi, and Boris Tishchenko.[15] The events in Kazan included lectures, chamber music, and a performance of *Alleluia;* and in the afternoon of the final day Sofia's former family home at 29 Ulitsa Telmana officially became the Sofia Gubaidulina Center for Contemporary Music (Tsentr sovremennoi muzyki Sofii Gubaidulinoi), an institute that to this day has remained rather modestly endowed. The concluding event was a televised performance of *St. John Passion,* conducted by Valery Gergiev with the musicians of the Maryinsky Theater.

The festivities in Moscow began the next day with another performance of *St. John Passion* in the Great Hall of the Conservatory. The actual anniversary concert was scheduled for the following day, October 24, 2001, and took place in the concert hall that was part of the array of buildings of the reconstructed Cathedral of Christ the Savior (Khram Khrista Spasitelia), now again Moscow's largest church. Bashmet played the Viola Concerto, Tonkha and Lips the *Seven Words* together with the Maryinsky Theater Orchestra directed by Gergiev. Many distinguished guests were present: Mstislav Rostropovich, Galina Vishnevskaya, Natalia Svetlova (Solzhenitsyn's wife), and the poet Bella Akhmadullina, who told Sofia after the concert that music can speak more profoundly than words. The acting minister of culture, Mikhail Shvydkoy, gave an address, and Vladimir Putin sent a congratulatory telegram. A conference at the Moscow Tchaikovsky Conservatory discussed Gubaidulina's music; the Goetheanum Ensemble of Dornach (Switzerland) staged a Eurythmic performance to Tonkha's cello music; Gennady Aigi read from his poems; and Gidon Kremer, Mark Pekarsky, Vladimir Tonkha, and others performed chamber music. The concluding concert in the Great Hall featured Pyotr Meshchaninov conducting the Russian National

Orchestra in a performance of the Concerto for Flute and Strings (with soloist Oleg Khudiakov) and the koto concerto, *In the Shadow of the Tree*, with Kazue Sawai, who had come from Japan. Both performances excelled in rhythmic precision. The second part of the evening's program—*Now Always Snow*, performed by the chamber chorus of the conservatory and the soloist ensemble of the Moscow Studio for New Music (Studiia novoi muzyki) under Igor Dronov—almost fell apart. The festival organizer suddenly let it be known that there were no funds for paying the soloist ensemble (the use of contributions by sponsors was always a murky affair). Things had drastically changed since the 1980s: Gubaidulina was now the cultural cynosure in both Kazan and Moscow, the central figure at concerts, receptions, and interviews. At the same time money had come to dominate everything, and the divide between rich and poor had widened enormously. Even at a time when professors at the conservatory received a meager one hundred dollars, concert halls in Moscow were available only for very high dollar rents, thus nipping many artistic initiatives in the bud.

St. John Easter and the Premiere of the Passion and Resurrection Cycle

In early spring of 2000—even before the performance of *St. John Passion*—propitious circumstances made it possible to make plans for a Hamburg performance of the two-work Passion and Resurrection cycle that would include the premiere of *St. John Easter*. Norddeutscher Rundfunk celebrated the fiftieth anniversary of its annual music series, "das neue werk," with numerous concerts spanning two seasons, from January 2001 until June 2002, and featuring the works of Pierre Boulez, Hans Werner Henze, and Krzysztof Penderecki together with two composers living in the Hamburg area, György Ligeti and Sofia Gubaidulina. Richard Armbruster, the young and talented new manager of the series, had planned the performance of *Passion* and *Easter* for March 16, 2002, at St. Michael's Church (St. Michaelis Kirche; popularly known as "Michel") in Hamburg.

The events of *St. John Passion* conclude with Christ's words, "It is finished." The Resurrection that follows was, in the words of Paul, "unto the Jews a stumbling block, and unto the Heathens (Greeks) foolishness" (1 Corinthians 1:23), but for Gubaidulina it represented "not a *continuation* of completed events but their *transfiguration* and *transformation*. Whereas in the *Passion* the earthly existence of the Word Incarnate is completed and the circle of life is closed, *Easter* is the *opening up* of our soul, its transition to another dimension."[16] Because the events in *St. John Easter* are not earthly but spiritual, the Apocalypse of John stands in the foreground: spiritual eternity (verticality) devours—that is, conquers—earthly temporality (horizontality). According to Gubaidulina, after the breaking of the bread and the drinking of the wine there is a third event, the consumption of the book: "Take it [the book], and eat it up; and it shall make thy belly bitter, but it shall be in thy mouth sweet as honey" (Revelation 10:9). "And everything else," so the composer declared about *St. John Easter*, "is a process of *devouring*: VICTORY devours death; LIGHT devours infinite mourning and mortification; the final ANSWER devours the insoluble questions; . . . all candles are devoured by fire; all fires are transformed into LIGHT. With this apologia of the WORD that was 'in the beginning' and of the LIGHT as the origin of all things my work arrives at its completion. 'In my end is my beginning.'"[17]

St. John Easter consists of twelve parts that flow into each other *attacca* (without pause): 1. Easter Morning; 2. Mary Magdalene; 3. First Appearance of the Risen Christ to His Disciples: "Receive the Holy Spirit"; 4. "I do not believe"; 5. The Rider on the White Horse; 6. Second Appearance of Christ to His Disciples: "And doubt no longer"; 7. Intermedium; 8. "I am the living bread"; 9. "The darkness vanishes"; 10. Third appearance of Christ to His Disciples: "Farewell"; 11. Judgment; and 12. "And I saw a new heaven and a new earth."

The performance of both the *Passion* and *Easter* with more than two hundred musicians was the most costly of the anniversary productions in the Norddeutscher Rundfunk series "das neue werk," the traditional venue for new music in Hamburg. Valery Gergiev conducted the NDR chorus and orchestra, and added to them the soloists and chorus of the Maryinsky Theater as well as the St. Petersburg Chamber Chorus. Arrangements within the church were quite elaborate, with chorus and orchestra placed in the north gallery, which was large enough to accommodate all performers and offered excellent acoustics. But unpleasant complications marred the last few days of rehearsals. Although Gergiev had arrived on March 11, he interjected a quick trip to Moscow two days before the premiere to receive a prestigious award from Vladimir Putin. Contrary to an earlier agreement, he simply canceled rehearsals on March 14, instead of turning it over to a replacement, thereby insulting the composer and costing the musicians an important day of rehearsals.

The audience and the press came from far and wide to hear the premiere on March 16, 2002. Among them were several composers, such as Toshio Hosokawa from Japan and most of Hamburg's music elite. The sixteen hundred seats available to the public had been sold out, much to the dismay of those trying to buy last-minute tickets.

Following the ninety minutes of the *Passion* and a long intermission, *Easter* opens with the quiet and tender passages of "Easter Morning": the solo violin plays fifths in harmonics, the notes fading away like echoes; flutes enlarge the sound; then the choirs enter with the Easter greeting of the Orthodox liturgy— "Christ is risen from the dead." By doubling the events—the women and the disciples meet the risen Christ as recounted in the Gospel according to John, while prophetic images from the Apocalypse are also suggested—the emotional range changes as voices and instruments fuse and interchange. The bass recitative weaves in and out of highly expressive choral and orchestral passages, particularly in the long and central tenth part, "Third Appearance of Christ to His Disciples: 'Farewell,'" which enacts the ritual of the third supper. The twelfth and final part, "And I saw a new heaven and a new earth," turns back to the beginning of St. John Easter, now on a higher, spiritualized plane. New timbral colorations are introduced by means of a waterphone (see below) and chimes, along with flutes and piccolos in extremely high registers. The liturgical Easter hymn reappears amid solo passages sung by the tenor and bass. After the choir's repetition of the austere "In the beginning was the Word" from the opening of the Passion, the work concludes with the words "Holy, holy, holy is the Lord, Almighty God of all creation."

The grandeur of St. Michael's Cathedral enhanced the compelling intensity of the performance, and the audience celebrated the composer, the conductor, and the performers with several minutes of standing ovations. NDR's series, "das neue werk," had rarely before presented works of Russian music, let alone music in the spirit of the Orthodox Church. Reflecting on the event some two years afterward, Richard Armbruster, who had scheduled the premiere, would write, "Looking back, I am still struck by the spiritual power of this work. In its deeply sincere and highly intellectual spirituality as well as with its frank piety it projects a voice that is unique in contemporary music. There is no other work like it, and all of us were aware of its uniqueness when we staged that huge performance in Hamburg. Church music in Hamburg during the Easter season is traditionally dominated by performances of Bach's great Passions. Suddenly there was an entirely new work in that context, one that attracted audiences from large parts of northern Germany. In this sense, Hamburg's Protestant cathedral was an excellent venue for the premiere. I personally was and continue to be fascinated by the highly intellectual conception of the textual dimension of the work, as it challenges one to think about the story of Christ's Passion. With some works of art, one simply feels deeply grateful that they exist—and Sofia Gubaidulina's oratorio is one of them."[18]

Gubaidulina's arrangement for the last part of St. John Easter included a waterphone in the percussion section. Related to both the Tibetan water drum and the African kalimba (thumb piano), this instrument of relatively recent invention has a circular, flat resonator that is filled with water and equipped with a slender neck that serves as a handle and for water intake. Bronze rods tuned to a combination of microtonal and diatonic relationships are arranged around the outer edge of the resonator. The player bows the rods, or strikes them by hand or with a mallet, while swinging the instrument around, thus producing reverberant, shimmering glissando sounds. Some listeners are reminded of the haunting sounds of the humpback whale. When Gubaidulina was searching for new sounds in preparation for the Passion-Resurrection cycle, she happened to see and hear a waterphone for the first time in New York. During a break in rehearsals for *Two Paths,* the solo percussionist of the New York Philharmonic, Christopher Lamb, remained on stage to play the waterphone in anticipation of the forthcoming premiere of Tan Dun's Concerto for Water Percussion, in which Lamb performed as soloist. The instrument immediately piqued Gubaidulina's curiosity and, with Laurel Fay's assistance as a translator, she walked up to the stage and communicated with Lamb, mostly in gestures, but with the result that he gave her his card and the address in New York City where she could buy the instrument. A couple of days before her return to Europe after the premiere of *Two Paths* in April 1999 she bought her first waterphone.

The instrument had been invented and developed in the 1960s by Richard Waters, an American multimedia artist living in Hawaii, and it quickly became popular among California artists. Waters has meanwhile built by hand more than one thousand waterphones of varying sizes, giving particular attention to the difficult process of tuning each instrument. He has improvised with other musicians and exhibited the instrument in galleries. In April 2001 Laurel Fay ordered a second instrument from Waters for Gubaidulina and had it shipped to Germany. Not long after the performance of the Passion-Resurrection cycle in Hamburg's "Michel," Gubaidulina wrote *On the Edge of the Abyss,* a work for seven cellos and two waterphones, which she presented as a gift to Victor Suslin on his sixtieth birthday.

Travels, a Big Prize, and a Work for the Boston Symphony Orchestra

From May to September 2001 Gubaidulina took brief trips to France, Sweden, Denmark, Japan, Russia, England, and the Netherlands. From October through December she concentrated on a new orchestral work for the Boston Symphony Orchestra. Because of the extensive amount of time it had taken to complete the Passion-Resurrection cycle, other commissioned pieces were postponed, among them a work for the French festival Rencontres d'Ensembles de Violoncelles in Beauvais. Since the 1990s a large number of cello ensembles had emerged, and many works have been and continue to be written for them by such composers as Pierre Boulez, Kaija Saariaho, Augusta Read Thomas, and Arvo Pärt. As a center for these activities, the Beauvais festival had commissioned a work from Gubaidulina in the 1990s, but the premiere scheduled for May 2000 had to be canceled. Only in the spring of 2002, after finishing *St. John Easter,* did Gubaidulina write *Mirage: The Dancing Sun* [*Mirazh: Tantsuiushchee solntse*]. Written for eight cellos, it was performed by L'Octuor de Violoncelles de Beauvais in the presence of the composer on May 10, 2002.

As is so often the case with artists who have reached a certain level of fame and received several initial honors, Gubaidulina now began to attract distinctions and prizes like a magnet. Between May 2002 and January 2003 she was given three important awards. On May 27 she traveled to Stockholm to receive, together with Miriam Makeba from South Africa, the Polar Music Prize [Polarpriset] 2002 from the hands of the King of Sweden at a gala event. The Polar Prize, an award of international distinction like the Japanese Premium Imperiale, is given to artists who have significantly contributed to breaking down barriers between different musical worlds. Hence each year the prize goes to two recipients, who in prior years included Paul McCartney, Ray Charles, and Bob Dylan as well as Pierre Boulez, Karlheinz Stockhausen, and Iannis Xenakis. On her return trip Gubaidulina stopped over in Copenhagen to participate in the presentation of *Essential Time,* a film portrait dedicated to her.

During the summer Gubaidulina traveled to the East, first to Japan and then to Russia. She revisited Tokyo to spend several days at the Tokyo Summer Festival 2002, attending the July 9 performance of *Now Always Snow,* which shared the program with a poetry reading by Genadi Aigi. Daniel Reuss conducted the outstanding Collegium Vocale Gent from Belgium and the Nomad Ensemble.

Back in Germany, on August 17, 2002, at a festive occasion in Kiel, Gubaidulina was awarded the Grand Cross of the Order of Merit of the Federal Republic of Germany [Große Verdienstkreuz des Verdienstordens der Bundesrepublik Deutschland]. She was now a German citizen as well as a citizen of the State of Schleswig-Holstein, and hence eligible for the highest distinction awarded by the German government for contributions to the common good. (The year before, on March 22, 2001—the anniversary date of Goethe's death—Gubaidulina had received the Goethe Medal in Weimar [Goethe-Medaille der Stadt Weimar].) The next day, August 18, 2002, she was on her way to Russia accompanied by a small German film crew and by Irina Parfyonova, a Russian journalist living in Berlin.

Parfyonova, while she was listening to the *St. John Passion* at the Berliner Philharmonie, had conceived the idea of making a film about Sofia Gubaidulina, her music, and her religious beliefs. The journalist felt a strong connection between Gubaidulina's music and the atmosphere of the island of Valaam in Lake Ladoga that she had often visited. A group of about thirty islands clusters around Valaam, with its All-Saints Cathedral and Monastery of the Transfiguration of the Savior [Khram vo imia Vsekh Sviatykh i Spaso-Preobrazhenskii monastyr'], a center of Orthodox faith and a destination for pilgrims that dates from the eleventh century. Built on the model of Jerusalem, the island has a river Jordan, a Garden of Gethsemane, a Mount of Olives, and a Tomb of Jesus. A number of nineteenth-century artists were inspired by its atmosphere. In Nikolai Leskov's *Enchanted Wanderer* [*Ocharovannyi strannik* (1872)], a novice at the monastery tells the story of his life as he crosses Lake Ladoga onboard a ship headed for Valaam. Painters like Ivan Shishkin and Nikolai Roerich have used the island as a subject for painting. And Pyotr Tchaikovsky, in a melancholy mood after a visit to Valaam, probably chose "Land of Gloom, Land of Mist" ["Ugriumyi krai, tumannyi krai"] as the title for the second movement of his First Symphony (*Winter Reveries* [*Zimnie grëzy*]). During the Soviet era, the monastery was used as a home for invalids and the disabled, with the church buildings used for storage. In the 1990s the monastery was restored to its original use, and today around two hundred people live on the islands, including about twenty-five monks during the warmer seasons and somewhat fewer during the winter.

Despite the pressure of work, Gubaidulina was glad to take the trip to Valaam to experience its special atmosphere, to feel close to nature, the surrounding water, and the rocks. The harmonious relationship between the setting and eight hundred years of Christian monastic tradition had remained a fond memory for her. As early as the 1970s she had visited the island from the Union of Composers creative retreat [Dom tvorchestva] in Sortavala, on the banks of Lake Ladoga near the Gulf of Finland. Of course, no ferry service was available at that time, as the Communist regime disapproved of the Christian history of Valaam, but, by happenstance, some wealthy people from St. Petersburg who owned a yacht offered to take her to the island. Now, in 2002, Irina Parfyonova had made all the necessary arrangements, including obtaining Church permission to do the filming. After a three-hour drive from the St. Petersburg airport, a boat from the monastery was waiting for them in Prioserk, and five hours later they reached Valaam. The German film crew, directed by Daniel Finkernagel, had already shot some footage during rehearsals of the Passion-Resurrection cycle in Hamburg and was now working on the conclusion of the documentary. It would show Gubaidlina on her visit to Father Vasily, a monk living in a *skit* (hermitage) on one of the secondary islands. The film does not show her asking the question that has always troubled her: whether she has the right to compose music that is not for specific use by the Church. But, as it happened, Father Vasily, though unprompted, answered in the affirmative. *Passionen eines Lebens* was broadcast on ZDF/ARTE television for the first time on January 11, 2003. An appealing and evocative film, it was generally successful, even though Irina Parfyonova, in retrospect, had second thoughts about some of its details: "The treatment of Gubaidulina's Orthodox faith, her childhood, and the icons—all of that was too direct and lacked nuance. Moreover, communication with the German crew, who were outsiders to that world, was generally something of a problem."[19] She did, however, like the cinematic images of Valaam that are the high point of the film.

St. John Passion and St. John Easter again dominated the events of the next three weeks in the summer and early fall of 2002. Soon after her return from Valaam, Gubaidulina flew to England, where Gergiev conducted the Passion-Resurrection cycle at the London Proms in Royal Albert Hall in the afternoon of August 25. Like so many of Gergiev's concerts, the event was something of a tour de force, as he and the musicians of the Maryinsky Theater had performed Musorgsky's *Boris Godunov* the night before and would do Prokofiev's Third Piano Concerto and Shostakovich's Fourth Symphony only a few hours after the Passion-Resurrection concert. Gubaidulina was pleased with the performance, even though the concert hall accommodating several thousand people was only a little more than half full—it has standing room for fifteen hundred. The reviews in the London papers were generally unenthusiastic.

As part of the festivities for Gergiev's fiftieth birthday, the Passion-Resurrection cycle was twice performed in Rotterdam on September 15 and 16, 2002. Besides his role as director at the Maryinsky Theater, Gergiev was also principal conductor of the Rotterdam Philharmonic Orchestra, but it was the St. Petersburg orchestra that he conducted in the Rotterdam performances of *St. John Passion* and *St. John Easter*. Initially he had planned to place the orchestra in the pit and the chorus on stage enacting the events in motions and gestures. The entire performance was to be enhanced by light and color effects arranged by the Russian lighting designer Gleb Filshtinsky, under the general direction of Alexander Galibin. Gubaidulina, however, objected to this plan and felt, in particular, that projections for the performance should show either medieval or modern art but nothing from any periods in between. In the end, the audience saw only projections of subdued colors and abstract images while listening to the music and words. In gratitude for Gergiev's initiative—without him the many performances of the *Passion* and the entire cycle would have been impossible—Gubaidulina dedicated the work to him. Also, in response to a commission by the Eduard van Beinum Stichting, by request of the Rotterdam Philharmonic Gergiev Festival, she took the fifth part of *St. John Easter, The Rider on the White Horse* [*Vsadnik na belom kone*], and arranged it as a separate orchestral work, this time with the waterphone in the percussion section. Gergiev conducted the Rotterdam Philharmonic Orchestra in the premiere on September 21, 2002.

Gubaidulina spent the following months focusing on the orchestral work for the Boston Symphony Orchestra and finished it just as 2003 was beginning. In January 2003 she was honored with yet a further distinction: the editors of the most influential record and CD publications in seven countries voted her the "Living Composer 2003" at the music fair "Midem" in Cannes. Moreover, the Stuttgart CD recording of *St. John Passion* received first prize in the category of nineteenth/twentieth-century choral music. At the award ceremony in Cannes, a reporter asked Gubaidulina: "Why did you not compose *The Passion and Resurrection according to St. John* as an a capella work?" To which she replied: "That would have been possible if I had written music only for the story of the Passion. But the addition of the Apocalypse of St. John created a new dimension that exceeded the limitations of a choir."

Finally, at the end of April 2003, Gubaidulina flew to Boston; she was by now a familiar figure in the New England music world. On her second visit six years earlier, when Bernard Haitink had conducted her Viola Concerto, the Boston Symphony had requested an orchestral work from her. She was pleased to accept the assignment from such a distinguished orchestra, and she chose a theme that had been on her mind ever since the 1970s. As she later commented:

> Quarter tones, as well as the conventional chromatic twelve tones, are really a violation of nature. For instance, when a horn player plays chromatically, he must re-form the natural tones of his instrument with his mouth. I have thought much about this, and my new work for Boston reflects my thinking. . . . To this day the problem has not been resolved, and it will never be resolved because we live in the tension between the material and the spiritual parts of our existence—and this is the cause of much pain. In my own work, the problem is not resolved but only demonstrated. In the twentieth century the path of a creative individual was free and open, but now in the twenty-first century that's past—one must now search still further and in greater depth.

The conflict becomes quite evident in the new twenty-minute work when the French horn and the cello play the same melody in a duet—the horn in natural tones, the cello in chromatics. Chromatic *glissandi* in the accompanying strings, however, resolve this particular conflict, as the sounds of the strings are part of both the natural overtone series and the tempered scale. The end of the work is marked by the delicate, light sounds of the *cymbales antiques* for which the piece is named: *The Light of the End* [*Svet kontsa*].[20]

Kurt Masur was the guest conductor of the Boston Symphony Orchestra's premiere of *Light of the End* in Symphony Hall on April 17, 2003. Placed between Prokofiev's First Symphony (*Classical*) and Tchaikovsky's Sixth Symphony (*Pathétique*), Gubaidulina's work was the center of an all-Russian program and impressed with its strong natural vitality. The public rehearsal and all three performances were sold out, and many young people were in the audience. On the morning before the premiere Masur, now conducting Gubaidulina's third large work, said:

Sofia Gubaidulina is a woman who has always affected me deeply in new ways. And this piece is even more dramatic and expressive than all the other works by her that I know and have conducted. That does not diminish the other works in any way, but the enormous splendor that she projects here gives it a special dimension. The work is a mirror image of her beliefs, and what she presents in it is, so to speak, the ebb and flow of life with its obligations and passions. But at the end there is the prospect of hope and light—just as the title of the piece suggests, the light that will shine for each of us in the end.[21]

The morning following the premiere, Gubaidulina was at the Longy School of Music in Cambridge, across the Charles River, to attend an event arranged by the Boston Symphony Orchestra. She had been expected by a group of composition students who were joined by fellow students from Harvard. They listened carefully to a recording of the previous night's performance with two copies of the score at hand, and Gubaidulina patiently answered the students' questions, with Laurel Fay acting as interpreter.

Back in Appen, she was able at last to get to the bayan piece long ago requested by Friedrich Lips. Playfully alluding to the fact that she and Lips were born under the same sign of the zodiac, Gubaidulina titled the new piece *Under the Sign of Scorpio [Pod znakom skorpiona]*, and explained in the subtitle: "Variations on six hexachords for bayan and large orchestra." Lips played the premiere on October 10, 2003, in Stockholm, with Manfred Honeck conducting the Swedish Radio Symphony Orchestra (Sveriges Radios Symfoniorkester). Among other commitments of long standing was a trombone concerto for the Swedish trombonist Christian Lindberg, a creative musician of the first order who also composes music and has played more than seventy premieres of works dedicated to him by such composers as Luciano Berio, Arvo Pärt, Alfred Schnittke, Tōru Takemitsu, and Mark-Anthony Turnage. But because of Gubaidulina's preoccupation with the Passion-Resurrection cycle, the plans for this work also had to be changed. As the Raschèr Saxophone Quartet had also repeatedly asked for a piece, Gubaidulina discussed the situation with everyone concerned and finally wrote a work for trombone and four saxophones, eventually adding cello, double bass, and tam-tam. In her search for an appropriate kind of music for Lindberg, she had listened to his recorded performances, and in the end wrote a work that included a "transformation"—the title she eventually chose for it. In the first part of *Transformation [Vewandlung]*, the score leaves the trombonist considerable improvisational freedom. At this performance, the tam-tam was placed at center stage, with cello and bass to the right and the saxophone quartet to the left. Lindberg entered the hall wearing a red jersey and a clown's cap to play a few notes. He sashayed about, flirted with a woman in the audience, and asked her companion to leave. With the audience breaking out in laughter, he continued playing, the saxophone quartet replied to him, he brazenly interrupted them, and the first part ended in a fortissimo passage. Then the "transformation" took place: the trombonist—now dressed in a black suit suggesting his tragic fate—played melodic and expressive thematic ideas. Then the piece evolved into a coordinated performance of the seven instruments and ended in a single beat on the tam-tam. Up to that point the percussionist—dressed in the red robe and cap Gubaidulina had worn when she received her honorary doctorate in Kazan—had been sitting silently at his instrument. Lindberg was delighted with it all, and the premiere on March 14, 2004, in Turku, Finland, was a great success. "But," the composer later said, "humor is something that didn't come easy for me; depth and tragedy are more my nature."

For the foreseeable future Gubaidulina is committed to many commissioned works. In the fall of 2004 she was working on a new flute concerto for Sharon Bezaly, the winner of the "Young Artist 2003" award in Cannes. It is scheduled for its premiere with the Göteborg Symphony Orchestra under the direction of Mario Venzago. Also, at the request of Steven Sloane, the principal conductor of the Bochum Symphony Orchestra, Gubaidulina will be composer in residence for their 2004–2005 season. Despite major cutbacks in funding for cultural events, the conductor—who originally came from Los Angeles—will perform six of her works in the course of the year, among them the world premiere of a Concerto for Cello and Orchestra scheduled for January 27, 2005. At the request of the composer, Vladimir Tonkha arranged Gubaidulina's Viola Concerto of 1996 for cello and is to be the soloist for the new premiere.[22]

Fourteen Years since 1990

Fourteen years have passed since Sofia Gubaidulina immigrated to Germany, years in which life has dramatically changed in both East and West, not least regarding mutual understanding and interaction between the two former opponents. In the West the enthusiasm that once welcomed perestroika has long since flamed out. In Russia, a cool skepticism now prevails toward what is generally seen as the single-minded economic and pragmatic attitude of the West. At the same time, however, that very pragmatism has been adopted by a large portion of the younger generation of Russians as a modus vivendi in a tense "struggle for survival." The continuation of building cultural bridges to this ever mysterious giant empire—bridges that would span the distance between European and Asian cultures—will require great patience and persistence. Fourteen years ago those in both East and West who expected a thorough transformation of Russia in short order were blind to prevailing realities. It will take many more years to pay off the heavy mortgage of seventy years of Communist administration and ideology, and the West has only a dim understanding of the purgatory through which two generations of Soviet citizens had to pass.

Sofia Gubaidulina's life has run parallel to the phases that have marked the Soviet system: she lived in Kazan during the Stalin era; she studied in Moscow and was exploring the directions of her future life when Khrushchev was in power; during the Brezhnev period she belonged to a small group of nonconformist composers, struggling under hardships. Not until Gorbachov was she allowed to travel, and when the Soviet Union collapsed, she emigrated and settled in Germany.

Today Gubaidulina lives and composes in the small northern German village of Appen. When still a child, she had decided to make music her life, and now her works have achieved worldwide renown. By ancestry and education she is deeply and equally rooted in both East and West, but her works are such an intricate fusion of Russian, Oriental, and European culture that her music is no longer simply "Eastern" or "Western" but speaks a universal language that can be understood by all humanity.

The radical changes occurring in our times have raised many questions in Gubaidulina's mind, and as she looked back on the condition of the arts during the twentieth century, she said in January 2003:

> Art in the twentieth century has had many good and fruitful effects, but at the beginning and at the end it revealed two negative aspects, as I see it. At the beginning I think of Jean Cocteau, especially as a theater director who wanted his actors to amaze and astonish their audiences. He was more concerned with polish and effect than with an inner truth. That is also true of today's videos, where all that matters is clever effect and stimulation. A TV editor told me recently: "An image has to change every eight seconds." And now at the end of the century they say, "We don't need art, what's it good for?" because for many people life is all about entertainment and making money. Both strike me as errors because true art, for me, is essentially religious. Art originates in man's spiritual essence, and it can return mankind to that origin.

Appendix A.
Chronology of Gubaidulina's Life

1931

Born on October 24, in Chistopol on the Karma (Tatar Autonomous Soviet Socialist Republic), daughter of the Tatar geodetic engineer Asgad Masgudovich Gubaidullin (1903–1996) and the Russian teacher Fedosia Fyodorovna Elkhova (1903–1992); the following spring the family moves to Kazan, the capital of the republic.

1937–1939

Attends the Children's Music School in Kazan, having been admitted at an earlier age than the standard.

1939–1946

Attends public school and the Children's Music School; first childlike attempts at composition.

1946–1949

Attends music "gymnasium" (secondary school); first composition lessons with Nazib Zhiganov.

1949–1954

Studies piano at the Kazan Conservatory under Leopold Lukomsky, and, as of 1952, under Grigory Kogan; first trip to Moscow as her teachers' guest; starting in 1952, takes composition as an elective under Albert Leman; in 1954 meets geology student and poet Mark Liando.

1954–1959

Studies composition at the Moscow Conservatory, first with Yury Shaporin and, beginning in 1955, with Nikolai Peiko; continues piano lessons with Yakov Zak until 1957; January 22, 1956, marriage to Mark Liando; summer 1958, moves from student residence to Tomolino, a Moscow suburb; final examination in

June 1959; November 11, 1959, birth of daughter Nadezhda (Nadia); in the early 1960s, dissolution of the relationship with Mark Liando.

1960–1963

Graduate studies under Vissarion Shebalin, who withdraws after a year because of illness and dies on May 25, 1963; returns to the student residence of the Conservatory on Srednii Kislovskii pereulok; joins the Composers Union in 1961; December 15, 1962, first composer's evening at Gnesin Hall with *Phacelia* and *Chaconne*.

1963

Freelance composer as of summer; room on Leninskii Prospekt; wins first prize with *Allegro rustico* in all-union competition of young composers; becomes acquainted with the dissident Nikolai Bokov and, during the winter of 1963–64, with Maria Yudina.

1964

Begins to earn a living by composing film music; by 1989 composes a total of about twenty-five documentaries, animated films, and features.

1965

After more than twenty youthful compositions as a student, composes Five Etudes for Harp, Double Bass, and Percussion Op. 1; official premiere, May 20, 1967, in the Small Hall of the Moscow Conservatory; musical collaboration with Mark Pekarsky and Boris Artemiev; in the summer, marriage to Nikolai Bokov.

1966

Moves to Studentcheskaia ulitsa.

1967

Travels to International Biennial for Contemporary Music in Zagreb.

1969

Rents her own apartment at No. 2 Pugachevskaya ulitsa; experiments at the Moscow Electronic Studio; becomes acquainted with the music theoretician and pianist Pyotr Meshchaninov.

1970

Travels to Warsaw Autumn festival; baptism in the Russian Orthodox Church; Maria Yudina dies, November 19; during the winter of 1970–71, begins a new cycle of works with *Concordanza.*

1971

Premiere of *Concordanza,* Royan Festival, April 4; premiere of *Night in Memphis,* Zagreb Biennial, May 13.

1972

Becomes acquainted with the poet Gennady Aigi; separation from Nikolai Bokov.

1973

Enters into partnership with Pyotr Meshchaninov (they marry in the summer of 1991); premiere of *Detto II* in the Small Hall of the Moscow Conservatory, May 5.

1974

Begins musical collaboration with Valery Popov; *Steps* receives honorary mention by the Italian Society for Contemporary Music in Rome; beginning in the summer, Nadezhda lives with her mother (until 1979).

1975

Travels to Prague to work with Marek Kopelent and Paul-Heinz Dittrich on *Laudatio pacis;* Shostakovich dies August 9; beginning of improvisations with Viacheslav Artyomov and Victor Suslin (until the summer of 1981); for stage appearances, the three call themselves Astraea; beginning of musical collaboration with Friedrich Lips.

1977

Premiere of *Dots, Lines, and Zigzags,* East Berlin, February 22; Astraea travels to Baku in October; beginning of musical collaboration with Vladimir Tonkha; during the winter of 1977–78 beginning of a new cycle of works with *Introitus;* Gidon Kremer suggests that she "write a violin concerto."

1979

Unofficial premiere of Flute Quartet, Athis Mons (near Paris), February 15; premiere of *In croce*, Kazan, February 27; premiere of First String Quartet, Cologne, March 24; meets the poet Francisco Tanzer in Moscow; premiere of *Percussio di Pekarski*, Paris, October 22; blacklisted, along with six other composers, by Tikhon Khrennikov in November, the start of two especially difficult years.

1980

Premiere of *Detto I*, Moscow Autumn festival, October 14.

1981

Premiere of *Offertorium*, Vienna, May 30; premiere of *Descensio*, Paris, also May 30; Victor Suslin emigrates in July.

1982

First Russian performance of *Offertorium*, Great Hall, Moscow Conservatory, April 15; premiere of *Seven Words*, Moscow Autumn festival, October 20.

1983

Takes a new step in artistic collaboration with Pyotr Meshchaninov after *Perception;* begins composing in rhythm of form.

1984

In August, first trip to the West to attend the Helsinki Festival; commission of an orchestral piece from the Berlin Festival Weeks, the first major commission from the West.

1985

In July, radio production of *Perception* by West German Radio Cologne; first broadcast, January 1, 1986.

1986

With all travel restrictions lifted, can attend all concerts abroad; during the summer, first trip to Lockenhaus to attend premiere of *Perception*, July 11; premiere of *Stimmen . . . verstummen . . .*, Berlin Philharmonic, September 4; first trip to England for Huddersfield Festival.

1987

Premiere of *Hommage à T. S. Eliot,* Kölner Philharmonic, March 25; receives Music Prize of the Fondation Prince Pierre de Monaco for overall compositional work; in September, first trip to the United States to attend Sound Celebrations, Louisville, Kentucky, and visit to New York; in November, first trip to Paris for a performance of *Offertorium;* composer's concert, December 3, House of Architects, Moscow, with an exhibition of paintings by Vladimir Yankilevsky.

1988

In May, meets John Cage at the USSR's Third International Music Festival, Leningrad, also the venue for a performance of a revised version of *Hour of the Soul;* trip to Leipzig for a concert in her honor; receives Koussevitsky International Record Award for CD of *Offertorium.*

1989

Concert in her honor, Continuum Series, New York, April 22; in May, first trip to Japan for concerts in Kobe and Tokyo; meets the composers Yuji Takahashi, Toru Takemitsu, and Toshio Hosokawa, as well as the koto master Kazue Sawai; during the summer, guest at the Almeida Festival (London) and the Holland Festival (Amsterdam); attends Bad Kissingen summer festival for premiere of *Steps,* June 22; premiere of *Pro et Contra,* Louisville, November 3; later that month, Composer in Residence at Wien Modern festival.

1990

In January, first Gubaidulina Festival of the USSR, Sverdlovsk (Ekaterinburg); in January, guest of Musica Nova festival, Brisbane, Australia; premiere of *Alleluia,* Berlin Philharmonic, November 11.

1991

In February, attends concerts in Canada, followed by emigration; settles in Germany, first as a grant recipient in Worpswede, sponsored by the State of Lower Saxony, and then in Schreyahn/Wendland; premiere of *Aus dem Stundenbuch,* Helsinki, August 27; in July, guest at the Davos Music Festival, where Astraea (with a new cast) performs improvisations; sixtieth-birthday festivals and concerts in Torino, Heidelberg, Hanover, Bochum, and Hamburg; performance of *Prayer for the Age of Aquarius,* Teatro Carlo Felice, Genoa, December 27; receives the awards Premio Franco Abbiati and Heidelberger Künstlerinnenpreis.

1992

Transfers scores and sketches to the archives of the Paul Sacher Stiftung, Basel; in July, buys a house in Appen, near Hamburg; in September, fourth trip to Japan for koto lessons from Kazue Sawai; receives Koussevitsky International Record Award for CD of *Stimmen . . . verstummen . . .*, and also Russian State Award.

1993

Performance of *Offertorium* at the 250th Anniversary Celebration of the Gewandhaus Orchester, Leipzig, March 11; premiere of *Now Always Snow,* Amsterdam, June 12; in August, Composer in Residence at Mozarteum, Salzburg; in November and December, attends concerts in St. Petersburg and Kazan.

1994

Several premieres: String Quartet No. 4, Carnegie Hall, New York, January 20; *And: The Festivities at Their Height,* Las Palmas, February 1; *In Anticipation,* Stockholm, February 12; *Dancer on a Tightrope,* Washington, D.C., February 24; and *Figures of Time,* Birmingham, November 29.

1995

Early in the year, three-week sojourn in Paris to attend Festival Présences, dedicated to her; at the festival, premiere of Music for Flute, Strings, and Percussion, February 18; receives Ludwig-Spohr Preis of the city of Braunschweig.

1996

Following performances and workshops in San José, California, visits Moscow for a number of concerts in April; during the 1996–97 season, concerts in London, Huddersfield, Zurich, and Bochum in celebration of her sixty-fifth birthday.

1997

Premiere of the Viola Concerto, Chicago, April 17; during the summer, Visiting Composer, Tanglewood, Massachusetts; in September, guest at the Festival Donne in Musica, Fuggi; receives Kulturpreis of the city of Pinneberg.

1998

Premiere of *Canticle of the Sun,* Frankfurt am Main, February 9; in June, Gubaidulina Festival days, Dornach (Switzerland); in July, guest at the Centre Acanthes, Villeneuve-lez-Avignon; receives Praemium Imperiale in Japan.

2000

Premiere of *St. John Passion,* Stuttgart, September 1; becomes member of the Ordre Pour le Mérite; in November, Gubaidulina Festival, Royal Philharmonic, Stockholm.

2001

Premiere of *Risonanza,* Amsterdam, April 4; receives Goethe Medaille, Weimar; seventieth-birthday performances in several countries, most notably the International Festival Sofia Gubaidulina, Kazan and Moscow.

2002

First performance of the entire Passion-Resurrection cycle, including the premiere of *St. John Easter,* Hamburg, March 16; receives the Polar Preis and the Grosses Verdienstkreuz des Verdienstordens of the Federal Republic of Germany.

2003

Chosen as Composer of the Year at the International Music Fair "Midem," Cannes; premiere of *The Light of the End,* Boston, April 17; premiere of *Under the Sign of Scorpio,* Stockholm, October 10.

2004

Premiere of *Transformation,* Turku (Finland), March 14.

Appendix B. List of Works

Sources: Catalogue of Works, Musikverlag Sikorski (Sikorski Music Publishers Archives); Valentina Kholopova's List of Works, in the Russian edition of Kholopova/Restagno (see chap. 1, n. 6); Sofia Gubaidulina's manuscript list of works up to 1979 and her notebook; and the author's research and personal collection of concert programs. All uncertain references are indicated by a question mark. Concerts within the Composers Union are designated by MMMK [Moskovskii molodëzhnyi muzykal'nyi klub] (Moscow Youth Music Club), directed by Grigory Frid, and NPKM [Novye proizvedeniia kompozitorov Moskvy] (New Works by Moscow Composers), directed by Edison Denisov. The given year always refers to the time of a work's completion. Musikverlag Sikorski, Hamburg, has the publishing rights to most of Gubaidulina's works, including those published early in the composer's career by the Soviet state publishing houses "Sovetskii kompozitor" (Moscow) and "Muzyka" (Moscow). A few works were published by Boosey & Hawkes (B&H), London; Chant du monde (Ch), Paris; G. Schirmer, Inc. (GS), New York; Ricordi (Ri), Milano; Fazer (Fa), Espoo, Finland; and Berben Editioni Musicali (Be), Ancona, Switzerland. The following other abbreviations are used: C = conducted by; D = dedicated to; J = juvenalia; O = occasional piece; P = premiere; RR = radio recording; SG = Sofia Gubaidulina; T = text by; U = unfinished work; and W = withdrawn work.

Published Works

Phacelia [*Fatseliia*] (1956). Vocal-Symphonic Cycle comprising six songs for soprano and symphony orchestra
T: Mikhail Prishvin, arranged by Mark Liando, in Russian
1. "The Wasteland"; 2. "The Blue Feathers"; 3. "The Aeolian Harp"; 4. "The First Flower"; 5. "The Wild Rose Blooms"; 6. "River under the Clouds".
P: Moscow, 1957: Tamara Petrova, soprano; orchestra (?); C: Emin Khachaturian (version for soprano and piano)

Piano Quintet (1957), in four movements
P: Moscow, November 1958: Komitas Quartet; SG, piano

Serenade [*Serenada*] (1960?) for Six-String Guitar

Chaconne [*Chakona*] (1962) for Piano
D: Marina Mdivani
P: Moscow, December 15, 1962: Marina Mdivani, piano

Allegro rustico (1963) for Flute and Piano
P: Moscow, October 1963: Eduard Shcherbachev, flute; SG, piano

Sonata for Piano, in three movements (1965)
D: Genrietta Mirvis
P: Moscow, March 13, 1966 (MMMK): SG, piano

Five Etudes for Harp, Double Bass, and Percussion (1965), in five movements
P: Moscow, April 21, 1966 (MMMK): Vera Savina, harp; Boris Artemiev, double bass; Valentin Snegiryov, percussion

Sonata for Two Percussionists (1966), in three movements
D: Mark Pekarsky
P: Moscow, December 27, 1991: Nikolai L'govsky and Ilya Vlasov, percussion

Pantomime [*Pantomima*] (1966) for Double Bass and Piano
D: Boris Artemiev
P: Moscow, May 17, 1978 (?): Boris Artemiev, double bass; Olga Günter, piano

Night in Memphis [*Noch' v Memfise*] (1968/1988/1992), Cantata for Mezzo-Soprano, Male Chorus (on prerecorded tape or live from the rear of the concert hall), and Chamber Orchestra in seven movements
T: Ancient Egyptian, translated into Russian by Anna Akhmatova and Vera Potapova
P: Zagreb, May 13, 1971: Eva Novšak-Houška, soprano; Zagreb Radio Symphony Orchestra; C: Igor Gjadrov

Musical Toys [*Muzykal'nye igrushki*] (1969), fourteen piano pieces for children
P (?): Moscow, March 1, 1973 (MMMK): SG, piano

Rubaiyat [*Rubaiiat*] (1969), Cantata for Baritone and Chamber Orchestra
T: Omar Khayyam, Hafiz, Khaqani, translated into Russian by Vladimir Derzhavin
P: Moscow, December 24, 1976 (NPKM): Sergei Yakovenko, baritone; soloists of the Moscow State Symphony Orchestra; C: Gennady Rozhdestvensky

Vivente—non vivente (1970) for ANS Tone Synthesizer and Prerecorded Natural Sounds

Concordanza (1971) for Instrumental Ensemble
P: Royan (France), April 4, 1971: Musica Viva Pragensis; C: Zbynek Vostrak

String Quartet No. 1 (1971), in one movement
P: Cologne, March 24, 1979: Arcis Quartet

Toccata-troncata (1971) for Piano

Fairy-Tale Poem [*Poema-skazka*] (1971) for Symphony Orchestra
P and RR: Moscow, November 21, 1971: Moscow Radio Symphony Orchestra;
C: Maxim Shostakovich

Music for Harpsichord and Percussion Instruments from Mark Pekarsky's Collection [*Muzyka dlia klavesina i udarnykh instrumentov iz kollektsii Marka Pekarskogo*] (1972) in two movements
D: Boris Berman and Mark Pekarsky
P: Leningrad, April 5, 1972: Boris Berman, harpsichord; Mark Pekarsky, percussion

Roses [*Rozy*] (1972) for Soprano and Piano, five songs
T: Gennady Aigi, in Russian
1. "A Dream: The Path across the Field"; 2. "Migrating Bird"; 3. "Roses on the Hills"; 4. "A Field in Midwinter"; 5. "And: The Roses Are Wilting"
P: Moscow, March 1, 1973 (MMMK): Lydia Davydova, soprano; SG, piano

Steps [*Stupeni*] (1972/1986/1992) for Symphony Orchestra and Speaker
T: Rainer Maria Rilke, in German or in Russian translation
P (1972 version): Berlin, December 19, 1990: Berlin Radio Symphony Orchestra;
C: Gerd Albrecht
P (1986 version): Bad Kissingen (Germany), June 22, 1989: Prague Symphony Orchestra; C: Jiri Belohlávek
P (1992 version): Stockholm, March 25, 1993: Royal Stockholm Philharmonic Orchestra; C: Gennady Rozhdestvensky

Detto II (1972) for Cello and Instrumental Ensemble
D: Natalia Shakhovskaya
P: Moscow, May 5, 1973: Chamber Ensemble; C: Konstantin Kremets

Counting-Out Rhymes [*Pesenki-schitalki*] (1973) Five Children's Songs for Voice and Piano
T: Yan Satunovsky, in Russian
1. "Once upon a Time"; 2. "The Crane"; 3. "A Character from a Fairy Tale"; 4. "Counting-Out Song"; 5. "The Cuckoos"

Ten Etudes (Preludes) for Solo Cello (1974)
D: Vladimir Tonkha
P: Moscow, December 12, 1977: Vladimir Tonkha, cello

Invention [*Inventsiia*] (1974) for Piano

Quattro (1974) for Two Trumpets and Two Trombones
P: Moscow, November 22, 1974: Leonid Chumov and Fyodor Grigin, trumpet; Anatoly Skobelev and Anatoly Nesterenko, trombone

Hour of the Soul [*Chas dushi*] (1974), Poem for Large Wind Orchestra and Mezzo-Soprano (Contralto)
T: Marina Tsvetaeva, in Russian
P: Bolzano (Italy), September 11, 2004: Nathalie Stutzmann, mezzo-soprano; Windkraft Tirol; C: Kasper de Roo

Rumore e silenzio (1974) for Harpsichord/Celesta and Percussion
D: Alexei Liubimov and Mark Pekarsky
P: Leningrad, April 16, 1975: Mark Pekarsky, percussion; Alexei Liubimov, harpsichord/celesta

Concerto for Bassoon and Low Strings (1975) (at least four cellos and three double basses) in five movements
D: Valery Popov
P: Moscow, May 6, 1976: Valery Popov, bassoon; soloists of the Moscow State Symphony Orchestra; C: Pyotr Meshchaninov

Laudatio Pacis (1975), Oratorio for Soprano, Alto, Tenor, and Bass, Reader, Two Mixed Choirs, and Orchestra (without strings) in nine movements
T: Amos Comenius, in Latin
Collaborative composition with Marek Kopelent and Paul-Heinz Dittrich (movements 2, 4, and 8 by SG)
D: UNESCO, on the occasion of its thirtieth anniversary
P: Berlin, September 3, 1993: Central German Radio Chorus and Symphony Orchestra; C: Daniel Nazareth

Sonata for Double Bass and Piano (1975)
P: Moscow (Moscow Autumn) 1975 (?): Anatoly Grindenko, double bass; SG, piano

Concerto for Symphony Orchestra and Jazz Band (1976) with Three Sopranos (amplified with echo) and Tape Recording
T: poem by Afanasy Fet, in Russian
P: Moscow, January 16, 1978: Radio Moscow Pops Orchestra; C: Alexander Mikhailov

Light and Darkness [*Svetloe i tëmnoe*] (1976) for organ
P: Leningrad, May 21, 1979: Alexei Liubimov, organ

Two Ballads (1976) for Two Trumpets and Piano

Dots, Lines, and Zigzags [*Tochki, linii i zigzagi*] (1976) for Bass Clarinet and Piano
D: Josef Horák and Emma Kovárnová
P: East Berlin, February 22, 1977: Josef Horák, bass clarinet; Emma Kovárnová, piano

Trio for Three Trumpets (1976)

Hour of the Soul (*Percussio di Pekarski*) (1976/1988) for Solo Percussionist, Mezzo-Soprano, and Large Orchestra (revision of the version for Wind Orchestra of 1974)
T: Marina Tsvetaeva
D: Mark Pekarsky
P (1976 version): Paris, October 22, 1979: Christoph Caskel, percussion; Marie-Louise Gilles, mezzo-soprano; West German Radio Symphony Orchestra; C: Antoni Witt
P (1988 version): Leningrad, May 26, 1988: Mark Pekarsky, percussion; Lina Mkrchan, mezzo-soprano; Leningrad Philharmonic Orchestra; C: Timur Mynbaev

Misterioso (1977) for Seven Percussionists
D: Vladimir Steinmann
P: Moscow, April 5, 1977: Percussion Ensemble; C: Vladimir Steinmann

On Tatar Folk Themes [*Po motivam tatarskogo fol'klora*] (1977), Three Cycles of Five Poems for Soprano, Alto, and Bass domras, and Piano
P (?): Zurich, December 8, 1996: Guzel Mukhametdinova, domra; Josephine Sokolskaya, piano

Lamento (1977) for Tuba and Piano

Song without Words [*Pesnia bez slov*] (1977) for Trumpet and Piano

Quartet for Four Flutes (1977)
P (?): Moscow, October 11, 1978: Irina Loben, Alexander Korneyev, Alexander Munshin, Oleg Cherniavsky, flute

Duo-sonata for Two Bassoons (1977)
D: Valery Popov
P: Moscow, May 17 (?), 1978: Valery Popov and Alexander Kochetkov, bassoon

Introitus (1978), Concerto for Piano and Chamber Orchestra
D: Alexander Bakhchiev

P: Moscow, February 22, 1978 (NPKM): Alexander Bakhchiev, piano; chamber orchestra; C: Yury Nikolaevsky

Sonatina for Flute (1978)

Sounds of the Forest [*Zvuki lesa*] (1978) for Flute and Piano

Te salutant (1978), Capriccino for Large Pops Orchestra
P (?) and RR: September 16, 1978: Radio Moscow Pops Orchestra; C: Alexander Mikhailov

Detto I (1978) for Organ and Percussion
P: Moscow, October 14, 1979: Tatiana Sergeeva, organ; Victor Grishin, percussion

De profundis (1978) for Bayan
D: Friedrich Lips
P: April 8, 1980 (MMMK): Friedrich Lips, bayan

Jubilatio [*Iubiliatsii*] (1979) for Four Percussionists
D: Mark Pekarsky
P: Moscow, January 13, 1979: Ensemble Mark Pekarsky

In croce (1979) for Cello and Organ
D: Vladimir Tonkha
P: Kazan, March 27, 1979: Vladimir Tonkha, cello; Rubin Abdullin, organ
P: (1991 version for cello and bayan, arr. Elsbeth Moser): Hannover, November 16, 1991: Christoph Marks, cello; Elsbeth Moser, bayan
(Version for cello and bayan, arr. Friedrich Lips)

Two Pieces for French Horn and Piano (1979)
1. *There, in the Distance* [*Tam, vdali*]; 2. *The Hunt* [*Okhota*]

Garden of Joy and Sorrow [*Sad radosti i pechali*] (1980) for flute, harp, spoken voice ad lib.
T: Francisco Tanzer, in German
D: Francisco Tanzer
P: Moscow, February 9, 1981 (NPKM): Sergei Bubnov, flute; Irina Kotkina, harp; Mikhail Goudimov, viola
(Version for flute, harp, and cello, arr. Vladimir Tonkha)
(Version for violin, harp, and cello, arr. Gidon Kremer)

Offertorium (1980/1982/1986), Concerto for Violin and Orchestra
D: Gidon Kremer
P (1980 version): Vienna, May 30, 1981: Gidon Kremer, violin; Austrian Radio

Symphony Orchestra; C: Leif Segerstam

P (1982 version): West Berlin, September 24, 1982: Gidon Kremer, violin; Young German Philharmonic; C: Charles Dutoit

P (1986 version, BBC Studio production): London, November 2, 1986; Gidon Kremer, violin; BBC Symphony Orchestra; C: Gennady Rozhdestvensky

Descensio (1981) for Three Trombones, Three Percussionists, Harp, Harpsichord/Celesta, and Piano/Celesta (Ch)
D: Pyotr Meshchaninov
P: Paris, April 30, 1981: Ensemble 2e2m; C: Paul Méfano

Rejoice! [*Raduisia!*] (1981/1988), Sonata for Violin and Cello, in five movements
D: Natalia Gutman and Oleg Kagan
P: Kuhmo (Finland), July 26, 1988: Oleg Kagan, violin; Natalia Gutman, cello

Seven Words [*Sem' slov*] (1982) for Cello, Bayan, and Strings, in seven movements
D: Vladimir Tonkha and Friedrich Lips
P: Moscow, October 20, 1982: Vladimir Tonkha, cello; Friedrich Lips, bayan; Ricercar Chamber Orchestra; C: Yury Nikolaevsky

Perception (1981/1983/1986) for Soprano, Baritone, Seven String Instruments (2.2.2.1), and Prerecorded Tape, in thirteen movements
T: Francisco Tanzer and fragments from Psalms, in German
1. Einsicht; 2. Wir; 3. Pizzicato I; 4. Dezember; 5. Pizzicato II; 6. Begegnung; 7. Am Meer; 8. Col Legno I; 9. Ich; 10. Ich und Du; 11. Col Legno II; 12. Montys Tod; 13. Stimmen
D: Francisco Tanzer
P (one part of the 1981 version as *Five Miniatures for Baritone and Seven String Instruments* [*Piat' miniatiurov dlia baritona e semi strunnykh instrumentov*]): Moscow, February 1, 1982: Sergei Yakovenko, baritone; members of the Tula Philharmonia Orchestra; C: Yury Nikolaevsky
P (1986 version): Lockenhaus (Austria), July 11, 1986: Jutta Geister, soprano; Charles Naylor, baritone; Philip Hirschhorn and Isabelle van Keulen, violin; Kim Kashkashian and Neithard Resa, viola; Thomas Demenga and Richard Duwen, cello; Alois Posch, double bass; C: Dennis Russell Davies

In the Beginning There Was Rhythm [*V nachale byl ritm*] (1984) for Seven Percussionists
D: Mark Pekarsky
P: Tallinn (Estonia), October 1984: Ensemble Mark Pekarsky

Quasi hoquetus (1984/1985), Trio for Piano, Viola, and Bassoon
D: Mikhail Tolpygo, Valery Popov, and Alexander Bakhchiev

P: Moscow, January 16, 1985: Mikhail Tolpygo, viola; Valery Popov, bassoon; Alexander Bakhchiev, piano
(Version for Piano, Viola, and Cello, arr. Vladimir Tonkha)

Hommage à Marina Tsvetaeva [*Posviashchenie Marine Tsvetaevoi*] (1984) for *A Capella* Chorus on Poems by M. Tsvetaeva, in five movements
T: Marina Tsvetaeva, in Russian
1. "The Day's Burden Has Sunk Beside the Waves"; 2. "The Horse"; 3. "The Glory of the Trumpets"; 3. "Interludium"; 4. "The Garden"
P: Stockholm, November 27, 1989: Swedish Radio Chorus; C: Gustav Sjökvist

Letter to the Poet Rimma Dallosh [*Pis'mo poetesse Rimme Dalosh*] (1985) for Soprano and Cello
T: SG, in Russian

Et exspecto (1985), Sonata for Bayan
D: Friedrich Lips
P: Moscow, November 29, 1987: Friedrich Lips, bayan

Symphony: *Stimmen . . . verstummen . . .* (1986) for Orchestra, in twelve movements
D: Gennady Rozhdestvensky
P: West Berlin, September 4, 1986: Moscow State Symphony Orchestra; C: Gennady Rozhdestvensky

Hommage à T. S. Eliot [*Posviashchenie T. S. Eliotu*] (1987) for Soprano and Instrumental Octet (clarinet, bassoon, horn, two violins, viola, cello, and double bass)
T: T. S. Eliot, in English
P: Cologne, March 25, 1987: Christine Whittlesey, soprano; Eduard Brunner, clarinet; Klaus Thunemann, bassoon; Radovan Vlatkovic, French horn; Gidon Kremer and Isabelle van Keulen, violin; Tabea Zimmermann, viola; David Geringas, cello; Alois Posch, double bass

Witty Waltzing in the Style of Johann Strauss [*Ein Walzerspass nach Johann Strauss*] (1987) for Soprano (vocalization) and Instrumental Octet (clarinet, bassoon, horn, two violins, viola, cello, and double bass)
P: Cologne, March 25, 1987 (interpreters as under *Hommage à T. S. Eliot*)
P (1989 version for Piano and String Quartet): Moscow, December 30, 1989: Gidon Kremer and Tatiana Grindenko, violin; Vladimir Mendelssohn, viola; Thomas Demenga, cello; Marc Marder, double bass; Vadim Sakharov, piano

String Quartet No. 2 (1987)
D: Sibelius Quartet

P: Kuhmo (Finland), July 23, 1987: Sibelius Quartet (Yoshiko Arai and Jaakko Vuornos, violin; Jouko Mansnerus, viola; Seppo Kimanen, cello)

String Quartet No. 3 (1987) (B&H)
P: Edinburgh, August 22, 1987: Arditti Quartet (Irvine Arditti and David Alberman, violin; Levine Andrale, viola; Rohan de Saram, cello)

Two Songs on German Folk Poetry [*Zwei Lieder nach deutschen Volksdichtungen*] (1988) for Mezzo-Soprano, Flute, Harpsichord, and Cello
T: Folk rhymes, in German
1. "Streitlied zwischen Leben und Tod"; 2. "Wenn der Pott aber nu en Loch hat"
D: Roswitha Sperber
P: Heidelberg, June 22, 1988: Roswitha Sperber, mezzo-soprano; Willy Freivogel, flute; Peter Schumann, harpsichord; Reimund Korupp, cello

Trio (1988) for Violin, Viola, and Cello (Ch)
D: In memory of Boris Pasternak
P: Paris, March 4, 1989: Members of the Moscow String Quartet (Evgeniya Alikhanova, violin; Tatiana Kokhanovskaya, viola; Olga Ogranovich, cello)

Answer without Question [*Otvet bez voprosa*] (1988) collage for three orchestras (Prokofiev, Overture for Chamber Orchestra Op. 42; Shostakovich, Eight English and American Folk Songs; Charles Ives, Fourth Symphony)
D: Gennady Rozhdestvensky
P: Moscow, January 4, 1989: Moscow State Symphony Orchestra; C: Gennady Rozhdestvensky

Rejoice before God [*Jauchzt vor Gott*] (1989) for Mixed Chorus and Organ
T: Psalms, in German
P: Cologne, June 8, 1990: Cologne Radio Chorus; Wolfgang Gehring, organ; C: Robin Gritton

Pro et contra (1989) for Large Orchestra (GS)
P: Louisville, November 3, 1989; Louisville Symphony Orchestra; C: Lawrence Leighton Smith

Alleluia [*Alliluiia*] (1990) for Mixed Chorus, Boy Soprano, Organ, and Large Orchestra, and Color Organ ad lib. (four players), in seven movements
T: Russian Orthodox liturgy, in Russian
P: Berlin, September 11, 1990: Philipp Cieslewicz, boy soprano; Thomas Trotter, organ; Leipzig Radio Chorus; Berlin Philharmonic Orchestra; C: Simon Rattle
P (with "light organ"): New York, February 18, 1994: Concert Chorale of New York; American Symphony Orchestra; C: Leon Botstein

Can You Hear Us, Luigi? Here's a Dance, Which an Ordinary Wooden Rattle Will Dance for You [*Slyshish' li ty nas, Luidzhi, vot tanets, kotoryi stantsuet dlia tebia obyknovennaia dereviannaia treshchotka*] (1991) for Six Percussionists and Six Percussion Instruments
P: Moscow, February 23, 1991: Ensemble Mark Pekarsky and SG

From the Book of Hours [*Aus dem Stundenbuch*] (1991) for Cello, Orchestra, Male Chorus, and Female Reader of Verses by Rilke (Fa)
T: Rainer Maria Rilke, in German
D: Vladimir Tonkha
P: Helsinki, August 27, 1991: Vladimir Tonkha, cello; Estonian Men's Chorus; Helsinki Philharmonic Orchestra; C: Eri Klas

Even and Uneven [*Chët i nechët*] (1991) for Seven Percussionists (incl. Harpsichord) (Ri)
D: Mark Pekarsky
P: Turin, September 18, 1991: Ensemble Mark Pekarsky; SG, harpsichord and percussion

Lauda (1991) for Alto, Tenor, Baritone, Speaker, Mixed Chorus, and Large Orchestra (as the third part of the ballet music *Prayer for the Age of Aquarius*, to be performed only together with *Pro et contra* and *Alleluia*)
P: Genoa, December 27, 1991: Patricia Adkins Chiti, alto; Oleg Orlov, tenor; Georgy Zastavni, baritone; Galina Vishnevskaya, speaker; Latvian State Chorus (Riga); Teatro Carlo Felice Orchestra (Genoa); C: Mstislav Rostropovich

Silenzio (1991); Five Pieces for Bayan, Violin, and Cello
D: Elsbeth Moser
P: Hannover, November 16, 1991: Elsbeth Moser, bayan; Kathrin Rabus, violin; Christoph Marks, cello

Tatar Dance [*Tatarsmii tanets*] (1992) for Bayan and Two Double Basses
D: Victor Suslin
P: Hitzacker (Germany), July 25, 1992: Elsbeth Moser, bayan; Wolfgang Güttler and Alexander Suslin, double bass

Dancer on a Tightrope [*Tantsovshchik na kanate*] (1993) for Violin and Piano
P: Washington, February 24, 1994: Robert Mann, violin; Ursula Oppens, piano

Now Always Snow [*Teper' vsegda snega*] (1993) for Chamber Ensemble and Chamber Chorus on Verses by Gennady Aigi, in five movements
T: Gennady Aigi, in Russian
D: Gennady Aigi

P: Amsterdam, June 12, 1993: Schönberg Ensemble, Chamber Chorus of the Netherlands; C: Reinbert de Leeuw

Meditation on the Bach Chorale "Before Thy Throne I Step Herewith" [*Meditation über den Choral "Vor deinen Thron tret ich hiermit" von J. S. Bach*] (1993) for Harpsichord and String Quintet
P: Bremen, September 30, 1993: Robert Hill, harpsichord; members of the German Chamber Philharmonic (Bremen)

. . . Early in the Morning, Right Before Waking . . . [*. . . Rano utrom pered probuzhdeniem . . .*] (1993) for Three Seventeen-string Kotos and Four Thirteen-string Kotos
D: Kazue Sawai
P: Tokyo, June 4, 1994: Kazue Sawai Koto Ensemble

And: The Festivities at Their Height [*Und: Das Fest ist in vollem Gang*] (1993) for Cello and Orchestra
D: David Geringas
P: Las Palmas (Gran Canaria), February 1, 1994: David Geringas, cello; Finnish Radio Symphony Orchestra (Helsinki); C: Jukka-Pekka Saraste

String Quartet No. 4 (1993) with Prerecorded Tape (Color Organ ad lib.)
D: Kronos Quartet
P: New York, January 20, 1994: Kronos Quartet (David Harrington and John Sherba, violin; Hank Dutt, viola; Joan Jeanrenaud, cello)

In Anticipation [*In Erwartung*] (1993) for Saxophone Quartet and Six Percussionists
D: Raschèr Quartet and Kroumata Ensemble
P: Stockholm, February 12, 1994: Raschèr Saxophone Quartet (Carina Raschèr, Harry Kinross White, Bruce Weinberger, Kenneth Coon) and the percussion ensemble Kroumata (Anders Loguin, Roger Bergström, Ingvar Hallgren, Anders Holdar, Leif Karlsson, and Johann Silvmark)

An Angel . . . [*Ein Engel . . .*] (1994) for Mezzo-Soprano and Double Bass on a poem by Else Lasker-Schüler
T: Else Lasker-Schüler, in German
D. Ulrich Eckardt
P: Berlin, May 28, 1994: Maria Kowollik (mezzo-soprano); Alexander Suslin (double bass)

Figures of Time [*Figury vremeni/Zeitgestalten*] (1994) for Symphony Orchestra (B&H)

D: Simon Rattle
P: Birmingham, November 29, 1994: City of Birmingham Symphony Orchestra;
C: Simon Rattle

From the Visions of Hildegard von Bingen [*Aus den Visionen der Hildegard von Bingen*] (1994) for Contralto/Mezzo-Soprano
T: Hildegard von Bingen, in German
D: Alfred Schnittke
P: Ludwigsburg, Germany, July 6, 1997: Stephanie Haas

Music for Flute, Strings, and Percussion (1994)
D: Pierre-Yves Artaud
P: Paris, February 18, 1995: Pierre-Yves Artaud, flute; National Orchestra of France; C: Charles Dutoit

Le Grand Tango (1995) (by Astor Piazzolla) arranged for violin and piano (Be)
P: San Francisco, October 22, 1995: Gidon Kremer, violin; Vadim Sakharov, piano

Quaternion (1996) for Four Cellos
D: Vladimir Tonkha
P: Moscow, April 11, 1996: Vladimir Tonkha, Elena Zhulyova, Vladimir Zhulyov, Mikhail Shumsky, cello

Gallows Songs à 3 [*Galgenlieder à 3*] (1996), Fifteen Pieces for Mezzo-Soprano, Double Bass, and Percussion on poems by Christian Morgenstern
T: Christian Morgenstern, in German
1. "Die Mitternachtsmaus" 2. "Das Nachdenken"; 3. "Das ästhetische Wiesel"; 4. "Das Knie"; 5. "Das Spiel I"; 6. "Das Spiel II"; 7. "Die Beichte des Wurms"; 8. "Improvisation"; 9. "Der Tanz"; 10. "Das Gebet"; 11. "Das Fest des Wüstlings"; 12. "Der Psalm"; 13. "Fisches Nachtgesang"; 14. "Nein!"; 15. "Das Mondschaf"
D: Patricia Adkins Chiti
P: Huddersfield, November 25, 1996: Patricia Adkins Chiti, mezzo-soprano; Marta Ptaszynska, percussion; Alexander Suslin, double bass

Gallows Songs à 5 [*Galgenlieder à 5*] (1996), Fourteen Pieces for Mezzo-Soprano, Flute, Percussion, Bayan, and Double Bass
T: Christian Morgenstern, in German
1. "Die Mitternachtsmaus"; 2. "Das ästhetische Wiesel"; 3. "Das Knie"; 4. "Die Beichte des Wurms"; 5. "Improvisation"; 6. "Die Prozession"; 7. "Der Tanz"; 8. "Das Gebet"; 9. "Das Fest des Wüstlings"; 10. "Das Spiel I"; 11. "Das Spiel II"; 12. "Fisches Nachtgesang"; 13. "Nein!"; 14. "Das Mondschaf"
D: Ensemble "that"

P: Hannover, May 23, 1997: Ensemble "that" (Elena Vassilieva, soprano; Carin Levine, flute; Edith Salmen-Weber, percussion; Elsbeth Moser, bayan; Wolfgang Güttler, double bass

Impromptu (1996) for Flute, Violin, and Strings
D: Irena Grafenauer and Gidon Kremer
P: Cologne, January 16, 1997: Irena Grafenauer, flute; Gidon Kremer, violin; German Chamber Philharmonic (Bremen)

Concerto for Viola and Orchestra (1996) (GS)
D: Yury Bashmet
P: Chicago, April 17, 1997: Yury Bashmet, viola; Chicago Symphony Orchestra; C: Kent Nagano

Ritorno perpetuo (1996) for Harpsichord
D: Elżbieta Chojnacka
P: Warsaw, September 27, 1997: Elżbieta Chojnacka, harpsichord

Canticle of the Sun [*Sonnengesang*] (1997) for Cello, Chamber Chorus, and Two Percussionists
T: St. Francis of Assisi, in Old Italian
D: Mstislav Rostropovich
P: Frankfurt (Main), February 9, 1998: Mstislav Rostropovich, cello; Kaunas State Chorus; percussionists of the Lithuanian National Orchestra; C: Robertas Šervenikas

In the Shadow of the Tree [*V teni dereva*] (1998) for Koto, Bass Koto, Zheng (amplified), and Orchestra
D: Kazue Sawai
P: Tokyo, April 14, 1999: Kazue Sawai, koto, bass koto, and zheng; NHK Symphony Orchestra; C: Charles Dutoit

Two Paths (A Dedication to Mary and Martha) [*Dva puti (Posviashchenie Marii i Marfe)*] (1998) for Two Violas and Orchestra (GS)
P: New York, April 29, 1999: Cynthia Phelps and Rebecca Young, viola; New York Philharmonic Orchestra; C: Kurt Masur

St. John Passion [*Johannes-Passion/Strasti po Ioannu*] (2000) for Soprano, Tenor, Baritone, Bass, Small and Large Mixed Chorus, and Large Orchestra
T: Gospel according to John and Revelation (Apocalypse) of John, in Russian and Church Slavonic
P: Stuttgart, September 1, 2000: Natalia Korneva, soprano; Victor Lutsiuk, tenor; Fedor Mozhaev, baritone; Gennady Bezzubenkov, bass; St. Petersburg Chamber

Chorus; Chorus and Orchestra of the Maryinsky Theater, St. Petersburg; C: Valery Gergiev

Risonanza (2001), Concerto for Organ, Three Trumpets, Four Trombones, and Six String Instruments
D: Reinbert de Leeuw
P: Amsterdam, April 18, 2001: Schönberg Ensemble; C: Reinbert de Leeuw

St. John Easter [*Johannes-Ostern/Paskha po Ioanu*] (2001) for Soprano, Tenor, Baritone, Bass, Small and Large Mixed Chorus, Organ, and Large Orchestra
T: Gospel according to John and Revelation (Apocalypse) of John, in Russian
P: Hamburg, March 16, 2002: Natalia Korneva, soprano; Victor Lutsiuk, tenor; Fedor Mozhaev, baritone; Gennady Bezzubenkov, bass; St. Petersburg Chamber Chorus; Chorus of the Maryinsky Theater, St. Petersburg; North German Radio Chorus and Orchestra; C: Valery Gergiev

Reflections on the Theme B-A-C-H (2002) for String Quartet
D: Brentano String Quartet
P: Dartmouth, N.H., October 2, 2002: Brentano String Quartet

Mirage: The Dancing Sun [*Mirage le soleil dansant/Fata Morgan: Die tanzende Sonne/Mirazh: Tantsuiushchee solntse*] (2002) for Eight Cellos
D: Octuor de Violoncelles de Beauvais
P: Beauvais, May 10, 2002: Octuor de Violoncelles de Beauvais

On the Edge of the Abyss [*Na kraiu propasti*] (2002) for Seven Cellos and Two Aquaphones
D: Victor Suslin
P: Moscow, February 28, 2003: Vladimir Tonkha, cello; Gnesin Institute Cello Ensemble; SG and Victor Suslin, aquaphone

The Rider on the White Horse [*Vsadnik na belom kone/Der Reiter auf dem Weissen Pferd*] (2002) for Large Orchestra and Organ
D: Valery Gergiev
P: Rotterdam, September 15, 2002: Rotterdam Philharmonic Orchestra; C: Valery Gergiev

The Light of the End [*Svet kontsa*] (2002) for Large Orchestra (GS)
P: Boston, April 17, 2003: Boston Symphony Orchestra; C: Kurt Masur

Under the Sign of Scorpio [*Pod znakom Skorpiona*] (2003), Variations on Six Hexachords for Bayan and Large Orchestra
D: Friedrich Lips

P: Stockholm, October 10, 2003: Swedish Radio Symphony Orchestra; C: Manfred Honeck

Transformation [*Verwandlung*] (2004) for Trombone, Saxophone Quartet, Cello, Double Bass, and Tam-tam
D: Christian Lindberg and the Raschèr Saxophone Quartet
P: Turku, March 14, 2004: Christian Lindberg, trombone; Raschèr Saxophone Quartet; musicians of the Turku Philharmonic Orchestra

Works Published in Soviet Collections (with year of publication)

A Little Song about the City at Daybreak [*Pesenka ob utrennem gorode*] (1965) for Two Solo Voices or Two-part Chorus

Toccata (1969) for Six-string Guitar

On a Spring Day [*V letnii den'*] (1973) for Voice and Piano (Bayan)

Prelude (1978) for Trumpet and Piano

Echo [*Ekho*]; *Game* [*Naigrysh*] (1979) Two Piano Pieces for Children

Fairy Tale [*Skazka*]; *Elegy* [*Elegiia*] (1979); Two Pieces for Trumpet and Piano

A Little Tatar Song [*Tartarskaia pesenka*]; *Holiday* [*Prazdnik*];*The Suyumbika Tower* [*Suiumbika*] (1979); Three Pieces for Two Trumpets

Thumbelina [*Diuimovochka*] (1984) Piano Piece for Children

Unpublished Works

Epipe (1946), Variations on a Tatar Theme for Piano (J)

Concerto for Violin and Orchestra (1952?) (J)

Little Blades of Grass Wilt and Dry in the Field [*Vianet, sokhnet v pole travushka*] (1954) two choruses after Russian folk songs (J)

Variations for String Quartet (1955?) (J)

Symphony (1958) in E major, in three movements (J)

Concerto for Piano and Orchestra (1959) (J)

The Magic Flute [*Volshebnaia svirel'*] (1960) ballet music in one act (J)

Four Pieces for Electronic Instruments (Four Miniatures . . .) (1960) (J)

Intermezzo (1960) for Eight Trumpets, Sixteen Harps, and Percussion (version for Eight Trumpets, Two Pianos, and Percussion, 1960?) (J)

Triumph [*Triumf*] (1963?) Overture for Symphony Orchestra (J)

Adagio and Fugue (1963?) for Violin and String Orchestra (J)

The Jolly Tsar [*Tsar' vesel'chak*] (1963?), one-act opera (J)
T: Jan Satunovsky

The Wave Runner [*Begushchaia po volnam*] (1963), ballet music in five acts after a story of the same title by Alexander Grin (J)
Libretto: Mark Liando

Sayan [*Saian*] (1967) for Voice and Piano (W)
T: Velimir Khlebnikov

Detto I (1969) for Solo Organ (W)
P: Moscow, 1974; (?) Tebenikhin, organ

Tiento (1972) for Cello and Ensemble (second movement of *Detto II*) (W);
D: Natalia Shakhovskaya
P: see *Detto II*

Adagio (1975?), ballet music for orchestra (O)

Bacchanal [*Vakkhanaliia*] (1978) for Soprano, Saxophone (Clarinet) Quartet, Bayan, and Percussion (W)
T: Boris Pasternak
P: Moscow, December 10, 1978: Anna Soboleva, soprano; Saxophone Quartet Lev Mikhailov; Vladimir Dolgopolov, bayan; Mark Pekarsy, percussion; C: Pyotr Meshchaninov

Crossroads [*Perekrëstok*] (1977), incidental orchestral music for Vasil Bykau's play of the same title (O)
P: London 1981: BBC Symphony Orchestra; C: Gennady Rozhdestvensky

March (1981) for Symphony Orchestra, composed in collaboration with Edison Denisov and Alfred Schnittke (O)
P: Moscow, April 16, 1982: Orchestra of the Ministry of Culture of the USSR; C: Gennady Rozhdestvensky

Heads or Tails [*Orël ili reshka*] (1983), Directions for Improvisations on the Book of Changes, *I Ching* (O)
P: Moscow, April 1983: Valentina Ponomaryova, voice; Lev Mikhailov, clarinet

and saxophone; Sergei Letov, saxophone; a group of amateur musicians; SG, flexatone

Whispering Games [*Sheptalki*] (1984), Two Orchestral Songs from the film *The Cat That Walked by Himself* [*Koshka, kotoraia guliala sama po sebe*] (O)

Two Etudes for Double Bass (1994) (U)
D: Alexander Suslin
P: Lockenhaus (Austria), July 6, 1995: Alexander Suslin, double bass

Film Music

We Explore the Ocean [*My otkryvaem okean*] (1964); documentary; unknown director

Anna Golubkina (1964); documentary (Moscow); Arkadi Levitan

Believe It or Not [*Khotite, ver'te—khotite net*] (1964); feature (Yalta); Igor Usov and Stanislav Chaplin

Lenin's Three Springs [*Tri vesny Lenina*] (1964); documentary (Moscow); unknown director

The Vertical Line [*Vertikal'*] (1967); feature (Odessa); Stanislav Govorukhin and Boris Durov

Mowgli [*Maugli*] (1967–1971); animated (Moscow); Roman Davydov
—*The Roller Bird* [*Raksha*] (1967)
—*The Abduction* [*Pokhishchenie*] (1968)
—*Akela's Last Hunt* [*Posledniaia Okhota Akely*) (1969)
—*The Battle* [*Bitva*] (1970)
—*The Return to Humankind* [*Vozvrashchenie k liudiam*] (1971)

The Wizard Blacksmith [*Kuznets-koldun*] (1967); animated (Moscow); Perch Sarkisian

Name Day [*Den' angela*] (1968); feature (Odessa); Stanislav Govorukhin

White Explosion [*Belyi vzryv*] (1969); feature (Odessa); Stanislav Govorukhin

Novellas about the Cosmos [*Novelly o kosmose*] (1973); animated (Moscow); Lev Atamanov

Mowgli [*Maugli*] (1973); montage of five earlier Mowgli films; Roman Davydov

The Everyday Life of Dr. Kalinikova [*Kazhdyi den' doktora Kalinnikovoi*] (1973); feature (Moscow); Victor Titov

Inseparable from Us (in Chuvash); documentary (Kazan); Anatoly Surukh; screenplay by Gennady Aigi

When Our Habits Change [*Kogda meniaiutsia nashi privychki*] (1974); animated (Moscow); unknown director

A Man and His Bird [*Chelovek i ego ptitsa*] (1975); animated television film; Anatoly Solin

The Treasure [*Klad*] (1976); feature (Sverdlovsk); Olgerd Vorontsov
The Puppet Show [*Balagan*] (1981); animated puppets; Ideya Garanina

Rishad—Zify's Grandson [*Rishad—vnuk Zify*] (1981); feature (Moscow); Mark Osepian

The Great Samoyed [*Velikii samoed*] (1981); feature (Moscow); Arkady Kordon

Three Days of Feast (*The Return of Feelings*) [*Tri dnia prazdnika* (*Vosvrazhchenie chuvstv*)] (1982); feature; Mark Osepian

The Academic Chair [*Kafedra*] (1982); television film (Belorus); Ivan Kiasashvili

The Scarecrow [*Chuchelo*] (1983); feature (Moscow); Rolan Bykov

The Kreutzer Sonata [*Kreitserova sonata*] (1987); feature (Moscow); Mikhail Shveitser and Sofia Milkina

The Cat That Walked by Himself [*Koshka, kotoraia guliala sama po sebe*] (1988); animated (Moscow); Ideya Garanina

The Sand-Storm Tribe [*Smerch*] (1988); feature; Bako Sadykov; screenplay by Chingiz Aitmatov

The Anna Akhmatova File [*Lichnoe delo Anny Akhmatovoi*] (1989); semi-scholarly documentary; Semyon Aranovich

Diary of a Madman [*Zapiski sumashedshego*] (1990); television film; Tatiana Magar (Ukraine); music by SG and Alfred Schnittke; first broadcast: January 7, 1991

Theater Music

The Gambler [*Le Jouer/Igrok*] (1963) by Jean-François Régnard; unknown director

Only Telegrams [*Tol'ko telegrammy*] (1966) by Valery Osipov; Taganka Theater; directed by Teodor Vulfovich

Let's Settle the Score with Fame [*Svecti schët so slavoi*] (1971) by Yakov Volchek; Mossoviet Theater; unknown director

Crossroads [*Perekrëstok*] (1977) by Vasil Bykau; Taganka Theater; directed by Yury Liubimov and Boris Glagolin

Notes

Interviews conducted by the author are indicated by location and date; other communications by phone, fax, letter, or e-mail are identified only by date. All comments made by Viktor Suslin (since 1985) and Pyotr Meshchaninov (since 1991) are undated. Comments by Gubaidulina without specific place or date citation are derived from various conversations with the author. Russian titles are transcribed according to standard scholarly practice.

1. Ancestors

Editor's note: Asgad Gubaidullin spelled his name, transliterated from Russian, as shown here. His daughter Sofia, however, adopted the common Russian spelling of her name and patronymic, which transliterates as the familiar Sofia Asgatovna Gubaidulina—the "t" instead of "d" in her patronymic and a single "l" in her surname—the form used throughout this book.

1. Sofia Gubaidulina, "Moia zhizn' sostoit iz voprosov" [My life consists of questions], *Izvestie Tatarstana press daidzhest* (1992): 6.

2. Gennady Aigi, "Meine Erinnerungen an Sofia Gubaidulina" (unpublished manuscript); narrated January 4, 1998, and revised by Michael Kurtz, November 1999; in the author's private possession.

3. Göran Fant, "Bön för vattumannens tidsalder" (interview with Sofia Gubaidulina), *Forum Järna* 6 (February 1992): 40.

4. Ibid.

5. Asgad Gubaidullin, "Avtobiografiia" [Autobiography] (unpublished manuscript).

6. Valentina Nikolaevna Kholopova and Enzo Restagno, *Sofia Gubaidulina* (Moscow: "Sovetskii Kompozitor," 1996), 10. This book is in two parts: part 1, entitled *Zhizn' pamiati* [Life of memory] consists of extensive interviews with Gubaidulina conducted by Enzo Restagno, some of which were published independently in Italian as *Gubajdulina a cura di Enzo Restagno* (Torino: E. D. T., 1991); Restagno's conversations with Gubaidulina, translated into Russian, thus make up part 1 (pp. 1–98). Part 2, entitled *Shag dushi* [A step of the soul], is an autonomous research monograph by Kholopova devoted to theoretical/analytical studies of Gubaidulina's music. Hereafter quotations from this book are cited as Kholopova/Restagno.

7. Lilia Olliviers, *Anton Webern's Illegitimate Children* (film script), Sikorski Music Publishers Archives.

8. In the poet's own words, "I was born the same year as Charlie Chaplin, Tolstoi's *Kreutzer Sonata,* Hitler, the Eiffel Tower, and, I believe, Eliot. That summer, all of Paris was celebrating the centennial of the storming of the Bastille. It has been and continues to be a tradition to celebrate Midsummer's Eve during the night of my birth. I was named Anna in honor of my grandmother Anna Egorovna Motovilova, whose mother, the Tatar princess Akhmatova, was a descendant of Ghengis Kahn. Without thinking that I wanted to become a Russian poet, I chose her surname as my *nom de plume*" (Jelena Kusmina, *Anna Achmatowa* [Berlin, 1993], 16).

9. The First Five-Year Plan, which began in October 1929, was given an official starting date of March 1928.

10. Michael Heller and Alexander Nekrich, *Geschichte der Sowjetunion* (Königstein, 1981), 1:252, 2:393.

2. Childhood and Youth, 1932–1949

1. Maria Bogatyryova, "Ot bednosti nichego khoroshego ne byvaet" [Nothing good comes from poverty] (interview with Sofia Gubaidulina), *Moskovskii komsomolets,* July 26, 1991, 4.

2. Victor Yuzefovich, "Ob uchiteliakh, kollegakh i o samoi sebe" [About teachers, colleagues, and about myself] (interview with Sofia Gubaidulina), *Muzykal'naia aka-demiia* 3 (1994): 8.

3. V. Gor'kin, "V prekrasnom i iarostnom mire muzyki" [In the beautiful and savage world of music] (interview with Sofia Gubaidulina), *Komsomolets Tatarii,* March 8, 1981, 2.

4. Ibid.

5. Sofia Gubaidulina, unpublished address at an anniversary celebration of the Children's Music School in Kazan.

6. Rena Seiko, "Tonkaia sfera" [The delicate sphere] (interview with Sofia Gubaidu-lina), *Miloserdie* 2 (1990): 24.

7. Yuzefovich, "Ob uchiteliakh, kollegakh i o samoi sebe," 8.

8. Ibid.

9. Maria Bogatyryova, "Ot bednosti nichego khoroshego ne byvaet" [Nothing good comes from poverty] (interview with Sofia Gubaidulina), *Moskovskii komsomolets,* July 26, 1991, 4.

10. Sofia Gubaidulina in a conversation with Michael Kurtz.

11. Bogatyryova, "Ot bednosti nichego khoroshego ne byvaet," 4.

12. D. Liubin, "Moi vpechatleniia" [My impressions], *Komsomolets Tatarii,* June 7, 1940.

13. *Editor's note:* Mikhail Fabianovich Gnesin (1883–1957) was a noted Russian-Soviet composer and piano pedagogue, respected for the high quality of his teaching pieces for children.

14. Lilia Olliviers, *Anton Webern's Illegitimate Children* (film script), Sikorski Music Publishers Archives.

15. Interview with Natalia Segel, Kazan, April 13, 1992.

16. Andrei Ustinov, "*Chas dushi* Sofii Gubaidulinoi" [Sofia Gubaidulina's *Hour of the Soul*] (interview with Sofia Gubaidulina), *Muzykal'noe obozrenie* 3 (1994): 10.

17. Semyon Gurary, "*Chas dushi* Sofii Gubaidulinoi" [Sofia Gubaidulina's *Hour of the Soul*] (interview with Sofia Gubaidulina), *Vechernaia Kazan'*, May 11, 1988.

18. Vladimir Agopov, "Sävellyksen syvin kerros voi olla akustisesti kuulumattomissa," *Kulttuurivihkot* 2 (1984): 14–18.

19. *Editor's note:* Called the Union of Soviet Composers (Soiuz sovetskikh kompozitorov), until 1957; afterward, the Union of Composers of the USSR (*Soiuz kompozitorov SSSR*). These were the names of the nationwide organization, which comprised all the statewide composers unions in each of the constituent republics of the Union of Soviet Socialist Republics (Soiuz sovetskikh sotsialistichekikh respublik). The statewide unions simply bore the name of the relevant republic, for example, the composers union of the Russian Federation was called the Union of Composers of the RSFSR (Soiuz kompozitorov RSFSR). There were also separate chapters of the RSFSR Composers Union in Moscow and Leningrad. Since the demise of the USSR, the statewide organization of each former Soviet republic has essentially been preserved in the independent states. In the interest of simplicity, the nationwide organization will sometimes be referred to as the Composers Union. References to statewide composers unions will include the name of the relevant state. Chapters associated with cities will, of course, include the city name.

20. Sofia Gubaidulina's memoirs of Shostakovich, as recorded by Elizabeth Wilson in *Shostakovich: A Life Remembered* (Princeton, N.J., 1994), 305; hereafter, cited as Wilson.

3. At the Kazan Conservatory, 1949–1954

1. Maria Veniaminovna Yudina, *Luchi bozhestvennoi liubvi: literaturnoe nasledie* [Radiant beams of divine love: literary legacy], prep. and ed. Anatoly Kuznetsov (Moscow and St. Petersburg, 1999), 25.

2. Stalin once ordered his underlings to bring him a recording of Mozart's Piano Concerto in A Major, K. 488. Because no such recording existed, they scrambled together an orchestra that very night and made a recording with Maria Yudina at the piano. Yudina had her choice of conductors. The following day, after Stalin had listened to the single-issue recording, he sent an envelope containing thousands of rubles to the soloist. Yudina replied in a letter to Stalin, thanking him and asking permission to use the money for the reconstruction of a destroyed church. She also informed him that she would pray for him and for the forgiveness of his sins. When Stalin received this letter the order for Yudina's execution had already been signed, but Stalin gave no sign of displeasure and the pianist was never touched. See Krzysztof Meyer, *Schostakowitsch* (Bergisch-Gladbach, 1995), 235–238; and Solomon Volkov, *Testimony: The Memoirs of Dmitri Shostakovich* (New York, 1979), 194. Anatoly Kuznetsov, the Yudina scholar and editor of her writings and letters, ascribes this event to the war years of 1943–44; he states that the conductor was "either Sergei Gorchakov or Alexander Gauk."

3. Maria Yudina gave a second concert in Kazan at about this time, but there is no extant program and the exact date has not been established. Gubaidulina remembers that the concert was an all-Beethoven affair.

4. Victor Yuzefovich, "Ob uchiteliakh, kollegakh i o samoi sebe" [About teachers, colleagues, and about myself] (interview with Sofia Gubaidulina), *Muzykal'naia akademiia* 3 (1944): 8.

5. Interview with Albert Leman, Moscow, April 20, 1992.

6. "From the Memoirs of Sofia Gubaidulina" (original contribution).

7. Mark Liando, "Zvezda nad snegamu, avtobiografiia" [A star over the snow: autobiography] (unpublished manuscript).

8. Ibid. Frezi Grant was the exotic heroine of Alexander Grin's romantic fantasy *The Wave Runner* [*Begushchaia po volnam*].

9. Ibid.

10. Ibid.

4. At the Moscow Conservatory, 1954–1959

1. Interview with Andrei Volkonsky, Aix-en-Provence, December 18–20, 1998.

2. Ibid.

3. Interview with Elizaveta Tumanian, Moscow, October 11, 1998.

4. Kholopova/Restagno, 17.

5. Interview with Nikolai Peiko, Moscow, April 15, 1992.

6. Ibid.

7. Mark Liando, "Zvezda nad snegamu, avtobiografiia" [Star over the snow] (unpublished manuscript).

8. Ibid.

9. Interview with Henrietta Mirvis, Moscow, October 12, 1998.

10. Valentina Kholopova, "Sofia Gubaidulina als Studentin und Doktorandin des Moskauer Konservatoriums" (original contribution).

11. Wilson, 306.

12. Vladimir Agopov, "Sävellyksen syvin kerros voi olla akustisesti kuulumattomissa," *Kulttuurivihkot* 2 (1984): 14–18.

13. Wilson, 306.

14. Interview with Nikolai Peiko, Moscow, April 15, 1992.

15. Mikhail Chulaki, "Novaia molodaia porosl'" [New, young growth], *Sovetskaia muzyka* 8 (1959): 18–19.

16. Valentina Kholopova, "Sofia Gubaidulina als Studentin und Doktorandin des Moskauer Konservatoriums" (original contribution).

5. Searching for Her Own Way, 1959–1965

1. Interview with Olga Stupakova, Moscow, October 12, 1998.

2. Mark Liando, "Zvezda nad snegamu, avtobiografiia" [Star over the snow] (unpublished manuscript).

3. The performance of this work in the Small Hall of the Conservatory is dated January 29, 1961, in Leonid Talokin and Irina Alpatova, ed., *Drugoe iskusstvo—Moskva*

1956–66 (Moscow, 1991), an informative work but generally unreliable in assigning dates. The program also included Volkonsky's *Suite of Mirrors* [*Siuita zerkal*] and *Musica stricta* (with Maria Yudina at the piano), and Denisov's Sonata for Violin and Piano.

4. According to his own testimony, Volkonsky had performed this piece at an earlier, semi-official occasion.

5. Kholopova/Restagno, 46.

6. Victor Suslin, "Auskunft über Sofia Gubaidulina," Program for *Offertorium*, Berlin, September 24, 1982.

7. Interview with Henrietta Mirvis, Moscow, October 12, 1998.

8. Wilson, 307.

9. Sofia Gubaidulina, "Werkeinführung der Chaconne" (Sikorski Music Publishers Archives).

10. Original contribution by Werner Barfod.

11. These numbers are given in Boris Schwarz, *Music and Musical Life in Soviet Russia, Enlarged Edition, 1917–1981* (Bloomington, Ind., 1983), 399–400.

12. Victor Bobrovsky, "Otkroite vse okna" [Open all the windows], *Sovetskaia muzyka* 2 (1962): 23–28.

13. Rubin Shaverdian, "Avtorskii kontsert S. Gubaidullinoi [*sic*] i A. Nikolaeva" [A meet-the-composer evening with S. Gubaidulina and A. Nikolaev], *Sovetskaia muzyka* 3 (1963): 78–80.

14. According to Gubaidulina, a hierarchy of payments went along these lines: popular science films, thirty rubles per minute; documentaries, forty rubles per minute; children's films, sixty rubles per minute; and features, eighty rubles per minute.

15. Viktor Bobrovsky, "Otkroite vse okna" [Open all the windows], *Sovetskaia muzyka* 2 (1962): 23–28.

16. Sofia Gubaidulina, "Moia zhizn' sostoit iz voprosov" [My life consists of questions], *Izvestiia Tatarstana press daidzhest* (1992): 6.

17. Interview with Nikolai Bokov, Paris, June 3 and 5, 1999, and August 1, 2000.

18. Ibid.

19. The exact date is not known.

20. Alexander Ivashkin, *Alfred Schnittke* (London, 1996), 62.

21. Kholopova/Restagno, 19.

22. Ibid., 40.

23. Interview with Henrietta Mirvis, Moscow, October 12, 1998.

6. A Late Artistic Birth, 1965–1970

1. Artem Vargaftik, "Noty sushchesvuiut chtoby oni zvuchali" [Notes exist in order to sound] (interview with Sofia Gubaidulina), *Muzykal'naia zhizn'* 11 (1998): 16.

2. Andrei Ustinov, "*Chas dushy* Sofii Gubaidulinoi" [Sofia Gubaidulina's *Hour of the Soul*] (interview with Sofia Gubaidulina), *Muzykal'noe obozrenie* 3 (1994): 10.

3. Olga Bugrova, "'Dano' i 'zadano'" ["What's given" and "what's assigned"] (interview with Sofia Gubaidulina), *Muzykal'naia akademiia* 3 (1994): 2.

4. Letter to Michael Kurtz, April 29, 1994.

5. Göran Fant, "Bön för vattumannens tidsalder" (interview with Sofia Gubaidulina), *Forum Järna* 6 (February 1992): 40.

6. Novalis, *Werke* (Cologne, 1996), 2:103.

7. Kholopva/Restagno, 122.

8. Maria Bogatyryova, "Ot bednosti nechego khoroshego ne byvaet" [Nothing good comes from poverty] (interview with Sofia Gubaidulina), *Moskovskii komsomolets,* July 26, 1991, 4.

9. V. Gor'kin, "V prekrasnom i iarostnom mire muzyki" [In the beautiful and savage world of music] (interview with Sofia Gubaidulina), *Komsomolets Tatarii,* March 8, 1981, 2.

10. Interview with Mark Pekarsky, Moscow, December 29, 1997, and October 9, 1998.

11. Václav Kučera, *Nové proudy v sovetské hudbe* (Prague, 1967), 36.

12. Interview with Boris Artemiev, Moscow, June 5, 1999.

13. Interview with Mark Pekarsky, Moscow, December 29, 1997, and October 9, 1998.

14. *Ogonyok [Ogonëk]* 25 (1988): 30.

15. Kholopova/Restagno, 123.

16. Ibid.

17. Ibid.

18. Interview with Vera Gubaidulina, Moscow, October 10, 1998.

19. Interview with Grigory Frid, Moscow, December 30, 1997; and October 14, 1998.

20. Interview with Václav Kučera, Prague, October 26,1994.

21. Besides discussing Schnittke, Denisov, and Gubaidulina, the book also includes commentary on, for example, Leonid Hrabovsky, Arvo Pärt, Valentin Silvestrov, Kuldar Sink, Sergei Slonimsky, Boris Tishchenko, Veljo Tormis, and Andrei Volkonsky.

22. H. H. Stuckenschmidt, "Zwei Welten der Musik in Zagreb," *Melos Zietschrift für neue Musik* 7/8 (1967): 270–274.

23. Ibid.

24. Ibid.

25. Interview with Nikolai Bokov, Paris, June 3 and 5, 1999, and January 8, 2000.

26. Eduard Artemiev was working on film scores, among them Tarkovsky's *Solaris* [*Soliaris*] and *The Mirror* [*Zerkalo*].

27. For Alexander Nemtin, the completion of Scriabin's *Prefatory Act* [*Predvaritel'noe deistvo*] from the original sketches for the *Mysterium* [*Misteriia*] became the labor of a lifetime.

28. Kholopova/Restagno, 183.

29. Marina Drozdova, *Uroki Iudinoi* [*Yudina's lessons*] (Moscow, 1991), 184.

30. In June 1941 this church was ordered closed, but a week later Hitler's army invaded Russia, and Stalin had other things to worry about. Other members of the intelligentsia besides Maria Yudina attended this church: Rostropovich attended on several occasions in the early 1970s and, probably because of him, so did Solzhenitsyn, who was

married there in 1974. The oldest icon in the church (at the lower left of the iconostasis, next to the door of the chancel), depicting Our Lady of Kazan, is by Simon Ushakov.

31. Maria Yudina's note (1968); Lenin Library, OR, RGB, F 527 M.V. Yudina/Box 4 *ed. khranenaiia* 9.

32. Interview with Jürgen Köchel, Bochum, April 21, 1999, and January 14, 2001.

33. Ibid.

34. Interview with Elizaveta Tumanian, Moscow, October 11, 1998.

35. Interview with Valentina Kholopova, Moscow, October 13, 1998.

36. Kholopova/Restagno, 145.

7. Finding the Legato in the Staccato of Life, 1970–1975

1. Program, "Huitième Festival International d'Art Contemporain de Royan" (no page).

2. Dorothea Redepenning, "Concordanza," CD booklet CPO 999164–2.

3. Kholopova/Restagno, 50.

4. Ibid., 51.

5. Interview with Boris Berman, March 25, 2001.

6. Gennady Aigi, "My Memories of Sofia Gubaidulina," unpublished manuscript.

7. Ibid.

8. Ibid.

9. Detlef Gojowy, ed., *Augustyn Bloch* (Cologne, 1999), 10–11.

10. Interview with Grigory Frid, Moscow, December 30, 1997, and October 14, 1998.

11. Michael Kurtz interviewing Sofia Gubaidulina, "It Seems to Me There Is Something That Exists Outside Me, Something That Helps Me and Guides Me" (interview with Sofia Gubaidulina), in *Annäherungen IV an sieben Komponistinnen,* ed. Brunhilde Sonntag and Renate Matthei (Kassel, 1988), 52.

12. Interview with Grigory Frid, Moscow, December 30, 1997, and October 14, 1998.

13. The score shows Rilke's lines in Russian translation above the original German text. For the first version of this work, Gubaidulina had selected a passage from the Old Testament: "For the dust must return to the earth, as it was, and the spirit unto God, who gave it" (*Ecclesiastes* 12:7).

14. Konrad Onasch, ed., *Lexikon Liturgie und Kunst der Ostkirche* (Berlin and Munich, 1993), 210–213.

15. Nikolaj Berdjajew [Nikolai Berdyaev], *Der Sinn des Schaffens* (Tübingen, 1929), 129.

16. Fedor Stepun, *Mystische Weltschau: Fünf Gestalten des Russischen Symbolismus* (Munich, 1964), 144–147.

17. In addition to Ligeti, the jury consisted of the composers Mario Bartolotto, Sylvano Bussotti, Aldo Clementi, Christobal Halffter, and Klaus Huber.

18. In second place was *Limbale,* by Davide Anzaghi (Italy) and in third place *Seul Ensemble* by Maurice Weddington (United States).

19. *Detto I* is a work for organ solo that was written and withdrawn in 1969; in 1978 Gubaidulina wrote a second version for organ and percussion.

20. Kholopova/Restagno, 53. Valentina Kholopova relates this work to the Communion, the last of the four variable parts of the Roman Catholic Mass (see Kholopova/Restagno, 136). The Proper consists of the Introit, Offertory, Gradual, and Communion. However, according to her own comments to the author, the composer did not have the Proper in mind when she wrote this piece. It is possible that she expressed herself differently when she spoke with Kholopova.

21. Interview with Natalia Shakhovskaya, Moscow, October 11, 1998.

22. Interview with Pyotr Meshchaninov, Moscow and Appen.

23. The composer later withdrew the second movement, titled *Tiento.*

24. Interview with Natalia Shakhovskaya, Moscow, October 11, 1998.

25. Interview with Nikolai Bokov, Paris, June 3 and 5, 1999, and January 8, 2000.

26. At that time Gubaidulina had heard only a recording of Schnittke's First Symphony.

27. Kholopva/Restagno, 181.

28. From Marie Louise Bott, "Kein Buch—ein Lied, eine Stimme," *Individualität* 28 (December 1990): 82.

29. Dorothea Redepenning, ". . . reingewaschen durch Musik . . .," *Neue Zeitschrift für Musik* 1 (1990): 21.

30. Ibid.

31. Interview with Leonid Chumov, Moscow, October 12, 1998.

32. Ibid.

33. See Kholopova/Restagno, 146: "When the work, however, was presented onstage, its playful moments, in the perception of listeners, acquired a touch of the comic, the buffo."

34. Interview with Leonid Chumov, Moscow, October 12, 1998.

35. The four students were Evgeny Pan and Anatoly Sizonov (trumpets) and Alexander Gorobets and Vadim Akhmetgareev (trombones).

36. Interview with Jean-Pierre Armengaud, Paris, January 7, 2000.

37. Alexander Ivashkin, *Alfred Schnittke* (London 1996), 128.

38. The program lists only the names of the composers and the instrumentalists. Neither the organizers nor the performers recall the specific works that were played. Possibilities include the Piano Quintet or the First String Quartet on August 3, and *Allegro rustico* or the Serenade for Guitar on August 4, 1975.

39. Concert program of the premiere, Berlin, September 3, 1993.

40. Wilfried Brennecke, "Der ersehnte Friede," concert program of the premiere.

41. Pyotr Meshchaninov had gone to great lengths to organize this concert in the Composers Union. The program listed not only *Concordanza* but also *Roses,* with soprano Lydia Davydova and the composer at the piano. About ten days before the performance, Gubaidulina noticed by chance that her works had been stricken from the program. She called Evgeny Makarov, the head of the Artistic Council, to complain about "this mess,"

because the musicians had already rehearsed and received their pay, but nobody had been notified. Only after she threatened to go public with this scandal was the ban rescinded. *Concordanza* was a great success and was played again as an encore. The production of *Roses* was less successful, as the pianist, owing to the stressful situation, played poorly.

42. Kholopova/Restagno, 71.

43. Interview with Valery Popov, Moscow, October 14, 1998.

44. Jean-Pierre Armengaud, *Entretiens avec Denisov* (Paris 1993), 87–90.

45. Interview with Victor Suslin, Appen and Hamburg.

46. Kholopova/Restagno, 70.

47. Ibid., 161.

8. Composing and Improvising, 1975–1979

1. Interview with Viacheslav Artyomov, Moscow, April 16, 2001.

2. Victor Suslin, "Neue Musik in der UdSSR," radio manuscript, Westdeutscher Rundfunk, July 1984.

3. Ibid.

4. Kholopova/Restagno, 72.

5. Dorothea Redepenning, an interview with Sofia Gubaidulina, in *Russische Avant-garde—Musikavantgarde im Osten Europas, Dokumentation—Kongressbericht* (Heidelberg 1992), 33.

6. The program states: "Ensemble with Folk Instruments." The other musicians were Vladimir Martynov (composer), L. Makhashvili, and Julia Karabanova.

7. Interview with Viacheslav Artyomov, Moscow, April 16, 2001.

8. Ibid.

9. Gennady Aigi, "My Memories of Sofia Gubaidulina," unpublished manuscript. In this instance, Aigi's recollection is not entirely accurate. This first meeting took place before February 1977. The photograph showing Gubaidulina, Silvestrov and his wife, Aigi, and Kuznetsov (see p. [149]) was taken in February 1977 and certainly does not show their first meeting. The premiere of the Concerto for Symphony Orchestra and Jazz Band did not take place until January 1978.

10. Interview with Pyotr Meshchaninov, Moscow and Appen.

11. The Russian original uses the diminutive form *notki* in reference to the "music," lending the word a particularly innocent, yet also ironic, meaning.

12. Original contribution by Sergei Yakovenko.

13. Communication with Frangis Ali-Sade, May 7, 2001.

14. Victor Suslin, "Neue Musik in der UdSSR," radio manuscript, Westdeutscher Rundfunk, July 1984.

15. *Editor's note: kemancha,* sometimes *kyamancha* [*kiamancha*], is a bowed string instrument with a hemispherical resonator common among the peoples of the Caucasus and the Middle East.

16. Olga Bugrova, "'Dano' i 'zadano'" ["What's given" and "what's assigned"] (interview with Sofia Gubaidulina), *Muzykal'naia akademiia* 3 (1994): 2.

17. Andrei Ustinov, "*Chas dushy* Sofii Gubaidulinoi" [Sofia Gubaidulina's *Hour of the Soul*] (interview with Sofia Gubaidulina), *Muzykal'noe obozrenie* 3 (1994): 10.

18. Kholopova/Restagno, 59–62.

19. For some time Vladimir Tonkha played only nine etudes in his concerts, omitting No. 8, "Arco-pizzicato," as it had the same theme as No. 9, "Pizzicato-arco."

20. "Sofia Gubaidulina und die Verwandlung der Zeit," program brochure, Dornach, Switzerland, June 10–14, 1998.

21. Friedrich Lips, "Kazhetsia eto bylo vchera," *Narodnik* 1 (1999). English translation by Herbert Scheibenreif, "It seems like yesterday"; available at www.accordion-cd.co.at/?show=en_artikel_scheintgestern.

22. Ibid.

23. Ibid.

24. Interview with Friedrich Lips, Moscow, January 13, 2001.

25. Ibid.

26. Transcription of a tape recording of the workshop concert, November 6, 1994, Krefeld, Germany.

27. Joseph Smits van Waesberghe, ed., *Musik des Mittelalters und der Renaissance*, vol. 3, *Musikgeschichte in Bildern* (Leipzig, 1969).

28. Interview with Alexander Bakhchiev, Moscow, October 17, 1998.

29. Ibid.

30. Other works issued by Melodya were Hindemith's *Kammermusik Nr. 3*, Webern's *Opus 11*, and Denisov's *Three Pieces for Cello and Piano*.

31. A program sheet of a performance on May 17, 1978, indicates that Valery Popov and Vsevolod Brenner performed the Sonata on that date. Popov, however, insists that he performed the premiere with Kochetkov. It is possible either that Kochetkov rather than Brenner played in the May performance or the performance was canceled and did not take place until November with Popov and Kochetkov.

32. Hannelore Gerlach, *Fünfzig sowjetische Komponisten der Gegenwart* (Leipzig and Dresden, 1984), 163.

33. Interview with Rubin Abdullin, Kazan, April 13, 1992.

34. Kholopova/Restagno, 57–60.

35. Ibid., 63.

36. Interview with Tatiana Sergeeva, Moscow, October 16, 1998.

37. Kholopova/Restagno, 76.

38. *Editor's note:* These included *Leaves* [*List'ia*], a cycle of five poems selected from Tanzer's collection of poems, and *Blätter*, for soprano and string trio, composed in 1978.

39. Interview with Jürgen Köchel, Bochum, April 21, 1999, and January 14, 2001.

40. Ibid.

41. Interview with Christoph Caskel, September 11, 1999.

42. Review by André Lischke, *Russkaia mysl'*, November 22, 1979 (English translation based on Detlef Gojowy's translation from Russian to German).

43. Interview with André Lischke, Paris, January 8, 2000.

44. Gérard Condé, "Jeunes compositeurs soviétique," *Le Monde*, November 2, 1979.

45. *Sovetskaia kul'tura* 94 (November 23, 1979).
46. Interview with Asgad Gubaidullin, Kazan, April 13, 1992.
47. Interview with Dmitri Smirnov, London, February 26, 2001.
48. Interview with Victor Suslin, Appen and Hamburg.
49. The program consisted of the following works: Jean-Claude Eloy, *Equivalence;* Claude Lefebvre, *Etwas weiter;* Paul Méfano, *Interférences;* and Pascal Dusapin, *Le Bal* (premiere).

9. *Offertorium*—A Musical Offering, 1979–1981

1. Interview with Gidon Kremer, Cologne, December 12, 1999.
2. Wolf-Eberhard von Lewinski, *Gidon Kremer* (Mainz/Munich, 1982), 26–29.
3. Kholopova/Restagno, 79–80.
4. Ibid.
5. Joachim Kaiser, quoted in Lewinski, *Gidon Kremer,* 13.
6. Vladimir Agopov, "Sävellyksen syvin kerros voi olla akustisesti kuulumattomissa," *Kulttuurivihkot* 2 (1984): 14–18.
7. The Offertorium in the Proper of the Roman Catholic Mass includes the offering of the sacrifice, that is, the gifts of the bread and wine, the body and blood of Christ. The equivalent in the Russian Orthodox Church is the Anaphora (a Slavonic term derived from Greek that is translated into Russian as *prinoshenie*—gift or offering).
8. Kholopova/Restagno, 82–83.
9. Letter to Francisco Tanzer, September 14, 1979.
10. Ibid., May 12, 1980.
11. Ibid., August 4, 1980.
12. Interview with Irina Kotkina, Hamburg, January 26, 2000.
13. Interview with Rolan Bykov, *Sovetskaia kul'tura,* October 26, 1991.
14. Interview with Francisco Tanzer, Düsseldorf, May 8, 1998, August 12, 1998, and November 12, 1999.
15. Friedrich Lips, "Kazhetsia eto bylo vchera," *Narodnik* 1 (1999). English translation by Herbert Scheibenreif, "It seems like yesterday"; available at www.accordion-cd.co .at/?show=en_artikel_scheintgestern.
16. It has not been possible to reconstruct exactly how the first score of *Offertorium* reached the West or to know when Gubaidulina received confirmation that Kremer had received the music. In the first half of 1980 Sikorski mailed a prospectus of Gubaidulina's compositions—including *Offertorium*—to all West German radio stations, to promoters and experts of contemporary music, and to VAAP. Gubaidulina later recalled that she gave the score "illegally" to Jürgen Köchel during the 1980 Moscow Autumn festival. Before his departure for Moscow, however, Köchel had already received a score from Jörg Polzin, who worked for Ariola-Eurodisc and had maintained close contacts with Kremer since first successfully inviting him to West Germany in 1975. Polzin had probably received the score from Kremer, but neither remembers the details, although Kremer thinks that the publisher sent him the score. Certainly by no later than June 1980 Kremer knew about

the work that had been written for him and discussed it with Universal Edition in Vienna, which in turn immediately informed VAAP. The score in Polzin's possession had been produced either by VAAP very soon after the completion of the composition, that is, in the spring of 1980, or "illegally" at Gubaidulina's request. According to her recollection, Denisov was familiar with unofficial channels for copying scores.

17. Interview with Gidon Kremer, Cologne, December 12, 1999.

18. H. H. Stuckenschmidt, "Alter Rausch und neue Schönheit," *FAZ*, June 1, 1981.

19. Michael Kurtz, "It seems to me there is something that exists outside me, something that helps me and guides me" (interview with Sofia Gubaidulina), in *Annäherungen IV an sieben Komponistinnen,* ed. Brunhilde Sonntag and Renate Matthei (Kassel, 1988), 52.

10. The Rhythm of Musical Form, 1981–1985

1. Letter to Francisco Tanzer, July 3, 1981.
2. Diethelm Zuckmantel, "Eine Sternstunde," *Rheinische Post,* November 4, 1981.
3. Interview with Yuri Nikolaevsky, Bochum, January, 28–31, 1999.
4. Letter to Francisco Tanzer, October 31, 1981.
5. Yuri Nikolaevsky conducted the Tula Chamber Orchestra of the Tula Regional Philharmonic Society [Tul'skii kamernyi orkestr, Tul'skoi oblastnoi filarmonii], with Sergei Yakovenko as soloist. The Soviet premiere took place in Leningrad on October 30, 1986, and a first Moscow performance a few years later—both with Sergei Yakovenko and Nelli Lee. Yakovenko later commented:

> As for my participation, together with Nelli Lee, in the performance of *Perception,* the combination of objective and subjective circumstances did not permit me to be up to the task. The main reason was my lack of familiarity with the German language. It is impossible to understand and interpret an exceedingly difficult and subtly wrought work when one is frustrated and shackled by foreign texts. Also, the rehearsals were hasty and carelessly conducted—we showed up for the premiere at the Moscow House of the Artist [Tsentral'nyi dom khudozhnika] without having gone through the entire work with the conductor and the musicians. Everything was improvised (in the bad sense of the word) and sloppy, and on top of everything there were organizational problems—a lack of practice space, a constant turnover of musicians. . . . The performance in Petersburg was more dignified, but I did not get the same sense of satisfaction and delight as I did with *Rubaiyat.*

Another successful performance took place on December 13, 1991, with Nelli Lee and Ruben Lisitsian in the famous "December Evenings" series at the Pushkin Museum ["Dekabr'skie vechera" v GMII im. A.S. Pushkina].

6. Letter to Nikolai Bokov, December 7, 1981.
7. As quoted by Sofia Gubaidulina.
8. Ibid.

9. Leonid Boblev's Concerto for Violin, Piano, and Strings and the premiere of Mark Milmann's First Chamber Symphony.

10. As quoted by Sofia Gubaidulina.

11. A reproduction of a page from a program brochure of "Moscow Autumn" 1982, with signatures of the meeting, appears in *Alfred Schnittke zum 60. Geburtstag, eine Festschrift* (Hamburg: Sikorski, 1994), 221. In that reproduction Artyomov's name is missing from the program. The name does appear, however, in a Russian-language diary of Elena Firsova and Dmitri Smirnov, published on the Internet at www.smirnov.fsworld.co.uk/denfrag6.html, and dated October 18, 1982. Despite Peter Michael Hamel's suggestion in the text below, Alexander Knaifel was most likely not present. Neither Jürgen Köchel nor Dmitri Smirnov remember his being there, and Hamel, when asked again, said he was not entirely sure about Knaifel's presence.

12. Ibid., 220–221.

13. Letter to Victor Suslin, March 13, 1983.

14. Gubaidulina also had another title for this withdrawn work: "Even and Uneven." It is not the same as, or in any way related to, *Even and Uneven [Chët i ne chët]*, a 1991 piece for seven percussionists.

15. Interview with Valentina Ponomaryova, Moscow, April 17, 2001.

16. Interview with Rolan Bykov, *Sovetskaia kul'tura*, October 26, 1991.

17. R.-M. Borngässer, "Und wieder wird gejubelt, wenn Stalin winkt," *Die Welt*, December ?, 1985.

18. Jelena Bonner, *In Zweisamkeit vereint* (Munich, 1991), 141–142.

19. Interview with Igor Ganikovsky, March 21, 2001.

20. Letter to Victor Suslin, December 1, 1983.

21. Raimo Koivisto, "Iloa olemassaolon tuolla puolen," *Kainun Sanomat*, July 28, 1988.

22. Olga Bugrova, "'Dano' i 'zadano'" ["What's given" and "what's assigned"], *Muzykal'naia akademiia* 3 (1994): 2.

23. Sybille Jacobsen and Sigrun Witt, "Etwas Helles und Himmlisches" (interview with Sofia Gubaidulina), *Flöte Aktuell* (March 1997).

24. Valeriia Tsenova, *Chislovye tainy muzyki Sofii Gubaidulinoi* [The numerical secrets of Sofia Gubaidulina's music] (Moscow, 2000). German translation: *Zahlenmystik in der Musik von Sofia Gubaidulina* (Berlin, 2001).

25. Interview with Veijo Varpio, Helsinki, August 28, 1995.

26. Performance of August 23: Gubaidulina, *Offertorium;* Shostakovich, Eighth Symphony. Performance of August 24: Denisov, *Peinture;* Kancheli, Fifth Symphony; Schnittke, Faust Cantata [*Seid nüchtern und wachet . . . (Istoriia doktora Ioganna Fausta)*].

27. Interview with Veijo Varpio, Helsinki, August 28, 1995.

28. Seppo Heikinheimo, "Tikhon Khrennikov in Interview," *Tempo* 173 (June 1990): 19.

29. Vladimir Agopov, "Sävellyksen syvin kerros voi olla akustisesti kuulumattomissa," *Kulttuurivihkot* (The deepest level of composition may be inaudible) 2 (1984): 14–18. This interview, conducted in Finnish, in which she speaks at length about her life and work,

is among the earliest and most important published conversations with Gubaidulina. To clarify her concept of vertical and horizontal time, she told the following two parables.

> In Oriental parables the teacher sends his student to fetch water. The student draws water from the well and becomes absorbed in his own thoughts. After he has poured the water into the container, he returns to the village. But the teacher is no longer there, and all his contemporaries are hoary old men—a hundred years have passed. In another parable the teacher sends his student to fetch water. The student draws it from the well, but just then along come a storm and flood. The student is carried off far away from home to some other island among strangers. He marries, has children, and life goes on. Then another storm returns him to the same shore and well from which he was snatched away. He sees the well, draws the water, and returns to the village. His teacher says: 'So you brought some of the water?' In the first instance, a hundred years of astronomical time pass, but the experienced, essential time was only the brief moment of fetching the water. In the second story, years and decades of experienced time pass, whereas the astronomical time lasted only as long as the moment of fetching the water.

30. Kalevi Aho, original contribution (in German); abbreviated with the author's permission.

31. Interview with Pyotr Meshchaninov, Moscow and Appen.

11. Travels, Travels, and More Travels, 1985–1991

1. Letter to Victor Suslin, May 13, 1986. The ellipsis is Gubaidulina's.

2. Semyon Gurary, "*Chas dushi* Sofii Gubaidulinoi" [Sofia Gubaidulina's *Hour of the Soul*] *Vechernaia Kazan'*, May 11, 1988.

3. Interview with David Geringas, Dortmund, December 14, 1999.

4. Interview with Hans-Ulrich Duffek, Hamburg, March 7, 2000.

5. The *Times*, February 28, 1987. However, the performance, arranged by Gerard McBurney, was less than successful. As Gubaidulina's name was unknown, only a small audience of about forty had gathered at St. John's Smith Square. Contemporary music has had to fight an uphill struggle in England.

6. Program brochure, "Tage Neuer Musik," Beethoven Halle, Bonn, June 26, 1988, on the occasion of the performance of *Offertorium*, under the direction of Dennis Russell Davies.

7. Rozhdestvensky wanted to perform the Berlin works also in East Germany to "keep them fresh," but this was not permitted under the contractual arrangements for the premiere of Gubaidulina's work for the Berliner Festwochen.

8. Interview with Irina Kotkina, Hamburg, January 26, 2000.

9. Interview with Reinbert de Leeuw, Amsterdam, November 7, 1999.

10. Stepen Plaisow, director of the section for contemporary music at BBC 3, had initiated the commission.

11. Interview with Gerard McBurney, London, May 14, 1999, and February 27, 2001.

12. Letter to Victor Suslin, December 6, 1986.

13. Interview with Gerard McBurney, London, May 14, 1999, and February 27, 2001.

14. Interview with David Geringas, Dortmund, December 14, 1999.

15. Interview with Seppo Kimanen, Helsinki, June 22, 1999.

16. Ibid.

17. Semyon Gurary, "*Chas dushi* Sofii Gubaidulinoi" [Sofia Gubaidulina's *Hour of the Soul*] (interview with Sofia Gubaidulina), *Vechernaia Kazan'*, May 11, 1988.

18. At that time the Moscow String Quartet, founded by Evgeniya Alikhanova, included in its repertoire all three of Gubaidulina's quartets and later added the fourth.

19. Interview with Vladimir Yankilevsky, Paris, January 7, 2000.

20. Interview with Laurel Fay, New York, April 1–10, 1998.

21. *Sovetskaia Muzyka* 7 (1988): 4–5.

22. Original contribution by Laurel Fay (typescript).

23. Gubaidulina had too many other commitments to accept a commission from the Old Opera in Frankfurt, and for the same reason she declined a request for a work for voice and chamber ensemble from the Davos Festival in Switzerland. A commissioned piece for cello and winds for Warsaw Autumn fell through, and a request from the Berlin Festival Weeks for a piece for bayan, cello, and a third instrument later became *Silentio*, composed for the Hannover Society for New Music. Finally, a viola concerto requested by Ricordi in Milano did not materialize.

24. György Ligeti won the 1988 prize for his overall work as a composer. Besides Gubaidulina, the jury consisted of the composers Narcis Bonet, Charles Chaynes, Henri Dutilleux, Lawrence Foster, Jean Français, Christobal Halffter, Betsy Jolas, Virgilio Mortari, Andrzej [Panufnik], and Aribert Reiman.

25. Bernhard Holland, "A Soviet Composer's Works Speak as to a Friend," *New York Times*, April 24, 1989.

26. Interview with Yuji Takahashi, Kamakura, April 19, 2000.

27. Ibid.

28. Valdislav Dunaev, "Dve vstrechi v Santori kholle" [Two meetings in Santory Hall (Tokyo)], *Sovetskaia kul'tura*, April 14, 1990.

29. Interview with Toshio Hosokawa, Tokyo, April 24, 2000.

30. Interview with Kazue Sawai, Tokyo, April 24, 2000.

31. Dunaev, "Dve vstrechi v Santori kholle."

32. Max Loppert, "Gubaydulina," *Financial Times*, July 16, 1989.

33. Elmer Schönberger, "Introduction," program brochure, Holland Festival (1989), 6.

34. The request for a small work for this festive religious service was not unusual; Arvo Pärt and Alfred Schnittke also contributed compositions to it.

35. Laurel Fay, "Das Licht als Symbol in Gubaidulinas *Alleluja*," in *Symbol—die Suche nach dem Spirituellen in der sinnlichen Erscheinung: Dokumentation der Referate des Symposiums vom 12./13.6.1998 im Rahmen der Musik- und Kulturfesttage 'Sofia Gubaidulina und die Verwandlung der Zeit'*, ed. Michael Kurtz (Dornach, 1999).

36. Ibid.

37. Ibid.

38. In the 1990s Noklaevsky conducted Gubaidulina's music in both Italy ("Torino Settembre Musica") and Tokyo.

39. Conversation with Michael Kurtz, March 27, 1989.

40. Andrei Ustinov, "*Chas dushi* Sofii Gubaidulinoi" [Sofia Gubiadulina's *Hour of the Soul*], *Muzykal'noe obozrenie* 3 (1994): 10.

41. Anne Välinoro, "Tummasta löyty monta sävyä," *Aamulehti,* August 4, 1990.

42. Fred R. Banks, "Brisbane," *Musical Times,* November 1990.

43. Ibid.

44. Letter to Laurel Fay, August 20, 1990.

45. Laurel Fay, Dornach (Switzerland).

46. Interview with Ulrich Eckardt, Berlin, July 9, 1997.

47. Enzo Restagno, original contribution (typescript).

12. Worldwide Fame, Worldwide Demand, 1991–1996

1. Lutz Lesle, "Grenzgängerin des Glaubens" (interview with Sofia Gubaidulina), *Allgemeines Deutsches Sonntagsblatt,* August 7, 1992.

2. Ibid.

3. Jukka Määttänen, "Gubaidulina's neues Werk, eine Kreuzfahrt zwischen dem Schönen und Schrecklichen," *Uusi Suomi,* August 29, 1991. (German translation, Sikorski Archives.)

4. *Quasi hoquetus, Hommage à T. S. Eliot, Music for Harpsichord and Percussion Instruments from Mark Pekarsky's Collection, Light and Darkness, In croce,* String Quartet No. 3, and *Garden of Joys and Sorrows.*

5. Interview with Gidon Kremer, Cologne, December 12, 1999.

6. Interview with Mstislav Rostropovich, Cologne, February 12, 1999.

7. The agreement specifies that all scores and sketches, including future works, would become the property of the foundation, which would properly archive and make them available to researchers.

8. Instead of the orchestra of the Teatro Carlo Felice, the Schleswig-Holstein Musik Festival orchestra—a group of gifted music students from all over the world—played at this performance.

9. In response to the author's request for a contribution to this book, Kazue Sawai sent the previously printed text from the program of the New York premiere of . . . *Early in the Morning, Right before Waking* . . .

10. Kholopova/Restagno, 161.

11. Interview with David Geringas, Dortmund, December 14, 1999.

12. Interview with Bruce Weinberger, Weimar, April 26, 1996.

13. Christopher Morley, "Russian Star Who Must Be Heard," *Birmingham Post,* November 28, 1994.

14. Interview with Simon Rattle, Berlin, September 20, 1999.

15. Interview with Jean-Pierre Armengaud, Paris, January 7, 2000.

16. Original contribution by Pierre-Yves Artaud (manuscript).

17. Interview with Mayumi Miyata, Tokyo, April 24, 2001.

18. Alain Galliari, "Sofia Goubaïdoulina en Acanthes," *Diapason* (Paris), July 1998.

19. Bashmet's comments about the origin of the commission may lead to misconceptions. The commission by the Chicago Symphony Orchestra had nothing to do with Ricordi but was the result of the actions of Schirmer and Laurel Fay. The orchestra requested a work for solo string instrument and orchestra, but it was Gubaidulina who chose the viola and Bashmet as the soloist for the premiere.

20. Interview with Yuri Bashmet, Cologne, April 29, 2000.

21. Richard Dyer, "A Magical 'Metaboles' Stars at Tanglewood," *Boston Globe,* August 16, 1997.

22. Sofia Gubaidulina, program brochure for the premiere of *Canticle of the Sun.*

23. Stefan Schickhaus, *Frankfurter Rundschau,* February 11, 1998.

24. Interview with Charles Dutoit, Düsseldorf, September 25, 1999.

25. Interview with Kazue Sawai, Tokyo, April 20, 2000.

26. Interview with Kurt Masur (Michael Kurtz and Jurriaan Cooiman), New York, May 3, 1999.

27. Cynthia Phelps, e-mail to Michael Kurtz, October 17, 2004.

13. The Center of Life

1. Interview with Christian Eisert, April 25, 2001.

2. Sofia Gubaidulina, Letter to Christian Eisert, February 23, 1996, printed in the program brochure for *Passion 2000* (Stuttgart 2000), 34–35.

3. Annette Eckerle, "Den Menschen ist der Sinn des Lebens abhanden gekommen," *Stuttgarter Nachrichten* (September 1, 2000).

4. *Editor's note:* Gubaidulina evidently did not understand that Roman Catholic doctrine holds views similar to those of the Orthodox Eastern Church in believing that in repeating the actions of Jesus at his last supper when he gave his disciples bread and wine, saying, "This is my body" and "This is my blood," the elements of the bread and wine passed by the priest to those receiving communion are turned miraculously into the literal substance of Christ himself, that is, as an actual fact that has taken place in the real world.

5. Kholopva/Restagno, 65–66.

6. Sofia Gubaidulina, Letter to Helmut Rilling, March 5, 1996.

7. This description of the Easter liturgy in Margarita Woloschina's autobiography, *Die grüne Schlange* (Stuttgart, 1954), 75, is based on late-nineteenth-century customs. Not much has changed since then. After seventy years of dictatorship and the difficult period that followed, the Church is again experiencing considerable popularity. The first televised Easter service was broadcast in the early 1990s, and nowadays politicians of all persuasions find it necessary to attend church and be photographed in the company of a priest.

8. Program brochure, *Passion 2000*, 251–252.

9. The figures of Lazarus and John are most likely the same person. See Johannes Hemleben, *Evangelist Johannes* (Reinbeck/Hamburg, 1972), 37–48.

10. Program brochure, *Passion 2000*, 251–252.

11. Interview with Christian Eisert, April 25, 2001.

12. Concerto for Viola, *Stimmen . . . verstummen . . .* , *And: The Festivities at Their Height, Pro et Contra, Figures of Time, Steps, Offertorium, Seven Words, Perception, Now Always Snow,* String Quartets No. 3 and No. 4, *Hommage à T. S. Eliot, Silenzio, In croce, Rejoice!* and *Galgenlieder à 5.*

13. Single works were performed in South Korea (*Offertorium*, with violinist Hae-Sung Kang and the Changwon City Orchestra under the direction of Duk-ki Kim) and in Malaysia (*Detto II*, with members of the Malaysian Philharmonic Orchestra, conducted by Kevin Field).

14. At the request of Cecilia Cartellieri, Reinhard Flender composed *Sofia Orthi*, for two cellos, percussion, and piano. Peter Michael Hamel's contribution was *Neunundvierzig Grad Celsius*, songs with a Russian theme from texts by Evgeniya Ginsburg for alto, percussion, and double bass.

15. Victor Suslin, *Tone-B* for cello and piano; Yuji Takahashi, *For Sofia Gubaidulina* for violin, cello, and bayan; Boris Tishchenko, *Mysterious Ancestral Relations*, (puzzle) canon in countermovement for percussion ensemble and stopwatch; and Dmitri Smirnov, *Saga* for cello.

16. "Sofia Gubaidulina Comments on *St. John Passion* and *St. John Easter*," NDR Program Brochure, 8.

17. "In my beginning is my end" is the first sentence of T. S. Eliot's "East Coker" (No. 2 of "Four Quartets"), with which Gubaidulina was thoroughly familiar ever since her preparations for *Hommage à T. S. Eliot*. It is thematically related, of course, to the Revelation of St. John the Divine, 1:8, "I am Alpha and Omega, the beginning and the ending."

18. Personal note from Richard Armbruster to the author.

19. Irina Parfenova in an e-mail to the author, August 12, 2004.

20. The American music critic Keith Powers commented on the title in "Old Friends Shed 'Light' on Work," *Boston Herald*, April 17, 2003, 49: "The Russian title makes a wordplay that can also imply 'End of the World.' . . . Gubaidulina confirmed this was intentional, but was quick to insist that, for her, the end of the world doesn't have to be cataclysmic, but instead can be unifying."

21. Kurt Masur in conversation with Michael Kurtz, April 17, 2003.

22. Besides the cello concerto, conducted by Yves Abel, the following works will be performed during the 2004–2005 season: *Offertorium* (with Antje Weithaas, violin), *Stimmen . . . verstummen . . .* , *Introitus, Seven Words,* and *Detto II.*

Bibliography

Earlier bibliographies have appeared in Valentina Nikolaevna Kholopova and Enzo Restagno, *Sofia Gubaidulina: Zhizn' pamiati* [(My) life of memory], Sofia Gubaidulina in conversation with Enzo Restagno; *Shag Dushi* [A step of the soul], a research monograph by Valentina Kholopova, Moscow: "Kompozitor," 1996. Restagno's conversations with Gubaidulina were previously published independently in Italian as *Gubajdulina* a cura di Enzo Restagno, Torino: E.D.T., 1991; and in *Sikorski informiert,* 3:1997. The names of Russian authors appearing in non-Russian publications are given in the transliterated form of the original publication, even if they vary from one publication to another; however, names in Russian publications, as well as Russian titles, are transcribed according to standard American transliteration practices.

Interviews (in alphabetical order)

Agopov, Vladimir. "Sävellyksen syvin kerros voi olla akustisesti kuulumattomissa" [The deepest level of composition may be acoustically inaudible]. *Kultuurivihkot* 2 (1984): 14–19.

Bargban, Efim. "Zhizn po vertikali" [A life of spiritual verticality], *Moskovskie novosti* 48 (December 14–20, 1999): 22.

Beyer, Anders. "Into the Labyrinth of the Soul." In *The Voice of Music: Conversations with Composers of Our Time.* Aldershot, 2000.

Bogatryova, Maria. "Ot bednosti nichego khoroshego ne byvaet" [Nothing good comes from poverty]. *Moskovskii komsomolets,* July 26, 1991, 4.

Bonnauré, Jacques. [no title]. MS (November 1987?), Archives of Chant du Monde Publishers, Paris.

Brand, Bettina. "Am Anfang war der Rhythmus." *Neue Berlinische Musikzeitung* 3 (1990): 33–37.

Bugrova, Olga. "'Dano' i 'zadano'" ["What's given" and "what's assigned"]. *Muzykal'naia akademiia* 3 (1994): 1–7.

Dalton, Jody. "Sofia Gubaidulina." *Ear Magazine* 14 (5) (July/August 1989): 25.

Dümling, Albrecht. "Auf dem Weg nach innen." *MusikTexte* 21 (October 1987): 8–11.

Dunaev, Vladislav. [Two encounters in Santori Hall with Sofia Gubaidulina and Yury Liubimov]. *Sovetskaia kultura,* April 14, 1990, 4.

Eckerle, Annette. "Den Menschen ist der Sinn des Lebens abhanden gekommen." *Stuttgarter Nachrichten,* September 1, 2000.

Fant, Jöran. "Bön för vattumannens tidsalder." *Forum Järna,* 6 (February 1992): 37–42, 56.

Galliari, Alain. "Sofia Goubaïdoulina en Acanthes." *Diapason* (Paris) (July 1998).

Gojowy, Detlef. "Wurzel, Stamm, Krone." In *Gegenwelten: Eine Dokumentation (10 Jahre Internationales Festival für neue Musik, 10 Jahre Kulturinstitut Komponistinnen),* ed. Roswitha Sperber, 201–204. Heidelberg, 1997.

Gor'kin, V. "V prekrasnom i iarostnom mire muzyki" [In the beautiful and savage world of music]. *Komsomolets tatarii,* March 8, 1981, 3–4.

Guarary, Semyon. "*Chas dushi* Sofii Gubaidulinoi" [Sofia Gubaidulina's *Hour of the Soul*]. *Vechernaia kazan',* May 11, 1988, 3.

Gubaidulina, Sofia. "Moia zhizn' sostoit iz voprosov" [My life consists of questions]. *Izvestiia Tatarstana press daidzhest* (1992): 6.

Hüppi, Astrid. "Ein Gespräch Sofia Gubaidulinas mit Astrid Hüppi." In *Das Konzert für Violine und Orchester 'Offertorium.'* [N. P.] Diploma thesis in Music History, December 1989.

J.-S. V. "Questions d'écriture," *La Lettre du Musicien* (March 1995): 38.

Jacobsen, Sibylle, and Sigrun Witt. "Etwa Helles und Himmlisches." *Flöte Aktuell* 3 (1997): 11–16.

Koleskin, R. "Dukhovny opyt festivalia" [The spiritual experience of the festival]. *Vecherny sverdlovsk,* January 27, 1990, 1.

Kurtz, Michael. ". . . mir scheint, dass ausser mir etwas existiert, das mir hilft und mir etwas zu sagen hat." In *Annäherung IV: an sieben Komponistinnen,* ed. Brunhilde Sonntag and Renate Matthei, 47–55. Kassel 1988.

Lukomsky, Vera. "The Eucharist in My Fantasy." *Tempo* 206 (September 1998): 29–35.

Polin, Claire. "Interviews with Soviet Composers. II. Firsova, Gubaidulina, Loudova, Smirnov." *Tempo* 151 (December 1984): 3–16.

Redepenning, Dorothea. "Sofia Gubaidulina im Gespräch." In *Musikalische Avantgarde. Musikavantgarde im Osten Europas,* 31–38 (Heidelberg 1992).

Salkina, Marina. "I Prize Solitude above Everything." *Music in the USSR* (July/September 1991): 6–8.

Seiko, Rena. "Tonkaia sfera" [The delicate sphere]. *Miloserdie* 2 (1990): 23–24.

Serrou, Bruno. "Le 'présent infini' et le temps de l'art. . . ." *La Lettre du Musicien* (March 1995): 38–39.

Stähr, Susanne. "Komponieren ist immer ein spiritueller Akt." Program brochure, Gütersloh '98, 14–18.

Sykes, Julian. [no title]. *Le Nouveau Quotidien,* March 14, 1997.

Ustinov, Andrei. "*Chas dushi* Sofii Gubaidulinoi" [Sofia Gubaidulina's *Hour of the Soul*]. *Muzykal'noe obozrenie* 3 (1994): 9–10.

Vargaftik, Artem. "Noty sushchesvuiut chtoby oni zvuchali" [Notes exist in order to sound]. *Muzykal'naia zhizn'* 11 (1998): 16.

Yamaguchi, Masao. "The 'Echo' of Folk Instruments." Broadcast on March 1, 1998, as part of the Cultural Program *Stage Entrance,* NKH Television, Tokyo.

Yusefovich, V. "Ob uchiteliakh, kollegakh i o samoi sebe" [About teachers, colleagues, and about myself]. *Muzykal'naia akademia* 3 (1994): 8–9.

Zeichner, Jürgen. "Durch neue Musik wird der Kirchenraum sehr lebendig." *WAZ,* January 25, 1997.

Zimmerlin, Alfred. "Im Saal soll etwas Phantastisches erscheinen." *Neue Züricher Zeitung,* December 5, 1996.

Works on Music

Alfred Schnittke zum 60. Geburtstag: Eine Festschrift. Hamburg, 1995.

Armengaud, Jean-Pierre. *Entretiens avec Denisov.* Paris, 1993.

Aronovsky, M. *Ruskaia Muzyka i XX vek* [Russian music and the 20th century]. Moscow, 1997.

Artyomov, Viacheslav. Booklet with Texts, Reviews, and Lists of Works. 1997.

Burde, Tamara. *Zum Leben und Schaffen des Komponisten Alfred Schnittke.* Kludenbach, 1993.

Danuser, Hermann, Hannelore Gerlach, and Jürgen Köchel, eds. *Sowjetische Musik im Lichte der Perestroika.* Laaber, 1990.

di Vanni, Jacques. *Trente ans de musique soviétique.* Arles, 1987.

Drozdova, Marina. *Uroki Iudinoi* [Yudina's lessons]. Moscow, 1997.

Fay, Laurel. *Shostakovich: A Life.* New York, 2000.

Frid, Grigory. *Muzyka, obshchenie, sud'by: o Moskovskom molodëzhnom muzykal'nom klube: stat'i i ocherki* [Music, relationships, destinies: About the Moscow Youth Musical Club: articles and essays]. Moscow, 1987.

———. *Muzyka! Muzyka? Muzyka: Muzyka i molodësh'* [Music! Music? Music: Music and youth]. Moscow, 1991.

Gerlach, Hannelore, ed. *Fünfzig sowjetische Komponisten der Gegenwart.* Leipzig and Dresden, 1984.

Gojowy, Detlef, ed. *Augustyn Bloch: Ein Komponistenleben in Polen.* Cologne, 1999.

Hakobian, Levon. *Music of the Soviet Age, 1917–1987.* Stockholm, 1998.

Hillier, Paul. *Arvo Pärt.* Oxford, 1997.

Ho, Allan, and Dmitry Feofanov. *Biographical Dictionary of Russian/Soviet Composers.* Westport, Conn., 1989.

Internationales Musik-Festival Komponistinnen. *Russische Avantgarde. Musikavant-garde im Osten Europas.* Heidelberg, 1992.

Ivashkin, Alexander. *Alfred Schnittke.* London, 1996.

Ivashkin, Alexander, and Josef Oehrlein. *Retrospektive.* Schweinfurth, 1997.

Kholopov, Yuri, and Valeryia Tsenova. *Edison Denisov.* Moscow, 1993.

Kholopova, Valentina, and E. Chigarëva. *Al'fred Shnitke: ocherk zhizni i tvorchestvo* [Alfred Schnittke: An essay on his life and work]. Moscow, 1990.

Kholopova, Valentina, and Entso Restan'o [Enzo Restagno]. *Sofiia Gubaidulina: Zhizn' piamiati: Sofiia Gubaidulina beseduet s Entso Restan'o Shag dushi: monografiches-koe issledovanie Valentiny Kholopovoi* [Sofia Gubaidulina: A life in memory: Sofia Gubaidulina talks with Enzo Restagno. A step of the soul: A research monograph by Valentina Kholopova]. Moscow, 1996.

Komponistinnen Gestern—Heute, 1985–89: Festival International Heidelberg. Heidelberg, 1989.

Kremer, Gidon. *Oase Lockenhaus.* Salzburg, 1996.

———. *Obertöne.* Salzburg, 1997.

Kučera, Václav. *Nové proudy v sovetské hudbe.* Prague, 1967. Lemaire, Frans C. *La musique du XXe siècle en Russie.* Paris, 1994. von Lewinski, Wolf-Eberhard. *Gidon Kremer.* Munich, 1982.

Kuznetsov, Anatoly, ed. *Mariia Veniaminovna Iudina: Stat'i, vospominaniia, materialy* [Maria Veniaminovna Yudin: Articles, reminiscences, materials]. Moscow, 1978.

Meyer, Krzysztof. *Schostakowitsch.* Bergisch Gladbach, 1995. de la Motte-Haber, Helga, ed. *Musik und Religion.* Laaber, 1995.

Pestalozza, Luigi. *La musica in URSS: Cronaca di un viaggio.* Milano, 1987.

Prieberg, Fred. *Musik in der Sowjetunion.* Cologne, 1965.

Rostropowitsch, Mstislaw, and Galina Rostropowitsch. *Die Musik und unser Leben.* Munich, 1987.

Schnittke, Alfred. *Über Leben und Musik.* Munich and Düsseldorf, 1998.

Schwarz, Boris. *Musik und Musikleben in der Sowjetunion von 1917 bis zur Gegenwart.* 3 vols. Wilhelmshaven, 1982.

Sperber, Roswitha, ed. *Gegenwelten: 10 Jahre Internationales Festival für Neue Musik; 10 Jahre Kulturinstitut Komponistinnen Heidelberg; 10 Jahre Heidelberger Festival Ensemble: Eine Dokumentation.* Heidelberg, 1997.

Tsenova, Valeryia, ed. *Svet. Dobro. Vechnost'. Pamiati Edisona Denisova. Stat'i Vospominaniia. Materialy* [Light. Good. Eternity. Remembering Edison Denisov. Articles. Reminiscences. Materials]. Moscow, 1999.

———, ed. *Underground Music from the Former USSR.* Amsterdam, 1997.

Wilson, Elizabeth. *Shostakovich: A Life Remembered.* London, 1995.

Yudina, Maria Veniaminovna. *Luchi bozhestvennoi liubvi: literaturnoe nasledie* [Radiant beams of divine love: Literary legacy]. Prepared and edited by Anatoly Kuznetsov. Moscow and St. Petersburg, 1999.

Zenova, Valeryia. *Zahlenmystik in der Musik von Sophia Gubaidulina.* Berlin, 2001.

General Works

Bednarz, Klaus. *Mein Moskau.* Hamburg, 1985.

———. *Russland: Ein Volk sucht seine Zukunft.* Munich, 1994.

Belkina, Marija. *Die letzten Jahre der Marina Zwetajewa.* Frankfurt, 1993.

Bochum Museum. *20 Jahre unabhängige Kunst aus der Sowjetunion.* Bochum, 1979.

Bokov, Nicolas. *Déjeuner au bord de la Baltique.* Montricher, 1999.

Bokow, Nikolaj. *Wirren aus neuester Zeit oder: Die erstaunlichen Abenteuer des Wanja Tschmotanow.* Zurich, 1983.

Bonner, Jelena. *In Einsamkeit vereint.* Munich, 1991.

Bukowski, Wladimir. *Wind vor dem Eisgang.* Berlin, 1978.

Etkin, Efim. *Unblutige Hinrichtung.* Munich, 1978.

Feinstein, Elaine. *Marina Zwetajewa.* Frankfurt, 1993.

Florenskij, Pavel. *Die Ikonostase.* Stuttgart, 1988.

———. *Die umgekehrte Perspektive.* Munich, 1989.

Ganikowskij, Igor. *Werkmonographie.* Bönen, 1996.

———. *Werkmonographie, andere Werke.* Bönen, 1998.

Gille, Werner. *Wolgafahrt.* Munich, 1992.

Götz, Roland, and Uwe Halbach. *Politisches Lexikon Russland.* Munich, 1994.

Groys, Boris. *Zeitgenössische Kunst aus Moskau.* Munich, 1991.

Heller, Michael, and Alexander Nekrich. *Geschichte der Sowjetunion.* 2 vols. Königstein, 1981.

Hildermeier, Manfred. *Geschichte der Sowjetunion 1917–1991.* Munich, 1998.

Jaffé, Aniela, ed. *Erinnerungen, Träume, Gedanken von C. G. Jung.* Solothurn, 1971.

Jewtuschenko, Jewgeni. *Der Wolfpass.* Berlin, 2000.

Kappeler, Andreas. *Russland als Vielvölkerstaat.* Munich, 1993.

Kasack, Wolfgang, Jefim Erkind, and Lew Kopelew. *Ein Leben nach dem Todesurteil. Mit Pasternak, Rilke und Kästner. Freundesgabe für Konstantin Bogatyrjow.* Bornheim, 1982.

Konzelmann, Gerhard. *Die Wolga.* Hamburg, 1994.

Lewytskys, Boriys. *Politische Opposition in der Sowjetunion 1960–1972.* Munich, 1972.

Liando, Mark. *Al'fa nashikh zor'* [The Alpha of our drawnings]. Moscow, 1994.

Malzew, Jurij. *Freie Russische Literatur 1955–1980.* Berlin, 1981.

Mark, Rudolf A. *Die Völker der ehemaligen Sowjetunion.* Opladen, 1992.

Marx, Christa, and Adolf Karger. *Moskau.* Stuttgart, 1997.

Orlowa, Raissa, and Lew Kopelew. *Wir lebten in Moskau.* Munich, 1987.

———. *Zeitgenossen Meister Freunde.* Munich, 1989.

Plissezkaja, Maija. *Ich Maija.* Bergisch Gladbach, 1995.

Razumovsky, Maria. *Marina Zwetajewa.* Frankfurt, 1994.

Ruge, Gerd. *Weites Land.* Berlin, 1996.

Sacharow, Andrej. *Mein Leben.* Munich, 1991.

Scherrer, Jutta. *Requiem für den roten Oktober.* Leipzig, 1996.

Schlögel, Karl. *Moskau Lesen.* Berlin, 2000.

Simon, Gerhard. *Nationalismus und Nationalitätenpolitik in der Sowjetunion.* Baden Baden, 1986.

Sinjawskij, Andreij. *Der Traum vom neuen Menschen oder die Sowjetzivilisation.* Frankfurt, 1989.

———. *Iwan der Dumme.* Frankfurt, 1990. von Ssacho, Helene. *Der Aufstand der Person.* Berlin, 1965. von Ssacho, Helene, and Manfred Gruner. *Literatur und Repression.* Munich, 1970. Stepun, Fedor. *Mystische Weltschau.* Munich, 1964.

Thomas, Donald M. *Solschenizyn*. Berlin, 1998.
Thun, Franziska, ed. *Erinnerungen an Pasternak*. Berlin, 1994.
Waage, Peter Normann. *Der unsichtbare Kontinent*. Stuttgart, 1988.
Woloschina, Margarita. *Die grüne Schlange*. Stuttgart, 1954.
Yankilevsky, Vladimir. [*Retrospektiva*]. Moscow, 1996.

Index

Ida, *34*
idealism, 228
Igolinsky, Vladislav Grigoryevich, 205, 211
Impromptu (Gubaidulina), 235
improvisation: and Astraea, 157–158, 204; and
  Bleffert, 213; and folk instruments, 119–121;
  Heads or Tails, 170; "Meet the Composer"
  series, 102–103; and the Présences Festival,
  232; Sixth International Musik Festival Davos,
  219–220; on stage, 121–123
In croce (Gubaidulina), 136, 140, 152, 154, 238,
  255
In Erwartung (Gubaidulina), 224, 225, 227
In the Beginning There Was Rhythm (Gubaidu-
  lina), 73, 182, 238
In the Shadow of the Tree (Gubaidulina), 232,
  241–245, 256
Intermezzo for Eight Trumpets, Sixteen Harps,
  and Percussion, 52
International Bach Festival, 246–247
International Festival "Donne in Musica—Gli
  Incontra al Borgo," 238–239
International Festival of Contemporary Music,
  141
International Festival Sofia Gubaidulina, 255
International Tchaikovsky Competition, 56, 106
Into the Depths of Time (Hosokawa), 255
Into the Storm (Khrennikov), 20
Introitus (Gubaidulina), 134–137, 140, 150, 213
IRCAM, Institut de Recherche et Coordination
  Acoustique/Musique, 143, 231
Ishi, Maki, 243
Ishii, Mitsu, 232
Islam, 3–4, 60
Italian Society for Contemporary Music,
  105–106
Ito, Ken, 221
Ivan the Terrible, 2, 9
Ivanova, Victoria, 135
Ivashkin, Alexander Vasilievich, 64, 137, 254
Ives, Charles, 190, 203

Japan, 204–206
Japan Broadcasting Corporation Symphony
  Orchestra, 241–245
"Jauchzt vor Gott," 207–208
jazz, 63, 126, 225
Jelinek, Hanns, 65
Jews and Judaism, 1
Johannes Passion (Bach), 248, 251
Joker King (Gubaidulina), 51
Jolivet, André, 128
Joueur, Le (Régnard), 51
Journey into the Whirlwind (Ginsburg), 14
Jubilatio (Gubaidulina), 189
Juilliard Quartet, 227
Jung, Carl Gustav, 69–70

Junge Deutsche Philharmonie, 156–157
Junge Kammerphilharmonie Klangwerk, 255
Jungle Book (Kipling), 79

Kabakov, Ilya Iosifovich, 198
Kabalevsky, Dmitri Borisovich, 37, 38, 64, 183
Kachkyn (Zhiganov), 18
Kagan, Oleg Moiseevich, 153–154, 167, 177, 179,
  195, 210, 236
Kaiser, Joachim, 149
Kako, Takashi, 243
Kammermusikfest, 184
Kancheli, Giya Alexandrovich, 177, 234
Kandinsky, Wassily, 197
kanón, 119
Kantor, Thomas, 38
Karelia, 182–183
Karsky, Michel, 129
Kashkashian, Kim, 187
Kasparov, Yury Gazarovich, 146
Kataev, Vitaly V., 110, 111
Katz, Arnold Mikhailovich, 55, 127
Kazan, 9–10, 27, 255, 266
Kazan Conservatory, 2, 11–12, 22–30
Kazan khanate, 2
Kazan Music Gymnasium, 18–19
Kazan University (Yevtushenko), 87–88
Keldysh, Georgii Vsevolodovich, 45
Kelemen, Milko, 77
kemancha, 130
KGB *(Komitet gosudarstvennoi bezopasnosti),* 14,
  67, 92, 107–109, 122
Khachaturian, Aram Ilich, 20, 179
Khachaturian, Emin Levonovich, 41
Khachaturian, Karen Surenovich, 66, 89
Khaqani (Persian poet), 81
Khayyam, Omar, 81
Khlebnikov, Velimir, 86
Kholopov, Valentina, 82–83, 86, 91, 214, 302n20
Kholopov, Yury Nikolaevich, 82–83, 86, 102
Kholopova, Valentina Nikolaevna, 43, 46, 71
Khôra (Dusapin), 231
Khrennikov, Tikhon Nikolaevich: and Armen-
  gaud, 114; and artistic repression, 20, 100–101,
  101–102; and dodecaphony, 64; and *Dots,
  Lines, and Zigzags,* 129; and Helsinki Festival
  Weeks, 178–179; and the Huddersfield festival,
  190; impact on SG's career, 152; and Köchel,
  89; and the Paris-Moscou exhibition, 145–146;
  and perestroika, 211; and *Phacelia,* 56–57; and
  Shostakovich's death, 117; and travel restric-
  tions, 204; and Vienna Festwochen, 155
"Khrennikov Seven," 145–146
Khrushchev, Nikita Sergeevich, 36, 59, 67, 266
Khudiakov, Oleg Valentinovich, 256
Kikta, Valery Grigoryevich, 152
Killmayer, Wilhelm, 168, 169

Born in 1948 in Essen (Ruhr), MICHAEL KURTZ studied English, American Studies, and Geography in Bochum and Tübingen. He was a Waldorf School teacher for many years, doing research in contemporary music (Stockhausen, Globokar, Gubaidulina, Saariaho, Hosokawa, among others). In 1990 he became the founder and artistic director of the Bochum performance series "Begegnung der Kulturen" (A meeting of cultures), which encompassed projects on Russia, Japan, the Czech Republic, and Finland. Since the summer of 2001 he has served as music specialist in the Department of Spoken and Musical Arts at the Goetheanum in Dornach, Switzerland. His writings include texts for the Salzburg Festival, Radio France, and the Royal Philharmonic Orchestra (Stockholm), as well as interviews and contributions to encyclopedias and other reference works. He is author of *Stockhausen: Eine Biographie* (1988), the standard biography of the German composer (English translation, 1992), and of *Die Musik der zweiten Jahrhunderthälfte* (1993), an essay with questions and responses by thirty composers and others. He is currently working on a retrospective view of twentieth-century music presented in biographical portraits of selected composers.

www.ingramcontent.com/pod-product-compliance
Lightning Source LLC
Chambersburg PA
CBHW070449100426
42812CB00004B/1251